Russia and Germany
A Century of Conflict

WALTER LAQUEUR

An Encounter Book

LITTLE, BROWN AND COMPANY • BOSTON • TORONTO

Published simultaneously in Canada
by Little, Brown & Company (Canada) Limited

PRINTED IN THE UNITED STATES OF AMERICA

CONTENTS

DENMARK
Copenhagen
North Sea
Baltic Sea.
Rig[a]
Hamburg
Danzig
Kaliningrad
Bremen
EAST
BERLIN
HOLLAND
Dortmund
Poznan
WEST
Cologne
Leipzig
Warsaw
LUX.
Dresden
Wroclaw
Prague
CZECHOSLOVAKIA
Krakow
FRANCE
Stuttgart
Brno
Lvov
Munich
Danube
Vienna
SWITZ.
Zurich
AUSTRIA
ITALY
Budapest.
HUNGARY

North Sea
DEN.
Riga
Moscow
Hamburg
Danzig
NETH.
Berlin
Warsaw
RUSSIA
RUMAN[IA]
BELG.
LUX.
GERMANY
POLAND
Bucharest
FRANCE
Prague
Danube
Munich
AUSTRIA-
SWITZ.
Vienna
Rostov
BULGAR[IA]
HUNGARY
Milan
Budapest
MONTENEGRO
Belgrade
RUMANI[A]
ITALY
Adriatic Sea
SERBIA
Danube
Bucharest
Black Sea
ALBANIA
BULGARIA
Rome
Sofia
Istanbul
GREECE
Ankara
TURKEY
JRF
Athens
Miles
0 100 200

BOUNDARIES 1914

BOUNDARIES after 1945

PREFACE

THIS IS A STUDY of what Russians and Germans have thought of each other in this century and of the fateful consequences of their interacting ideas. It deals briefly with the historical origins of Russophobia in Germany, and of anti-Germanism in Russia, and in greater detail with the confrontation of Nazism and Bolshevism that culminated in the Second World War. It is concerned with the history of ideas and attitudes as they shaped the political consciousness of millions of people in Central and Eastern Europe, thus decisively affecting the history of our time.

Like most historical studies, this book was nurtured in archives and libraries, but it was not conceived there. My own interest in Russian–German relations goes back a long time. It may be many years before all the facts are known, but I am convinced that by the time a definitive study of the subject is written most people will have ceased to care about it. I envy the historian who will know so much more than we do, but his work may lack one essential dimension: the feeling of immediacy, that special point of focus possessed by those who lived through the period. Hitler has been dead for almost twenty years, and Stalin for more than ten; a generation has grown up to whom these figures and their time are as unreal as the First World War was to my own.

One summer evening a few years ago I listened to community singing in one of Moscow's parks of 'rest and culture'. I like Russian songs and most of those I heard that evening were familiar, but the last was unknown to me. When I asked what it was a friend said, 'Nabat Bukhenvalda, the Tocsin of Buchenwald – don't you know?' There could have been no greater incongruity than that between Buchenwald and this peaceful scene in a Moscow park, the cheerful Russian boys and girls singing their song with apparent unconcern about its text and meaning. Then I recalled that most of those present had probably been born after the Second World War. Buchenwald to them – and to their contemporaries in the west – was little more than a name.

Nazism, Fascism, Stalinism are turning into figures of speech. A British police sergeant who provides hard mattresses for the guests at his station is charged with using Gestapo methods. A lady who expresses highly controversial views on birth control in a newspaper is accused by an opponent of having issued a 'Hitlerian manifesto'. A playwright who feels slighted by a critic calls him a Fascist, or a Stalinist, or both. One winces, but it is a natural development in its way. That evening in the Gorki Park made me realize how fast the terrible events of the thirties and forties are receding into the past. They have inevitably become history, and for the young, distant history, a period about which their elders often talk, sometimes excitedly, but with which they have no personal link. Those who lived through the period will always remember it, and nothing can dim its vividness. Riding out of Moscow by tram on another visit I saw a little column that I must have passed several times before but had somehow never noticed. I was told that it marked the farthest point of advance of the German army in November 1941. I knew that the Wehrmacht had been very near the centre of Moscow, but that little landmark on the Volokolamskoe Chaussee – or was it the Mozhaisk highroad? – helped me to understand Russian attitudes towards Germany as much as any document or book I have consulted. Similarly, a walk along the Wall in Bernauer Strasse in Berlin is not merely instructive in itself; it is almost essential for realizing the full significance of some of the events that have taken place in our time.

It took the Germans five months to reach Volokolamskoe Chaussee; the Russian advance towards Bernauer Strasse was slower but its effects have been lasting. The map of Europe has changed utterly as a result of the war unleashed by Nazi Germany; eight hundred years of German history have been undone. It is still too early to assess the full implications of these historical changes, but it is probably not too early to discuss their causes.

Russian–German relations have been one of the key issues in world affairs for the last hundred years, and they remain so despite Europe's diminished importance on the international scale. I hope I shall not be rebuked for failing to provide a systematic diplomatic history, but concentrate instead on the metapolitics of Russian–

German relations. One should know as much as possible about the diplomatic negotiations between these two countries; but the more I studied the period, the more I became convinced that this was not really the most important aspect of German–Russian relations. On the whole the diplomats really had very little scope for their activities, since, to put it bluntly, they did what they were told to do. This, at any rate, was the state of affairs in Germany after 1933 and in Russia after 1917. But even before those dates the importance of diplomatic initiatives should not be overrated. It is my conviction that what Germans and Russians thought about each other, their civilizations, ways of life, and political systems mattered much more in the long run than all the diplomatic reports. I am aware that some British and American students will be reluctant to accept this, but one should bear in mind the fact that 'ideological' factors (in the widest sense) were important in European politics long before they began to influence American foreign policy.

It is comparatively easy to write diplomatic history, especially after the opening of archives; the whole traffic of notes, memoirs, and meetings takes place in a small world of professionals and can be retraced with reasonable accuracy. The image of another nation is something far more complex and elusive. All kinds of influences, operating on many levels, help to shape it, and behind these influences there are usually traditions reaching back over a long period of time. The Nazi attitude to Russia, for instance, cannot be understood without reference to certain trends in German (and Russian) thought before 1917.

Basically, this book is a study in mutual misunderstanding. The Nazis never really understood what Marxism (which they so frequently invoked) was really about, and they completely misjudged the Soviet Union. The Communists, on the other hand, have to this day stubbornly refused to re-examine their well known and profoundly mistaken appraisal of Fascism, ignoring the factual evidence that has long been available.

These misunderstandings and misjudgments provide, in my view, essential clues for understanding how Hitler and Stalin behaved. I have dealt only very briefly with topics and periods – such as Soviet–German relations between 1939 and 1941, and German rule in Russia during the Second World War – that have been thoroughly investigated and on which we now have definitive studies.

I attribute more importance than other writers on the origins of

National-Socialism have done to the impact of (pre-Soviet) Russian influences and of certain circles of the Russian emigration. I felt at one stage less certain than I do now about the significance of the *Protocols of the Elders of Zion* and their first sponsors in Germany. Yet the evidence is overwhelming, and I now believe that the Russian sources of National-Socialism have hitherto been overlooked simply because they have been insufficiently studied.

Some of my research is based on interviews, but much more is based on the study of the contemporary literature. It proved far more difficult than I had anticipated to obtain early Nazi and certain Russian *emigré* publications, and the same holds for certain Russian materials, both pre-1917 and Soviet, some of which are apparently no longer available. Of greatest value was the perusal of the German files and microfilms covering the activities of the German Foreign Ministry, the Nazi Party, the SS (and the political police), as well as other institutions. These files and microfilms cover events in Germany not only during the Nazi period but frequently date back to the twenties, and, as far as the German Foreign Ministry is concerned, much earlier. They also shed much light on developments in other European countries. This study is partly based on materials that have not yet been used or published, but I have no doubt that I over-looked at least some material that would be relevant and perhaps important. I have sometimes felt lost in the maze of many millions of pages and microfilm frames, as, I suspect, has many a student before me. This is perhaps unavoidable in view of the enormous mass of material, and the frequent absence of research tools.

Some of my research and visits to other countries were made possible by a grant awarded by the Rockefeller Foundation, to which I should like to express my thanks; I should also like to thank the Warden and Fellows of St Antony's College, Oxford, for administering the grant, and extending to me their hospitality. I have used archives and libraries in many cities but owe special thanks to two because I tried the patience of their staff more than all the others: the Wiener Library, and the Foreign Office Library, both in London. To Mr Philip Mairet I owe thanks for suggesting improvements in style; the advice and assistance given by Mrs Jane Degras has been invaluable.

Chapter 1

RUSSIAN–GERMAN ATTITUDES

'I SAY, AS VOLTAIRE SAID of God, that if there were no Germans we should have to invent them, since nothing so successfully unites the Slavs as a rooted hatred of Germans.' Thus Bakunin, exactly one hundred years ago, in a letter to his sister-in-law. A love-hate relationship unique perhaps in history has prevailed between Russia and Germany over many centuries; every now and then, from the time when Alexander Nevsky defeated the Teutonic Knights on Lake Peipus to the days of the Warsaw Pact, Germany has been branded as the enemy *par excellence*.

But there was no nation the Russians admired more; the Germans were the masters, the teachers, the ideal to be imitated by successive generations of young Russian intellectuals. The romantic hero of the Russian novel was often more German than Russian in character. Of Lensky (in *Eugene Onegin*) it is said that he studied in Germany, that he was an admirer of Kant, and grew up as a poet under the skies of Schiller and Goethe. From distant Germany he brought home the fruits of scholarship, dreams of freedom, a burning and questioning spirit, a passionate language, and long dark locks of hair. German influence extended from the far left to the extreme right; even pronounced Germanophobes like Bakunin and Herzen had been shaped by it in their formative years. Pobedonostsev, we are reliably told, always carried around with him a copy of Goethe's *Faust*.

There was a similar ambivalence in German attitudes: a traditional fear of Russia mixed with contempt. Friedrich II was afraid of the Russians who (he wrote to his brother in 1769) '*dans un demi siècle feront trembler tout l'Europe*' (which did not prevent him from using Russian assistance at the most critical turning point in his war). Ranke taught that there was a great and unbridgeable divide

13

between West and East, and he has had his followers. Marx and Engels were very much children of their time in their negative judgments on Russian history – not just on the Tsarist government. But this was by no means the only trend in German public opinion; the conservatives who regarded Russia as a bulwark against revolutionary movements (the Russian alliance is our last refuge, King Friedrich Wilhelm IV told the brothers Gerlach); Bismarck and the other *Real-Politiker* who regarded Russia as Germany's natural ally; Nietzsche, for whom Russia was the very antithesis of 'European particularism and nervousness', and who regarded the integration of the Germanic and Slavic races as the most desirable prospect for the future. The ideological proponents of a German–Russian alliance were by no means to be found only on the extreme right – there is a whole chain of thinkers, from Bruno Bauer, an early friend of Marx, to Thomas Mann (during the First World War) and the National Bolsheviks of Weimar Germany, who regarded the common rejection of the West as a firm basis for such an alliance. 'Are the Russian and the German attitudes towards Europe, Western civilization, and politics not closely akin? Haven't we Germans also our Slavophiles and Westerners?' Thus Thomas Mann in 1917.

The pro-Russian tradition in German politics goes back to the eighteenth century. Russia's struggle against Napoleon in alliance with Prussia and Austria made it Germany's saviour; Tauroggen, the little place in East Prussia where General York reached an agreement with the Russians in 1812 without authorization from his king, has ever since been a catchword in German politics; together with Rapallo it is now frequently used by the East German communists – but not only by them. From Tauroggen there is a direct line to Bismarck's coalition with Russia. There is an influential school of German historians which maintains that the day when the alliance with Russia was permitted to lapse was the most fateful day in German history.

There was a school of thought, too, which from the time of the wars against Napoleon, and particularly after 1850, favoured an *Ostorientierung*. The inclination towards close collaboration between Russians and Germans was to be found over the entire political spectrum, from the extreme right to the radical left. The organs of the extreme right in Wilhelmian Germany, such as the *Staatsbürgerzeitung* (and even the *Kreuzzeitung*) used to take much of their ideological fare, and even much of their news, from the Russian *Novoe*

14

Vremya, and vice versa; collaboration between Russian and German anti-Semites was particularly close. 'We are proud to have provided ideological weapons to our friends in the neighbouring country,' wrote one of the racialist German newspapers around the turn of the century. The 'ideological weapon' was the famous 'Chief Rabbi' speech at the Jewish cemetery in Prague, which in a more accomplished and embellished form returned to Germany in 1919 as the even more famous *Protocols of the Elders of Zion* and began their triumphal travels throughout the world from Berlin. During the First World War Dubronin, head of the 'Black Hundreds', declared that the victory of the Hohenzollerns would be a far lesser evil than the victory of democracy in Russia.

Collaboration on the left was even closer. The Russian socialists looked up to their German comrades as their guides and mentors and frequently as the arbiters in their internal quarrels. Russian was the language into which some of the works of Marx and Engels were first translated. Nowhere were they more avidly read or their prescriptions more zealously observed. Right up to the outbreak of the First World War Berlin was the main source of inspiration for the various Russian socialist factions; many a Soviet historian has been in trouble for recalling that there was no basic quarrel between Lenin and Kautsky before 1914, and it is well known what exclusive importance the Russian Bolsheviks attached after 1917 to the outbreak of the German revolution, which they regarded as of greater significance than their own.

Not all Russians thought the Germans were demi-gods. The very fact that successive Tsars introduced so many innovations from Germany produced a hostile reaction. As far back as the seventeenth century Yuri Krizhanich, the precursor of Panslavism, opposed the introduction of the 'crazy' customs and manners of the Germans that were to replace the time-honoured and praiseworthy customs and institutions of Russia. The Petrine reforms brought many more Germans to Russia; Ernst Johann Buehren, Duke of Courland, better known as Biron, gave his name to a whole period in Russian history – the reign of a small group of unscrupulous German courtiers around the Empress Anna Ivanovna. Biron's reign, it is true, did not last long, but those who overthrew him were named Muennich and Ostermann; the German influence was there to stay. The appointment of so many Germans to leading positions provoked great resentment, but the practice was continued, for the class of educated Russians was too small to fill the growing number of posts. Many Russian aristocrats, moreover, looked with disdain on the state service as an occupation not fit for gentlemen. For Germans, on the other hand, the question of double loyalties did not really arise; until well into the nineteenth century foreigners served in both the Russian administration and the army without being required to take an oath of allegiance.

Leading diplomatic posts in the Russian foreign service were held almost exclusively by Germans: Meyendorff and Budberg in Berlin; Lieven and Brunnow in London; Stackelberg in Vienna; von Schroeder in Dresden; Nesselrode and Giers and von Pahlen. The only exception at the time was the envoy in Paris, Pozzo di Borgo. General Ermolaev's reply when Alexander I asked him to name his own reward for his services is well remembered: 'Sire, do make me a German . . .'

Nicholas I trusted only two men: one was Benckendorff, head of the famous third department (and, incidentally, Countess Lieven's brother). The other was von Rochow, the Prussian envoy at his court, to whom he told things that even his own foreign minister did not know. About his own subjects he said: '*Ces Russes me font toujours de guignon . . .*' But the foreign service was not the only German domain: the Wrangels and Kleinmichels, Plehves and Neidharts, Rennenkampfs and Kauffmanns had an unassailable position in the civil administration and the army, and infiltrated even the Holy Synod. So strong was the position of the Germans in Russian public life that even the anti-German movement could not manage without them. F. F. Vigel (Wiegel) was the author of a tract published in 1844 entitled *La Russie envahie par les Allemands.* And when the Panslavist movement came to the fore in the sixties, two of its main ideologists were Miller and Hilferding. The libretto to Russia's national opera *A Life for the Tsar* (or *Ivan Susanin* since the Revolution) was provided by yet another German, Gustav von Rosen. But Germans were not only diplomats, generals, and professors. At a lower social level there were the Swabian settlers and the many artisans in the cities. Before the First World War there were some fifty thousand Germans in St Petersburg, twenty thousand each in Moscow and Saratov, and at least ten thousand in Odessa. These Germans had their own churches (St Peter and St Anne in the capital), their own theatre (the only permanent German theatre outside Germany), and of course their own newspapers and clubs. The businessmen went to the Schusterklub, the artisans to Die Palme.

The contempt of the Russian nobleman for the *petit-bourgeois* German whose orderly, pedantic ways were so diametrically opposed to his own *shirokaya natura*, is admirably expressed in Gogol's *Nevsky Prospekt*: 'Schiller (at the age of twenty) had already planned his future in a most thorough and methodical way and never, in any circumstances, did he deviate from the course he had set himself. He resolved to get up at seven, to lunch at two, to be punctual in everything, and to get drunk every Sunday. He resolved to save a capital sum of fifty thousand and this was as certain and irrevocable as fate itself . . . In no circumstances did he increase his expenses and if the price of potatoes went up, he did not spend a penny more on them but merely bought less potatoes . . . His exactness was such that he made it a rule never to kiss his wife more than twice in twenty-four hours and to make sure he did not kiss her three times he never put more than one teaspoonful of pepper in his soup.' Such judgments were fairly typical in Russian nineteenth-century literature. The practical, efficient, and energetic Stolz in *Oblomov* is at the same time hopelessly uninteresting and flat – very much in contrast to the hero of the book. Perhaps the most savage attack on the Russkie Nemtsy was made by Herzen (in a series of articles in *Kolokol*, starting October 1859), in which they were described as arrogant, brutal, evil, and unwilling and unable to understand Russia and the Russians. This German upper class was convinced that '*s nashim bratom nichevo bez palki ne sdelaesh*'; '*Man muss der Bestie den Russen herausschlagen.*'

From the time of Fonvizin, the German private tutor had become the laughing stock of Russian literature. Turgenev describes how his father threw his German tutor bodily from the second floor window of their mansion after the miscreant had dared to administer corporal punishment to his pupils, who seem to have more than deserved it. The German tutor was philistine and petty, he was in brief, like all other Germans, a *meshchanin*, and there was nothing the Russian upper class despised more. For the Germans were essentially a middle-class people. They lacked the arrogance of the British, the elegance and intellectual facility of the French, the natural grace of the Italians. Since Russia had never possessed a middle class of any numerical or political significance, bourgeois virtues and bourgeois social ideals were utterly strange to them. The Germans were industrious and clean, but basically they appeared quite stupid to the

Russians, for they had sold their soul to the devil for a penny, as described in some detail in Saltykov-Shchedrin's story of the 'Boy with his Pants on and the Boy without Pants'.

The Boy with his Pants on, filled with compassion, tries to persuade The Boy without Pants to stay behind in Germany, to become a defector, as we now say. 'Herr Hecht,' he says, 'would take you on as a labourer. Just think, how do you sleep, how do you eat at home? Here you'd get a good piece of felt to sleep on and peas and bacon even on weekdays.'

'Not bad,' answers the Russian, 'but is it true, German, that you have sold your soul for a penny?'

'You have in mind Herr Hecht? But my parents receive a fixed wage from him.'

'That's what I say; you have sold your soul for a penny.'

The German boy, understandably, gets rather indignant: 'But excuse me, worse things are told of you; it is said that you have given away your soul for nothing.'

'Yes,' says The Boy without Pants with pride, 'yes, we have. But for nothing, not for a penny; that is the point. And what I have given away for nothing, I can take back again. You are a dolt, kolbasik, aren't you?'*

This contempt never extended to German culture. If Tolstoy and Dostoevsky were more widely read in Germany than in any other Western country, the impact in Russia of German philosophy, literature, and the arts (from Schelling to Johann Strauss) was unique. The Russian Academy of Sciences was a German institution, its mouthpiece, the *St Petersburger Zeitung*, a German newspaper. Under Peter I, Russian students began to appear in increasing numbers at German universities, German scientists laid the foundations of the study of the natural sciences in Russia, and Schloezer and Mueller were the precursors of a Russian national school of historiography. More and more Russian travellers appeared in Weimar and Stuttgart where Russian Grand Duchesses resided; later on Baden Baden, Bad Homburg, and Karlsbad became the most fashionable meeting points for these visitors from the East. German writers and philosophers were even more admired than in their own country; every Russian traveller wanted to meet them and to talk to them. When Karamzin was interrogated at the gates of Weimar as to the purpose

* I am indebted to Victor Frank for some concise formulations ('Russians and Germans', in *Survey*, October 1962, p. 72).

of his visit he countered by impatiently asking the sentry: 'Is Goethe here? Is Herder here? Is Wieland here?'

Schiller's influence on the Russians was greater than that of any other contemporary writer, while Hegel's impact went deeper there than in Germany. That the Russian Westerners were strongly influenced by German thought we know from Herzen and many other contemporaries. But even those who had serious political reservations about the Germans, the Slavophiles and those who later adopted *Pora domoi* as their watchword, received their main impulses from German culture. Samarin, for instance, wrote: 'To every Russian who has studied there, at least in my time, Germany is also a kind of motherland whose milk has long nourished them.' The Russian intelligentsia was more alert to all that was new and progressive and fashionable in Germany than the German intellectuals themselves. There was a Psychoanalytical Institute in Moscow before there was one in Berlin; important new German books were almost immediately translated into Russian, occasionally in larger editions than the original. German belles-lettres around the turn of the century had no great achievements to their credit, nor was Germany at that time the centre of modern painting. Yet German literature continued to be the main formative influence for leading Russian poets such as Bely and Pasternak. Russian painters such as Kandinsky or Yavlensky preferred to settle in Munich rather than Paris. It was said at the time that the Russians had always preferred to import from France fashionable dressing gowns, chocolates, cheap novels, and mistresses; but from Germany they imported ideas.

The cultural traffic was not one way. Leibniz was fascinated by Russia, a country which he compared to a *tabula rasa*, and in which he thought more good could be achieved than in the West. Herder believed that the Russians were more peaceful than the Germans; the Slavs had been the stepchildren of history, but this would change in the course of time, and the Ukraine might become one day a new Hellas. About himself, Herder wrote that during his stay in Riga he had become a 'real Russian patriot'. (Many years later, in the Nazi period, this eighteenth-century Russophilia was severely condemned.) Klinger and Lenz, two prominent members of the group that entered German literary history under the name 'Storm and Stress', lived for many years in Russia though neither was very happy there. The enormous impact of the Russian realist novel in Germany has been noted. The names of two remarkable women should be

19

mentioned in this context: Malwida von Meysenburg helped Wagner and Nietzsche to know and understand the great Russian writers; Wagner had some first-hand knowledge of the country, having served as director of the Riga Orchestra in 1837. Lou Andreas Salomé travelled with Rilke to Russia. After two extensive trips Rilke began to write poems in Russian and wrote to her: 'That Russia is my homeland is one of the great and mysterious certainties of my life.' Similar sentiments were expressed by Morgenstern; and the greatest German novelist of the twentieth century concluded that never had humanity found a deeper expression than in Russian literature, by which he and all his contemporaries had been profoundly impressed beyond all political argument.

Then came the war and the revolution. Nicky and Willie, who had written each other so many and such affectionate letters, disappeared. But the Eastern orientation remained a very important factor in German policies, both domestic and foreign. In Soviet thinking, too, a special place was reserved for Germany from the very beginning. The German proletariat, Lenin wrote in his farewell letter to the Swiss workers in April 1917, was the 'most faithful and reliable ally of the Russian and international proletarian revolution'. Radek in Berlin in 1919 did not find it difficult to make converts to his thesis that Russia and Germany now had more common interests than ever, and that the logic of history compelled them to work together – not against each other. The Western Allies wanted to keep them apart. At the Versailles peace conference Lloyd George had circulated a confidential memorandum:

> The greatest danger that I see in the present situation is that Germany may throw in her lot with Bolshevism and place her resources, her brains, her vast organizing power at the disposal of the revolutionary fanatics whose dream is to conquer the world for Bolshevism by force of arms. This danger is no mere chimera.

Clemenceau was not impressed, but Rathenau was, though he did not take the revolutionary nonsense very seriously. Prussia, after all, was the kernel of Germany, and Prussia had always gravitated towards the East; this pull towards the East had been tempered only by the fear of being overwhelmed by the Russian colossus. But as the result of the war and the civil war Russia had been very much weakened and there was no immediate danger. True, there was the fear of Communism. 'We are on the eve of the German October', *Pravda* had written in December 1917. 'History is repeating itself; Berlin streets look like Petrograd streets on the eve of the revolution.' But history did not repeat itself. The Spartakist revolt failed and thus the way was opened to Rapallo, to German–Soviet economic exchanges, and to military collaboration between the Reichswehr and the Red Army. Rathenau and Brockdorff-Rantzau, Seeckt and Krupp (who was one of the first to supply machines to Russia), all reached the conclusion that a revision of the Versailles treaty could be achieved only through collaboration with Russia. This was not the policy of the Social Democrats, but among some of the centre parties and in particular those on the extreme right, Russia became very fashionable indeed. When Lenin wrote 'Even the blackest reactionaries and monarchists in Germany said that the Red Army would save them', he was reporting fairly accurately the state of affairs at the time of the Soviet–Polish War.

This re-orientation in foreign policy had its ideological and cultural parallels. There was a Dostoevsky boom, the like of which had not been witnessed before, and some shrewd observers realized that it had something to do with current politics. Moeller van den Bruck developed his theories about the right of the young peoples and their coming victorious struggle against the decadent West; Moeller by a strange coincidence was the German translator of Dostoevsky. Ernst Niekisch, mentor of the National Bolsheviks, preached a synthesis between the spirit of Potsdam and the spirit of Moscow, and declared war on Rome, Paris, and places west.

For Spengler, Russia was the only country which had a future, unlike America and the European states. But Spengler leads us to the Third Reich and the Nazis, who, as we all know, were bitter opponents of Russia. As Goebbels put it at the Reichsparteitag in 1936: 'From the very first hour of our political thinking we have carried on the struggle against this world danger with utter ruthlessness.' Goebbels' memory was short: eleven years before he had written a widely discussed article, 'The Russian Problem', in a periodical edited by Gregor Strasser, which was very much in line with the ideas then held by the National Bolshevists: 'Russia is our natural ally against the devilish temptations and the corruption of the West.' He was called to order by Alfred Rosenberg, then the party's chief ideologue, whose hatred of all things Russian was indeed above suspicion. Rosenberg's *obiter dicta* about Russia and Communism are found in the *Mythos* and in countless brochures and booklets: Bolshevism is the revolt of the Jewish and Mongolian races against the German (aryan) element in Russia; it is the revolt of the steppe, the hatred of the nomads for everything great, heroic, racially healthy; all big things in Russian history had been achieved by Germans or those of German blood, but the revolution of 1917 had exterminated the aryan element. A *rapprochement* with Russia was out of the question; the Germany of the day was not a German Reich, strong and self-confident, nor did the Jewish-Soviet Government represent the Russian people. To the Nazi ideologists, all leading Soviet statesmen were Jews: Lenin and Tomsky, Lunacharsky and Rakovsky, Kuibyshev and Krasin, Beria and Manuilsky among them. Whoever was not a Jew was a Chinese. Rosenberg developed an elaborate theory about the leading role of Chinese silk merchants in the Russian revolution. While other observers of the Soviet scene engaged in political speculation and social analysis, the Nazis' Russian experts were preoccupied with another kind of scientific investigation which hardly left them time for anything else. They tracked down the 'real' (Jewish) names of all Soviet leaders; Lunacharsky, for instance, became Mondschein – for who did not know that 'luna' was 'moon' in Latin? This, by and large, was the level of Nazi Sovietology.

Hitler himself as a young man had imbibed the traditional feelings of superiority *vis-à-vis* the Slavs. He was very much influenced in the early twenties by the Balts in his party (such as Alfred Rosenberg and Scheubner-Richter), who told him that Bolshevism was not an ideology but a Judaeo-Masonic conspiracy. This fitted in well with his prejudices and simplified matters; it made an ideological confrontation unnecessary. Russia and Bolshevism were to be exterminated. Yet he had a sneaking admiration for Stalin, as will be readily seen from his *Table Talk*; whenever he wanted to commend a particularly intransigent and militant party member (such as, for instance, Roland Freisler, the German Vyshinsky), he called him a 'real Bolshevik'. The alliance of twenty-two months in 1939–41 produced strange results on both sides; Goebbels, in his (secret) instructions to the German press, ordered the German–Russian reconciliation to be described as 'total and final', and Mr Molotov talked about a friendship that had been cemented in blood. Ribbentrop cabled home from Moscow that he had been given a royal welcome and felt himself 'among old party comrades'.

But in the end Hitler's intuition prevailed; the German army got its marching orders and the SS got its way with the doctrine of the *Untermensch*. The results are known.

Nazi–Communist relations from the late twenties are a study in misunderstanding. The Nazis refused to understand what Communism was all about; the Russians analysed and discussed at great length 'German fascism' – they did not like the term 'Nazism' or 'National Socialism'. But they were hopelessly wrong about it from beginning to end. They regarded it as the praetorian guard of monopoly capitalism, and Hitler as the instrument of Thyssen; when Thyssen was sent packing, this was just too bad for the facts – it was theory that mattered. They never even began to understand that National Socialism was a real mass movement, that extreme German nationalism had an enormous appeal and was a political factor of the very greatest importance, that Hitler was nobody's servant, and that in a totalitarian state the economy too is directed from above. They really seem to have thought that the German workers (and perhaps the peasants too) would soon be up in arms against Hitler. They failed to realize what should have been clear from their own experience, that a totalitarian state with its monopoly of the means of mass communication and indoctrination could easily succeed in neutralizing the great majority of the population and winning over large numbers to active collaboration with the regime. It was no accident (to borrow a phrase from the Communist jargon of the time) that Stalin was not prepared in June 1941.

In the West since the Second World War there has been an enormous literature on Hitler and Nazism; too much, perhaps, in particular at the popular level. There has been a certain morbid fascination with certain aspects of Nazism, as some observers have rightly noted. In the Soviet Union not a single book dealing with the Nazi regime, the party, its leaders, the SS, the Gestapo, the concentration camps, was published for many years – strictly speaking there was not even a history of Germany covering that period (apart from lecture courses). It would be fascinating to go, in some detail, into the real reasons for this apparent reluctance to deal with Nazism and the Third Reich.

The Russians were unprepared for the German onslaught in June 1941 in more than one sense. Sholokhov, in his *Nauka Nenavisti*, has described the shock experienced by Soviet citizens when they realized that the behaviour of the Germans in the occupied territories was very far indeed from their traditional image of the civilized and orderly German; they could not at first believe the news about mass killings, mass robbery, and brutal oppression. They had always held the Germans in special esteem (as Stalin had told Emil Ludwig in a famous interview: the Germans were solid, reliable, sober people who could be trusted). There had been some anti-Fascist literature, novels by Feuchtwanger, Friedrich Wolff, and Bredel (temporarily withdrawn from circulation in 1939), and the Soviet newspapers announced from time to time that the Communist Party and the working class of Germany were suffering severe persecution. But according to Bolshevik dogma the working class and the Communist parties of all capitalist countries had to suffer, so there was perhaps not so much to choose between Hitler, Daladier, Chamberlain, and FDR.

These misconceptions were rudely shattered during the first months of war. Alexei Tolstoy and Ilya Ehrenburg became the spokesmen of the new line, though Ehrenburg was restrained during the last phase of the war. On the German side, meanwhile, the most unbridled racial chauvinism prevailed, of which the famous *Untermensch* brochure is a perfect illustration.

When the war ended the Soviet Union emerged as one of the two strongest powers in the world, whereas divided Germany had ceased to exist as a major active factor in world politics. Its eastern third was gradually absorbed into the Soviet bloc, while West Germany joined NATO. Soon Russia was to become a nuclear power; as far as Moscow was concerned the German danger had ceased to exist. West Germany was now a small and vulnerable country in the centre of Europe that could be wiped out by half a dozen bombs. And yet the German menace continued to exist for some of the Western Slavs, who feared that a strengthening of Germany could somehow bring about a change in the *status quo* on its eastern frontiers. German revanchism also remained a favourite talking point for some British and American observers, who chose to interpret Soviet policy in Germany as a purely defensive reaction provoked by the fear of a Germany seeking revenge. The Russians were probably not displeased that such an impression had been created in some quarters abroad. They regarded Germany as the greatest post-war prize to be won in Europe. Stalin was willing to forgive the Germans; in 1949 he wrote to the East Berlin comrades that Russia and Germany had suffered more than any other country during the war and close cooperation had become imperative. As he had said earlier, Hitlers come and go, but Germany remains. But East Germany proved a disappointing starting point for winning over the whole of Germany. Soon it became all too obvious that the frontiers of Central Europe could be changed only as the result of a new war.

Even so, Germany continued to be of importance in Soviet foreign policy in two ways: If the Germans were so deeply concerned about German unity, the argument ran, then they could have their unity – at a price. For several years Soviet declarations about German unity remained ambiguous; only comparatively recently has it been stated that German unity is both impractical and undesirable. In these circumstances the potential 'Russian party' in West Germany received a fatal blow even before it had asserted itself; there was to be no new Rapallo or Tauroggen; the Russians were not willing to play. They could not sacrifice Ulbricht, nor were they able to disregard the susceptibilities of their brother Slavs in Warsaw and Prague.

The dimensions in German–Slav relations have changed, but the two peoples have clearly not reached the end of the road. Geography, the past, common interests, and quite a few unsolved problems bind them together, or at any rate make it impossible for them to ignore each other. Neither the much admired German romantic hero nor the much despised German philistine of the nineteenth century exists any longer; and the great-grandchildren of Ivan Karamazov do not spend much of their time nowadays discussing the ultimate questions of good and evil. But the Russian–German problem still persists and, for all we know, will still be with us in one form or another for a long time to come.

Chapter 2

'DE MORIBUS RUTHENORUM'

RELATIONS BETWEEN Russia and Germany have been close for a very long time. Intimacy, however, may breed not only friendship, but also contempt or open hostility. Russia has had friends and partisans in Germany, but also bitter enemies. Anti-Russian schools of thought, varying in character and motivation, have at certain times dominated German opinion, though in other periods they have attracted little public support. It is a serious error to exaggerate the importance of these attitudes, still more so to argue, as has been done, that there has been nothing but enmity between the two countries. On the other hand, little is to be gained by trying to minimize a tradition of distrust so deeply rooted in history: any discussion of German–Russian relations that tried to leave this awkward factor out of account would be not merely incomplete but dangerously misleading.

During the Middle Ages there was little contact between the two countries. Alexander Nevsky's defeat of the Teutonic Knights in 1242, which figures so prominently in all Russian history books, passed almost unnoticed in Germany. During the fourteenth and fifteenth centuries much of Russia was under the Tatar yoke. The first real confrontation came only in the sixteenth century, with Ivan IV's drive towards Livonia. The atrocities said to have been committed by the Russians during the invasion of 1558, were bewailed in a number of books, of which one by Timann Brakel, the preacher of the German community in Dorpat, was probably the best known. Yet these impressions were mainly confined to the Baltic Germans; most other educated Germans heard about Russian conditions for the first time from the report of Herberstein, who visited Moscow twice as the German emperor's envoy. Herberstein was very unfavourably impressed by some aspects of life in Russia, notably the despotic rule of the Tsar and the acquiescence of most of the population. This image of Russia dominated German thinking for centuries after. Another German sixteenth-century chronicler, Heinrich von Staden, called for a crusade against Russia and has, for this reason, been called a precursor of the war of intervention against the Soviet Union.[1]

This kind of genetic research into the history of ideas is of doubtful value unless its findings are put into their proper setting. Historians who go back far enough into the history of a people and include in their investigation everything that was done, said, or written, regardless of its intrinsic importance, can find proof for almost any thesis. There were indeed manifestations of Russophobia in Germany before the nineteenth century but so there were in France and England; the question whether Muscovy belonged to Christendom or was beyond the pale, was much discussed in the fifteenth and sixteenth centuries, and by no means only in Germany. Conversely, traces of anti-Germanism can readily be detected in Russian history; for centuries the Russians did not feel very friendly to Westerners, or to foreigners in general. The Prussian (later the German) government and ruling classes were certainly not permeated with the hatred and contempt for Russia that has sometimes been alleged. On the contrary, friendship with Russia was for many years a pillar of Prussian foreign policy; indeed, some critics thought this one-sided pro-Russian orientation very unfortunate for Germany.[2] The Cossacks, at any rate, were cordially received in Berlin in 1813, and when Tsar Nicholas I died in 1855, the Berlin *Kreuzzeitung* wrote, 'Our Emperor is dead' . . .

Anti-Russian feeling was to be found mainly on the left. From the seventeen-nineties there was considerable sympathy with the Poles, most of whom had come under Russian rule following the occupation and division of their country. After 1815, moreover, Russia loomed as the great bulwark of reaction and despotism, the main bastion of the 'Holy Alliance'. German nationalists, not without good reason, regarded Russia as a major obstacle to the unification of their homeland. For many years German democrats proclaimed the necessity of a war against Russia. Freiligrath, the revolutionary poet, wrote about the two camps into which the world was divided; everyone would have to stand up and be counted, and the free people of the West, under the oriflamme of liberty, were to defeat the slaves of the East in a last, decisive battle.* German freedom and unity would be achieved only after the overthrow of Russia.

In this confrontation between the revolutionary West and the reactionary East, German democrats usually equated Tsarist rule with the Russian people. If there was a Russian public opinion at that time, it certainly did not make itself widely heard in the West. Even Russians who were enemies of the Tsarist regime generally regarded the Polish question as a family quarrel between Slavs (as Pushkin put it), which strengthened Western democratic suspicions that the Russian opposition, weak as they were, could not be trusted; they were all thinly disguised Panslavists who wanted to conquer Europe. Even if Russians took an unequivocal stand on the Polish question, as Herzen and Bakunin did, they could not allay the fears and suspicions of men like Marx and Engels. German radical public opinion was anti-Russian, precisely because Russia was the trusted friend of their own government, particularly of Prussia. Russia opposed any reform, helped to suppress free thought, and acted, whenever it could, as Europe's censor and gendarme. Never was this more clearly felt than when Russian troops suppressed the revolution of 1848 in Hungary; for the German left, Russia was thenceforth a counter-revolutionary nation. The Russians (those 'aggressive Western Chinese', as Moses Hess called them), had all the faults but none of the virtues of primitive people. They were barbarians; their victory would plunge Europe into perpetual night and a Slav invasion would spell the destruction of all civilization and culture.†

These views were shared by most Democrats and Liberals at the time and had no more extreme exponents than Marx and Engels, whose main foreign political slogan in 1848–9 was war against Russia. Such a war would free the German nation and cleanse it of the sins of the past. The hatred of Russia (as Engels wrote to Bakunin) was the first revolutionary passion of the Germans. Russia was the enemy *par excellence* and the Germans should not be deflected from their purpose by vague references to a future in which Russia too would be democratic.

Marx and Engels remained staunchly anti-Russian throughout their lives, although they greatly admired the leaders and heroes of

* 'Zwei Lager zerklueften heute die Welt
Und ein hueben, ein drueben nur gilt.'

† Hess developed his ideas about Russia and Europe mainly in his *Europaeische Triarchie* (Leipzig, 1841), and his exchange of letters with Herzen.

28

the young Russian revolutionary movement. In their extreme distrust of all Russian influences they were given to exaggeration and unwarranted suspicion; Palmerston was certainly not a Russian agent, as they thought for a long time he was. They did not differentiate between the Tsarist regime and the Russian people. They welcomed, of course, the emergence of a socialist opposition in Russia in the seventies, but on the whole they regarded Russia as a country from which nothing good could possibly come to the rest of mankind. Its history was interpreted by Marx in very unfavourable terms. What could be expected of a people whose character had been formed during centuries of Mongol, Tatar, and Tsarist despotism? In their view Russia had made territorial conquests far beyond its natural frontiers; all revolutionary democrats and socialists thought it was an elementary demand of historical justice that the Poles and all other subjugated peoples should be liberated after the defeat of Tsarism. Many years later Marx's and Engels' views on Russia became a source of embarrassment to Soviet historians, who have argued that they were not Russophobes but merely abominated the Tsarist regime. Yet their unfavourable comments concerned not only Tsarist foreign policy but also Russian history, Panslavism, and even the Russian national character. There was also the fact that Marx and Engels, like most nineteenth-century thinkers, had been quite ready to subordinate the fate of small peoples to that of big 'revolutionary' nations. After all, the right of self determination for *all* peoples is a discovery of the twentieth, not the nineteenth century.

Marx's and Engels' views on Russia were by and large shared by the German democrats and, of course, by the socialist groups of the fifties and sixties. At the time of the Crimean War there was a strong movement in these circles to join in the battle against Russian autocracy, to make it a war of the Romano–Germanic peoples against the Slavs – the Poles always excepted because they had put their freedom above their Slavdom (as Friedrich Engels had said some years before).

The growth of a strong opposition within Russia towards the end of the nineteenth century naturally had its effect upon this attitude of the German left. Yet even then, Tsarism remained for the socialists the most abominated enemy in Europe. Engels, as well as Bebel and Wilhelm Liebknecht, continued to justify a revolutionary war against Russia in the eighteen-nineties. Plekhanov, the leader of the Russian Social Democrats, acclaimed the notion of such a war in

29

1893, and said that the German army would come as a liberator to Russia, even as the armies of revolutionary France had freed the Germans themselves a hundred years earlier.[3] It was not until the revolution of 1905 that the downfall of Tsarist rule became a credible possibility in the eyes of the German left wing. But the movement of revolt was defeated and many German socialists had no very high opinion of the Russian comrades whose perpetual internal conflicts were a source of anxiety to the whole international socialist movement. When the First World War broke out, German Social Democracy, almost without a dissenting voice, stood for what their spokesmen called the defence of Western (and especially German) civilization against corruption by primitive Russia.[4] In the name of culture and progress they joined in the war against Tsarist despotism, as a cause that coincided with the interests of the proletariat. Their war aims included the liberation of all the Tsar's non-Russian subjects – not only of the Poles, but also the Finns, Balts, White Russians, Moldavians, etc. The right wing of the party went even further and demanded annexations in the East; on the idea of splitting-up Russia, we shall have more to say.

Socialists and radical democrats were not, however, the only German enemies of Russia. There were the Russophobes on the right, mostly of German–Baltic origin, few perhaps in number but influential in the formation of German public opinion. Their enmity towards things Russian was a far more complex phenomenon than the hostility of the left; even the most militant among them had been influenced to a certain extent by Russian culture, and, generally speaking, by the more attractive features of Russian life. Theirs was more of a love-hate relationship in which, admittedly, hate prevailed in the end.

When Baron Haxthausen visited Russia in the eighteen-forties he found much anti-German feeling, but it was explained to him that the real culprits were the German Balts, who were so haughty and always pushed themselves to the fore. Their position was indeed a difficult one. They were a privileged, educated minority which tended to monopolize certain sections of the country's administration and of the army, but these were often routine jobs in provincial centres which the Russian aristocracy would not have wanted anyway. Haxthausen did not think that the antipathy was mutual: 'Among the Germans there is not the slightest antipathy to the Slavic peoples; on the contrary there is a palpable inclination towards them.'[5] About a decade later Herzen wrote his famous essay on German Russians and Russian Germans, but closer examination shows that his attack was directed primarily against the Balts and other German citizens of the Russian empire, who by that time were becoming the scapegoats *par excellence*. The privileges enjoyed by the Balts came under attack, and their cultural, educational, and religious autonomy was slowly whittled away. If they had until then a low opinion of some aspects of life in Russia and the way things were managed, their bitterness now became systematic and pronounced; it found eloquent expression in the works of Baltic publicists, some of whom attained positions of influence in Germany.* While a German–Baltic peasant was quoted as having interpreted the russification campaign as an attempt 'to replace our clean, well-fitting coat with their shabby and lice-infested sheepskin', his more sophisticated contemporaries complained of an 'invasion des Tatares'.[6]

This strained relationship between the Russians and the German Balts can be traced back to the eighteen-sixties and the emergence of Panslavism. The Panslavists entertained the ideal of a Russia that should extend 'from the Nile to the Neva, from the Elbe to Cathay' (Tiuchev). They also advocated the russification of both Slav and non-Slav minorities throughout the Russian empire. Carl Schirren, the spokesman of the German Balts, indignantly rejected these Russian claims to a world mission in an open answer to one of the leaders of Panslavism. Nobody would deny, he wrote, that the Russians were a very gifted people, but seriousness, moderation, and perseverance were not among their virtues. They were excessively subject to moods and emotions; they lacked manly principles. Was there any other people in the whole world so blind to the discrepancy between its real abilities and its aspirations?[7] Schirren also referred to what he called the destructive tendencies of the Panslavists and their polemics against Western civilization. There was a danger, he thought, that it would all end in a revolutionary war in the worst sense, a *Kulturkrieg*.[8] These charges were to be levelled time and again in later years. There is no denying that some of the leading spirits of Panslavism preached a holy war against the West. At the same time a tendency to generalize about the Russian national character can

---

* It was not confined to the Balts either; the growing Russian antipathy towards the Germans was widely noted. Fontane says about one of his heroes in *Cécile* (1886) that he fought with the Russians at Plevna, but resigned from Russian service in view of the 'growing Russian hate for everything German'.

already be detected, an eagerness to attribute certain qualities and characteristics to the whole Russian people. This tendency found its classic expression, and its culmination, in a book written about the same time as Schirren's warning, but published several decades later. This was Victor Hehn's *De moribus Ruthenorum*, the diary of a natural scientist of Baltic–German origin, and it is of the very greatest significance in this context. It is symptomatic of the frame of mind in which many German experts then regarded Russia and some of its judgments and ideas were later adopted by National Socialism.[9]

Hehn had spent many years in various parts of Russia and found nothing to admire there. Custine's famous book reads, in comparison, like the prospectus of a travel agency persuading the public to visit Russia. One wonders, in fact, that Hehn stuck it for so long, and decided to emigrate to Germany only in the seventies. While other contemporary writers found fault with the Russian government and the ruling class, Hehn reached the additional conclusion that there was nothing in the myth of the unspoilt Russian peasant. The Russian lacked idealism and any depth of feeling and emotion. Even Pushkin's talent was imitative; it lacked moral depth and there was a streak of frivolity in it. The Russians really were the Chinese of the West; the age-old despotism had enervated them, and they had no conscience and no honour. They were ungrateful and loved only those they feared. They had no perseverance, were corrupt, and were the world's greatest liars. They had no genuine talent, and had not produced a single statesman of real stature. The Russians lacked the gift of putting two and two together, and lost their heads in an emergency; no Russian was able, for instance, to become a railway engine driver. Hehn did not like their looks any more than their characters; he discussed at great length their lifeless skin and their brutal faces. Russian lack of cleanliness, the prevalence of fleas, their unhygienic toilet habits, were another source of despair to him. 'The Russian,' he wrote, 'is civilized only in the presence of others.' They had invented nothing; they could be deleted from the list of civilized nations without any loss to mankind.[10] They could be compared with the Japanese students who were sent to the West to study modern technique but had no creative genius of their own, no soul, no fantasy; such was the 'terrible inability' of a people that could not advance mentally beyond the stage of a German secondary school pupil. The educated Russian, too, was a miserable creature, and at the same time a great danger for Europe. There were so many Slavs, perhaps there would be a new battle of Chalons? If the Mongols had reached Silesia, the Russians could well advance up to the Atlantic coast.

Hehn was sarcastic about the Russian susceptibility to the latest intellectual fashions: of course they jumped at every new idea (such as socialism), they had no tradition, no roots, no culture of their own to fall back on. All they possessed had been imported from abroad. In a very interesting passage he discussed Chernyshevsky's socialist views: socialism and communism presupposed a very high stage of social and cultural development. For that reason Russia was the least likely place for such an experiment. Strict orders and the whip could induce the Russians to commit acts of heroism. They presented a wonderfully malleable mass for any sort of masters – whether Varangians, or German NCO's. But could freedom and humanity grow and develop in these conditions?

Hehn's observations cannot be simply dismissed as the ravings of a German chauvinist. He was a liberal, and much of his bitter criticism of Russia stemmed from his opposition to Tsarist autocracy, but towards the end of his life his liberalism went sour – he became an extreme conservative and anti-Semite. In this respect his political biography was not at all unique. He saw some of the problems very clearly, as his remarks on socialism indicate. He had no illusions about the rôle of the Germans in Russia who (he said) led a semi-colonial existence. In the eyes of the Russian people they were on the side of the suspicious and bloodthirsty rulers, supporters of the corrupt court and the obscurantist church; they had no sympathy with the sufferings of the Russian people. Hehn was not a racialist; he lived in an age in which culture and civilization counted for more than race. On the contrary, he and some other German anti-Russian writers of the late nineteenth century express bewilderment that, though there was some racial affinity between Germans and Slavs, there was such a cultural disparity between them. Much of what Hehn reported was undoubtedly correct and was said by contemporary Russian writers as well; at the very time when Hehn was writing in his diary, Chernyshevsky called his people 'a miserable nation, a nation of slaves, from top to bottom nothing but slaves'. Yet in contrast to the Russian radicals Hehn saw no redeeming features at all, no prospect of change and improvement.

Quite independently of the Balts there was a school of thought among German right-wing thinkers in the late nineteenth century which was anti-Russian by conviction, and advocated German expansion eastwards. Constantin Frantz, one of Bismarck's chief critics, wanted to see Prussia wage war in the east on the grand scale, with three great armies marching upon Warsaw, Riga, and Vilna, and occupying all the territory up to the Dvina.[11] Even more sweeping in his demands and conceptions was Paul de Lagarde, who in many respects was the ideological godfather of the Nazi movement. He regarded Russia as potentially the greatest menace to Germany and the chief obstacle to Germany's drive to the east. Lagarde wanted the Russians and southern Slavs to be cleared out of Poland and the Black Sea region, which should be conquered for German colonization. The Germans were a peaceful people but they had a mission to fulfil; obstructed, they had a right to use force.[12] Friedrich Lange, another well-known racialist of the early days, called upon Germany to advance into 'these nerveless territories', conquer them and change them into German lands.[13] The Lagardes and Langes were outsiders; they made a certain impact on public opinion but upon German policy they had little, if any, influence in their time. Their ideas were, however, taken up in the middle nineties by the Pan-Germans, that famous political group which stood for German expansionism in its most aggressive form. The Pan-Germans anticipated many of the basic tenets of Nazism, such as their teaching of the racial superiority of the German people and its mission to rule the world, their contempt for law and international treaties, the belief that might always precedes right and the conviction that occasional wars are highly desirable as a form of mental and physical hygiene for the nation. Latter-day historians have offered conflicting assessments of the political importance of the *Alldeutsche*; some regard them as a comparatively small group of eccentrics and cranks who never had any real influence on German politics; others believe they can detect their hidden hand in many fateful decisions of German foreign policy. It is the belief of the present writer that the direct influence of the Pan-Germans on national policy was limited and brief (important only during the First World War), but that their influence on public opinion, particularly in certain sections of the middle class, was considerable. This influence is not always easy to estimate; many German teachers, to give but one example, were strongly influenced by the *Alldeutsche*, but they had no ways or means of expressing their views outside their schools and universities; the great organs of the press were not at their disposal. Their very considerable indirect influence was felt much later, when those born between 1880 and 1900 entered German politics. Thus, indirectly, the Pan-Germans did a good deal towards conditioning German minds for the reception of National Socialism.

The Pan-Germans were convinced that Germany was surrounded by enemies – a projection of their own feelings upon the neighbours of the Reich – and believed that the Greater Germany they envisaged, which was to extend 'fon Boonen bis Narwa, fon Bisanz bis ans Schwarze Meer', would be won only by force of arms. (Boonen, incidentally, was Boulogne, and Bisanz was Besançon.) One Pan-German spokesman demanded, in 1893, that the Baltic lands should be restored to Germany.[14] Predicting future events in Europe during the next two decades, which was a favourite sport in these circles, an anonymous author announced, in 1895, that Germany's new eastern frontier would lie along the line Narva – Pskov – Vitebsk to the bend of the Dnieper, and from there eastwards to the Don. Not only the whole of the Ukraine and the Crimea were to be incorporated in the Reich, but the entire Saratov region as well.[15]

Some Pan-German authors, such as Tannenberg and the president of the association, Heinrich Class (writing under the pseudonym Daniel Fryberg) advocated the evacuation of the (Slav) local population from the areas in the east after their conquest by Germany.[16] They repeated time and again that the destruction of the strongest Slav power, Russia, was an essential preliminary to the building of Pan-Germany in Europe.[17] The same anonymous writer advised the German leaders not to be unduly worried by considerations of international law; the more brutal the treatment of the defeated, the more lasting would be the ensuing peace. In ancient times defeated peoples had been physically destroyed; in modern times this could no longer be done. 'Nevertheless one could think of conditions which would approach such destruction very closely indeed.'[18] Racial enmity between Slavs and Germans, said Class, was a fact of the greatest political significance; it sprang from dissimilarities of national character, which had their roots in the different racial origins of Russians and Germans. This was 1913, and Class, the president of the Pan-German Association, had good news to add: war with Russia was impending.[19] The *Alldeutsche* attacked all Germany's neighbours with equal vehemence; in their view there was nothing to choose between Russians and other Slavs, whereas one of the basic

35

tenets of the liberal imperialists was that the Poles and the Ukrainians must be wooed by Germany in order to win their support to defeat Russia. This division of opinion was to reappear later. Hitler, too, believed that he could defeat all enemies in the East and West single-handed, whereas some of his more far-seeing advisers realized comparatively early that such a policy was bound to end in disaster.

The First World War gave fresh impetus to German anti-Russian feeling; among its most vocal mouthpieces were three Balts, Theodor Schiemann, Johannes Haller, and Paul Rohrbach. The first two were prominent historians, the third a leading political publicist and advocate of the idea of *Mitteleuropa*. Haller and Rohrbach survived both Kaiser and Fuehrer. They did not join the Nazi Party and were to a certain extent critical of Hitler and what he stood for; yet there is no doubt that their writings strongly influenced a whole generation of German nationalists. Rohrbach, who was the most influential, started early in the 1914–18 War to advocate the partition-ing of Russia. He urged that the 'Russian colossus' should be dissected into its 'natural historical and ethnic components' – Finland, Poland, Bessarabia, the Baltic provinces, the Ukraine, the Caucasus, and Turkestan. Russia, he argued, could be divided up like an orange, without a cut or a wound, whereas Germany or France would not survive such an operation.[20] Yet Rohrbach was no Pan-German or racialist. On various occasions he referred to Russian persecution of the Jews as further evidence of Tsarist brutality and Russian back-wardness. He fought a running battle against the Pan-Germans, whose demands, he maintained, lacked both moderation and realism and had done immeasurable harm to the German cause throughout the world.[21] Rohrbach's imperialism was national-liberal in inspira-tion, based on a feeling of cultural rather than racial superiority. If Pan-German propaganda reached tens of thousands of Germans, Rohrbach's political travelogues were even more widely circulated; he was probably the most widely read German foreign political commentator in the first two decades of the century.

Rohrbach's theories on the artificial character of the Russian state were not exactly novel; they could be traced back to a casual remark in Haxthausen's famous book, according to which Russia was geographically subdivided into four colossal separate regions. Haxthausen did not draw any far-reaching political conclusions from this observation of his, but others did. There had been an influ-ential group in Berlin during the Crimean War, the so-called *Wochen-*

blattspartei, which advocated a similar policy. One of their spiritual heirs was Theodor Schiemann, Professor of Russian History, who believed that the Russian empire was a more or less synthetic creation, including as it did a conglomeration of various incompatible races and peoples, held together only by Tsarist despotism. The first big shock, so he argued, would wreck the Russian empire and bring about its dissolution. Schiemann, not a very effective speaker, produced a great number of booklets and pamphlets and had considerable influence at court (he carried on a correspondence with the Kaiser), among the army general staff, and even in the Foreign Ministry. He was in favour of a separate peace with the British in order to gain a free hand in the East, for there were not many spoils of victory to be had in the West, whereas the prospects for expansion in the East seemed almost limitless.[22]

Professor Haller's professional speciality was the Middle Ages, which did not prevent him from participating with much gusto in the discussion of topical problems. A little book with the suggestive title *The Russian Menace in the German House* was his main contribution to this debate.[23] The two main theses of his works were that Germany had to expand in its natural direction, which was to the east, and that Russia was historically outside the European family of nations and its cultural and political traditions.

In what way did the Russians differ? The First World War was the heyday of speculation about Panslavism, Dostoevsky and the Russian soul, both on the literary and the political levels; the litterateurs wrote like politicians and the political commentators like essayists evaluating Dostoevsky. Most of them stressed the imponderabilia of the Russian soul, its deep instinctive rejection of the occidental Roman–German culture, and the nebulous Byzantine–Slav *folie de grandeur* which was allegedly in the blood of every Russian – 'that fantastic, boundless, specifically instinctive attitude'.[24] The adjectives were usually the same; nobody made it quite clear what all this really meant, apart from the fact that it was something destructive, aggressive, and very dangerous. This view of the matter reappeared in much of the writing of the time, and was absorbed and simplified by Nazi writers such as Rosenberg, Schickedanz, and Georg Leibbrandt.

Having established some of these ideological antecedents, it remains to note that Russophobia in pre-1918 Germany was only one of a number of currents of thought about Russia, and not even, on the right, the dominant one. Otto Hoetzsch, one of the leading pro-Russian commentators both before and after 1918, vigorously criticized the anti-Russian propagandists even in the middle of the war.[25] It was perhaps symptomatic that Hoetzsch succeeded the Russophobe Schiemann, in November 1914, as the chief commentator of the *Kreuzzeitung*. Schiemann treated the whole of Russian culture with contempt, and became so anti-Russian after the outbreak of war that he soon got out of touch with his readers, who consisted mainly of staunch Prussian junkers.[26] If some militant German publicists proposed to dismember Russia into its 'natural' components, it is only fair to recall that some Allied statesmen and publicists also spoke in favour of various schemes to 'carve up Hunland'. German historians contributed their share to the conception of the 'Asiatic' origins of Russia, yet Henri Massis, with his *Defence of the Occident*, and the 'Eurasians', a Russian *emigré* school of thought, became in later years even more closely identified with this theory.[27]

To sum up, German Russophobia was a complex phenomenon; it existed on the left as well as on the right, not to mention the specific contribution made by the Baltic Germans. In a similar way, anti-Germanism in Russia was endemic both among Panslavists and among some revolutionaries. Russophobia certainly dominated German left-wing thought until the end of the First World War; on the right it was an influential but never a really dominant school of thought. The motives of left-wing Russophobia had, of course, nothing at all to do with the considerations that made the Pan-Germans and national-liberals think in terms of expansion towards the east, yet indirectly it had an undoubted effect upon public opinion. National Socialism got most of its ideas on Russia from the Balts and the Pan-Germans, but it also owed a considerable if unacknowledged debt to such national-liberal propagandists as Rohrbach. The Russophobia remained but the ideological justification was somewhat modified. The one new idea that was added by the Nazi writers in the nineteen-twenties and thirties was the concept of 'racial chaos': the idea that the deplorable state of the Russians was the result of some inferior blood mixture. Thus the German cultural mission in the East of 1914 became a racial mission in 1933.

Chapter 3

'WE ARE BIGGER PEOPLE
THAN THE GERMANS'

'THE RUSSIAN BATTLE of Dorking' was the title of an article published in a British journal in 1902; it described the surprise and anger of a Russian citizen who had fallen asleep in 1897, and awoke only after thirty years, when he found that in the meantime his country had been taken over by the Germans. There had been only six weeks of war, six weeks in which the Germans, owing to their decisive superiority, especially in the scientific field, had completely crushed the Russians. The Tsar's empire had been truncated; Finland and Bessarabia, for instance, were no longer part of it, and the capital had been moved to Nizhny Novgorod. What remained of Russia was a German dependency, while the Jews were almost everywhere in charge of local government. The native Russians were reduced to the status of hewers of wood and drawers of water.[1]

It was a fantasy (and one not very skilfully elaborated) which reflected certain fears that had been entertained in Russia for a long time. There had been apprehension of a 'German invasion' as far back as 1840, although at that time Germany was still weak and disunited.[2] This fear was in part symptomatic of a feeling of resentment that had its roots far back in history, earlier than the time of Peter the Great; in part it was a reaction against the Petrine reforms that had brought so many foreigners to Russia, where they soon assumed leading positions in the state and the army. With them they imported German customs and the German language; Russia had a German Government when, shortly before her death, the Empress Anna appointed her favourite Biron (Buehren) regent. Biron was soon ousted by Muennich, and Muennich by Ostermann, until Elisabeth, Peter's daughter, overthrew this clique with the help of the palace

39

guards. Even if Biron had been a wise and competent statesman instead of an adventurer, he was a German and therefore unacceptable to most Russians. Though the *Bironovshchina* did not last many years, it is remembered to this day as a particularly brutal and corrupt episode in Russian history and a symbol of foreign domination and exploitation.[3] It is by no means certain that Russian government was in fact any less arbitrary or corrupt before or after the *Bironovshchina*, nor indeed did the number of Germans in high places diminish in the second half of the eighteenth century.[4] But Russian resentment against foreigners in high positions, fanned by the old nobility and the newer gentry alike, was the first assertion of Russian nationalism. National consciousness and nationalism do not grow in isolation; they develop in contrast to, or in conflict with, some outside enemy. Certainly up to 1812 the German was the foreigner *par excellence* to the Russians – the others did not matter, or were too far away to be of any consequence.

Schloezer and Mueller, two German historians who had removed to Russia, were, in contrast to Biron, exemplary citizens. They won fame as the first to treat the study of Russian history as a scientific discipline, but they soon found themselves under attack by Lomonosov in the Academy of Sciences. Lomonosov thought that Russian history could and should be written only by Russians. Foreigners were bound to treat the subject without emotion, without heart, and without patriotic feeling; they would depict medieval Russia as a country of savages, and would describe Russian history as a chain of murders, robberies, treason and pillage. Thus the controversy began about the origins of Russia; most foreign scholars maintained that Russia's first rulers had been Varangians, of Germanic, not Slavic stock. All Russian patriots took violent exception to this 'Norman' theory.[5] The Germans were disliked but they continued to be needed in Russia – as technical specialists, merchants, private tutors, and above all in the army and the civil service. The higher posts usually went to the Baltic Germans, while tutors, technicians and artisans were often newcomers from Germany proper. The Russian aristocracy and the emerging intelligentsia showed little eagerness to join the state service; it was not very remunerative nor was it considered quite the proper thing to do; hence the growing number of Germans in state service. Some of the Tsars, such as Nicholas I, quite rightly assumed that the Germans were more pliable tools for carrying out their repressive and unpopular policies than the

Russians, who valued their independence more highly. The percentage of army officers of German extraction was particularly high; in 1812 there were no fewer than sixty generals of German origin. Even in the eighteen-eighties, at the height of the Panslavic propaganda, about 40 per cent of the posts in the higher command were held by Russians of German origin. In some ministries their share was even higher – 57 per cent in the Ministry of Foreign Affairs, 46 per cent in the Ministry of War, 62 per cent in the Ministry of Posts and Communications. Broadly speaking, a third of all high government officials, army and navy officers, and an equal proportion of the members of the Senate, were of German origin at a time when Germans constituted not more than one per cent of Russia's population.[6]

A German name did not, of course, invariably mean that the bearer was deficient in patriotism. They all were loyal subjects of the Tsar; quite a few families had been assimilated in everything but name and some had even adopted the Orthodox religion. But in most cases it was personal loyalty to the Tsar and there was no identification with the emergent nationalist movement. It was not really a matter of names; both Herzen and the early Slavophiles, when attacking the Germans, were willing to admit that quite a few of them had served Russia well, that the Gorchakovs and the Shuvalovs and others of true Russian blood were much worse than any Baltic baron. What they opposed was the whole 'German' system, 'a razor's edge passed between the heart and the head of the nation, a poison injected into the most sensitive fibres of the body';[7] 'l'empire knouto-Germanique', as Bakunin put it.

Anti-German feeling took various forms. Among the aristocrats there was contempt for the submissive, obsequious German. Bakunin ironically noted the inscription under the Prussian eagle affixed to a Berlin tailor's shop: *Unter deinen Fluegeln kann ich ruhig buegeln.* The awkward, clumsy German tutor had been a stock figure of ridicule – Vralman in Fonvizin's play *The Minor* was an early example. The same author had written in 1784, after a visit to Central and Western Europe, that 'everything with us is better, and we are bigger people than the Germans.'[8] Was this perhaps a first manifestation of the Russian *'shirokaya natura'* (as Professor Rogger has put it) as against the Germans' lack of humanity, feeling, and heart? But Fonvizin himself had come from a completely assimilated German family, which shows that caution is needed when generalizing about the 'Russian Germans'.

Russian aristocratic contempt for the German *meshchanin's* lack of elegance and *savoir vivre* remained constant throughout the nineteenth century, as was regretfully noted by a German ambassador.[9] Whilst there was admiration for everything that came from Paris, even while Moscow was burning in 1812, there was only contempt for all things German, even while the alliance with Prussia lasted.

Anti-German feeling among the intelligentsia had different sources and manifested itself in a different way. The impact of German philosophy on Russia was enormous, and it has already been noted that Schiller had an even greater influence on Russian than on German literature. Goethe and Schiller, however, were thought to belong to all mankind; they did not make the Russians any better disposed towards contemporary Germany. When Johann Kohl, the author of an early Baedekerlike guide-book, visited Moscow around 1840, he had an interesting meeting with the writer and historian Polevoi: 'Of Schiller and Goethe he spoke with the warmest enthusiasm, as well as of Herder's *Ideas* which, he said, were in the hands of all cultivated Russians. But speaking of Germany of the present day he raised his hands above his head and exclaimed: "My God, where has the genius of Germany hidden itself?" '[10]

Polevoi was no extremist; the early Slavophiles were far more outspoken. Ivan Kireyevsky, writing around 1850, compared Germany to a prison, or a coffin, in which people were buried alive. There was no nation on the entire globe so dull, soulless, and vexatious as the Germans; in comparison with them the Bulgarians were geniuses.[11] What displeased Kireyevsky and his friends was the lack of vitality of the Germans, their woodenness, their absence of any show of feeling – or perhaps they did not have any human feelings? The Germans, in brief, did not really *live*; an essential dimension was missing from their national make-up. Years later Russian Jews were to make similar complaints about their German co-religionists.

Slavophiles and Westerners in Russia quarrelled about most things but with regard to Germany, Herzen, an outspoken Westerner, shared to a great extent the feelings of the Slavophiles, partly for the same reasons. The Left, in addition, had other reasons for their dislike. Russian writers were never permitted to forget for long that the head of the 'third department' (the political police and the censorship) was named Benckendorf, and his successor Dubbelt, and that, generally speaking, the high German official was a symbol of restriction and of everything reactionary in Russia. Another contemporary observer,

Michelet, wrote: *'En Russie le peuple n'existe pas; il n'y a que le bureau et le fouet. Le bureau c'est l'Allemand, le fouet c'est le Cosaque.'* Since so many Germans had chosen to serve the Tsarist autocracy, quite a few Russian progressives formed the mistaken idea that this autocracy was a German importation. The struggle against the 'Russian German' became for some, like Herzen, almost an obsession.

Up to the eighteen-sixties the presence of so many Germans in Russia had been considered a domestic problem. The successors of Nicholas I did not show great preference for Germans; at Court there was a strong anti-German faction, and their share of the top positions gradually decreased. But it was now that Germany emerged almost overnight as a major factor in European politics and as a potential enemy of Russia. Gorchakov, the Foreign Minister, pursued a policy which, broadly speaking, was pro-German, just as Bismarck put great emphasis on the alliance with Russia, but popular opinion in Russia, which was beginning to exert a certain influence on foreign policy, was strongly anti-German. Katkov's influential *Moskovskie Vedomosti* had been alarmed by the Prussian victory over Austria in 1866; it had engaged in anti-German polemics ever since and advocated a *rapprochement* with France to counterbalance the growing power of a Germany united by Prussia. Katkov had strong public support, for there was a growing fear that Germany would soon reclaim the Baltic provinces and perhaps restore an independent Poland. Above all, the whole European equilibrium, as it had existed for so long, was upset by the emergence of a strong Germany. At the end of the Franco-Prussian War early in 1871, a German diplomat reported from St Petersburg that the attitude there was markedly hostile towards Germany; in part it stemmed from fear of the powerful neighbour, but it also reflected strong liberal and republican feelings 'up to the very highest society' which induced many people to sympathize with France.[12] The same considerations, and the belief that the autocrats should stick together against their enemies, induced the Tsar to pursue a pro-German policy. Katkov's propaganda, especially in later years, expressed the fears of powerful industrialists, especially those who felt themselves directly threatened by German competition and who demanded a policy of protectionism. Since these economic conflicts played an important part in the deterioration of relations between Russia and Germany in the last quarter of the nineteenth century and the years leading up to the First World War, they call for a brief description.

German industry, which had made rapid headway after 1870, wanted to export as much as possible to Russia, whereas the big land-owners in Germany resisted any liberal trade policy, which for them would have meant stiff competition with Russian wheat. In Russia, on the other hand, the great expansion of industry did not begin until later, and Russian industrialists felt that they needed state protection to develop a native industry against foreign competition. In the eighteen-eighties the Tsarist government adopted a protectionist policy, imposing heavy duties on most foreign products; Bismarck retaliated in kind by putting a heavy tax on the import of Russian grain to Germany. This customs war continued for years; the steep decline in trade between the two countries was accompanied by acrimonious attacks in the press. It was ended by a compromise in 1894 but the relations between the two countries had suffered lasting damage; Russia never completely regained the position it formerly held as Germany's main supplier of grain, while French capital and French and Belgian industry had to a certain extent replaced those of the Germans in Russia. The trade agreement of 1894 was, on balance, more favourable to Russia than to Germany, but Russian public opinion resented the economic treaty that replaced it ten years later, for it was argued that Russia, under pressure because of the war with Japan, had been forced to accept unfavourable conditions. Professor Mitrofanov wrote in 1914 that Russia had been a tributary of Germany for many years and public opinion would insist that the government should not repeat its former mistakes. Witte, too, thought that much of the anti-German feeling in his country had been caused by the resentment arising from unfavourable trading conditions.[13]

The rapid progress of industrial development in both Russia and Germany seemed irresistible, but there were grave forebodings in certain circles, both high and low, that felt excluded from its benefits, about its social and political effects. They hated the liberal *bourgeois* elements, which included more than a few Jews, who were growing in strength. There was a curious parallelism between German and Russian reactions to these changes. In both countries the anti-Semitic movement was a strange mixture of reactionary and populist, conservative and anti-capitalist sentiments.

Both monarchs and their families were anti-Semitic – the Romanovs more so than the Hohenzollern. They regarded the Jew as the agent both of capitalism and of socialism, of liberalism and of communism, in any case as undermining the established order. They had some vague ideas about promoting popular forces that shared their resentment of capitalism, liberalism, socialism, and of those who represented these trends. It was realized and openly admitted that between the monarchs there was a community of interest to defeat these enemies. Admiral von Hintze, a confidant of Wilhelm II in Moscow, wrote in a report to the Emperor a few years before the outbreak of the First World War that there was a common interest in holding down the Poles and the Jews. Unwilling to offend Albert Ballin and some other German Jews in the entourage of the Kaiser, he added, 'I have in mind international Jewry.' But he also wrote: 'The traditional friendship between Germany and Russia has, after all, grown on this very soil.'[14] Both monarchs believed in a Jewish world conspiracy, and were greatly impressed by the *Protocols of the Elders of Zion*. After the murder of the Tsar's family, three books were found in their house in Ekaterinburg – the Bible, *War and Peace*, and a Russian edition of the *Protocols*. And in the last letters of the Tsarina there was mention of that ominous sign of a new international brotherhood, the Swastika.[15]

Economic competition intensified the Russian–German antagonism, but was it really a decisive factor? If anti-German feeling flared up after 1876, and again after 1908, it was sparked off largely by political and military developments in the Balkans. Russian public opinion supported the aspirations of the Serbs and the Bulgarians. Aid committees were founded throughout Russia, and the news from the battlefields (and from the diplomatic front) was followed with great interest and enthusiasm, and the events and moods of the time can be clearly traced in contemporary Russian literature. This support for the southern Slavs was not entirely unconnected (to put it cautiously) with the traditional drive towards Constantinople, and it brought Russia into conflict with the Habsburg monarchy. A Panslav diplomat said at the time that the road to Constantinople passed through Vienna. Who would help Russia to achieve its aims in the Balkans? Certainly not Germany, Austria's ally.

The outcome of the Berlin Congress in 1878 did not improve matters; the general impression in St Petersburg was that Bismarck had led the senile Gorchakov up the garden path. This was an exaggeration, for though Bismarck was never quite so pro-Russian as he pretended to be, he did make an effort at the time of the Berlin Congress to prevent the emergence of a new 'Crimean coalition' against

Russia. This, however, was not recognized or appreciated by Russian public opinion, and many Russians then became firmly convinced that nothing good could come out of Germany. Some Russians, such as Dostoevsky, despite their personal dislike of the Germans, might admire the efficiency and other good qualities of Russia's western neighbour, and envisage a long alliance – for 'have not the Germans needed us much more than we have needed them?' But others reacted differently; one of them was Ignatiev, the Minister of the Interior, another Skobelev, the conqueror of Turkestan. In an interview in Paris he declared that the Russians were not masters in their own house – the foreigner was everywhere and everything:

> 'We are dupes of his policy, victims of his intrigue, and from his baneful influence we can only be delivered by the sword. Shall I tell you the name of this intriguing intruder, this oppressor of Russians and Slavs? You all know him as the author of the *Drang nach Osten*. He is the German. I repeat and entreat you never to forget that the German is the enemy. A struggle is inevitable between the Teuton and the Slav. It cannot be long deferred. It will be long, sanguinary, and terrible.'[16]

The press in both Russia and Germany played a central role in the deterioration of relations between the two countries. Their exchanges followed a recurrent pattern. *Novoe Vremya*, for instance, would publish a sensational article about the 'Organization of German espionage in Europe', in which Bismarck was accused of striving for German world rule.[17] Similar articles were written by Prince Meshchersky in the *Grazhdanin* or the *Moskovskie Vedomosti*; soon many other papers followed suit. Meanwhile, some Russian general would give an interview to one of the revanchist papers in Paris or publish a pamphlet about the desirability of a Russo-French alliance to defeat Germany. Later, the German press would launch a counter-attack, drawing attention to the Russian military build-up in Poland or elsewhere. Russian diplomats in Berlin, and German diplomats in the Russian capital, would find themselves spending much of their time commenting on some newspaper article, denying or explaining it, continually preoccupied with the press.[18]

One is sometimes tempted to suspect that but for the existence of the press, the First World War would never have happened. Every two or three years there was a scare and many people, including some in high positions, persuaded themselves that war between the two countries was just around the corner. Then would follow a temporary *détente*, until the publication of some new sensational item about Russian (or German) political intentions and military plans created a new crisis. This went on, almost without interruption, throughout the forty years before the First World War. Schweinitz, for many years the German ambassador in Russia, noted in his diary that never and nowhere had the press exerted a more negative influence on foreign policy than in Russia; in other countries the press was merely one of the factors that shaped public opinion, but in Russia it was the only one, and the government hardly ever saw fit to defend policy against its unbridled attacks.[19] Schweinitz forgot to add that the German press was no better, and that some of the publications of the *Alldeutsche* after 1890 were, if anything, slightly worse. Yet the attacks in the press did not come out of the blue and one cannot attribute them all to the sensationalism of journalists given to exaggeration or flights of fantasy. To a large extent these papers only printed what they thought the public would like to read or, in some instances, what they were paid to publish by various supporters. With or without the press, after 1880 war against Germany would have been more popular in Russia than war against any other nation – just as war against Russia had many enthusiastic advocates in Germany before 1914.

Bismarck, Wilhelm II, and most German diplomats thought that the revolutionary Panslavists were natural allies of republican France, and suspected that many educated Russians would actually welcome a war because it would lead to the overthrow of the existing order.[20] Some highly placed Russians shared this conviction; Giers, for instance, said in 1888 that all those who wished to overthrow the regime wanted war. This was no doubt an exaggerated view, but not altogether wrong, for ultimately Tsarism *was* overthrown following two military defeats; if the desire among the Russian opposition for a war was probably less deliberate and conscious than the Germans assumed, it did nevertheless exist. Nor were the fears of a German attack restricted to the extreme nationalists; as far back as 1868 Herzen had written about the approach of the learned Barbarians – everyone knew whom he meant, and his feelings were shared by many liberals.

Following the advice of some of his counsellors, Wilhelm II decided, in 1890, not to renew the Reinsurance Treaty. This led to a reorientation of Russian foreign policy and eventually to a military convention with France. Much has been written about that fateful decision. It has been argued, for instance, that Russia would have been compelled to turn to France in any case, since there was not enough surplus capital in Germany to assist Russia's industrialization. But in 1890 the initiative was the Kaiser's; Russian diplomacy made great efforts to renew the treaty. Germany's economic position in Russia remained quite strong; in the years before the First World War Germany was Russia's most active trade partner by far, taking about one third of all Russia's exports and supplying almost half of her imports. If there was friction with Germany, the possibility of conflict with England was certainly as acute. In later years the Kaiser reached the conclusion that war between Slavs and Germans was inevitable and that its outbreak was merely a question of time.[21] But in his early days he was far more cautious, and did not want war with Russia 'merely to satisfy a hundred crazy Junkers', as he said on one occasion. If so, his decision in 1890 was most probably a gesture of self-assertion, an act of defiance against Bismarck who had dominated German foreign policy for so long; he wanted to show his people and the whole world that he was going to pursue his own policy.

But once the formal tie had been severed, one thing led to another and relations continued to deteriorate. Public opinion in Russia had been unfriendly towards Germany even while the two countries were allies, and it became more hostile after opposing camps had been formed. When Austria took over Bosnia and Herzegovina in 1908, there was tremendous indignation in Russia, and German activities in Turkey (the Liman von Sanders mission, for instance) created more suspicion and ill-will.

Germany had few well-wishers in Russia and the majority of them belonged to the extreme right wing. The Tsar and his family were certainly not anti-German. In a remarkable interview with the German ambassador in 1908 the Tsar's praise of the German national character contrasted sharply with his assessment of his own people, of whom he spoke in derogatory terms.

If the Tsar did not think highly of Russians, many a Russian patriot was suspicious of the Romanovs; for some old aristocratic families they always remained foreigners. The liberal and centre parties and large sections of the aristocracy and the army were anti-German; Witte's attitude was exceptional. Among the socialists there was perhaps some sympathy for Bebel's Germany, but certainly not for the Kaiser's. Anti-German feeling was manifested among many sections of the intelligentsia during the First World War, in a number of books and articles that purported to show how 'from Kant to Krupp' (to quote the title of one of the most widely discussed) the Germans had been up to no good. Around 1910 many leading Russians and Germans had formed the firm notion that a war between the two countries was inevitable. The reasons that made them think so seem almost inexplicable fifty years later; perhaps it was the result of boredom, the desire for change at almost any price. These leaders and leading citizens did not of course envisage the holocaust that was to follow, but instead imagined a short and not too bloody war, that would somehow absorb the excess energies and purify the air. True, many Russians realized that the house of Romanov would probably not survive a second unlucky war, but this prospect does not appear to have concerned many of them. Somebody would take their place; in any case, few thought in terms of a Russian defeat.

Symptomatic of the lack of political imagination and of the flippancy that prevailed in both countries, is a report that was submitted to the Kaiser in 1910. During the meeting of the two emperors in Potsdam in November 1910, an anonymous German source, probably a fairly high-ranking officer, reported a conversation he had had with members of the Tsar's entourage who were hostile towards Germany. The Russians argued that there were economic conflicts that could not be resolved. Germany was basically an industrial country, which the Junkers had artificially made into a country producing agrarian products. 'We Russians have to buy your industrial products but you close your borders to our grain exports. Your press being in the hands of Jews is almost uniformly anti-Russian.' It was a distorted picture but apparently a widely accepted one. The German answered, 'Judging by what you say, war is now a possibility. Well, we shall do our duty. But this should not prevent our having a very nice get-together at the Ritz in Paris after the war, when we shall tell each other what it was like on the other side.' (*Und wir koennen uns dann erzaehlen wie es hueben und drueben war.*)[22] It is not known if the meeting at the Ritz ever took place; if it did, those present were undoubtedly wiser and sadder men.

Chapter 4

THE RISE OF NATIONAL SOCIALISM
PART I: HITLER'S MENTORS

VICTORY CAME to extremist parties in a number of European countries in the wake of the chaos during and after the First World War. Movements of the radical left and right had existed in Europe before 1914, but only the destruction of the war, the ensuing political and economic crises, and the fatal weakening of the traditional forces turned them into strong contenders for political power. Italian Fascism and German National Socialism were counter-revolutionary movements, but it would be misleading to interpret them as nothing more than that. The nationalist wave which brought them to power was set in motion by the extreme right, but their dynamism led them towards a totalitarianism far beyond the traditional concepts of left and right.

The first confrontation between Nazism and Bolshevism took place in 1919, when the young Soviet regime was struggling for its very existence against both native enemies and foreign invaders, and when the Nazi Party was no more than a regional group of little political consequence. What Hitler thought of Russia and Communism at the time seemed unimportant, for he was far from being a leading figure even on the Munich scene, let alone in German affairs. But it was, in fact, of the greatest relevance, for it was between 1919 and 1923 that Hitler's world outlook and that of his party were shaped. He hated Jews and he had the traditional dislike of Austrian nationalists for the Slavs. But, these two basic ideas or prejudices apart, Hitler in 1919 was still largely an 'unwritten page'. By 1923 his opinions had crystallized and to the end of his life they did not undergo any substantial change.

A study of the formative political influences that shaped Hitler's view of Communism and the Soviet Union during this period of apprenticeship seems at first sight to involve no particular difficulties. Most of the *dramatis personae*, their doings, sayings, and writings, are known and can be documented in considerable detail. There are, however, complications of a different character; the investigator is drawn on to seemingly remote topics. The impact on Hitler and his party of some German Balts and their friends of the extreme right wing of the Russian emigration was anything but negligible in the early years. Hitler himself, many years later, said jokingly that the early *Voelkischer Beobachter* should really have been called *Muenchener Beobachter – Baltische Ausgabe*.* The Russian sources of National Socialism cannot be analysed without reference to events and movements in pre-revolutionary Russia, such as the proto-Fascist 'Union of Russian People', just as the tremendous impact of the *Protocols of the Elders of Zion* cannot be discussed except in the broader framework of collaboration between right-wing extremists in Russia and Germany dating back to the eighteen-eighties. This in its turn brings up such problems as the origins of Fascism and modern anti-Semitism. The transition from religious to racial anti-Semitism was a very clear process in Germany, whereas in Russia the link between the extreme right, the religious establishment, and the monarchy was much closer. The Russian extreme right wing never fully emancipated itself; it took some hesitant steps towards social demogogy and Fascist methods, but essentially it remained reactionary in an old-fashioned way, and therefore much more restricted in its social and political appeal. The same is true of the German Balts who played such a conspicuous part in the early years of the Nazi

---

* *Hitler's Secret Conversations* (Signet Edition), p. 602. The only writer who has drawn attention to the great importance of the 'Russian roots' of National Socialism is Henri Rollin (*L'Apocalypse de Notre Temps*, Paris 1939). This work is most important for the genesis of the *Protocols* and their dissemination. Yet it is almost totally unknown, because it appeared a short time before the Nazi invasion of France and most copies were destroyed as a result. I am most grateful to Prof. Norman Cohn, who has made a study of the origins of the *Protocols*, for having brought this book to my notice. Rollin was, to the best of my knowledge, the first to have stressed the impact of the 'message' brought to Germany from Russia by men like Vinberg and Shabelsky-Bork. His book, which contains an enormous amount of documentation, has obvious weaknesses; the author felt more at home describing events in Russia and France, but was less familiar with German affairs. Even so, this work, published in the winter of 1939, is of greater value than much of the literature on Nazism that appeared after the Second World War, and it is to be greatly regretted that it has not been reissued and translated.

movement; men like Scheubner-Richter and Rosenberg (despite his anti-Christian sentiments) were essentially extreme conservatives. They made an important contribution to the policy and the ideology of National Socialism – but the more radical, revolutionary inspiration of Nazism originated elsewhere. Their impact on Hitler was very great indeed while it lasted; yet Hitler, who was an astonishingly quick learner, was also extremely selective. He realized at once, for instance, the enormous possibilities of the *Protocols* and the doctrine of the 'hidden hand', and made this his own; at the same time he refused to take Rosenberg's general theories quite seriously and had a very low opinion of the right-wing Russian *emigrés* after they had shown their political ineptitude in 1919–22. But this is anticipating events; in 1920 Hitler was no more than the leader of one of many splinter groups, whereas the *Volksdeutsche* from Riga and the Russians from Moscow, with their greater political and financial resources, seemed to him important potential allies.

In 1919–20 many Russian refugees reached Central Europe in the wake of the defeated White armies, but only a minority was politically minded, and even fewer were 'ideologists'. Of these few some had belonged in Russia to the extreme right or had turned to the right during the civil war; they now settled in Berlin and Munich and sought contact with like-minded parties and political personalities. In this search they met and collaborated with the leaders of the extreme nationalist and racialist factions such as Count Reventlow, Field-Marshal Ludendorff, anti-Semitic groups, and the anti-Bolshevik leagues that had sprung into existence in 1917–18. None of these had a mass following, but reports were circulating about a new group that had just come into being in Munich and had assumed the name National Socialist German Workers' Party; it was said to be headed by an extremely capable ex-soldier who showed every promise of making his small splinter party the great and long-awaited political party of the extreme right. Some of the Baltic refugees from the Russian revolution went to reconnoitre and ended by joining it; after a short while they took leading positions in the new party. They also brought along some of their Russian friends, who were suitably impressed by the ex-lance-corporal, an excellent and forceful speaker. They, too, decided to help the new party. The combined impact of Balts and *emigré* Russians was felt on many levels. There was, to begin with, their ideological influence; the Russians contributed some important planks to Nazi ideology, as will be shown below. They also gave political guidance and financial assistance that may have been of decisive importance at certain critical junctures in the troubled early history of the Nazi Party. After all, as Hitler later said, the Nazi Party at that time was a very fragile growth.

In the search for the origins of German National Socialism some highly abstruse and improbable influences have been prominently featured, but the more tangible and substantial impact of refugees from Russia has usually been overlooked. There are two reasons for this oversight: the historians of the Nazi movement have not usually been interested (and sometimes perhaps not qualified) to interpret influences from the East; language barriers and the great difficulty in tracking down the historical sources may have played their part. There is another, perhaps more relevant explanation: later events over-shadowed these early developments. The influence of the Balts faded in later years; von Scheubner-Richter was killed as early as 1923, and Rosenberg, after proving himself an utter failure as a politician and organizer, rapidly lost stature. In a similar way the right-wing Russian emigration became expendable from the Nazi point of view after the Hitler party had become a mass movement. After the late twenties the relationship between these two groups was rather one-sided. Certain sections of the Russian emigration came under the spell of Nazism, but they no longer had any influence on Hitler, who regarded them as political failures if not outright nuisances.

These later developments should not, however, hide the fact (as they have done) that at one time Scheubner-Richter was Hitler's main political aide, that Rosenberg's theories strongly impressed Hitler in his formative period, even if he did not formally acknowledge the debt, and that, in general, the influence of certain Russian circles – who imported into Germany the *Protocols of the Elders of Zion* and made cash contributions to the Nazi treasury – was very strong between 1919 and 1923. Writing fifteen years later, a member of this group claimed that this 'modest bookshop' (Mauerstrasse 15 in Berlin, where the *Protocols* could be bought in Russian and German), 'known only to a few at first, lost in one of the many Berlin thorough-fares, was nevertheless the headquarters of the splendid popular movement which ten years later brought Adolf Hitler to power'. Of Scheubner-Richter the same writer said that 'he literally laid the foundations for the movement which brought Hitler to power'.[1] Such claims are, of course, exaggerated; everybody in 1933 wanted to climb on the Nazi bandwaggon and to appear an *'alter Kämpfer'*. But below the bombast and the historical embroidery there is an element of truth that deserves examination.

In January 1919, a few weeks after the end of the First World War and the overthrow of the monarchy in Germany, Anton Drexler, a Munich locksmith, founded in a suburban beerhall a new political group, the *'Deutsche Arbeiterpartei'*. Political organizations mushroomed at that time, most of them small and insignificant; Drexler's was undoubtedly one of the least important, for even many months later it had no more than half a dozen members. This diminutive group did not escape the attention of the local Reichswehr command which supervised and, to a certain extent, collaborated with all the extreme right-wing factions. On September 12, 1919, Adolf Hitler, lance-corporal with the temporary and unofficial rank of political officer (*Bildungsoffizier*), proceeded to the Sternecker, a Munich pub, to report to the army authorities about Drexler's group. After the meeting he decided, not without hesitation, to join it.[2] Hitler soon became its main propagandist; his appearances as a speaker were extremely successful and attendance at party meetings grew steadily; but it was only in July 1921 that Hitler assumed its leadership; before that date it had been run by a committee.

The party continued to grow and spread from Munich to some other Bavarian cities; the Storm Troops (SA) were founded to terrorize the party's opponents, and in January 1923 the Nazis held their first *Reichsparteitag*, or national congress, in Munich. The party had remained regional (Bavarian) in character, but its fame spread throughout Germany and Adolf Hitler had become a national figure in German politics before the unsuccessful *putsch* of November 1923 which temporarily put an end to Nazi activities.

It is not easy to reconstruct in detail the political platform of the early Nazi Party; admittedly its programme was published as early as February 1920, and the party organized countless meetings and demonstrations; but the records of its early days are incomplete. In most instances only summaries of speeches have been preserved. Only in December 1920 did the party acquire its official press organ, the *Voelkischer Beobachter*. In broad outline the general orientation of the party was fairly clear: it stood to the extreme right, its main propaganda was directed against the 'November criminals' (the Social Democrats and Democrats) who had stabbed the victorious

German Army in the back and accepted the Versailles Treaty; it stood for a bigger Germany (*Grossdeutschland*), and it was, above all, anti-Semitic, since 'the Jews are the source of all our evils'. There were many such groups in Germany at the time; the Nazi Party stood out as being more radical in its approach, more unbridled in its propaganda.

Hitler has generally been described as a rabid anti-Communist from the very first hour; the success of his party in Munich has in effect been explained as the reaction of the middle class (and the lower middle class) against the shortlived Soviet republic in the Bavarian capital in April 1919. Closer investigation suggests doubts; Hitler and the Nazi Party in the very early days by no means regarded Communism as their main enemy and the chief danger for the German people. This conviction came only in the later twenties, when the danger of Communism had in fact receded. Among the propaganda theses formulated by Hitler, the 'struggle against Marxism' took third place, after the fight against the Jews and the peace treaties.[3] 'Marxism', moreover, meant, in nine cases out of ten, the ruling Social Democrats, not the Communists. This appears, *inter alia*, from a curious and little known book by Dietrich Eckart, *Bolshevism from Moses to Lenin: A Dialogue between Adolf Hitler and me.*[*] Dietrich Eckart, an early member of the party, a critic and poet of sorts who contributed largely to party funds, was one of the main formative influences on Hitler during the early period. But despite the suggestive title, this book (which presents the two leaders thinking aloud) contains practically nothing about Communism; there are observations on Jewish history, the *Talmud*, and various other subjects including social democracy from Ebert to Martov – but nothing on Bolshevism. This is perhaps not altogether surprising, for the Nazi attitude towards the German Communists, whom they sought to influence and if possible to win over, was by no means as consistent as subsequently described. Thus, for instance, Dietrich Eckart and Gottfried Feder appeared in Nuremberg in the autumn of 1919 in an unsuccessful attempt to win adherents among the local Communists.[4] Several months later Eckart said in a speech at a party assembly in Munich that the Communists of German origin did not lack

---

[*] Munich 1924. The conversations were actually written down in 1922–3. A second part was promised but never materialized. Eckart died in 1924 while Hitler was in Landsberg prison. Hitler said about Eckart in 1942: 'He shone in our eyes like the polar star . . . at the time, I was intellectually a child still on the bottle.' *Hitler's Secret Conversations*, p. 222.

idealism; unconsciously and unintentionally they, too, were working for the common good – meaning Germany's salvation.[5] In an article entitled 'German and Jewish Bolshevism' in his own journal, Eckart came out squarely for what he defined as 'German Bolshevism', summoning the well-to-do to give up their profits;[6] like Hitler, he had endorsed Feder's appeal for the destruction of the 'yoke of interest' (*Brechung der Zinsknechtschaft*) which was first propagated in Eckart's newspaper and then became an ill-starred plank in the Nazi Party programme.

Count Reventlow, subsequently a leading Nazi figure in Berlin and member of the Reichstag, showed similar vacillations: he was one of the main propagandists of the *Protocols* in Germany,[7] but this did not prevent him from flirting for a time with Radek and even writing for the *Rote Fahne*, the central newspaper of the German Communists. Similar inconsistencies can be detected even in the appearances of Hitler at that time. At a meeting with Austrian National Socialists in Salzburg in August 1920, he declared that he would prefer to be hanged in a Bolshevik Germany rather than attain salvation (*selig werden*) in a French Germany.[8] At a public meeting in Munich in February 1921 he said that he would rather five hundred thousand rifles were given to the (German) Communists than delivered to the Entente.[9] These were no accidental slips; a close investigation of early Nazi literature and activities shows that the Communist issue was in those days a subsidiary question for Hitler and his political friends. In 1921 a gradual change set in which continued in 1922 and which had more or less reached completion when Hitler wrote *Mein Kampf* in 1924. For his gradual anti-Communist indoctrination, Hitler owed most to Alfred Rosenberg, a Baltic *emigré* and a Russian citizen who had arrived in Munich in the winter of 1918–19 and joined the Nazi Party when it still had fewer than two hundred members. Textual conformity can be established between Hitler's early anti-Russian and anti-Communist speeches, the relevant passages in *Mein Kampf*, and the writings of Alfred Rosenberg.[10] Max Erwin von Scheubner-Richter, another refugee from Riga, also had much influence on Hitler*, and through him Hitler came to know

---

* On S.-R.'s influence most historians are agreed, from the early anti-Nazi, Konrad Heiden, who wrote that S.-R. 'entirely dazzled Hitler and won a fateful political influence over him' (*Adolf Hitler*, Zurich, 1936, p. 115), to the most recent chronicler, G. Franz-Willing, who certainly cannot be accused of an excessive anti-Nazi bias. He reports that Hitler exclaimed after S.-R.'s death in 1923: 'All are replaceable, but not he' (*loc. cit.*, p. 133).

some leading right-wing Russian *emigrés*, who had at that time established their headquarters in Munich – the most promising choice for a Russian Koblenz.

From these quarters Hitler adopted the idea of anti-Bolshevism as a central plank in Nazi ideology and propaganda and equated Bolshevism with World Jewry. Whether and to what degree Hitler really believed in all this (as Rosenberg and Scheubner-Richter, fanatical anti-Communists, undoubtedly did), and to what extent he merely regarded it as a useful myth in his domestic policy, and a good weapon in his foreign policy, is another question.

Whether Hitler believed in his own propaganda or not, what matters in this context is the effect it had. Throughout his political life Hitler had a sneaking admiration for Stalin and Russian Bolshevism, though not for the German Communists. Goebbels and some other Nazi leaders reacted in a similar way. Very different was the attitude of the German Balts such as Rosenberg and Scheubner-Richter; they had been the first to be confronted with Bolshevism and they wanted no compromise or half-hearted measures against it. They were greater German patriots than the *Reichsdeutsche* themselves, as were the German nationalists in Austria. In the Baltic this was a comparatively recent development; until about 1905 they had been loyal subjects of the Tsar but since the revolution of 1905 this traditional loyalty had been wearing thin. There had been, in fact, a fairly radical switch of ideological and political allegiances by the leaders of the Baltic Germans during the decade between 1905 and 1914.[11] Not all these German Balts followed their leaders, but the group as a whole felt itself in great danger from the rising wave of Latvian and Estonian nationalism on the one hand and from the radical socialist attacks on their dominant political and social positions on the other.*

Both the revolution of 1905 and the repression following it had been more violent in the Baltic than in any other part of the Russian empire. Many baronial manor houses were destroyed by peasants and workers in the uprising of 1905, and in the 'pacification' that followed seven hundred agitators were sentenced to death, in addition to the hundreds killed without formality.[12] Among the Balts the feeling

* Neither Scheubner-Richter nor Rosenberg came from aristocratic families; the former adopted the 'von' and the hyphenated name on his marriage to Mathilde von Scheubner, who, incidentally, was his senior by some eighteen years.

of isolation grew, and they realized that the Tsar, their traditional protector, would not be able to help them much longer. In these circumstances a *rapprochement* with Germany was the logical conclusion. There had been, of course, close cultural ties all along. These were now complemented by an ideological reorientation. It was only natural that the Baltic Germans should show particular interest in the racial and imperialist trends that were enjoying a revival in the Wilhelmian Germany of the day. Members of leading families such as Stackelberg and Manteuffel-Katzdange preached extremist nationalist doctrines both at home and in the Reich. It was in this political climate that the Rosenbergs, Scheubner-Richters, and their whole generation grew up between the turn of the century and the Russian Revolution. They welcomed the occupation by the Kaiser's armies during the First World War, and after the great debacle of 1919 many of this generation preferred to migrate to Germany, particularly those intellectuals among them who were not tied to the Baltic countries by estates or business interests.

The Balts, one of the smallest German tribes, were also one of the most cultured and vocal of all German groups. Their political influence in Germany was out of all proportion to their number. Some had been prominent writers or advisers on foreign policy in Wilhelmian Germany (such as Theodor Schieman, editor of the influential *Kreuzzeitung*, or Paul Rohrbach, the most popular and persuasive of the apologists of German imperialism). They were now joined by a sizeable group of younger and far more radical compatriots. Even the few Baltic liberals who had advocated co-operation with the Russian democrats back in 1905 were influenced by this radicalization and were to play a fateful role in Weimar Germany.[13] Embittered by their experience as individuals and as a group in Courland and Livonia, these German Balts felt a mission to warn the German people against the dangers looming from the East. In Adolf Hitler and his party they found pupils only too willing to learn.

Scheubner-Richter

Scheubner-Richter is the great mystery man of early Nazi history. Much confusion persists about his antecedents, his profession, his activities during the First World War; everything, in fact, concerning this man, who hardly every appeared in the limelight, is shrouded in secrecy.* He was killed in the Hitler *putsch* in November 1923, and thus became one of the earliest martyrs of the Nazi movement. He should have entered Nazi hagiography as one of its patron saints, as did Dietrich Eckart. Yet in the Third Reich he was more than half forgotten, though he had been one of Hitler's closest confidants. Arm in arm he went with Hitler on that fateful march on November 9, 1923; when he was hit by a bullet, his fall dislocated Hitler's shoulder. Hitler perhaps did not want to be reminded in later years of one who had helped him so much in the early days and who had been closest to him in the hour of danger†.

Max Erwin von Scheubner-Richter was born in 1884 into a German Baltic family. As a young man he served with a Cossack regiment and helped to organize the German settlers' 'self-defence' in the 1905 revolution. Around 1910 he went to Germany, studied engineering at Munich, served in an aristocratic Munich regiment, the *Chevaux legers*, and became a German citizen. Politically he was not active during this period; he was influenced by the then fashionable teachings of Friedrich Naumann, who coupled a belief in a strong German national mission with vague socialist leanings. Scheubner-Richter combined considerable assurance with linguistic facility and an ability to make friends and influence people;‡ he seemed cut out to be a diplomat. He saw service on the Western Front but was soon called to serve his adopted country in a minor diplomatic function (consul in Erzerum). The *grand seigneur* also had a pronounced adventurous streak in him, and engaged in various perilous expeditions to mountain Kurds and other tribes in darkest Turkey not far from the battle front.

Following another Munich intermezzo, Scheubner-Richter graduated from the local engineering institute. In 1918 he was called to the German Army Headquarters in the Baltic countries (*Oberost*) to take

* Heiden (*op. cit.*, p. 115) mistakenly calls him an actor by profession; Alan Bullock (*Hitler*) thought that S.-R. was a Russian agent who passed to the German side during the First World War. Even a recent historian (H.H. Hofmann, *Der Hitlerputsch*, Munich 1961) calls S.-R. an elderly East Prussian; he was neither.

† A biography by a friend that is almost entirely devoted to his activities during the First World War was published during the Third Reich by a provincial publishing house: Paul Leverkuehn, *Posten auf ewiger Wache. Aus dem abenteuerlichen Leben des Max von Scheubner-Richter* (Essen 1938). Dr Leverkuehn was seconded to the German foreign service in Turkey during the First World War and again as intelligence agent during the second. He compares S.-R. with the German 'Lawrences', the Wassmuths, von Hentigs, etc.

‡ In Richard Hughes' novel *Fox in the Attic*, Natasha says about him, Poor Max-Erwin – she'd met him at parties: he had so much charm (p. 225).

charge of the press bureau in Riga. At first the position of the German units on this sector changed very little after the Russian Revolution; unlike the German armies in the West, these had not been defeated in battle and their leaders were extremely reluctant to give up the conquered territories. Scheubner firmly believed in a German revival. 'There will be a new Germany five years hence,' he told August Winnig. He was a determined opponent of the revolutionary movement; his attempts to indoctrinate the German soldiers and to fortify them against Bolshevik influences through a number of newspapers (*Das Neue Deutschland*) and other publications were not, however, very successful. Under the pressure of the Red Army and the newly independent Latvians, the German units were eventually compelled to retreat and it fell to Scheubner-Richter to negotiate with Stuchka, the head of the local Red Army units.

Like most of his contemporaries, Scheubner-Richter had been a member of Rubonia, the Riga students corps. Under him in *Oberost* there served another member of Rubonia, Arno Schickedanz,* who one day drew his attention to correspondence with a third companion of their youth – Alfred Rosenberg, an architect and painter who had shortly before settled in Munich. Rosenberg dabbled in German right-wing and Russian *emigré* politics and wrote to Scheubner-Richter about his negotiations with big South German firms willing to make contact with General Wrangel, then established in South Russia. The German businessmen wanted to trade with the territory under his control and, if necessary, extend economic assistance. Was not Scheubner-Richter, with his many connections and languages, the right man to visit Wrangel and to act as liaison officer with the White Armies? He got as far as the Balkans in 1920 but Wrangel's army was then in full retreat, and the plan was abandoned. Scheubner-Richter had, however, come to know the leading personalities of the Russian emigration during the trip, especially those on its monarchist, extreme right wing. The more he thought about it, the more it

---

* Schickedanz subsequently emerged as a Nazi ideologist, closely following, in his *Der Sozialparasitismus im Voelkerleben* (1927), the theories developed by Alfred Rosenberg. According to Otto Strasser (interview, Munich, May 1962), Schickedanz quarrelled with Rosenberg in the twenties, but this did not prevent his becoming Rosenberg's right hand, first in the *Voelkischer Beobachter*, later in the administration of occupied Russian territories. He was appointed Nazi governor for the Kuban and Caucasus region but never reached his destination. Together with his whole family Schickedanz committed suicide in 1945.

appeared to him that the attempt to introduce democratic reforms in Russia had been the source of the evil; there could be only two forms of government in Russia, he wrote – *Tsarism or Bolshevism*: it was as simple as that.[14] Any attempt to rule Russia through bourgeois liberals such as the Cadets, let alone the moderate socialists, was doomed to failure.

After his return to Germany, Scheubner-Richter decided to continue the collaboration with the Russian right-wing extremists. There was a short Berlin interlude. In March 1920 a group of army generals and right-wing politicians attempted to overthrow the Weimar Republic, and Scheubner-Richter was their candidate for heading the information service. However, by the time he reached Berlin, the Kapp *putsch* was over and all that remained for him was to return to Munich. He was to have been brought to trial by the Reich government for his part in the conspiracy, but the charges against him were dropped, perhaps owing to the intervention of influential friends, or because the Berlin judges realized that the Munich authorities who granted refuge to all right-wing political refugees from the north would not extradite him anyway.

From his old acquaintance Rosenberg, Scheubner-Richter heard about the existence of the small but rapidly growing National Socialist German Workers' Party. In October 1920 he was introduced to its leader. On 22 November he attended a meeting and soon after joined the party together with his wife. Scheubner-Richter was very favourably impressed by the hypnotic power emanating from this lower-class ex-lance-corporal; soon he was to describe him as the 'prophet of *völkische* Deutschland'.[15] The admiration was mutual; Hitler gained a very favourable impression of the *grand seigneur*, who moved easily in all spheres of society. True, he was not an ideologist like Rosenberg or a deep thinker, but then he was so much more a man of character than Rosenberg, the awkward bohemian. He was not much of a public speaker – but on that score Hitler needed no help. What he badly wanted, and what only Scheubner-Richter could offer, was an eminently respectable upper-class contact man who was also a capable organizer, devoted to the movement, who could get money and, more important still, who had useful political contacts. Later, as Fuehrer of a mass movement, the upper-class contacts would matter little – the big bankers and industrialists would implore him to take their money. But the breakthrough from almost total obscurity to a prominent place on the national scene could not be achieved without money and contacts; in this respect Scheubner-Richter's assistance was of the very greatest importance. He was a genius at procuring funds and this at a time of economic crisis when money was not at all easy to come by in Germany. He is said to have received it from the former Bavarian monarchs, the house of Wittelsbach, as well as from one of the two pretenders to the Tsardom of Russia, Prince Kyrill of Coburg. Kyrill's wife, Victoria Feodorovna, put at Ludendorff's disposal an 'enormous sum' between 1922 and 1924 for distribution among the German right-wing extremist organizations.[16] Other notable contributors included Russian industrialists (mainly oilmen) who had transferred part of their funds to Germany, such as Gukasov, Nobel, Lenisov, and others, and Baron Koeppen, General Biskupsky's cousin,[17] who is said to have ruined himself by his contributions to these causes.

There were close relations between the Scheubner-Richter family and the Coburg pretenders; Scheubner-Richter's wife, Mathilde, later recalled how she went with the Archduchess Victoria, Kyrill's wife, to watch the SA, Germany's future saviours, at one of their military exercises in a Munich suburb.[18]

There were useful German contacts as well: church dignitaries, members of the Bavarian aristocracy, bankers and leaders of heavy industry such as Reusch-Haniel and Thyssen. Unlike other members of the Hitler party, Scheubner-Richter was himself a rich man and since he did not demand money for himself but for what seemed to him a worthy cause, he went about it with perfect ease and conspicuous success.*

Even more important perhaps were Scheubner-Richter's political contacts, which included practically everyone prominent at that time in German right-wing politics; he was particularly close to Ludendorff and Poehner, the Munich police chief, and as a former officer

---

* According to an internal Bavarian government memo, Scheubner-Richter had 'enormous sums' at his disposal. This source did not exclude the possibility that the Hitler *putsch* had somehow been indirectly supported by Moscow: 'Moscow benefits from the fascist struggle against the national government in Bavaria. Moscow's tactics are always geared to a premature action by the 'Whites'. The communist-voelkisch *rapprochement* in Berlin in August 1923 is still vividly remembered, so is the fraternization between nazis and communists in Munich after the putsch.' The writer also draws attention to the presence of many ex-communists in Scheubner-Richter's Kampfbund and the participation of many recent arrivals from Russia's former Baltic provinces (Aktenvermerk of the state Ministry of the Exterior, dated *cir.* November 15, 1923, reprinted in Deuerlein (ed.), *Die Hitlerputsch*, pp. 386–90). These suspicions were most probably unfounded, but it is interesting that they should have arisen at all in a secret report.

he had direct access to the local Reichswehr command which followed Hitler's activities with much sympathy and occasionally gave positive support. Thus the first *Reichsparteitag* in Munich (January 1923) had been held with the backing of the local Reichswehr against the strong opposition of the civilian government. Earlier, Scheubner-Richter had helped Hitler several times to evade prison on charges of conspiracy and attempted revolt. But most of his time and energy was devoted to work among the Russian exiles.

In 1920 many Russian *emigrés* still refused to accept their defeat and exile as final. They hoped that the Soviet government would somehow be overthrown from within, or collapse as the result of its own incapacity, or perhaps be ejected as the result of some new foreign intervention. There was, consequently, a great deal of activity in the centres of the Russian emigration. But there was also a great deal of dissension, of personal and political strife, of mutual recrimination, not only between left, right, and centre, but also within each faction of the emigration. The *emigrés* accused each other of weakness and cowardice, if not outright treason, in their past and present behaviour; they quarrelled about their present foreign political orientation and the shape of the Russia that was to emerge after the successful counter-revolution.

On the extreme right wing, too, conditions in 1920 were pretty chaotic. One group had opted for Germany and preached German-Russian co-operation in the fight for a new Russia. But there were degrees of collaboration; Prince Bermont-Avalov in Berlin, for instance, was considered to be to all intents and purposes a German agent. He had raised a small army in the Baltic in 1919 to fight together with the German *Freikorps* against the Bolsheviks. His enemies, who were extremely numerous, doubted both his princely origin and his military qualifications. Another group, also centred in Berlin, consisted mainly of former members or sympathizers of the *Soyuz Russkovo Naroda*, the Black Hundreds of Tsarist days, who regarded everyone slightly more liberal than themselves as a traitor to the Russian cause. But many conservatives regarded these extremists as mere scum, foreign agents or provocateurs, not much better than the Bolsheviks. There were bitter disputes about their foreign political orientation; instinctively, many Russians disliked the Germans and distrusted German intentions with regard to Russia's future. How can we possibly co-operate with Ludendorff, they asked, the very man who brought Lenin to Russia in a sealed railway compartment? Eventually there were even two pretenders to the throne of the Tsar; Grand Duke Kyrill Vladimirovich, who had married a German princess, Victoria, settled in Coburg, and followed a pro-German orientation, and Grand Duke Nikolai Nikolaevich in France, who was pro-French and had the support of the majority of the right-wing emigration.

Scheubner-Richter was the main organizer of the great monarchist congress in Bad Reichenhall in late May 1921, the most ambitious attempt to bring all Russian right-wingers together on one platform. As usual, Scheubner-Richter himself kept in the background; he welcomed the participants and the work of his Munich association was warmly commended by some of the delegates, but he left the Russians to thrash out their own problems, in the hope that they would find common ground. The Reichenhall congress was a landmark in the history of the Russian emigration, but Scheubner-Richter's hopes were not fulfilled.

Nevertheless, he continued to give much of his time to the uphill task of trying to unite this right-wing Russian emigration into one effective political organization that would join forces with the German right, in particular the Hitler movement, in the struggle for a new Russia. He founded a German–Russian politico-economic association, which set out *inter alia* to promote German–Russian trade (with the future Russia) and published its own newsletter. This German–Russian association, called at first The Bridge (*Die Bruecke*), became better known under the name *Aufbau* (*Reconstruction*), and published a periodical with this title. It was a right-wing popular front, an alliance of various political groups, including some eminently respectable persons such as Cramer-Klett, who represented the interests of the Vatican in Bavaria. But the key positions were held by a number of trusted friends, who, as it happened, had all been members of the same student corporation back in Riga; Scheubner-Richter, von Kursell, Schickedanz – only Alfred Rosenberg was missing. Aufbau put stress on its work on economic collaboration, but *Vorwaerts*, the German Social-Democratic paper, was undoubtedly right when it called this an attempt to mislead the public:[19] what economic co-operation could there possibly be so long as Aufbau declined to do any business with the Soviet government?[20] Scheubner-Richter opposed the Rapallo policy; this line would not be dangerous if the German people were led by a strong government; in the given circumstances it might be fatal.[21] He thought that the White Armies had failed because they had not been ruthless enough; they had accepted moderate socialists in their ranks instead of treating them like Bolsheviks.[22] Scheubner-Richter made the Jews, and in particular the 'Elders of Zion', responsible for the dissension in the Russian emigration, and advocated the adoption of the strongest measures against Communists: Communists should be hanged, exterminated, as in Italy;[23] he thought highly of Mussolini, who had made his opponents drink castor oil, and expressed the hope 'that the principles of Italian Fascism will become self-evident in Germany too'.[24] But the German right-wingers were not militant enough for this task, and Scheubner-Richter urged them to march on Berlin 'to save German earth from the red terror'.[25] Germany's saviour he came to see in Hitler; quoting a Russian *emigré* paper (*Nakanune*), Aufbau predicted that Hitler was the only man in Germany who would achieve something in that winter of 1923. He was a clever man and had a large following among the down-and-out and the persecuted. Hitler's struggle would decide the fate not only of Germany, but of Europe, possibly of the whole world: 'This struggle will be waged under the slogan Soviet star *versus* Swastika. And the Swastika will prevail.'[26]

Those lines were written a few weeks before Hitler's first and unsuccessful bid for power. They expressed an optimism that was not altogether genuine; Scheubner-Richter could not fail to observe that his predictions about Russia had not come true; the Soviet regime had not been overthrown. In an article he wrote for the central Nazi newspaper he now called on his party comrades to learn from the Russians how to act.[27]

Legend has it that Scheubner-Richter was the main organizer of the *putsch* of November 1923, and most historians have accepted it. He was the secretary of the *Kampfbund*, the chief organization of all extreme right-wing organizations in Munich, and acted as liaison officer between Ludendorff and Hitler. The idea to march on Berlin was his, but the initiative was Hitler's. In September Scheubner-Richter had developed his strategy in some detail; he thought there was no point in further clashes with the police. The 'national revolution' would come *after* the Nazis and their allies had gained in a legal, or semi-legal way, the key positions in the state, namely, the command of the police force; the political situation was such that decisive action would have to come sooner or later. The National Socialists would be successful if they cleverly exploited the psychological factor; it would be a hazardous, to be sure, but any action involved risks. The risk would be comparatively small, and if the action had the support of popular opinion, the more legal it would appear.[28] But according to the evidence given many years later by his widow, Scheubner-Richter did not feel too happy in these days of October and early November 1923. He had been the target of many attacks; the Catholic press had called him a political impostor and demanded that he be thrown out of Bavaria: 'We do not envy the Hitler Guard this addition ... if the names of the leadership of the Hitler movement were published, it would be seen that three-quarters are not Bavarian names; they are men who ten years ago did not even know that Giesing is a suburb of Munich.' Hitler had to defend Scheubner-Richter against these attacks in a letter to Kahr.[29] In early November 1923 Scheubner-Richter was quite despondent; whenever Germany had a chance to rise again, he said, somebody committed an act of utter folly. On the eve of the *putsch* he went to bed early, and when Hitler telephoned and asked to see him he was reluctant to commit himself. But when Hitler came in person the old magic worked and his enthusiasm returned. Scheubner-Richter went off to take part in the meeting with Hitler, Weber, Poehner, Ludendorff, and the other main figures in the attempted coup. There was agreement to act at last; in the middle of the hectic preparations he came home for a few minutes: 'Everything went smoothly, quite beyond expectations, without bloodshed. I have still a lot to do and shall not be home tonight.'[30]

The events of those twenty-four hours, from the meeting in the Hofbraeuhaus where the uneasy coalition Hitler-Kahr-Lossow was established, to the march on the Feldherrnhalle, have been reconstructed in detail.[31] Scheubner-Richter, as usual, acted as liaison officer – this time between Hitler, Ludendorff, and the monarchist leaders. In the fateful march to the Feldherrnhalle he walked beside Hitler, wearing his uniform of an officer of the *Chevaux legers*, spiked helmet, pincenez and all. He was one of the first to be hit by police fire; falling to the ground, he drew Hitler with him, thus perhaps saving his life.

The *putsch* collapsed within a few minutes; the masses in their enthusiasm did not sweep Hitler to power (as he had hoped), and some of his right-wing allies deserted him. It was followed by a big trial, and by Hitler's stay in Landsberg prison, where he wrote *Mein Kampf*. When he emerged from prison he had to start almost from scratch, but conditions were propitious and it did not take him long to establish the Nazi Party as a powerful political instrument. At Scheubner-Richter's funeral all the nationalist leaders who had not been arrested in the wake of the *putsch* were present, and many of them paid homage to the life work of the dead leader of Aufbau and the *Kampfbund*.[32] They promised to carry on the good work, but without Scheubner-Richter's dynamic personality Aufbau soon began to decline. It was banned for a short time by the Bavarian government, but its influential backers soon had the ban revoked. Then the question of Scheubner-Richter's successor came up. General Biskupsky had been in charge of the Russian department of the organization and had followed with suspicion for a long time the doings of the Ukrainian section, headed by Butenko, an engineer, and Colonel Poltavetz-Ostranitsa, an extremist figure in Ukrainian-Cossack politics.[33] On this issue there were profound differences of opinion between the Russian right-wing extremists and their German friends, who wavered between support for a restoration on the Tsarist pattern and a division of Russia on ethnic lines, flirting with Skoropadski and other minority leaders. Ludendorff, who had the financial strings in his hands, suggested two candidates as successor to Scheubner-Richter, Arno Schickedanz and Otto von Kursell. Both were natives of Riga, and had belonged to the same students' corporation. Von Kursell was a painter; he had provided the drawings for some of the earliest anti-Semitic pamphlets of Dietrich Eckart and Rosenberg. Less politically inclined and slightly older than Schickedanz, he was believed to be more experienced, and was chosen as Scheubner-Richter's successor. But soon there were fresh intrigues: Biskupsky accused Kursell of siding with the Ukrainian separatists against the Great Russians.[34] Aufbau split into a 'Russian office' headed by Biskupsky, and a Ukrainian centre, led by Kursell. These two institutions ceased to exist after a few months. By late 1924 nothing remained of Scheubner-Richter's great projects; Biskupsky devoted all his time to Russian *emigré* politics, Kursell became an academic painter, to return to politics after 1933, and Schickedanz went to work under Rosenberg at the *Voelkischer Beobachter*. Scheubner-Richter's widow continued to be a fanatical adherent of Hitler's party; for several years she worked in one office with Himmler, starting a press clipping service for the use of the Fuehrer.

Some of Scheubner-Richter's contemporaries believe that had he lived he would not have retained his place at the top of the Nazi Party and the Third Reich. This is very probable; Scheubner-Richter was essentially an extreme conservative who, unlike Hitler, never ceased to believe in religion and monarchy. He lacked, in other words, the revolutionary and nihilistic impulse that was so prominent in the mental make-up of Nazis like Hitler and Goebbels. He also had enemies in the Nazi leadership; Goering, for instance, could not stand him.[35] He was an extremely useful, perhaps an indispensable, tool for Hitler in the early years, but there would hardly have been much need for him once the party had become a mass movement with supporters in all classes throughout Germany.

Ideologically, Scheubner-Richter's impact on Hitler was negligible; Rosenberg was a far greater influence during the early years, though Hitler, not a very grateful man at any time, never openly acknowledged this. Hitler, at any rate, was a quick learner; it did not need much to persuade him that as far as German domestic politics were concerned his Baltic collaborators were on to a good thing with their anti-Communism. The short-lived Bavarian Soviet republic had given his compatriots a serious fright; German Communist attempts to stage armed revolts elsewhere stood little chance of success but helped to rally support for the extreme right. In contrast to Mussolini, Hitler had never seriously studied Marxism; he was not sufficiently interested. Anti-Bolshevism did not play a central part in Nazi propaganda during its first phase; Hitler's views on Russia and Communism were moulded only between 1919 and 1924, with consequences that became apparent later on.

Alfred Rosenberg

Alfred Rosenberg, the chief ideologist of National Socialism, was also the leading party authority on things Russian. Born in the old Hanseatic city of Reval in 1893, he went (in the words of an official biographer) 'through all the sufferings of the German abroad'.[36] The predicament of the Baltic Germans after the revolution of 1905 has already been described; but all in all Rosenberg did not suffer in his childhood and adolescence much deprivation or unhappiness, private or collective. He came of a lower middle-class family of uncertain racial provenance, a fact that would be of little relevance for anybody but a philosopher of race.* He went to the local high school and later

---

* According to a communication in Rosenberg's personal file (No. 1259) in the Berlin Document Centre, one of his grandfathers (Martin Ros) was of Lettish origin, his grandmother, née Sire, hailed from France, and there were also rumours of Jewish and even Mongolian antecedents.

to the Riga technical college. The writers who made the strongest cultural and political impact on him, Nietzsche and Houston Stewart Chamberlain, were the usual reading matter at the time of young middle-class Germans; if the Balts as 'racial Germans' were perhaps more markedly political in their outlook, in other words more to the right, this was true of Austria too.

But the young Rosenberg who had visited Germany and France just before the outbreak of the First World War did not really think of politics as his vocation; his chief interests were cultural. He wanted to be an architect and a painter, and when the Riga university was moved to Moscow during the war, he too settled in the old Russian capital. There is nothing to show that he was particularly interested in the outcome of the war; in later years, when he had become a prominent personality on the German political scene, in the front ranks of a militarist party, his war record – or the absence of it – made him a vulnerable target for his political enemies.[37]

When the revolution of 1917 broke out in Moscow, Rosenberg was preparing for his diploma a design, fittingly enough, of an up-to-date crematorium with Romanesque vaults and a large colonnade as well as an adjoining graveyard. Of the historical events that were taking place around him he was hardly aware, and he recalls in his memoirs: 'If I attempted to give here a description [of the Russian Revolution] and the forces involved, I'd run the risk of including knowledge which I acquired only much later through the memoirs of Russians and Englishmen' (Buchanan, his daughter, and Sir Samuel Hoare).[38]

Rosenberg left Moscow, went to the Crimea, made his way back to Reval, returned to Moscow for his final examinations, and again went back to Reval, which a few days later was occupied by German troops. Rosenberg thought that the combined troops of the Russian generals would eventually prevail over the unorganized Bolshevik regime. 'But what was lacking was a leader, a slogan for the future. For the return of those who had been overthrown nobody wanted to fight.'[39] Rosenberg wanted to volunteer with the German Army, but was turned down as a Russian citizen in occupied territory – and because of his inability to provide any references in Germany. It was only with some difficulty that he received in November 1918 a permit to travel to Germany with the retreating German forces.

Rosenberg entered Germany as one of a great army of Russian *emigrés*. True, it was a home-coming of sorts. German had been his native language and Germany a second homeland. The German Revolution, in a way, hit him harder than the Russian Revolution: 'I did not want to carry on my future life between the fronts . . . I wanted to go to the Reich.' 1918 was the year of Rosenberg's political awakening; in 1919 and 1920 he laid the ideological foundations of his new political philosophy. By 1923 he had already published seven books and booklets and countless articles. It was very rapid progress by any standards.

According to an official biography Rosenberg came to Germany in 1918 in order to enlighten the Germans about the Russian Revolution and about Communism; but first he had to enlighten himself. He knew that he disliked what was happening in Russia, but would not have found it easy to explain why. The political education of Alfred Rosenberg can be followed with some accuracy from his diaries, parts of which appeared during the last phase of the Third Reich.

At the time of the 1917 revolution he was preoccupied with Schopenhauer and Wagner, Renaissance art and Indian philosophy. He developed in some detail his thoughts about 'Nirvana and personality', and wrote a draft for a book on the 'Philosophy of German Art' (which eventually became *The Myth of the Twentieth Century*). Around him the old world was dying and a new world being born, but the young architect from Reval does not seem to have reacted strongly one way or the other. True, there were some unfavourable comments on the Jews: 'This people hates everything that is not like itself, therefore there ought to be no tolerance towards it'; and on the Russians: 'I am interested in the juxtaposition of the Russian and the German,' Rosenberg wrote – and found moral weakness and lack of character in the Russians.[40] But these were the usual prejudices of the Balts which long before had found classic expression in a book by one of Rosenberg's compatriots, Victor Hehn, *De Moribus Ruthenorum*. The Russian was false, idle, unable to make a sustained effort; he was artistically gifted but morally unstable.

Rosenberg's attitude to the revolution of March 1917 was one of qualified enthusiasm; on one occasion he called it a deed of unheard of grandeur.[41] Everywhere he noted the conscious and serious attitude of all sections of the population. Fifteen months later he had become a fanatical anti-Semite and a rabid anti-socialist; politics had suddenly superseded art in his attention. He continued to write essays on 'personality', but they dealt exclusively with the 'idea of exploitation and destruction', the Jewish idea. He accused the Jews of trying to cause popular chaos by their smooth talk about human rights. Almost all left-wing socialists were Jews: 'Travelling through Russia, in spas and elsewhere, I saw Jewish students with *Pravda* in their hands lecturing in military hospitals.' Behind all these attempts at social and political destruction there was always the Jew.[42]

His thesis was not original – even some of the catchwords such as *Voelkerchaos* were taken from H. S. Chamberlain. Some of it is ill-digested Nietzsche; for instance, the references to the stupidity of an ignorant mass. Some is a typical romantic rejection of the industrial age: the activity of the industrial worker is said to be absolutely senseless, whereas the work of the peasant is purposeful and clear. *Pest in Russia* opens with a quotation from Goethe in which the Weimar sage expressed his fears about the prevailing use of machines: '*es waelzt sich heran wie ein Gewitter . . .*' This quotation, embodying the reaction of an 'artistic soul' against the 'soulless machine age', first occurs in an unpublished essay ('The Jew', written in Reval or Moscow in July 1918), which already included most of Rosenberg's ideas about Jewry and Bolshevism on which his later books were based.

Rosenberg's sudden conversion in 1918, his transformation from a slightly eccentric and not very original art critic and philosopher into a political thinker, appears in perspective a matter of some puzzlement. For those who did not live through that stormy period it is difficult to realize what passions were roused during the revolution. It is equally difficult to understand the psychology of those who believe they have discovered the hidden forces behind current events. There has been a strong inclination throughout history to look for a hidden hand whenever the suddenness or enormity of events transcends the comprehension of those who witness them. The French Revolution was one such occasion, the Russian Revolution another. Painstaking research into their political, social, and economic pre-history, and into the ideological developments in the decades preceding the revolution, the analysis of the political forces involved, rarely yielded clear and satisfactory answers, whereas the conspiratorial theory, relentlessly pursued, appealed to many contemporaries who had neither the patience nor the intellectual capacity for more serious investigation.

For Rosenberg, the artist, any such politico-social analysis was ruled out from the beginning; he was uninterested in economics and knew nothing of the history of the revolutionary movement in Russia, of socialism, Marxism, or other left-wing doctrines. He did know, somewhat vaguely, from his study of H. S. Chamberlain and the Black Hundred pamphlets, that the Jew was evil and was responsible for much of the world's misfortune. The Black Hundred had developed the concept of *Zhidomasonstvo* (the Judaeo-Masonic conspiracy), combining various sinister influences in one all-purpose slogan;* Rosenberg, because of his ethnic origin and cultural background, was able to link these ideas with the German racial doctrines. Having gained the key to the understanding of the revolution, he had no further interest in describing or analysing in detail what was wrong with revolutionary Russia, Socialism, or Communism; for him it was enough to show that Trotsky's original name was Bronstein, that Steklov's name was Nachamkes, and Kamenev's Rosenblum, that Kerensky was really Kirbis [*sic*], and that (according to Mommsen) on one day the Jews had killed 120,000 people in Cyprus. A serious confrontation with the Russian Revolution on this basis was impossible, but this was not what Rosenberg wanted. As he put it many years later: 'You cannot wage a big war in world history with a chance of lasting success if you accept the ideology and world outlook of the enemy as the framework of the battleground.' Consequently, only a very few of Rosenberg's many writings on Russia really deal with the subject under discussion. He is always preoccupied with quotations from the *Talmud*, the Zionist movement, or the impact of freemasons on the *Frankfurter Zeitung*. Rosenberg spent many hours in the Munich state library to find yet another fitting quotation from the *Shulkhan Arukh*, to 'unmask' yet another Jew in nineteenth-century France or England who had adopted a gentile name. For all we know the Russian expert of National Socialism did not read a single book or a single article by Marx or Engels.† His only fare on things Russian was the newspapers of the extreme right-wing *emigrés* such as *Novoe Vremya*, *Dvuglavy Orel* or *Prizyv*, which he used extensively in his own work.

Of pre-revolutionary Russia he knew, of course, more than the other Nazi leaders. He was taught Russian in school and had a very

---

* It had, of course, gained wide currency in France earlier, especially during the Dreyfus affair.

† The only work by Lenin he ever quoted was *State and Revolution*.

good knowledge of the language. He was well read in classical Russian literature, and in his early writings often quoted Dostoevsky and, to a lesser extent, Tolstoy. In one of his early books he enumerates some important Russian novels and says that only by reading them and by studying Russian folk songs and ikons can the outsider get a glimpse of the Russian soul.[43] Whether Rosenberg himself read all these books is not readily obvious; they cannot really have appealed to him, otherwise they would have had a more lasting effect on his views on Russia. In the early years he was sometimes willing to give Russia the benefit of the doubt, as, for instance, when he maintained that Russian Orthodoxy compared favourably with both the Catholic Church and freemasonry. In later years, however, his attitude hardened; there were few references to Russian cultural achievements but much abuse of Russian formlessness, lack of creativity, despotism, and servitude. In the *Mythos* he wrote that it had been a mistake to compel Russia to europeanize itself; in future Russia should see its centre of gravity in Asia; only then would it regain its inner balance. In Asia it had a mission to fulfil, not so in Europe.[44]

Rosenberg and Dietrich Eckart

When Rosenberg arrived in Munich in January 1919, he turned for help to the Russian *emigrés* committee which provided a room and vouchers for food. Most of his time he spent in the state library, reading up on Jewish history, the history of the Jesuits, the masonic orders, and similar topics. Through a fellow Baltic refugee, Mrs von Schrenck, he met Dietrich Eckart, a German writer and playwright, who was about to publish a magazine devoted to anti-Semitic and anti-Communist propaganda. Rosenberg has described his first meetings with this patron saint of National Socialism, who accepted him as a 'co-warrior against Jerusalem'.[45]

Eckart, who was also a poet of sorts, is now chiefly remembered for his translation into German of *Peer Gynt*. A heavy-set man who somewhat resembled another early Nazi leader, Julius Streicher, he was a *bona fide* anti-Marxist and anti-Semite, a heavy drinker who, from time to time, had to submit to cures in closed institutions. But Eckart, the bohemian, could not quite share Rosenberg's fanaticism and deadly seriousness, his utter lack of humour. Rosenberg wrote about Eckart that 'there always came, after days of full energy,

73

these pauses during which he retreated into himself, simply refusing to consider outward occurrences important enough. . . . Since Eckart was incapable of any sustained effort, I had taken care of all routine work from the very beginning and relieved him of most of his duties' (as editor of the *Voelkischer Beobachter*).[46] When the *Voelkischer Beobachter* was made a daily paper in March 1923, Rosenberg became editor. According to his version, Eckart no longer bothered to show up at the editorial department, and Hitler had told him (Rosenberg) that if he did all the work he might as well get the credit for it. Rosenberg had become a German citizen and thought he could now abandon the caution which had held him back from the limelight of German domestic politics. Eckart is said to have taken the appointment badly; Rosenberg himself reports that he was accused by his former mentor of ingratitude and that 'some resentment remained'.[47] Rosenberg's first published article was on 'Jewish Bolshevism', his first contribution to the *Voelkischer Beobachter* dealt with Zionism, to be followed by a series on the 'evils of freemasonry'. These remained the central topics in his writings throughout the early twenties. It may not be readily obvious why Zionism had to be brought in; only a few years before Rosenberg had expressed himself in favour of a Jewish state.[48] If he had now become anti-Zionist, it was mainly because he had become convinced that the Jewish national movement was merely a cloak for Jewish plans for world domination: 'The Weizmanns, Rothschilds, Warburgs, Schiffs, threaten us quite openly with world revolution, with Bolshevism, if they do not receive Palestine.' It was one of his main contentions that Bolshevism was not an aim in itself, but simply a means employed by Jewish financial capital to uproot the existing order, to destroy the national economies, to demoralize the peoples – and then to acquire the remainder for a song.[49]

Not many of his contemporaries in Germany shared his opinions; even on the extreme right there was pressure for a reconciliation with Bolshevist Russia. Rosenberg regarded it as one of his main tasks to call his compatriots to 'remain firm against the temptations from the East'; he was particularly scathing about Radek's success in winning support from German nationalist newspapers.[50] He strongly opposed the campaign to help the starving millions in Soviet Russia; the German workers stinted themselves of food in the belief that they were helping their Russian comrades, but most of this money was spent in Berlin and Stockholm luxury restaurants.[51] He had second thoughts about what ought to have been done in 1918: Moscow should have been taken by the advancing German Army; the annexationist peace treaty of Brest-Litovsk had not been far-reaching enough.[52]

Much of his material he drew from the extreme right-wing Russian *emigré* press, which he scanned regularly for comments friendly to the young Nazi movement. He evidently liked the reference in one such paper to the 'socialist tradition' linking Peter I to Adolf Hitler, noted approvingly that another Russian language periodical used the swastika on its cover, and quoted from a third the hope that Russia too would one day be able to boast of a Hitler movement.[53] During all those years there was only one modest attempt to discuss Communist ideology; in this Rosenberg tried to demonstrate at some length why Marxism was wrong. But there, too, the temptation to give the 'Jewish character of Marxism' as an explanation was too strong to be resisted, and with this rational discussion ended.[54]

Between 1919 and 1923 Rosenberg wrote and published no fewer than seven books, translated another,[55] and kept up a constant flow of articles. Some of the books were slight, all were repetitive, but as a result he became almost at once chief ideologist and chief propagandist of the Nazi Party; apart from the splenetic efforts of Dietrich Eckart and Feder's economic tract, his writings were the only ideological propaganda material of the party; *Mein Kampf* was published much later, and Geobbels was not yet even a member of the party. It is not difficult to imagine the impact these long pamphlets had on the party during its early, formative period. Moreover, Rosenberg the pamphleteer was far more intelligible than the philosopher of later years; the *Mythos* was widely sold but apparently was not read by a single leading figure in the Third Reich, not even Hitler.

At first glance the long pamphlets give the impression of immense erudition. When writing on the amorality of the *Talmud*, Rosenberg quotes the *Baba Meziah* and *Baba Kamma* as if he were a rabbi and son of a rabbi. When describing the crimes of freemasonry, references such as *Rivista della Massoneria Italiana* (1881) and *Le Globe*, Paris, November 25, 1830, are not infrequent. Elsewhere he refers to such sources as Beaulieu's *Histoire de Commerce de Lyon* (1838), André Favin's *Histoire de Navarre* (1612), the *Analecta Ecclesiastica* and the *Masonic Chronicle of Chicago*. (The only book in which

75

learned references are conspicuously absent is his *Pest in Russia*.)
Rosenberg had of course not read all these books in the Munich
library; he was a man in a hurry, and since any single one of the subjects he touched (for instance, the *Talmud*) would have required a
lifetime of study, he relied on a dozen standard works in each field.
He did not study the Talmud (he did not know a word of Hebrew or
Yiddish); his quotations are taken from the standard anti-Semitic
works such as Rohling and Eisenmenger, which had long been in
wide use.[56] Nor did he consult the many volumes of the *Archives
Israelites*, but found the references in Gougenot des Mousseaux's
book. He was simply a propagandist who collected quotations and
references, strung them together, and presented them in an up-to-date
framework. Apparently there was a demand for such literature; in a
country with a traditional weakness for footnotes this pseudo-
scholarship created an impression of original research not only on
the uneducated but also on considerable sections of what is in Germany frequently called the educated middle class. The great number
of pseudo-learned references is typical of the proponents of the conspiracy theory of history; in this respect Rosenberg did not differ
from the Nesta Websters, the Schwarz-Bostunichs, and the others,
before and since. After all, they had little straw with which to make
their bricks; the more unlikely their assertions, the more quotations
were needed.

Up to 1923 Rosenberg refrained from taking an active part in
German politics. In his writings, however, there was no such reti-
cence, and it is somewhat strange to read the ever-recurring tirades
against the strangers from Russia who had invaded Germany after
the First World War and wanted to dominate German politics.
Rosenberg chose to forget that he too was a Russian refugee. His
views on Russia are summarized in *Pest in Russia*, published with
seventy-five photographs in 1922. Its main thesis is that the clash
between Communism and capitalism is mere make-believe. Trotsky
knew that financial capitalism was not his real enemy – at most it
was a competitor. The real significance of the Russian Revolution was
the attempt of the Near Eastern racial underworld to overthrow
Europe (*Der Aufmarsch des vorderasiatischen Geistes gegen Europa*);
as such it is compared with the campaigns of Muslims, Tatars, Huns,
and other conquerors in ancient times and the Middle Ages. The Jews
take the most prominent place in this demonology; they are assisted
by the Armenians, the Chinese, the Latvians (against whom

Rosenberg seems to have nursed a private grudge), and even the Tungus.

Up to this point Rosenberg agreed with his friends of the extreme right-wing Russian emigration who also argued that the Russian Revolution was the work of foreigners. But he went further than they did in pointing to what he thought were the fatal weaknesses in the Russian character: indolence, ignorance, the chaotic anarchistic streak in many Russians, and the stupidity and insolence of the semi-intelligentsia. All this Rosenberg explained as the result of the racial bastardization of Russia under the Tatars, the 'fatal blood mixture'; the European and Asian characters are in permanent combat, the outcome of which cannot be predicted. As a result, Russia was even less able than Germany to resist the poison.

Such ideas about the racial inferiority of the Russians and the Slavs in general, were not exactly novel; they had been widely held among the Russian Germans long before the revolution. Nor were they entirely absent in Germany, although there was also the traditional Russophilia of the right and, after the First World War, the various National Bolshevik schools. Rosenberg regarded it as one of his main tasks to purge National Socialism of these deviations and it was due to him that Nazi policy from the very beginning rejected the very idea of an ideological confrontation or a political compromise.

This attitude gradually made his collaboration with the Russian emigration more and more difficult. The Russians, however right-wing, did not enjoy being told that they were racially inferior, nor were they pleased when Rosenberg developed his ideas about the division of the future Russia on ethnic lines. Up to 1923, while *Aufbau* existed, co-operation continued; there was, after all, the overriding common interest in fighting the Soviet regime. But after the Hitler *putsch*, the situation rapidly changed. The Soviets were now firmly in the saddle. Rosenberg was now deeply involved in German politics. While Hitler was in prison he was to lead the Nazi movement. He retained a few fellow *emigrés* who collaborated with him in *Weltkampf* (an anti-Semitic news service), but most of these were Russian Germans, Ukrainians, or belonged to other minorities. With the real Russians Rosenberg lost contact; he had antagonized most of them by what they considered his anti-Russian rather than anti-Bolshevik programme. In addition, he lost much of his interest in Russia as Rosenberg the pamphleteer gave way to Rosenberg the philosopher of history and cultural critic; he was now working on his magnum opus, the *Mythos*.

Rosenberg was basically a true believer. Unlike Goebbels, he was not a cynic, but really believed in his own propaganda; he reduced a very complex phenomenon like the Russian Revolution to a simple false thesis which prevented him from ever beginning to understand what it was all about. An innate and apparently total lack of humour prevented him from realizing how grotesque his own historical and political constructions really were.

Hitler soon became aware that Rosenberg was at best a heavy-going, plodding ideologist of doubtful value to the party; hence his gradual decline after 1930; but this in retrospect does not diminish his importance as the leading authority on Russia and Communism during the early formative years of the Nazi movement.

Chapter 5

THE RISE OF NATIONAL SOCIALISM
PART II: THE ELDERS OF ZION

The Black Hundred

HITLER AND ROSENBERG did not need the assistance of the Russian right-wing extremists to formulate a National Socialist political philosophy; they could even do without their expertise on the Jewish question, though they received some fresh inspiration from these quarters. But on one specific theme Rosenberg found the right-wing extremists absolutely indispensable, namely, the appraisal of the Russian Revolution and of Bolshevism in general. He studied their literature, regularly read their magazines and newspapers, and met many of their leaders in the emigration. His early writings on Russia were essentially the German version of the Black Hundred doctrine of the Russian Revolution, its causes and effects. He made some additions and innovations, but these were of no great consequence in the early years; they became of greater importance only later. Through Rosenberg and his friends National Socialism accepted a concept of Bolshevism that had evolved not in Germany but, somewhat ironically, in Russia itself before the revolution and during the civil war.

Who were the 'Black Hundred'? The *Soyuz Russkovo Naroda* (Union of the Russian People) had been founded in 1905 by a St Petersburg doctor, A. Dubronin, and for a while was a force to be reckoned with. George Louis, at one time French ambassador to Russia, wrote during the Stolypin era that 'The Black Hundred (the Union's military branch) are ruling the country and the government obeys them because it knows the Emperor is inclined to sympathize with them'. The Union has been called a proto-Fascist movement by both friends and critics; an American historian wrote

79

that in some respects it might be regarded as a 'forerunner of present-day Fascism',[1] and one of the most influential leaders of the movement, writing many years later, declared that 'in its spirit this Russian popular movement was almost similar to contemporary National Socialism'.[2] A closer look at the historical role of the Union of Russian People, as a connecting link between the old-fashioned and twentieth-century right-wing extremism, seems called for.

The Union and its forerunners, the *Russkoe Sobranie* (Russian Assembly) of 1901 and the *Soyuz Russkikh Liudei* (Union of Russian People) of March 1905, were founded to defend the regime against the revolutionary forces. The right-wing monarchists had their own traditional organizations, such as the Council of the United Nobility, but these were political clubs with restricted membership; a mass party was needed and it was to this end that Dr Dubronin founded his movement in St Petersburg in 1905. In the programme of the Union there was hardly an idea that had not been formulated by Nicholas I one hundred years earlier; the Union stood for the common good of the fatherland, the 'firm maintenance' of the old trinity of Orthodoxy, Autocracy, and Narodnost.[3] The only concession to later day political thought was the willingness of some of the Union's leaders to accept some form of consultative assembly (Soveshchatelny Zemskii Sobor) to advise the Tsar; not that the Tsar should be in any way compelled to take its advice; the Tsar had freedom of action, the people freedom of opinion – an old Slavophil maxim. In itself, however, such a programme was most unlikely to attract a great number of people at that late and critical date, and the Union tried to acquire the missing mass appeal by social demagogy, incitement against the intelligentsia and foreigners, and above all by its anti-Jewish campaign. The Union came into being at a time when it was already very difficult to form and hold together a mass organization solely on the basis of nineteenth-century articles of faith – some 'modern' elements were needed, and the Union was an attempt, albeit an unsuccessful one, to make the transition from the old conservative to the new totalitarian right.

No representatives of the Union had been elected to the first Duma, but quite a few of its members entered the second and third Duma. The Union, to be sure, was not parliamentarian; it resented this concession by the Tsar to popular opinion and rejoiced whenever the Duma was dissolved by decree. Some of its members were wholly averse to playing the parliamentary game, while others, including

Purishkevich and Markov II, thought that the elections, and their speeches in the Duma, provided after all a welcome and effective platform on which to air their views and to win new adherents to their cause.

Vladimir Purishkevich – Russian Fascist?

The driving force behind the Union of the Russian People and the Black Hundred was Vladimir Mitrofanovich Purishkevich, a Bessarabian landowner and former government official. He was the only outstanding leader on the extreme right and has been called the 'first Russian Fascist'.[4] For many years he was the most outspoken defender of the privileges of the monarchy and the aristocracy, but by origin he was by no means an aristocrat; his grandfather had been a village priest. From Kishinev he graduated with a study of oligarchic rebellions in ancient Greece – perhaps a first pointer to his later political inclinations. After having served as a local government official he moved in 1900, at the age of thirty, to the capital, where he worked in the Ministry of the Interior and soon became a special assistant of Plehve, then the strong man in Russian politics.

A flamboyant character, he had a knack of causing commotions and stirring up trouble; hardly a session of the Duma passed without his interruptions, mostly foulmouthed and often hysterical. There were likely to be disturbances whenever he appeared in public, whether at the theatre (protesting, for instance, against Oscar Wilde's *Salome*), or merely in a restaurant. He also had a knack of offending people (not only on the left) and felt unhappy if he did not produce a major scandal each week. But there was method behind all this. Purishkevich wanted to discredit the Duma, being basically opposed to parliamentarism; like Goebbels, he tried to break the system from within. (Like Goebbels, too, he wrote verse and novels.)

He was far more dynamic and purposeful than the average Russian politician of his day, as one opponent later put it; he had a talent for organization (yet another gift quite rare at that time and place) and a genius for obtaining money from various shady official and semi-official sources such as the funds of the secret police and the secret funds of various ministries. Millions of rubles passed through his hands between 1905 and 1917; as one political enemy said: 'Many right-wingers accepted bribes but Purishkevich was the only one to deliver the goods.' He was, in a way, the only one to understand the

81

spirit of the times; he realized that the old style conservatives and reactionaries were hopelessly out of step and unable to cope with a new and dangerous political situation. He tried, for instance, not without some success, to infiltrate the institutions of higher learning, in particular St Petersburg university, which were the bulwark of the left-wing revolutionary forces.

It was an uphill struggle, and Purishkevich, who was not deficient in political intelligence, came to realize, though late in the day, that he was fighting for a hopeless cause in the face of the imbecility of the ruling classes. He sensed the coming catastrophe; when he returned from the war front in November 1916, his speech in the Duma got a stormy ovation (for the first time in his life) from all sides – with the exception of his own friends of the extreme right. He was now convinced that Russia could be saved only by a desperate action; he joined the conspiracy to kill Rasputin and did in fact fire the mortal shots after the attempt by others to poison the monk had failed.[5]

Purishkevich never thought highly of his colleagues of the extreme right; even before the war he had quarrelled with most of them and established his own organization, the Union of the Archangel Michael. In 1914 he antagonized more people by his anti-German enthusiasm; quite a few leaders of the extreme right were either of German provenance, or, like Markov II, were pro-German in sentiment. Markov, for many years Purishkevich's colleague in the Duma, was said to resemble Peter I in his outward appearance. He was probably a more effective speaker than Purishkevich, but greatly inferior to him in intelligence and in charisma as a political leader.

At the time of the revolution Purishkevich tried to rally a few of his old comrades to organize a counter-revolution, but it was a vain attempt. He ended up in the Peter and Paul fortress, where he is said to have behaved with some dignity and passed his time writing bad poems (*Songs of an Unsubdued Soul*). He was released, or succeeded in escaping, and found his way to the White Army in the south. We shall deal with the last phase of his political activity – he died in 1920 – in another context.

In his feverish activity and his bombast Purishkevich somewhat resembles Mussolini and the younger Goering, but in contrast to the South and Central European Fascists of a later day he did not really find a suitable environment. Nor did he realize soon enough that the monarchy, the Church, and the ruling classes were too deeply compromised and that a successful Fascist movement could have emerged only independently of them, if not in actual opposition.

The Programme of the Black Hundred

The Union of the Russian People had no systematic doctrine or programme; ideologically, the Russian extreme right was even weaker than its counterparts elsewhere in Europe. But, in so far as it did exist, it included demands that were anathema to the traditional conservatives: limitation of the working day, raising the living standards of peasants, making cheap credit available to them and even providing for some form of agrarian reform. The Union tried hard to gain a foothold in the countryside and it made sweeping promises, assuming that it would never be called upon to honour them.[6]

According to Union propaganda, the Jews were the source of every evil in holy Russia. All Jews were revolutionaries, and all revolutionaries were Jews. They wanted to come to power to exploit the workers and peasants without mercy, and unless the Russian worker and peasant stood by his ruling class now, the ruling class would be powerless to help him once the power of the Jewish revolutionary-capitalist clique had been established. This was to become one of the main themes of Nazi propaganda, the conformity of interest between Jewish revolutionaries and Jewish capitalists, and the allegation that the former were acting as agents for the latter. Other propaganda themes to be resumed in later years, were the equation of revolution with world Jewry and the Freemasons (*Zhidomasonstvo*), which played an important role in extreme right-wing propaganda in Germany, France, and even England in the early twenties.[7]

As for the final solution of the Jewish question, Purishkevich suggested that all Russian Jews should be settled in the Kolyma region in the Arctic, whereas Markov II thought that all Jews 'down to the last' would be killed in the coming pogroms.[8] Meanwhile the Union contributed its share to the solution by organizing wide-scale pogroms and assassinating political opponents (such as the Duma deputies and journalists, Herzenstein, Karavaev, Jollos, etc.). They took a prominent part in the Beilis trial and on similar occasions, and the open support given to them by the government was a source both of strength and weakness. The Emperor thanked them for their 'most loyal activities' and the Tsarina also gave them open support.

It is estimated that in one year alone the government paid the Union two-and-a-half million rubles for its activities; Markov II admitted in his interrogation that he had accepted considerable sums for the Union press. The Union had the right to ask for a free pardon for any of its members arrested for participation in pogroms or similar crimes.

The Union had never been a group of high-minded idealists; an analysis of its social composition shows that its members were drawn largely from the flotsam and jetsam of the big cities. Its leaders were a curious mixture of the aristocracy, the clergy, merchants, and the more backward elements of the *petit bourgoisie*.

Among the leaders of the *Russkoe Sobranie*, a predecessor of the Soyuz, there were generals (Mordvinov and Zolotarev), journalists (I. Engelhard of the *Novoe Vremya*), artists (like Varlamov), and quite a few noblemen (Golitsyn, Volkonsky and the president of the organization, Count Shakhovsky). The *Soyuz Russkikh Liudei*, another predecessor, boasted among its leading members the historian Ilovaisky, Archbishop Anastasii and counts Golitsyn, Urussov, Meshchersky (editor of *Grazhdanin*), Sheremetev and Gagarin. The Soyuz, too, had a number of aristocrats among its leaders (Count Sherbatov, for instance), and also a number of intellectuals (such as A. A. Maikov, the son of the poet), and its leader Dr Dubronin.*

The financial support openly given by state and church enabled the Union to hire criminals to carry out its operations. In his memoirs Count Witte, a former prime minister, called the Union a body composed of 'plain thieves and hooligans'; 'the aims of the Black Hundred are usually selfish and of the lowest character. Their stomachs and pockets dictate their aspirations. They are typical murderers from the dark alleys.'[9] Of their leaders he wrote, 'Decent people do not shake hands with them and avoid their society.' A Nazi author, on the other hand, regretfully noted that the Black Hundred became, and remained, the bugbear of Russian society. 'It was a remarkable sign of the ignorance and the immaturity of the shady Russian intelligentsia that it considered anti-Semitism the worst stain on a man's character.'[10] Another weakness of the Union of the Russian People was its close identification with the Church. References to Orthodoxy appeared time and again in the programme of the movement and there were many churchmen in its leadership,

---

* Few contemporaries have much good to say of Dr Dubronin, the leader of the Soyuz. Nikolsky, himself a prominent member of the Russian Assembly, called him in his diary a 'coarse, repulsive animal' and a 'vile parasite'.

such as Antoni, Bishop of Volhynia, or Hermogen of Saratov, I. I. Vostorgov, Skvortsov, editor of *Kolokol,* and a missionary. Perhaps best known at the time was the monk Iliodor (Sergei Trufanov), probably the most effective rabble-rouser of his day, both by word of mouth and through a news-sheet *Pochaevskii Listok,* published from Pochaevskaia Monastery.* Not all churchmen were reactionaries; there were liberals and even socialists in the Orthodox Church of the day, and Dr Dubronin found it necessary to attack the Metropolitan of St Petersburg for 'revolutionary tendencies' and for his refusal to officiate at ceremonies of the Union of the Russian People.[11] Some bishops and lower clergy were reprimanded or even demoted temporarily for having identified themselves too closely with the Union. Iliodor, for instance, was called to order on one occasion in 1907 for having openly called for pogroms. However, far more frequently, pastors and congregations were strongly urged to participate in Black Hundred activities. 'Their emblems and banners are kept in churches so that to everyone it will be clear that the Holy Orthodox Church fully approves and blesses the high patriotic holy cause of the Union of Russian People and takes this work under prayerful protection.'[12]

On occasion the Union showed some independence: its leaders suggested that the Tsar should be 'nearer to the people' (another old Slavophil notion) and that the bureaucracy was impeding close ties between monarch and people. Attacks on the bureaucracy were in any case popular, and from time to time governors, ministers, and even the Chief Procurator of the Holy Synod (Count Tolstoy) were openly criticized.[13] Most of the mass movements of the day that had been sponsored by the government had a tendency to break away and become independent – up to a point (Gapon, the Zubatovshchina). The Union, on the whole, remained extremely *bien-pensant* – which was its undoing.

The Union was intended to serve as 'a shining example of justice and order to all men' (Nicholas II). In fact it became the meeting place of obscurantists of various classes with the criminal under-world and the *lumpenproletariat.* Its activity centred on the appearances of its leaders in the Duma; it also distributed a number of

---

* Iliodor was Rasputin's best friend at one time, but quarrelled with him and was defrocked in 1912 for various acts of disobedience, including the publication of the very compromising correspondence between the Tsar's family and their father confessor. He escaped abroad. See his *Sviatoi Chort* (Moscow 1917).

newspapers and periodicals that were not really widely read.* It organized occasional meetings and pogroms during its heyday between 1905 and 1910 but it was not capable (as a Nazi source already mentioned notes) of any sustained political or propaganda effort.[14] Its leaders were with one exception second rate – even measured by the modest standards of the day. They had at their disposal some new propaganda literature such as the *Protocols of the Elders of Zion*, first published by one of their members.[15] But even the *Protocols*, which later attracted so much attention, passed almost unnoticed at the time. The predicament the Union faced was similar to that confronting the extreme right wing in Germany and France around the turn of the century; the transition from the old-fashioned traditional right-wing ideology to a more streamlined social demagoguery that was no longer religious in inspiration but racialist or *voelkisch* and totalitarian; having been bitterly disappointed by the impotence of the monarchy, it parted company with the old conservative forces and gradually came to believe in a *fuehrer*. Stoecker's Christian-socialist movement in Germany in the nineties failed for reasons similar to those that explain the lack of success of the Union of the Russian People. It contained some of the necessary ingredients of social and national demagoguery for the establishment of a new type of movement, but its leadership was basically loyal to Emperor and Church and this loyalty made it incapable of effecting the requisite radical break with the past.

Nor should one belittle the obstacles in the way of a racialist (*voelkisch*) party in a country like old Russia, where half the people were of nationalities other than Russian. There was no precedent for such a doctrine, which would have antagonized half the population from the very beginning. In such a country an all-embracing doctrine was needed, not an exclusive myth, and the Black Hundred were very far from having found one. Around 1908 the Union had reached the zenith of its activities; from then on its influence rapidly declined. As far as the government was concerned it had not proved very efficient as a pillar of the regime. The revolutionary danger had lessened for the time being, and there was less need for the Union than before. The party began to disintegrate; Purishkevich split away and founded his own organization, the Soyuz Mikhail Arkhangela, while Dubronin and Markov II headed rival organizations,

* Though Purishkevich once reported that thirteen million brochures and leaflets had been distributed in a period of six months only.

each of which continued to carry the name Union of the Russian People. They denounced each other to the police for lack of patriotism or even 'Judophilia', as subsequently emerged when the Tsarist archives were opened after the revolution. There was a brief revival of activity in 1916 when the regime again found itself in dire straits. The longer the war lasted, the more apparent became the inability and corruption of the Tsarist government, and the more dissatisfaction grew. In this critical situation the Union was officially encouraged to resume its activities on a wider scale, but there was little it could do to combat the massive unrest. A few weeks before the March revolution the Union submitted its proposals to the government; there was little in them, apart from recommendations to counteract defeatism and, generally speaking, to take a strong-arm line.[16] After the fall of the Tsarist regime, the Union was banned and many of its leaders arrested and interrogated; its parliamentary deputies, however, like Markov II and Purishkevich, were not touched at the time. Purishkevich ran into some trouble in November 1917 when he was seized with a small group of fellow-plotters for trying to save the old regime. This group included some of the people who were in later years to play a part in the right-wing emigration in Germany and in the rapprochment with National Socialism, such as F. V. Vinberg, a retired colonel, and N. O. Graf, a captain of the Hussars. Also in this group was the young Duke of Leuchtenberg.[17] Most of them succeeded in escaping from Bolshevik-held territory and joined the White armies, in particular Denikin's forces in the south.

There the former leaders of the Union resumed their activities. In 1919 Purishkevich established a People's State Party (Narodno-Gosudarstvennaya Partiya) in Rostov, which tried to provide a link between the old right-wing extremism and a new, more efficient, organization on similar lines.* Vostokov, another 'old hand' in the Union, organized Bratstvo Zhivotvoryashchevo Kresta (Brotherhood of the Creating Cross). There were old style Black Hundred journals and newspapers like V Moskvu, which General Denikin, a witness not to be suspected of philo-Semitism, called a pogromist sheet.[18]

The main organization of the extreme right in the territory of the Southern army was the Union of Russian National Communities

---

* The programme of the party was published in Rostov in 1919. It is quoted in Gregor Schwartz Bostunitch, *Juedischer Imperialismus*, p. 409. I have not been able to locate a copy of the original.

(Soyuz Russkikh Natsionalnykh Obshchin) which, according to Denikin, was the most active and most widely diffused political organization in the rear of the Southern army;[19] the other main body was the Russian Assembly (*Russkoe Sobranie*), headed by Zamyslovsky, one of the old leaders of the Black Hundred, and the police general, Kommissarov, who was later Biskupsky's right hand man.* The political programmes of these groups were more or less identical with the platform of the old Soyuz Russkovo Naroda, though there were in addition some vague ideas about co-operation, possibly a corporative state, the promotion of native and the debarring of foreign capital. They wanted to establish 'communities' in the territories held by the White armies, and even in the emigration, but they did not specify the character of these communities. In the last resort, as General Denikin put it, these extremists were not concerned with the extremely difficult and complicated problems of positive reconstruction of the state and the social fabric, but reduced everything to an easy formula, intelligible to the dumbest – *Bei Zhidov, spasai Rossiyu* (Beat the Jews, and save Russia).[20] Denikin relates that these groups had great influence both in the ranks and among army officers who were confused by events around them.

The confusion and the officers' reactions are not difficult to explain. The Tsarist regime had crumbled and the traditional world of these men had disappeared almost overnight. But very few were inclined to look for the obvious reasons for the downfall of Old Russia – the almost unbelievable incapacity of the Tsar, of most of his ministers and the whole ruling class, the corruption, the lack of moral fibre, the obscurantism and the unwillingness to reform. This would have involved an admission of guilt on behalf of their class or caste, if not individual guilt – an admission of which only very few were capable; was it not much easier to look for less radical and painful explanations? It was at this juncture that the old propaganda of the Black Hundred fell on fertile ground. Before 1917 even confirmed rightwingers felt somewhat uncomfortable about the *Protocols* and other

---

* Subsequently he worked for the GPU. See V. Burtsev, *Protokoly Tsionistskikh Mudretsov* (Paris, 1938), p. 88. Kommissarov had been one of the chief organizers of the pogroms of 1905, was denounced in the first Duma and had to resign his seat temporarily. Later he was rehabilitated and appointed Stolypin's security officer. Still later he was responsible for Rasputin's well-being, which did not prevent him from participating in an unsuccessful attempt to poison Rasputin. See his long and detailed evidence in the third volume of *Padenie Tsarskovo Rezhima*.

items of Black Hundred propaganda, but after the revolution these were suddenly seen in a fresh perspective.[21] Had not the warnings about a conspiracy of Jews, freemasons, and foreign agents come true? Was it not a fact that there were very many foreign names behind the aliases of the leading Bolsheviks, and the heads of the other revolutionary parties?

Since the Jews in Russia, and in other East European countries, had been the object of so much oppression, it was only natural that they should join the revolutionary parties which promised to overthrow a regime that had been the cause of their sufferings, including the physical destruction of many of their number. That the Bolsheviks had a lesser percentage of Jews than the other revolutionary parties is of little relevance in this context; it certainly did not make much difference to the young officers and the White propagandists, who made Jewish Bolshevism their main propagandistic theme. It is found in the very first proclamations of the Kolchak and Denikin armies.[22] Apparently not satisfied with the fairly high number of Jews among the revolutionaries, they announced that Kerensky and Chernov were Jews too (their original names were given as Kirbis and Liberman respectively):[23] by these and similar operations they systematically 'de-aryanized' the leadership of the Russian revolution until in the end only Jews remained. These practices are noteworthy because they were widely used for export purposes (about which more below), and later perfected by the Nazi Party.

In a proclamation to the Don Cossacks it was said that with the victory of Lev Bronstein all the property of the Cossacks, peasants, and workers would be swallowed by the insatiable Chinese, the Latvians, the Jews, and the Communists.[24] This attempt to set up the Chinese, who played hardly any part at all in the Russian Revolution, as the chief bogeyman, is of some interest; it was immediately taken up by Alfred Rosenberg,* and later by Hitler himself.

Two other such fakes deserve mention because they, too, were subsequently exported abroad, repeated time and again in various languages, and produced a considerable literature.† According to one, the Russian Revolution had been engineered and financed by

* According to Rosenberg (*Pest in Russland*, Munich, 1922, p. 41), the Red Army was held together by the Jews with the help of Chinese silk merchants [sic] and Latvians.

† A correspondent later complained that under General Wrangel it was forbidden to circulate the *Protocols* (A. Doronin in *Vozrozhdenie*, November 6, 1934).

the New York banking house, Kuhn, Loeb and Co.; according to the other, the Tsar and his family had been killed by five Jewish hangmen. If it could be shown that Mr Jacob Schiff (who acted on behalf of the New York banking house) had paid the Communists, it would be obvious to all that the Russian Revolution was the work not of native revolutionaries, but of foreigners. Moreover, it would demonstrate that there was a united front of Jewish Communists and Jewish millionaires, both working for the same end – the establishment of Jewish rule. This motif was taken up as one of the basic tenets of Nazi propaganda, first by Alfred Rosenberg[25] and subsequently by Hitler and in Nazi literature in general. But it was also widely believed in other right-wing circles, both Russian and German, including those who hesitated to accept the *Protocols* at face value.* The fantasy boils down to the following: Jacob Schiff, either directly or through the German Jewish banker Max Warburg, is said to have given the Russian revolutionaries an unspecified sum (twelve million dollars according to one source), and thus saved the Bolsheviks at a critical moment – if, in fact, he did not make the revolution possible in the first place. Schiff (together with other American Jews) did indeed try to persuade the American government in 1905 to do something to alleviate the fate of the Russian Jews. He also negotiated with the provisional government (Milyukov) in 1917. With the Communists, needless to say, he had no dealings, and he certainly had no interest in their victory. The whole story was ridiculous, but it persisted in anti-Semitic literature for many years; the Nazis rehashed it and Father Coughlin frequently made use of it.[26] The Communists, who were apparently deeply irritated by these utterly baseless inventions, decided to reciprocate in kind; since the late thirties they have countered by arguing that not they but the Nazi movement had been financially supported by Kuhn, Loeb for many years prior to 1933, and that the 'national revolution' of 1933 was in fact engineered by the Wall Street firm and their (non-existent) roving European representative, Sidney Warburg. This *canard* is now part and parcel of Soviet historiography on Germany, though its spuriousness has been proved long ago.[27]

Those who argued in the early twenties that American Jewish financiers had sponsored the Bolshevik revolution pointed at the time

* It was believed, for instance, by Shulgin (of whom more below). See his *Chto nam v nikh ne nravitsya* (Paris 1930), pp 268–9.

to one piece of solid evidence: in an official document published by the American government in 1918, Mr J. Furstenberg informed Mr Scholak in Haparanda that Warburg, the German Jewish banker, knew everything about the overtures of comrade Trotsky.[28] It was quite a long time before it was established that these 'documents', the so-called *Sisson Papers*, were a forgery which had been sold to a credulous American diplomat by a White agent, motivated by financial or political reasons, or a mixture of both.[29] Meanwhile these 'disclosures' found their way abroad and helped to create an enormous literature.*

The story of the murder of Tsar Nicholas II by a group of five Jews apparently goes back to the report, on February 5, 1919, of a British general, Knox, who was with Kolchak in Siberia and who had received his information from Russian right-wing extremists or from Wilton, *The Times* correspondent.† Before it could be proved that the report was demonstrably false, it had been picked up in many countries, provided material for articles, speeches, and books,‡ and even King Alfonso of Spain had expressed his horror and revulsion. Most of this literature emanated from obscure little journals in Kiev, Rostov, and Novocherkassk; some was the voluntary contribution of certain British correspondents such as Marsden of the *Morning Post*, Wilton of the London *Times*, and some others about whose role more will be said presently. Nor can one disregard the part played by the OSVAG (Osvedomlitelnoe Agentstvo), Denikin's propaganda ministry. More moderate in tone than the propaganda of the Black Hundred, the policy followed by this agency was often not materially

---

* Among others, a special supplement of *La vieille France* (1920); Boris Brasol, *The World at the Cross road* (Boston 1921); Monseigneur Jouin, *Le péril Judeo-Maconnique'* (Paris 1921), Chapter 3; Netchvolodow, *loc cit.,* pp. 71–104; not to mention the countless articles in German and Russian right-wing periodicals. Max Warburg protested against these allegations (*C. V. Zeitung,* August 17, 1922), and brought an action against the German periodical *Der Hammer*, compelling it to withdraw its charges (April 1, 1923).

† General Knox to War Office in *Russia No. 1*, 1919. (A collection of reports on Bolshevism in Russia), (London) p. 41. Major General Alfred W. F. Knox was head of the British Military Mission in Siberia and his reports strongly influenced the Cabinet in London. Bruce Lockhart wrote of him to Balfour that 'his complete misunderstanding of the situation has been one of the chief reasons for our failure in this country' (Moscow, March 31, 1918). Milner MSS, see Richard H. Ullmann, *Intervention and the War* (Princeton 1961), p. 133.

‡ For instance, General Dietrichs in *Revue des deux mondes*, August 1920, Robert Wilton's book *The last days of the Romanovs* (see below), and countless articles in *Le Temps, Morning Post*, and other leading European newspapers. See also Chapters 2–4 in H. Rollin, *op. cit.*

different. The news items, the leaflets and cartoons distributed by OSVAG bore eloquent evidence to this effect.*

The *eminence grise* behind OSVAG was Vasili Shulgin, one of the most interesting figures on the Russian right. As editor of the influential Kiev paper *Kievlyanin*, he advocated the exclusion of the Jews from public life and frequently helped to incite pogroms. On two occasions his actions provoked the ire of his colleagues of the extreme right: in 1913, when he dissociated himself from the attempt to stage a ritual murder trial (the Beilis case), and again in 1917, when he was a member of the delegation that asked the Tsar to abdicate. His subsequent political career is not without interest. In the middle twenties he went on an illegal tour of Russia on behalf of an anti-Communist organization, without ever realizing that his trip had been stage-managed by the GPU, and that even the galleys of the book in which he described his trip had been read by the Soviet censor. In the thirties he withdrew from politics, spent the war years in Yugoslavia, and was arrested when the Soviet Army entered that country. Shulgin emerged from obscurity in 1961 with the publication of a long letter to Khrushchev in *Izvestia*, according to which he had become a Soviet patriot after many years in a labour camp. The case of Shulgin is more complicated than that of a rank and file right-wing extremist. Whilst Shulgin saw the reasons for the defeat of the White Army fairly clearly,† most others were utterly bewildered when their great offensive in the direction of Moscow suddenly came to a halt near Orel and Voronezh and turned into a rout. For them it was yet another victory of the hidden, infernal forces, and they were firmly resolved to continue their struggle against them from exile.

* For a description of OSVAG activities, see Aleksandr Drozdov, 'Intelligentsia na Donu', in *Arkhiv russkoi Revoliutsii*, Vol. II, pp. 50–7. A typical anti-Semitic poster circulated by OSVAG and reproduced in Schwartz-Bostunitch, *op. cit.*, p. 107, shows Trotsky, as a 'red devil' astride the Kremlin wall and a hecatomb of skulls. Schwarz-Bostunich, on whom more below, was a member of OSVAG and later political commissar in Wrangel's army. He became an SS leader in the nineteen-twenties.

† V. Shulgin, *1920 god* (Sofia 1922), pp. 7–14. Shulgin was undoubtedly the most gifted journalist of the right; David Zaslavsky is not unmindful of this in his *Rytsar chernoi sotni V.V. Shulgin*, published in Leningrad in 1924. Little did he expect that Shulgin's name would appear thirty years later alongside his own, as a contributor to a Soviet newspaper. In his *Pismo Russkim Emigrantam* (Moscow 1961), Shulgin quotes a private letter from a man (D. Zaslavsky?) who had once been his most bitter enemy but now, after Shulgin's conversion, welcomed him back to Russia.

I have dealt in what may seem excessive detail with the propagandist activities of the Black Hundred and their successors during the Russian civil war. These activities in themselves were of no great consequence; they reached comparatively few people, and at no stage did they have a decisive impact on Russian history. But, seen in a wider perspective, they were not entirely unsuccessful either; following its importation to Germany, some of this propaganda became part and parcel of the Nazi creed. We shall now turn to what was undoubtedly the most important East European contribution to Nazism – the famous *Protocols of the Elders of Zion*.

The Protocols of the Elders of Zion

Communism, in Nazi eyes, was a world conspiracy of revolutionary Judaeo-Masonic forces engineered by the hidden hand of the Elders of Zion. Ernst Werner Techow, one of the accused in the Rathenau murder trial in 1922, said in his evidence that a co-defendant had told him that Rathenau (the German foreign minister, and, incidentally, the head of one of Germany's biggest industrial concerns) belonged to the secret Bolshevist movement; he was one of the three hundred 'Elders of Zion', who were seeking to bring the world under the domination of the Jews. Two years before this event the *Protocols* had first been published outside Russia. They attracted enormous attention and many hundreds of thousands of copies circulated in Germany, the United States, and other parts of the world. Yet this same book, which was about to affect world history, had been known for many years in Russia, and Nilus, the man who appeared as its author, had complained in 1913: 'My book was published eight years ago and I cannot believe that it is taken seriously.'[30] Only outside Russia after the war did it become the great sensation. Nilus' biographer, somewhat blasphemously, quotes St Matthew in this context, '. . . it fell into good ground and brought forth fruit, some an hundredfold . . .'

The *Protocols* were thus the product of a combined, though not always planned, effort of the extreme right wing in Germany and Russia. This solidarity dates back to the eighteen-eighties. If Russian socialists co-operated with their German comrades, collaboration at the other end of the political spectrum was, if possible, even closer. For the German anti-Semites, the Tsarist regime was the realization of their dearest dreams; its most extreme representatives like

Stolypin, Plehve, and the Grand Duke Serge, they regarded as the greatest statesmen of the day. There was close collaboration between their press organs; almost daily, the *Staatsbuerger-Zeitung* reprinted material that had previously been published in Suvorin's *Novoe Vremya*. Sometimes these Western well-wishers even outdid the St Petersburg original, as, for instance, when they announced that the priest Gapon, who played a conspicuous part in the 1905 revolution, was really a Jew – an allegation which the Russian papers, for obvious reasons, did not care to repeat.[31]

By a strange twist of history, German anti-Semitism, which had been exported to Russia in the early eighteen-eighties, was re-imported into Germany from Russia after the First World War. In both countries there was a tradition of latent anti-Semitism, but the upsurge in Russia in 1880, and in Germany in 1920, was to a considerable extent affected by outside influences. It was widely believed by contemporary observers that 'this agitation in Germany' (in 1880) was the 'beginning of the whole thing, and that the fever of agitation only spread over the border into Russia after it had become epidemic from Berlin to Pomerania'.[32] Dubnow, the historian of East European Jewry, also mentions the impact of German anti-Semitism in both Poland and Russia.[33] Another historian noted that ever since Peter the Great the Russians had been looking to Germany as though hypnotized, and used to import their ideas from her. 'The idea of anti-Semitism, too, showed the full efficacy of its poison only in Russia. . . . The Berlin anti-Semitic leaders provided the necessary licence for the Russian hooligans. Stoecker, Ahlwardt, and their followers, became the real fathers of the Russian pogroms . . .'[34]

In 1882 some Russians had come to participate in the first congress of what was to become an anti-Semitic International; they were told by Stoecker, the German champion of the cause, that the Jewish question could be solved only in the manner the Turkish, Tatar, or Arabic [*sic*] question had been tackled in the Middle Ages.[35] In Germany, many anti-Semites had already outgrown the religious phase, or were about to do so, while Russian anti-Semitism remained religious in inspiration.* Even the Germans were still somewhat confused and in their manifesto they mentioned not only Aryan

---

* The existence of a Russian racialist group (Union of Christian Socialists) was mentioned for the first time by Gorky in *Novaya Zhizn*, May 20, 1918. It proclaimed the physical and moral superiority of the Aryan race; its slogan was: 'Anti-Semites of all peoples and countries, unite!'

peoples but also those who had *become* Aryan by accepting Christianity – an uneasy compromise between racial and religious anti-Semitism.[36] This did not prevent Russian anti-Semites from adopting much of the propaganda material put out by their German colleagues. It began fairly early; Wilhelm Marr, in his famous and frequently reprinted pamphlet on the victory of Jewry over Germandom, first published in the seventies, had predicted a Jewish revolutionary attempt to overthrow Tsardom in Russia and, having destroyed the last great bulwark of order, to establish their own regime.* The same theme – the prominent part of Jews in the revolutionary (then often called 'anarchist') movement – was taken up in the pamphlets put out by the indefatigable Theodor Fritsch, the Nestor of German anti-Semitism.[37] Probably the most effective piece of propaganda of this period was the Speech of the Chief Rabbi which, in an extended and improved form, became several decades later the *Protocols of the Elders of Zion*. This was an excerpt from a novel by a German writer, Hermann Goedsche, who in his younger years had to quit the state service following a number of unsavoury affairs. The novel, *Biarritz*, includes a chapter 'On the Jewish cemetery in Prague'; according to Goedsche, the Sanhedrin meets once every hundred years (by night, of course) at the grave of Simeon bar Yehuda, and discusses in great detail the Jewish plans for world domination. Goedsche's book was first published in 1869, but the German anti-Semites were not immediately aware of the propagandist possibilities of this piece of fiction. One of the first to use it was Theodor Fritsch, who published the passage, attributing it to a British gentleman named John Ratcliff (without revealing that this was Goedsche's pen-name). Fritsch had his doubts and added, 'Even if the speech was not delivered in this very form, even if it is only fiction, nobody will dispute that it aptly characterizes the aims of the Jews.'[38] In 1901 the Speech of the Chief Rabbi was reprinted again in Germany,[39] and this time the Russian authorities paid attention and had it published. Five years later the German anti-Semites announced with great satisfaction that they had supplied 'excellent weapons' to the neighbouring country. 'The Chief Rabbi speech has been distributed in millions of copies by the Russian government. . . .

---

* Marr had a revolutionary past to live down; he had been an enthusiastic follower of Wilhelm Weitling in his younger years: 'The Jewish elastic light-heartedness [sic] will precipitate a revolution in Russia the like of which the world has perhaps never seen'. *Der Sieg des Judenthums ueber das Germanenthum* (3rd ed., Bern 1879), p. 34.

We note with satisfaction that with the weapons of our ideological arsenal the Russian people can now liberate itself from its mortal enemy.'[40]

Biarritz was not the only precursor of the *Protocols*. In the eighties and nineties there was a whole literature on the 'hidden hand', as for instance the *Disclosures about the Assassination of Tsar Alexander II* by Major Osman Bey Kibridzli Zade, one of the most remarkable books ever written outside a lunatic asylum.* This is a collection of preposterous insults hurled against all Russian politicians and diplomats of the day, who had cheated the author of his due. Osman Bey had won the war single-handed against the Turks (in 1878), and by himself had defeated the revolutionary movement in Russia. But nobody acknowledged his merits and as a result he was reduced to begging and describes in considerable detail how he manages to obtain a few rubles from various Russian embassies, sometimes asking for charity, at others threatening blackmail. Osman Bey discovered that the Jewish world conspiracy was headed by the Alliance Israelite Universelle; the rabbis in East Germany, for instance, are nothing but disguised lieutenants and colonels of a forward assault group threatening Russia; the left flank of the Eastern Front is based on Koenigsberg, the chief commander being the local rabbi, Bamberger. 'A glance at the map suffices to show that this strategic plan, scheduled to enclose and cordon off the Russian frontier, is diabolically clever indeed.'[41] These and similar writings were taken at face value in the highest circles. After the revolution of 1917, a memorandum by Count Lamsdorf was found in the Russian archives (dated January 1906) fully endorsing Osman Bey's fantasy that the revolutionary movement in Russia was led by the Alliance Israelite Universelle and supported by the Rothschilds. Nicholas II added in his handwriting: 'I fully share the opinions here expressed.' Most anti-Semitic writers discarded the theory of the Alliance as the mainstay of Jewish political and military power around 1905, and transferred their attention to the world Zionist movement instead. Yet we find Alfred Rosenberg stressing the central role of the Alliance as late as 1919 in one of the earliest Nazi newspapers.[42]

All this was but a prelude to greater things to come, for after the revolution of 1917 a new theme appeared – the identity of interests between Jewry and Communism. As early as April 1919 one writer

* Published in Bern in 1886. The author was probably an apostate from Judaism of Rumanian origin by the name of Milliner.

referred to this 'eternal theme'.* Another reported that the 'real German anti-Semites are now compelled to take loans from their Russian colleagues!' Had the roles been reversed?

The exact origins of the *Protocols* imported into Germany in 1919 are not known and may remain unknown forever. It seems virtually certain that the Russian political police under General Orgeyevsky and Colonel Rachkovsky had a hand in its production, that it first appeared around 1895, and that it was originally written in French. It also seems certain that its political ideas are derived to a large extent from Maurice Joly's *Dialogues aux Enfers entre Machiavel et Montesquieu* (first published in Brussels in 1865), whereas much of its dramatics are taken from Hermann Goedsche's *Biarritz* (Berlin 1868–70). A great amount of critical intelligence has been invested in trying to solve the riddle of the greatest politico-literary hoax in modern history.[43] The present study, however, is concerned not with the people who wrote the *Protocols* but with those who read them and made political use of them. As for the study of their origins and authenticity, one likes to think that the prediction of Judge Meier, of Bern, has come true. In summing up the Bern trial of 1935, he said he hoped the day would come when people would no longer be able to understand how 'a number of extremely intelligent people tormented their brains in court for a fortnight about such ridiculous nonsense'.[44]

Even so, a short summary of the *Protocols* is necessary; they already belong to a bygone age and one can no longer take a knowledge of them for granted. They are an alleged verbatim record of twenty-four secret sessions of the heads of the world Jewish conspiracy, giving an outline both of their views and their intentions. It is their declared aim to overthrow all existing thrones and religions, to destroy all states and build on their ruins a Jewish world empire to be headed by an emperor from the seed of David. To this end the Jews use various secret organizations (such as the freemasons' lodges) but their main tools are democracy, liberalism, and socialism.

---

* *Mitteilungen*, April 16, 1919. The topic had first been taken up by the *Staatsbuergerzeitung* (February 3, 1918), referring to the victory in Russia of 'All-Jewish Communism'. Between Stoecker's days and the revolution of 1917 the identity of Jewish and revolutionary interests had been laboured in many books and pamphlets – at the greatest length perhaps in the work of a Czech clergyman, Rudolf Vrba, *Die Revolution in Russland* (1907–8); in two volumes Vrba collected all that had been said before on the subject, including of course the 'Chief Rabbi speech'.

The Jews have been behind all the upheavals in history (including, of course, the French Revolution), supporting the demand for the freedom of the individual; they are also behind the class struggle. All political assassinations are organized by them and, of course, all major strikes; they induce the workers to become alcoholics and try to create chaotic conditions by increasing food prices and spreading infectious diseases. They already constitute a secret world government, but since their power is as yet incomplete, they incite the peoples against each other with the intention of provoking a world war.

There is, however, a great difference between the tactics used to establish world power and their real aims. The Elders are by no means liberals or democrats; real happiness, they think, will be brought not by democratic principles but only by blind obedience to authority. Only a small section of the population will receive any education, for the spread of learning among the lower orders has been one of the main causes of the downfall of the Christian states. It will be the honourable duty of all citizens to spy and inform on each other. The government will put down without mercy those who oppose it. Its former co-conspirators (such as the freemasons) will be liquidated, some being killed, others exiled to punitive settlements overseas.

But what if the non-Jews discover this diabolical conspiracy in time? What if they attack the Jews once they have understood that all the disasters and intrigues are part of a gigantic master-plan? Against this last eventuality the Elders have a horrible ultimate weapon; soon all capitals will be undermined by a network of underground railways. In case of danger, they will explode the cities from these underground tunnels and all the governments, offices, archives, and all the non-Jews and their property will be destroyed.

This 'ultimate weapon' was too much even for the credulity of the Russian and the German editors of the *Protocols*. The Russian editors added a footnote, observing that at the moment there were no such underground tunnels in Russia but 'international committees were already at work to sponsor their building'.[45] The German editor, Theodor Fritsch, noted at this point that common sense revolted against the idea; it was probably a mere manner of speaking by which the author wanted to emphasize that the Jews would not be deterred from using even the most horrible weapons in achieving their aims. (It is probably fortunate that the *Protocols* were concocted in the pre-atomic age; the authors would undoubtedly have brought in the H-bomb instead of the rather clumsy and probably ineffective underground explosions.)

All in all, the world of the *Protocols* bore a surprising resemblance to the fantasy world of Tsar Nicholas I or Hitler in his *Table Talk*. Later commentators maintained that the world conspiracy as outlined in the *Protocols* was identical with Zionism which, apart from its avowed programme to establish a Jewish state in Palestine, had its much more ambitious secret designs. According to its early versions, the conspiracy was based on an organization quite separate from the Zionist movement;* some identified it with the Alliance Israelite Universelle, others defined it as not even specifically Jewish, but a working alliance between the Jews and the Freemasons. This briefest of possible outlines cannot possibly convey the full flavour of this hotch-potch of the most detailed absurdities; it is a document that has to be read, at least in part, to be believed.

It is the most detailed and the most absurd manifestation of the belief in a 'hidden hand', a central conspiracy which is behind all the world's evil and discontent. The 'conspiracy theory of history' is probably as old as historiography itself; at times it has appeared as a deep persecution mania fatally afflicting individuals and whole peoples. At other times it has seemed a rather harmless, if deluded, attempt to reduce events of very different origin and character to a common denominator.

In the modern age the Puritan revolution in England was attributed to a conspiracy; the books by Abbé Barruel (1797) and Chevalier de Malet (*Memoirs sur le Jacobinisme* 1817) on the origins of the French Revolution, gained wide currency. They wrote about a triple conspiracy of philosophers, freemasons, and *illuminati*; there was obviously no room for the Jews as yet, for they did not at that time play any part in French public life. Only in Gougenot des Mousseaux's book of 1869 (*Le Juif, le Judaisme et la Judaisation des peuples chrétiens* – translated into German, incidentally, by Alfred Rosenberg), is the anti-democratic and anti-liberal tendency coupled with systematic anti-Semitism; the Jews had meanwhile advanced to a position of a certain political and economic power and now qualified as a scapegoat. Between 1880 and 1914 the idea of a world conspiracy became an accepted article of belief on the extreme right in France, Germany, and Russia, and the *Protocols* were, in effect, anticipated

* For instance, by G. Butmi in his edition of 1906.

99

by a great number of publications in various languages which cannot be discussed in detail in this context.[46] But by and large the situation before 1918 was not propitious for the *Protocols*; in Russia less so than elsewhere. For Russian Jews were a downtrodden and oppressed minority, living, for the greatest part, in abject poverty. They bore no resemblance whatever to the rich and all-powerful Jews described in the *Protocols*. No wonder even Russian right-wingers rejected the *Protocols*, and even Stolypin, to whom an early draft of the document had been submitted by the political police, rejected it as unsuitable. We shall perhaps never know whether the *Protocols* were the means used by a *camarilla* headed by the Grand Duchess Elizabeth to induce the Tsar to get rid of M. Philippe, a French mesmerist and charlatan who had considerable influence at court at the time, or whether they were intended for use by the political police against certain liberal influences. With so many divergent interests at work, anti-Semitic police generals and scheming Grand Duchesses, informers and fakers trying to earn a dishonest ruble, religious maniacs, reactionary politicians, and plain crooks, it is about as easy to discover the real origin of the *Protocols* at this late date as to find a needle in a haystack.

Of the two Russian publishers of the *Protocols* one, Butmi (de Katsman) was a Bessarabian trickster, the other, Serge Aleksandrovich Nilus, was a somewhat more complicated character.* Our knowledge of Nilus's biography is, broadly speaking, limited to two sources, the French Count Armand Alexander M. du Chayla, and a Russian *emigré*, Count Zhevakhov, a shady character on the borderline of religious folly and quackery, of whom there were many in these circles.[47] Both these witnesses agree that Nilus, a landowner from Central Russia, led a rather dissipated life. According to Zhevakhov, revelation came to Nilus one day in middle age after seeing a comet in Kiev. Du Chayla offers a more prosaic explanation. Nilus had lost much money in French casinos; both his own resources and those of his first wife had been spent, and he was compelled to return to Russia to look for work, and eventually for a second wife. Both biographers agree that he gradually became afflicted by a severe persecution mania. His second wife, Ozerova, was a former

---

* Butmi's editions all appeared in the first decade of the twentieth century; Nilus's in 1905, 1911, and in January 1917, a few days before the February revolution. There were also a number of editions in Russian after 1917, of which more below.

lady-in-waiting to the Grand Duchess Elizabeth, and it is likely that the half-mad Nilus was chosen by these circles as a suitable instrument to publish and propagate the *Protocols*. Nilus' 'religious folly' was regretfully noted by some of the Russian popularizers of the *Protocols*, who complained that his persecution mania had a detrimental influence on his anti-Semitism. Schwartz-Bostunich, the 'missing link between the Black Hundred and the Nazis', said that despite his 'immortal achievement . . . ideologically we remain astronomically remote from a man who really expected the coming of the Antichrist and for whom the medieval devil was a real being'.[48] Nilus had published the *Protocols* as part of a bigger and much more ambitious work: *The Big in the Small; or the Anti-christ as a near political possibility*. This is an incredible gallimaufry of religious quotations, exact predictions about the coming of the Antichrist, and symbolical drawings, in particular of stars and snakes, which may be relevant in a psychiatric investigation but are of no interest in this context. Much of this pathological symbolism was subsequently taken over by the 'scientific' anti-Semites who had ridiculed Nilus; an enormous literature exists on such subjects as the signs found on the wall of the room in which the last Tsarina was killed, the emblem of the League of Nations, etc. While Nilus apparently believed in symbols *per se*, his successors tried to establish a link between them and the freemasons' emblems.

Nilus's first known edition of the *Protocols* was published by the official court printers in Tsarskoe Selo, his last by the printing shop of the Troitse-Sergeyevsky Lavra, Russia's foremost monastery, which shows that though neither the court nor the Holy Synod ever authorized or in any way promoted the *Protocols*, Nilus apparently had very highly placed well-wishers.

With the revolution of 1917 Nilus disappeared from the scene,* and the *Protocols* were taken over by professionals. After several new editions in South Russia, then in the hands of the White Armies, they were brought to Western Europe by Russian *emigrés* in 1919. The first German edition was sponsored by the 'League against Jewish Arrogance'; its leader was Gottfried zur Beek (*recte* Captain Mueller von Hausen), who had been Ludendorff's adviser and acted as editor.[49] This edition included only a small section of Nilus's book, namely, the *Protocols*, and sold about 120,000 copies in a short time; the number of brochures, leaflets, and reprints based on it went into

* Zhevakhov reports that Nilus died in 1930 in a Moscow suburb.

101

millions. Leading newspapers, like the *Kreuzzeitung* and the *Deutsche Zeitung*, serialized the *Protocols* or commented on them, and German aristocrats (including the Kaiser, by then in his Dutch exile) sent it to their friends, strongly recommending the book. There were many other German editions of the *Protocols*, above all those sponsored by Theodor Fritsch.[50] As a German commentator on the *Protocols*, Alfred Rosenberg made a name for himself; he published a great number of articles and booklets on the subject, some of which also achieved a wide circulation.[51] Within a fairly short time the *Protocols* were translated into many languages; they became the standard anti-Semitic text in most European countries and spread even to other continents. In Britain, for instance, there was the *Morning Post* adaptation, followed by a book edition by a reputable publishing house (Eyre and Spottiswoode), and countless pamphlet editions by 'The Britons', a pro-Fascist group. In France there were three translations within a couple of years, and more followed. There were Polish, Italian, even Chinese and Japanese translations, and the Latin Patriarch of Jerusalem, Barsalina, called on his flock to purchase an Arabic translation in the middle twenties; several more followed by the thirties and after the Second World War. The most widespread popularization was the one sponsored by Henry Ford which also sold several hundreds of thousand copies.[52] Ford also launched a newspaper devoted specifically to the study of the *Protocols*. He admitted later that he had ceased to believe in their genuineness. By 1923 there existed an international network of *Protocols* sponsors and students. They had their outlets in some of the Russian *emigré* papers, in Germany (*Der Hammer*, a proto-Nazi organ), in Britain (*The Patriot*, the *British Guardian*), the United States (*Dearborn Independent*), Italy, Hungary (*A ńep*), France (*La Vieille France*), Norway (*National Tidsskrift*), Denmark (*Dansk National Tidsskrift*), Poland (*Dwa Grosze, Pro Patria*), and other countries. There was a great deal of co-ordination and co-operation between these journals and their sponsors; the Anti-Semitic International worked a good deal more smoothly, in fact, than the fictitious 'Elders of Zion'.

How can one explain the enormous success of the *Protocols*? Forty years on it seems inexplicable that such a primitive fake could have been taken seriously by so many people for so long a time.* One is inclined to forget the specific post-war background against which the *Protocols* were read and believed. After many years of

* A complete exposure of the fraud was given in *The Times* in 1921.

peace and prosperity the general optimism of Europe had been rudely shaken. To many, the First World War came like a bolt from the blue; millions had died in a senseless slaughter and there had been unprecedented material destruction. Many millions found themselves without means at the end of the war and without much hope for the future. The war was followed almost everywhere by unrest, revolution, civil war, and economic disasters such as inflation and unemployment. In these circumstances many were looking for an answer, if possible a clear and easily intelligible answer, to their searching questions about the causes of these catastrophes and the unrest in the world in general. The Russian Revolution, an ominous and threatening event, had given rise to a great deal of brooding and speculation. And now a document had emanated from the very country in which these apocalyptic events had taken place – sufficient reason for many people to accept these startling explanations. So many disasters could not possibly have been unconnected and unplanned; surely there must have been a hidden hand somewhere behind it all. That the forgeries were primitive and unconvincing did not really matter in the last resort. 'The ignorant believed them because they were ignorant, and the partially intelligent because it was for the good of the reactionary cause to do so.'[53] If the *Protocols* were widely read and partly believed in the countries that had emerged victorious from the war, their success in the camp of the defeated – from the White armies of Russia to Weimar Germany – is all the more understandable. A scapegoat had to be found for the defeat. Who had really brought about the downfall of Tsarist Russia? Who had stabbed the undefeated German armies in the back? Was it not a fact that after the First World War the Jews were suddenly found in prominent positions in German and Russian politics as well as in the economic and cultural life of these countries? Russian and German right-wingers found that they did not have to blame themselves and their own shortcomings for their defeats, but an outside enemy – a solution that had psychologically much to recommend it.

But the *Protocols* offered more than an explanation; they were also a political slogan, a battle cry. Hitler did not believe in Christ; unlike Nilus he was certainly not afraid of the Antichrist. But he was shrewd enough to realize the enormous propagandist potential of the basic ideas of the *Protocols*. He refers to them in *Mein Kampf*; much of what he says in his *magnum opus* is based on this book. Some observers have gone further and argued that in his constructive programme

Hitler was in effect a pupil of the Elders of Zion.[54] Was not Hitler's conviction that might is right, his belief in dictatorship and terror, his opposition to democracy and constitutionalism closely modelled on the pattern of the Elders? Did not the *Protocols* in effect offer a key to Nazi policy? These parallels seem, however, somewhat far fetched. Hitler needed the *Protocols* for his struggle against the Jews, not as a blueprint for Europe's future.

Chapter 6

THE RISE OF NATIONAL SOCIALISM
PART III: PROLOGUE TO THE
FINAL SOLUTION

Hitler and the Russian Right Wing

THE PROTOCOLS had been brought to Germany by Russian *emigrés* after the revolution of 1917. Though few in number, these right-wing extremists were a very active and vocal part of the Russian emigration in Central and Western Europe, and their relations with the early Nazi movement deserve close study.

Divided into dozens of groups and parties, the Russian emigration had its own daily newspapers and publishing houses, schools and theatres, social clubs and ex-servicemen's organizations. To many interested observers it seemed that these men and women were only temporarily exiled from their homeland. The refugees from the French Revolution had, after all, returned to their native country albeit after many years. Nobody had paid much attention to the doings of Lenin, Trotsky, and their friends while they had been freely accessible in the cafés of Berlin, Vienna, and Zürich. Governments, parties, and intelligence services were resolved not to repeat this mistake, and the activities of the new Russian emigration were closely followed.

Most active among these well wishers of the right-wing Russian emigration were certain German sympathizers, who made an ambitious takeover bid for the political allegiance of this group at the Reichenhall congress in 1921; German sources estimated at the time, perhaps wrongly, that almost ninety per cent of the Russian *emigrés* subscribed to right-wing or monarchist tenets. The approaches came mainly from Scheubner-Richter and his Munich circle, which included several well-known politicians such as Cramer-Klett and

Hofrat Aman of the Bavarian Peoples Party, industrialists from Munich, Regensburg and Augsburg, and, above all, Ludendorff and Colonel Bauer, one of his closest collaborators in the German High Command and head of a semi-private intelligence service. Ludendorff's and Bauer's backing was intended to be a secret but it was in fact widely known and even commented upon in the press.[1] The aim of the German right-wing politicians was to restore the old German–Russian alliance; the Russians, for obvious reasons, wanted German financial and political backing. At Reichenhall they hoped to heal the splits and dissensions that continued to plague them.

Some one hundred and thirty representatives of the Russian emigration from various European countries convened in the restaurant 'Post' in the small Bavarian town of Reichenhall one early June morning in 1921. There were many well-known names and faces: Krupensky, who had been Marshal of the Moscow nobles; Volkonsky, a former vice-chairman of the Duma; Senators Bellegarde and Rimsky-Korsakov; ex-minister Trepov, ex-generals Zakharov (commander of the armies in the Far East) and Biskupsky. Among the clergy were Bishops Antoni of Kiev, Sergei, and Evlogii; among the politicians, Markov; among the ideologists, A. M. Maslennikov. The Balts were strongly represented by Baron Taube, Count Grabbe, Voelkersamb, and others. The congress got off to a good start (one German newspaper noted that whereas in St Petersburg no official business had been done before noon, the Reichenhall sessions started punctually each morning at ten o'clock), but the internal dissension proved stronger than the unifying factors, and in fact very little was achieved at the congress. Press comment was mainly hostile; a Social-Democratic paper called it an attempt to establish an alliance between the 'new Bavarians' (meaning Ludendorff, Scheubner-Richter and, perhaps, Hitler), and old Russians. The Communists, predictably, called it a 'congress of the Black Hundred', but even a staunchly anti-Communist paper dryly remarked that 'only a very narrow world waits for a message from Reichenhall'.[2] Spokesmen for the Russian democratic emigration commented that the claims and hopes of the monarchists assembled in Reichenhall were entirely unfounded; some simply dismissed them as mere Don Quixotes.[3] The course taken by the conference seemed to justify this scepticism.

All the participants agreed that economic reconstruction was a subject of the greatest importance, but what economic reconstruction was possible before the *emigrés* had regained political power? The question of the national minorities and the new border states that had emerged out of the old Russian empire was left open; there was some talk about a limited agrarian reform, but it all remained very vague. Many wanted to bring up the Jewish question but others thought that this would be unwise. Instead it was announced that the only salvation for Russian Jews was to collaborate in the restoration of the monarchy; if they failed to co-operate, the Russian people would put all the blame on them.[4] Nemirovich-Danchenko, who had been Wrangel's press officer in the Crimea and who was to write for Rosenberg in the *Voelkischer Beobachter* for many years, announced a new project on behalf of the *Aufbau* group at a press conference: Russia needed qualified German workers; their emigration to Russia should be carefully planned – not to exploit the workers, not to benefit capitalism, but to achieve the best for both countries.[5]

The German right wing were undoubtedly pleased when they heard that Markov had denounced the Versailles Treaty which (he said) had sold Russia down the river and was an insult to mankind.[6] This was all very well, but on the central issue there was no agreement. Even the extreme right could not see eye to eye with regard to an exclusive pro-German orientation, and they were not impressed by warnings in the German nationalist press that the Paris centre of the Russian emigration was not only French-dominated but also Jew-infested and infiltrated by the freemasons.[7] Nor was there unanimity among the *emigrés* with regard to the election of a new Tsar – both Kyrill (of Coburg) and Nikolai Nikolaevich (of Paris) had their supporters, and the pro-Germans did not succeed in pushing their candidate through. A semi-private German intelligence report of the time is highly revealing: Markov, it said, was thoroughly pro-German; Rimsky-Korsakov, the secretary of the congress, was not an outstanding personality but he, too, was quite reliable; others, like Senator Neidhart and Dolgorukov, were pro-French. The Russian *emigré* intelligence services were said to be quite indiscriminate in their contacts; their leaders, Hausmann and Freyberg, had established contact even with the Japanese . . .*

* Intelligence Report of Orgesch (Organization Escherich, a Bavarian Free Corps, dated June 10, 1921) in B.D.C. But Markov did not altogether justify the trust put in him by the German extreme right wing: he had been staunchly pro-German in his days in the Duma, but after Reichenhall he went over to the French camp, to switch his allegiance back to Kyrill and, incidentally, to the Nazis, only in 1929. Rimsky-Korsakov had been one of the spokesmen of the 'Union of the Russian People' before 1917; see 'Programma Soyuza Russkovo Naroda' in *Krasny Arkhiv*, 1 (20), 1927.

Thus, the Reichenhall congress ended without any tangible result; the participants returned to Berlin and Belgrade, Munich and Paris, and each continued to follow his own policy. The plan to unite the whole Russian emigration, or at least its extreme right monarchist wing, in one organization had failed. All that remained for many years to come was a myth – the remembrance of a great meeting at which unity had almost been achieved.

Vasili Biskupsky

Among those who did not give up after Reichenhall was General Vasili Biskupsky, who came to play a leading part in the Russian emigration both in the twenties and under Hitler. He had been known in Russia as an able officer and even better gambler. At the time of the revolution he was in command of the third army corps in Odessa; after the evacuation of the Ukraine by the White forces he had found his way to Berlin, and following the Kapp *putsch* (in which he appeared on the sidelines) he settled in Munich, then the Mecca of all right-wingers. He had known Ludendorff and Colonel Bauer, who regarded him as the most capable and reliable leader of the Russian *emigrés*. In Munich he set out to find more allies in the struggle against Bolshevism, and a friend subsequently described how they discovered Hitler one evening at a meeting in a Munich inn. 'Hitler gave the impression of a strong man who had great power over those around him,' one witness reports; the two came to know each other and their relation with each other became fairly close.* At about this time Biskupsky threw in his lot with the Kyrill faction in the Russian emigration and soon became its 'prime minister'.

According to some who knew him well, Biskupsky, a man of considerable cunning, was a schemer in the grand style, always engaged in some major financial or political intrigue. He pretended to have believed in the nefarious influence of the hidden hand, the Jews, freemasons, Jesuits, and other sinister international forces, since the

* Alexander Zakharovich Silaev, former Colonel in the Tsarist army and deputy governor of Kherson under Wrangel, in a conversation with Boris Nikolaevski, New York, December 22, 1947. According to the same source, Hitler at one time hid in Biskupsky's house and Biskupsky's wife, a well-known singer, pawned some of her pearls to enable him to make his escape. I am inclined to believe that Silaev's memory failed him on this point: it was Victoria Feodorovna, the wife of Kyrill, the claimant to the throne, who sold some of her valuables to help the young Nazi movement.

outbreak of the First World War.[8] But at least one witness maintains that Biskupsky was far too intelligent for this and was merely pretending to accept the basic articles of faith of the right-wing monarchist circles. According to the same source, Biskupsky 'cared no more about the fate of Russia than the future of Abyssinia'; he was interested in the excitement and the spoils of politics, not in ideology.* This may be an exaggeration, but it is certainly true that Biskupsky loved to plot and to scheme, mostly from behind the scenes, playing one Grand Duke against another in their ambitions for the throne. He plotted with Ludendorff, too, and concluded (as he later maintained) a secret agreement on Germany's and Russia's future. The exact contents of this 'Russian–German treaty of 1923' are unknown; Ludendorff, as far as can be ascertained, never referred to it. But Biskupsky in a conversation shortly after the German–Soviet Pact in 1939, said that the new pact 'did not affect the old agreement which was based on the frontiers of 1914'. He also said that the last paragraph of the 'treaty' provided for a 'people's monarchy' (Volksmonarchie).[9]

Among Biskupsky's young aides in Munich and Berlin, Shabelsky-Bork and Taboritsky attained some notoriety. Petr Nikolaevich Shabelsky-Bork was born in Terek in 1893, the son of a rich Caucasian landowner. He joined the Union of the Russian People early in life; there was, in fact, a family connection with this movement since his mother, E. A. Shabelskaya-Bork, was one of its leading members.† Shabelsky served in the war and the civil war as a young officer and together with his friend Taboritsky, founded in Berlin an organization on the pattern of the Black Hundred. They engaged in both literary and terrorist activities; Shabelsky-Bork helped to edit *Luch Sveta*, an extremist periodical, while Taboritsky bodily attacked Guchkov, the well-known politician and former head of the

* Snessarev: *Kyrill Pervy, Imperator Koburga*. This is a very revealing and damaging report by a well-known journalist who at one time closely co-operated with the 'Coburg' circle and with Biskupsky, but later fell out with them. His book is full of vituperation but also includes much that is apparently authentic. Snessarev had once before caused considerable harm to Russian right-wing prestige: in 1913 he broke with *Novoe Vremya*, the leading right-wing paper of which he had been an editor, revealing damaging details about corruption.

† She published a Black Hundred periodical in Petersburg, *Svoboda i Poryadok*; it was intended for working-class consumption and was financed by the local police. She also contributed editorials to Dubrovin's *Russkoe Znamya*. Vinberg called her 'the holiest and purest of Russian womanhood'. She tried to persuade Rasputin shortly before his death to leave Petrograd for the sake of Russia and the Tsar's family.

Octobrists in Tsarist Russia, in a Berlin street. Their most ambitious enterprise was the murder of Vladimir Nabokov on March 28, 1922. Leaders of the Constitutional Democratic Party had convened an *emigrés* assembly in Berlin in aid of the famine-stricken in Russia. When Miliukov had ended his lecture and the chairman asked the public to put their questions, the terrorists, headed by Shabelsky-Bork and Taboritsky, burst into the hall (the Berlin Philharmonia) singing patriotic Russian songs, and opened fire on the presidium. They intended to shoot Miliukov but instead hit Nabakov, who attempted to shield his fellow Cadet leader (with whom, incidentally, he disagreed on many important points). Miliukov saved himself by falling to the ground; Nabokov was mortally wounded.* At their trial, Shabelsky-Bork and Taboritsky denied membership of any political organization; they claimed that they were engaged in something like a romantic Caucasian vendetta and simply wanted to avenge the honour of the Tsarina, whom Miliukov had insulted in a speech during the war.

Shabelsky-Bork was sentenced to fourteen years hard labour; Taboritsky to twelve years. They were, however, released long before their terms were up, and again came to play a minor part in the fortunes of the Russian emigration in Germany.†

The Coburg Circle

Grand Duke Kyrill Vladimirovich (1876–1938), who proclaimed himself Tsar in August 1922, was first cousin to Nicholas II and therefore one of the 'rightful' pretenders to the Russian throne. His monarchist critics argued that the fact that his mother had not belonged to the true faith, and that he himself had married a woman who was not Orthodox, disqualified him; but according to his supporters Kyrill's rivals had all been discredited by their behaviour during the revolution and the civil war or were suspected of democratic and constitutional leanings. Kyrill had served without distinc-

* The report of the Shabelsky-Bork case (1922) by the public prosecutor has been preserved in the Berlin municipal archives.

† Shabelsky-Bork received a monthly salary from Rosenberg's office in 1933, for services rendered. He also helped in the same year to establish a Russian Nazi movement (letter to Schickedanz, March 14, 1933, National Archives, Washington, see chapter four, note 16, below). Taboritsky applied for some position during the early Nazi era, but was rejected as 'personally unreliable' by the Nazis. In 1938 he became assistant to General Turkul, leader of a pro-Nazi group in the Russian emigration.

tion in the Russian navy, went to Finland after the revolution, and eventually settled in Coburg where his wife's family had its possessions. Kyrill was a dull and unassuming man, not really interested in politics, who left the decision-making to his wife and his advisers.* His programme, first published in October 1922, was subsequently described as racialist–nationalist (*voelkisch*), very similar to the Nazi programme in character.[10] In fact, it was an old-fashioned manifesto with some vague statements about the desirability of 'Soviets without Communism' and promises that the peasants would keep the land they were working. Such concessions to the spirit of the times and the social revolution that had taken place were apparently considered necessary, but the programme did not go into practical details. On one point only were Kyrill and his advisers certain; they needed German help if there was ever to be a restoration, and they did their best to discourage the pro-Soviet orientation that was so fashionable in German right-wing circles in the twenties.

The very idea of trying to establish a Tsarist counter-government on traditional lines outside Russia was devoid of any sense of political realities; it soon became a farce. The majority of monarchists in the emigration, including the Supreme Monarchical Council, did not recognize Kyrill and a bitter struggle ensued between his supporters and those of the Grand Duke Nikolai Nikolaevich in Paris. Efforts were made to attract American help for the Coburg venture. (According to one source, three seats in the Coburg Regency Council were actually sold to America.) Among the Russian members of this exile government there was Kammerherr Matlev, whose reputation among his own compatriots was not very good, Colonel Dolivo-Dolinsky, head of the 'secret service', old Aleksei Bobrinsky, a general who edited the paper *Vera i Vernost*, and – most active of all – N. O. Graf, a captain of hussars who rose to be an 'admiral' in the emigration and who acted on behalf of Kyrill's group as head of the chancellery right up to the outbreak of the Second World War.†

---

* The 'Tsarina' was also apparently far more active in support of National Socialism than her husband. See Biskupsky to Schickedanz, March 22, 1933, National Archives, Washington, see chapter four, note 16, below.

† Nikolai Osvaldovich Graff had been Purishkevich's right-hand man in the student organization of the 'Union of the Russian people'; he was president of its branch at Petrograd university.

Collaboration and After

The collaboration between Russian *emigré* groups and the early Nazi movement came to an end with the failure of the Hitler *putsch* in 1923. Hitler's defeat had a sobering effect on the Russian extreme right; to make matters worse, the monarchical wave in Bavaria (and in Germany as a whole) was receding, a Labour government was in power in Britain, and France was contemplating recognition of the Soviet Government.[11] Munich ceased to be a centre of the Russian emigration and, outside the Kyrill faction, few Russian *emigré* politicians stayed on in Germany.[12]

Close relations between these Russian groups and the Nazis were not resumed after Hitler emerged from prison; a firm anti-Russian attitude developed and, in so far as the Nazis had a coherent policy on East European affairs, they supported the Ukrainian separatists.[13] Biskupsky tried, without success, to establish contact with various Nazi leaders, including Hitler. In a letter of September 21, 1932, he suggested they should 'co-ordinate their policy' regardless of ideological differences,[14] but received no satisfactory reply. When Nazi fortunes improved, Biskupsky tried hard to ingratiate himself with Rosenberg, who at the time was thought to be the future German foreign minister. He told Rosenberg that he had opposed his anti-Russian views but had always liked him personally; Rosenberg countered with a complaint that Biskupsky and his friends had not given sufficient consideration to legitimate German territorial aspirations in the East.[15] When the Nazis came to power, Biskupsky and his friends were quick to remind the new masters of Germany of their great services to the common cause in 1921–3. 'Dear' Alfred Voldemarovich (Rosenberg) and 'dear' Arno Gustavovich (Schickedanz) were bombarded with letters in Russian and German.* Above all these Russians wanted money; their situation was desperate. Biskupsky had been without any financial support since 1928 and Shabelsky-Bork was even more hard up. Biskupsky did not want to get something for nothing; he offered to organize a wide spy network in France. His organization there (the Mladorossy?) was to report to him in person and he was to be in direct contact with Rosenberg and Hitler. They had excellent contacts – with the French General Staff, the Second International, the Third International, and even the

---

* Some Russians addressed Rosenberg as Alfred Vladimirovich [sic] – for instance, V. Viktorov (*loc. cit.*). Rosenberg was probably not amused.

'Grand Orient'. Surely the Nazis must realize the importance of getting a constant flow of accurate information from the enemy country? Unlike previous German governments, the Nazis had read Colonel Nikolai (about espionage in the First World War) and would be willing to draw the necessary conclusions.[16] However, the German professionals apparently took a dim view of the efforts of amateur spies and at their instigation Biskupsky was arrested by the Gestapo and held prisoner from June to September 1933. This was not the end of his career; two years later he re-emerged on the political scene and was appointed head of the Russian emigration in Germany.

However, these later developments are outside the scope of this present study. Kyrill of Coburg and his family had been compelled to leave Germany in the middle twenties. According to their own version, this was the result of exorbitant financial demands made by the German tax authorities at the instigation of Hilferding, the Social Democratic minister. In fact, they were swindled out of much of their remaining property by a right-wing extremist confidence trickster who belonged to Ludendorff's circle.

Considerable sympathy for Hitler and Mussolini existed among Russian right-wing *emigrés* in the late twenties and, under the impact of the Nazi victory in Germany, a great number of small semi-Fascist or semi-Nazi groups sprouted in Germany and other countries. But the Nazis were indifferent to these potential allies, and did everything to discourage them.* They had needed allies in the early days, but after 1931-2 these Russians were more of a liability than an asset in Nazi eyes.

The majority of the Russian emigration had taken no part in the flirtation with the Nazis in the early twenties and they stayed aloof from the attempts to collaborate after 1933. Military leaders like General Denikin, and most of the political figures of the older generation, had their doubts about democracy, but the ideas of German National Socialism certainly did not attract them, and they thought it inconceivable that Hitler would be a trustworthy ally. At first sight the Russian emigration appeared a favourable breeding ground for sundry Fascist ideologies and movements. But in fact the state of affairs was far more complicated. German racialist theories did not

* Kyrill's faction had to discontinue its activities in Germany in October 1933; Kyrill's son, Vladimir Kyrillovich, who lives in Spain, is the rightful pretender to the Russian throne in the eyes of some remaining Russian monarchists.

find many supporters among the Russians, whatever their political persuasion; some 'right-wing' (Italian) type of Fascism might have found more sympathizers. But, ideological considerations apart, at least one essential factor was missing: in Germany and Italy Fascist movements had come to power as extreme nationalist mass movements in opposition to foreign enemies. The small Russian Fascist groups, on the other hand, had to put their hopes on the help of foreigners to get rid of the Bolshevik masters of Russia – not exactly a dignified position for extreme nationalists.[17] Nobody realized this more clearly than Hitler, who many years later recalled that he had quarrelled with Rosenberg about it as far back as 1921. 'I told him, "Rosenberg, mark my words, revolutions are made by people inside a country, not by those outside." Then came that Hetman (Skoropadski) and I asked Rosenberg: "What do you expect from that man?" "Well," he said, "he's organizing the revolution." I replied: "In that case he ought to be inside Russia." '[18]

Prologue to the Final Solution

A few extreme right-wing Russian *emigrés* joined the Nazi Party; others remained outside because they had certain reservations, or because they were refused admission. Their political activities were in any case of no great consequence; more important were their ideological efforts to bring the Black Hundred doctrine up to date, to digest the lessons of the war and the revolution. In so doing they had a certain, albeit limited, influence on National Socialism. Of particular interest in this context is the work of Fyodor Viktorovich Vinberg, a former Tsarist officer who lived in Berlin and published a number of books and edited several periodicals in the twenties. Vinberg was not a prominent figure in Russian political life; he had not been a member of the Duma nor did he belong to the inner councils of the right-wing emigration. Nevertheless, his publications are of considerable relevance because he was, in his own perverse way, the most logical and most outspoken of the entire group and because his writings apparently influenced Alfred Rosenberg and through Rosenberg, Hitler. Above all, he was the man who first brought the *Protocols* to Germany and published them there.

Born in Kiev, the son of a general commanding a cavalry division, he became an officer in the Imperial Horse Guards and ultimately attained the rank of colonel. He came into politics relatively late, shortly before the First World War, joining Purishkevich's group; he also wrote for some of the Black Hundred periodicals. Vinberg belonged to that small but influential group of russified Germans who played an important part in the politics and the administration of Tsarist Russia and in right-wing politics both before and after the revolution.* During the war their position in Russia was not easy, for they were suspected of treason. Vinberg certainly did not forgive Purishkevich his extreme anti-Germanism of that period.[19] These accusations against Vinberg and his friends were certainly false. They, of course, favoured a pro-German line in Russian foreign politics, but once hostilities had started they were certainly not disloyal to their sovereign and fatherland.

Vinberg was a most loyal and devoted subject of his Tsar and his writings are full of invective against all Russian politicians, particularly of the centre and the right, who had been deficient in this respect.† Shortly before the October revolution, Vinberg took part in a conspiracy to overthrow the provisional government, was arrested and sent to the Peter and Paul fortress.[20] There he had ample time to write his diaries and to bring some order into his ideas; like Hitler in Landsberg prison, he then and there prepared himself for his future political and publicist career. Vinberg was released, or escaped, in 1918, and went first to the Ukraine and later to Germany, where he systematically developed his ideas in the short-lived Berlin newspaper *Prizyv*, the yearbook *Luch Sveta* (*A Ray of Light*), published first in Berlin and subsequently in Yugoslavia, his book *Krestny Put* (*Via Dolorosa*), and a number of other writings. Vinberg's ideas can be summarized as follows:

1. The Jews are the source of all evil. They must be exterminated.
2. The liberals and the constitutional monarchists are responsible for Russia's ruin. Any form of democracy and republican regime is bad. A strong dictatorship is needed, for the people are stupid and bad and can never be trusted.
3. Russia and Germany must unite in order to crush the revolution.
4. The Catholic and Orthodox Churches must unite against the combined power of the Judaeo-masonic sects now operating as a new International.

* Such names as Baron von Taube, Meller, Schwartz, von Lampe, von Traubenberg, von Leuchtenberg, Talberg, von Manteuffel, Hartman, appeared rather frequently in these circles.
† His magnum opus starts with an ode to Nicholas II.

Vinberg sets out from the position of a partisan of the old regime but soon gives up some of its traditional articles of faith. He is violently opposed to all forms of parliamentarism and 'democratic squabble': there is a mixture of Nietzsche and social Darwinism unbecoming to a staunch royalist. In his 'Berlin letters' published in *Luch Sveta*, we learn that nature loves the strong, the brave, the agile, those who act and do not talk; she loathes weakness and democratic half measures.[21] Vinberg has only contempt for the masses, and his only criticism of Nicholas II is that the late Tsar unduly idealized the *muzhik*, and the Russian people in general,[22] who are really a good for nothing lot and deserve to be punished for having betrayed their Tsar. The people will always remain a blind, ignorant, senseless mass which has never and nowhere understood anything apart from the crudest material needs. The people is an 'anthropoid herd', a multifaced brute. What Rosenberg says of Jews and Jewish history can be traced, chapter and verse, to Vinberg's 'Berlin letters' of 1919: the Jewish religion is highly aristocratic; the Jews have been engaged for many hundreds of years in a struggle against the gentile aristocracies; they use in this fight democratic, liberal and socialist doctrines which act as a poison in the non-Jewish body politic. Thus they destroyed the Roman empire through the deadly injection of democratic-Jewish Christianity. The Jews themselves are immunized against the democratic virus by their religion and race. They use the natural laws of heredity and selection to perpetuate and to make more pronounced the qualities of their race. The *goyim*, on the other hand, have only recently begun to awaken to the importance of race. Socialism is in a way modern Christianity; it was invented by the Jews to achieve their ultimate aim – the triumph over the Aryan world. But is it not too late for any attempt to rescue the Aryan world? Three quarters of those who call themselves Christians are already caught in the Judaeo-masonic web; all the world's gold reserves are in their hands and three quarters of the world's press. At any moment their International is ready to strike in the direction chosen by the Sanhedrin; with the creation of an international army under the League of Nations they will receive the last instrument for carrying out their plans. Yet in spite of the mortal danger there is still a hope of salvation. The Aryan peoples must abandon their shortsighted and stupid politics and form a united front. As a good hunter should know the tastes and habits of his prey, so they should learn to think and act like beasts – only then will their hunting yield results. Those who have discovered the real meaning of Jewish religion – the establishment of their world rule – have no right to rest; their struggle for power must be equally cunning and ruthless.[23]

But what to do about the Jews? Vinberg is quite emphatic about this; the only solution is total physical extermination. There are two types of anti-Semitism. The 'higher', consisting of the promulgation of restrictive laws, expulsion, and other protective measures, and the lower, embodying total extermination. This anti-Semitism is terrible but it is effective and its consequences are beneficial. It cuts through the Gordian knot of the problem by destroying the Jews, the Judaized, and everything that smacks of Judaism. It comes from below, from the depths of the people (otherwise despised by Vinberg) but it is given them by God. The nest of vipers has to be destroyed so that no trace will be left.[24]

Vinberg died in February 1927,[25] and did not witness his ideas coming to fruition. His views are of historical interest because they constitute something in the nature of a half-way house between the old Black Hundred and National Socialism. His rejection of Christianity, while trying to preserve some private Christian myth, the adoption of the race theory (though not yet in a pseudo-scientific, elaborate form), the utter contempt for the masses, the intelligentsia, and in effect for all apart from the natural *élite*, the ideas of dictatorship and a radical solution of the Jewish question (more radical than anything Hitler or Rosenberg put on paper) – all this clearly led him far beyond the traditions of right-wing Russian political thought, such as it had been established by the Slavophiles and Pobedonostsev. The notion of Christianity as a democratic poison and as a precursor of Bolshevism was taken up by Alfred Rosenberg in his *Myth of the Twentieth Century*;[26] so was the idea that Jewry should be exterminated and not merely segregated and put in its place.

Vinberg's limitations as a forerunner of Nazism are at the same time obvious. With his belief in monarchy he failed to qualify (like Ludendorff) as a modern Fascist thinker; his contempt for the masses was not matched (as it was in Hitler) by a realization of the importance and the possibility of politically exploiting them. Vinberg and his like had fairly clear aims, but no idea how to realize them; he was a madman, but not a dangerous one. His Russian loyalties remained supreme despite his German origin. He could not, therefore, go along with the Nazi ideologists in writing off Russia as a country of *Untermenschen*. Nazi ideology was based, after all, on the superiority of the German *Volkstum*, of the Nordic race. Vinberg, as a Russian, could not possibly become the prophet of an exclusive racial myth.

Markov

There was a whole host of minor thinkers and writers in Berlin, Munich, and Belgrade, who propagated similar views with varying aptitude, intensity, and consistency. They had their own organizations, newspapers, periodicals, and publishing houses. Best known among them was undoubtedly Nikolai Yevgenevich Markov (known in the Duma as Markov II), whose very name had been a by-word in the last years of the Tsarist empire. Born in 1866, a landowner from the Kursk district, he represented the extreme right in the second, and in subsequent Dumas, heaping outrageous abuse on socialists, liberals, and, above all, right-of-centre deputies. The Russian equivalent of a Junker, his attacks on capitalism were even more violent and noisy than his charges against the socialists. He was the main exponent of a pro-German political orientation and throughout the war demanded a separate peace treaty with Germany.

After the revolution, Markov continued his activities in Germany; he headed the Russian Monarchist Union and helped to edit the *Dvuglavy Orel*, one of the leading periodicals at the time.* However, as a writer and ideologist Markov did not prove very effective; his main work, published in Russian in Paris and in a German edition in the Third Reich, is a collection of alarming reports about illuminist meetings, ritual slaughter, masonic plots, etc., from the death of Christ to the murder of Nikolai Romanov.[27] The only innovation is that Karl Radek appears in his work as the main agent of the Chief Rabbi of Constantinople. There was an enormous native anti-Semitic literature in Germany and foreign newcomers found it heavy going. Little notice was taken, therefore, of Markov in the Third Reich, and he spent his remaining years lecturing on the Russian emigration; an anti-climactic, though perhaps fitting, end to a politician who fancied himself a potential Russian Bismarck if not a new Peter I.

* His contributions were frequently published under the pen name 'Goi'.

118

Prizyv

On these ideological rubbish dumps, *Prizyv*, a daily newspaper published in Berlin, flourished for a brief period in 1919–20. The German right-wing extremist press was supplied for years with information first published in *Prizyv* during its nine months of existence.* The following typical story should suffice: At the time of an armed clash between Red Army units on the Estonian border, a letter had been found in the pocket of Sundel, the commander of the Russian unit; this was said to be a circular directed to the heads of departments of the international Jewish organization ('The Sons of Israel') informing them that the hour of victory was near. 'We are on the eve of world domination.'[28]

The paper called upon the Russian emigration to orientate themselves towards the German right rather than hope for any help from the Western powers. Anti-Semitic propaganda took pride of place; the editors proudly declared that theirs was the only Russian *emigré* paper not to have Jews on its staff. This was a somewhat incongruous announcement, for how could they square the talk about Judaeo-Bolshevism with the presence of so many Jews in the emigration? Indignantly the editors of *Prizyv* rejected charges of 'extremism'. 'Those who think we are too extreme ought to read the newspaper published in the rear of the White Armies,' they argued, 'Even the Constitutional Democrats are more outspoken than we are.'[29] *Prizyv* reiterated almost daily the editors' belief in the principle of Orthodoxy, and reported a great religious revival in the areas of Russia held by the White Armies. The victory of the counter-revolution in Hungary was a golden promise in the eyes of *Prizyv*, and so was the strengthening of the right-wing forces in Germany. The editors of the paper were involved in the preparation of the Kapp *putsch*, the attempt by right-wing extremists to overthrow German democracy in March 1920. As a result, *Prizyv* was banned by the Berlin authorities after the suppression of the coup.

Prizyv and some like-minded papers such as *Dvuglavy Orel* (*The Two-headed Eagle*) were avidly read by the Russian experts around Hitler such as Rosenberg and Scheubner-Richter.† Rosenberg,

---

* The first number appeared on June 22, 1919, the last on March 14, 1920.

† Rosenberg's many articles in these years were almost entirely based on his study of these newspapers. Sometimes he acknowledged his source (for instance, in *Auf Gut Deutsch*, December 30, 1919), more often he did not.

already a pupil of Houston Stewart Chamberlain, must have disliked the strong religious flavour of these publications, but as a source of information they were of the greatest value to him.

A few other spokesmen of this group deserve mention. Count (General) Cherep-Spiridovich had his headquarters in the United States; he was even more obviously a clinical case than some of his colleagues. He introduced himself in his books and pamphlets as 'The Slav Pope', 'The Slav Bismarck', 'The possessor of the faculty to foresee events' (Lord Alfred Douglas *dixit*)[30] and combined Barnum promotion techniques with propagation of the stories supplied by his European friends. The results have to be read to be believed. Even so, well-known men like Henry Ford and newspapers like the *Financial Times* in London took him seriously and helped him to reach a fairly wide public.

Another General, Nechvolodov, worked in France on lines broadly similar to those of Cherep-Spiridovich. Prince Gorchakov had a publishing house in Paris specializing in literature of the same kind – plots, ritual murder, etc. A great many publications of the kind came out in Yugoslavia. Evgenii Brant, in his 'scientific study' of ritual murder, brought all material published in European languages together in a three volume work.[31] V. Akhmatov, in a book that was strongly religious in inspiration, ended with the pious words, 'in the depth of my soul I still hope that in the not-too-distant future a Christian Messiah will arise to launch a crusade against Jewry'.[32] *Staroe Vremya* and *Novoe Vremya*, the main Russian *emigré* newspapers of this period, followed a similar line, though *Novoe Vremya* was less pro-German than the rest.

In Germany, Prince N. D. Zhevakhov, the biographer of Nilus, published his memoirs attacking even Markov for lack of anti-Semitic enthusiasm.[33] The elder statesmen of the extreme right, men like Krupensky or Bobrinsky, did not care to write books or articles in their old age. The same applies to A. A. Shirinsky-Shikhmatov who had been Pobedonostsev's understudy at the Holy Synod, and subsequently one of Russia's most reactionary local governors.[34] But old Shirinsky-Shikhmatov had a son, Yuri Alekseyevich, whose activities and subsequent fate are of some interest. The younger Shirinsky was the head of the Russian youth organization, 'the Council of National Thinking Russian Youth Abroad' in Berlin and Munich. He wrote under a pen name, Lukyanov, in the periodicals of this group, voicing somewhat heretical views such as opposition to foreign intervention in Russia and the demand for a 'revolutionary monarchist movement' – whatever that may have meant. Young Shirinsky-Shikhmatov was a prominent leader of the Berlin monarchist and right-wing extremist organizations and on their behalf he negotiated with a visitor named A. A. Yakushev (alias Fyodorov), who had come to Berlin from Moscow in November 1922 and was (he revealed) only outwardly a Soviet expert; in reality he represented the Russian monarchist opposition inside Russia. Thus a very fascinating chapter in the history of the Russian emigration started, for 'Yakushev' was as good as his word and brought on each visit important and apparently authentic information about the situation in Russia.[35] It took the Russian monarchists several years to discover that this apparent co-operation with the 'inner emigration' was in fact a hoax that was carefully stage-managed by the Soviet political police in a not unsuccessful effort to infiltrate the Russian emigration.[36]

The story of this attempt, the so-called 'Trust', is of no direct relevance in the present context. While it lasted there was real co-operation between these two camps and through the Berlin and Munich *emigré* centres some leading Nazis were apparently involved too. Hitler seems to have been distrustful of Russian *emigré* politics from a very early date and warned Rosenberg. But Scheubner-Richter continued to co-operate with the Supreme Monarchical Council. There were persistent rumours in Germany that Scheubner-Richter had in effect a direct wire to Moscow; the Free Corps commander, Captain Ehrhardt, claimed in 1923 to have been able to establish contact with the Soviet government via Scheubner-Richter.* It sounds most unlikely, but what really happened we may never know, for those prominently involved in these dealings have disappeared and have left no known records.

The literature produced by Vinberg and his friends flourished

---

* Bayrisches Hauptarchiv, Ministerium des Inneren 73700; see also August Winnig, *Heimkehr*, p. 179. The basis of these rumours was a report in the Russian *emigré* journal *Russkoe Delo* in Belgrade late in 1922, according to which General Komissarov had arrived in Munich for secret talks with Scheubner-Richter and Biskupsky. Komissarov had been one of the central figures in the Tsarist Okhrana between 1900 and 1917; he played a prominent part in the instigation of pogroms, in liaison with the Black Hundred, and, for a time, in the Rasputin affair. Later he was said to be working for the Cheka. This report, at once denied (*Aufbau*, February 7, 1923), was still quoted in exchanges between Biskupsky and Himmler twelve years later. See National Archives, Washington, EAP 161-b-12/139, folder 148.

throughout the twenties and thirties. It was not confined to Europe, and while all writers laboured the same general theme, each added some new variation. One author, writing in Shanghai in 1933, found that not only the YMCA was a branch of the Judaeo-masonic international, but the Boy Scouts and the Baptists were of similar inspiration.[37] Some of it outlasted the Second World War and there were a few late echoes of 'anti-Satanism' as it was then called in the early fifties. Its few proponents in the Russian right-wing emigration argued then that they were not against the Jews as such, but only against the sinister forces behind Jewry and the assimilationist Jews.

Schwarz-Bostunich

Among these preachers of a 'final solution', one went the whole way in accepting Hitlerism and identifying himself entirely with the Nazi movement. He became a confidant of Himmler and a friend of men like Heydrich, Ohlendorf and Karl Wolff, and a fairly high ranking member of the SS. To achieve this it was not enough, however, to accept Nazi ideology; he had to abjure his Russian origins and become an honorary racial German (*Volksdeutscher*). The case of Grigorii Schwarz-Bostunich is of some interest both as a contribution to the political psycho-pathology of our times and as an 'organic link' between the Black Hundred and the Nazi movement.

Bostunich was born in Kiev in 1883 into a well-to-do family.[38] He studied law and specialized in anti-Semitism and anti-masonic 'studies' from his early days. During the civil war he was a propagandist in Denikin's, later in Wrangel's army; after their defeat he went first to Belgrade but settled in Germany in the early twenties. His first publications were a commentary on the *Protocols* and a more substantial work on Freemasonry.[39] In effect, all his life from 1917 onwards was devoted to the study of secret societies and occult forces that had plagued the Aryan peoples.[40] He became the most prolific writer of anti-Jesuit, anti-anthroposophic, anti-masonic literature, and in his spare time he provided the philosophical rationale for Streicher's *Stuermer*, investigating the fatal attraction of Jewish men for German Aryan women and the terrible consequences of their intercourse.[41] 'My few friends and my many enemies,' he wrote in 1933, 'know perfectly well that I am quite unassailable because my references are accurate and I provide chapter and verse for my statements.'[42] Bostunich specialized in tracing Judaeo-masonic symbols in history; and since, according to him, masons and Jews used not merely the circle, the triangle, and the quadrangle, but also the cross, pentagram, hexagram, and even the swastika, there were but few signs, pictures, stamps, etc., which were found to be free of their pernicious influence. Typical of his philosophical-historical constructions were comments on a picture he had found somewhere, showing a snake (another famous Judaeo-masonic symbol) projected upon a map of Europe. This symbolized the successful attempts of the Jewish people to subvert all the states that constituted an obstacle to their way to world power: Athens in 429 BC; Rome of the Augustan age; Madrid under Charles V; Paris around 1700 under Louis XIV; Moscow in 1917. (The allegorical snake, which played a great rôle in Russian anti-Semitic literature and was imported into Germany in the twenties, had been invented by Liutstansky, a famous Russian apostate from Judaism who lived in the second part of the nineteenth century, became a Catholic priest, then a leading anti-Semite, and in the end offered the leaders of the Jewish community to withdraw publicly all he had written against them – for a suitable consideration.)

Bostunich did not really make an original contribution to either anti-Semitic or anti-masonic writings, but he collected all the inventions from many lands that had accumulated during the centuries and apparently sincerely believed that, if it had once appeared in print, even a lie became a scientific truth. He systematically dredged the sewers of European literature for items he thought would please his SS masters; but even they had some doubts about his methods. When it was suggested that the title 'professor' should be bestowed upon him during the Second World War, some of the SS chieftains, notably Ohlendorf, who had some academic training, commented that his approach was not really scientific; no German university volunteered, and he merely became an honorary SS professor.[43]

His conversion to National Socialism was gradual, though he argued in later years that he had been a fighter for the 'movement' since 1923; to his contemporaries in 1923 he was just a Russian *emigré* who had published an anti-Semitic play in his native language; it ended with the Jew, Zadok (chief of Dzerzhinsky's Cheka), crucifying a child, the son of a Russian general.* Around 1925 he came to

---

* *Luch Sveta*, Vol. IV; a German translation was published in 1936 in Graz, *Des Henkers Tod*: Bostunich continued to write plays in Nazi Germany without conspicuous success. Himmler opposed the showing of the *SS Bride*: the intention was said to be praiseworthy, the execution less so.

know Alfred Rosenberg and began to work for one of Rosenberg's anti-Semitic subsidiaries, the *Weltdienst* news agency. He changed his name to Schwarz-Bostunich and began to write in a somewhat halting German. Unlike some of his contemporaries in the extreme right wing, he did not stay with the Rosenberg circle but switched his allegiance to Himmler and the SS. This was a clever political move, for Rosenberg's influence was about to wane, whereas Himmler's star was very much in the ascendant.

What did the SS, the most *élitist* of all Nazi organization, find in this mad and half-crippled Russian that they promoted him to *Hauptsturmfuehrer* in 1935, and *Standartenfuehrer* in 1944 – fairly high ranks in the SS for a mere ideologist? Himmler was impressed by the fanatical personal devotion invariably shown by Schwarz-Bostunich. 'We have all come to like you,' Himmler wrote him in 1935.[44] Bostunich, for his part, stressed on every occasion that he was bound life and death to the 'magnificent SS.' He affirmed his undying devotion to Himmler and other SS leaders countless times. Bostunich undoubtedly had some of the old Austro-Ukrainian charm; he was apparently an excellent *raconteur* and very much in demand as a lecturer despite the fact that his German was not flawless. He toured Germany, and later also some of the occupied countries, with his standard lectures on Jewry and freemasons.

For all that, he was stark mad; from an early age he felt an urge to act as an informer and, what is more surprising, proudly announced this in public.[45] In a letter to the SS central office he reported that he was informing on enemies of the state wherever he found them and there is much evidence to the effect that he was telling the truth. He always felt persecuted; at one time during the early part of the war Heydrich, the Gestapo chief, had to send a professional pugilist to act as his bodyguard. When the Gestapo went to his house once on a routine check in his absence, Bostunich immediately called for Himmler's help against what he regarded as masonic intrigue.

By the late thirties Bostunich was one of the leading SS experts on the Jewish question and the highest authority for the anti-masonic struggle.* However, during the later part of the war his fanaticism was too much even for Himmler, who told him that the official line on freemasonry had been modified, that his lectures in future would have

---

* After 1935 he specialized more and more in the masonic field, presumably because the anti-Semitic field had become somewhat crowded and there was less demand there for his specialized services.

to be censored, and that he would not be permitted to appear in SS uniform. This was a heavy blow for Bostunich, who spent the latter part of the war trying to have the order rescinded. He attempted to find a secure place outside Berlin for his unique library of 15,000 volumes on Jewry and freemasonry. He also tried, without success, to convince Himmler that measures should be taken against smoking in public transport (especially by soldiers returning from the front), and to speed up the postal services. Himmler by that time had graver anxieties. Bostunich, by now in his sixties, and in a precarious state of health, was very much on his own when the end of the war came and with it the victory of the Judaeo-masonic forces.

The Bostunich case is of some significance because it shows, on one hand, the kinship between the Black Hundred ideology and Nazi thought, and at the same time indicates all too clearly the gulf between them. Nazism, with its belief in racial exclusivity, could not possibly accept in its inner ranks Russians (or any other non-Germans) however close they were ideologically. A few individuals, like Bostunich, could take the plunge and enter the ranks by becoming 'racial Germans', but this course was closed, needless to say, to any large group of people.

The Black Hundred impact on Nazism was limited, on the whole, to the early years of the Hitler movement. There was a very strong native Pan-German and anti-Semitic tradition in Germany – it could be argued that Hitler did not really need any outside assistance. Yet the fact remains that there were strong foreign influences: Balts like Rosenberg who had fled from Russia in 1918, and groups of right-wing extremist Russian *emigrés* who provided both ideological ammunition and material help. Under their influence an utterly distorted image of the Russian Revolution, the Soviet Union, and Russia and the Jews in general was created, in which Hitler and many millions of Germans came to believe. In later years it affected Nazi policy towards the Soviet Union and the Jewish question; during the Second World War these demented fantasies became reality in the extermination camps.

Chapter 7

BETWEEN MOSCOW AND WEIMAR

THE FIRST WORLD WAR sealed the fate not only of the Romanovs and the Hohenzollern; for a while both Germany and Russia ceased to be active factors in European politics. With the restoration of Poland in 1918 there was no longer direct physical contact between the two countries. Defeated Germany was in a state of constant turmoil, Russia in the throes of a ferocious and prolonged civil war. A power vacuum existed in Eastern and Central Europe. But the eclipse was only temporary; by 1920 Russia had again taken a leading place in the designs of German policy-makers, businessmen, and, inevitably, ideologists.

During the war Imperial Germany had tried to weaken Tsarist Russia by supporting the revolutionary movement there. On the whole this was done in a very amateurish way; the ability of Wilhelmian officers to engineer revolutions was strictly limited, and professionals who offered their services, such as Parvus, were not given much scope. In fact, these German offers of assistance probably did more harm than good to the cause of the revolutionaries. Tsarism was overthrown in March 1917 following a chain of defeats in the war, mounting distress and dissatisfaction on the home front, and through the incompetence of the old rulers of Russia. But it is at least arguable that the sealed train that brought Lenin and his comrades from Switzerland to the Finnish station changed history; without Lenin's guidance the Bolsheviks might not have tried their luck in November 1917; without his leadership they might not have survived the first critical months and years.

Brest-Litovsk was the first milestone in Soviet-German relations after the revolution of 1917. Against the advice of some of his closest political friends, Lenin gave ground in order to win time. Admittedly the German military leaders, whose counsel prevailed over the Foreign Ministry officials, made it very difficult for him. They not only wanted enormous territorial concessions and the grain of the Ukraine; they also demanded Russian military action against the Entente powers. Ludendorff thought the Bolsheviks could easily be overthrown, but from July 1918 the German military position deteriorated week by week, whereas the Soviet regime grew stronger. When the Armistice came in November 1918 the undefeated but demoralized German troops had to leave Russia without a battle.

At Brest-Litovsk Imperial Germany had been the victor; after Versailles, Republican Germany suddenly found she had interests in common with Russia: they were both outcasts, the pariahs of international politics; they both needed to work towards a revision of the peace treaties. Lenin believed that Germany's only means of saving herself was through an alliance with Russia, though many Germans were slower to realize the possible advantages of such an alliance. For the new Russia was no longer simply a national state with a traditional foreign policy; she had become the centre of world Communism, and at that time in Germany the small band of Communists had antagonized both the authorities and the public with their revolutionary slogans and activities; they were, in fact, an obstacle to a German–Soviet *rapprochement*.

Soviet-German diplomatic relations during the Weimar republic have been examined in some detail.[1] Suffice it to say here that even before the armistice of November 1918, there had been a Soviet ambassador, Adolf Joffe, in Berlin, and that after Joffe's expulsion Radek reached the German capital. Extensive contacts continued, almost without interruption, between German and Russian diplomats, businessmen and army officers. At the time of the Allied intervention in Russia and during the civil war, the official German attitude was one of neutrality – frequently of a pro-Russian neutrality. But the Russians expected more than that: when the news of the German revolution had reached Moscow, *Pravda* had announced that this was the next major stage of the world revolution. After the murder of Karl Liebknecht and Rosa Luxemburg and the defeat of Spartacus there was less cause for optimism. Bitter Soviet attacks on the German Social Democrats, now in power, were reciprocated from Berlin. The possibility of close Soviet-German collaboration, which had at one time seemed strong, was now remote. With the

Brest-Litovsk Treaty still fresh in mind, Moscow began to question whether Germany really differed in any way from the other imperialist powers.

It was the Versailles Treaty and the Polish question which brought about a reconciliation, despite ideological conflicts and political resentment. Even those Germans who stood for an *Erfuellungspolitik* were thinking of ways and means to improve Germany's status, politically and materially. Since the door to the Western world was bolted, a reorientation towards the East had its attractions. One year after Versailles, in April 1920, the Poles attacked in the Ukraine but were repulsed by the Red Army, which almost reached Warsaw. These Polish defeats were followed with considerable satisfaction in Germany; it was Poland, not Russia, which had profited from Germany's defeat, and which had designs on other German territories. Many a patriotic German professed his willingness to co-operate with the devil himself in order to confound the Poles: the Russians, on the other hand, were not looked upon as dangerous opponents. After the Polish campaign Lenin made an acute summary of the situation: the German bourgeoisie felt a real hatred towards Bolshevism and repressed it ruthlessly within Germany, yet they were impelled towards an alliance with Russia by the hard facts of the international situation. At the same time Russia's position was such that, to assist Germany – especially in the economic field – was to assist herself. Her security was assured so long as the imperialist powers remained disunited; hence her support for the German demand for a revision of the Versailles Treaty.

It took two years for this 'comradeship in misfortune' (as Churchill then called it) to ripen into a treaty. There was a German–Soviet trade agreement in May 1920 by which Berlin undertook to recognize the Soviets as the only government of Russia. During 1920 and 1921 German firms began to take an active interest in trade with Russia, applying for and obtaining a number of concessions for the exploitation of raw materials, in accordance with the foreign trade policy of the NEP. These concessions, however, were less important than the direct trade exchanges, which German businessmen found less complicated and more advantageous.

The great turning-point in Soviet-German relations came in 1922 with the Treaty of Rapallo. This hit the international scene like a bombshell, throwing some of the Allied governments into near panic, causing endless discussion in Berlin, and remaining to this day both a slogan and a symbol in German and Russian politics.* The facts, in the briefest detail, were these. At the Genoa conference in April 1922 the problems of reparations and international trade were to be tackled. Russia and Germany, although officially represented, found that they were expected to play a passive role. Russia refused to acknowledge her pre-war debts, and the Allies were unwilling to grant Moscow *de jure* recognition. In the early stages of the conference Chicherin and Rathenau and some of their closest advisers absented themselves for a day and signed a treaty at nearby Rapallo which provided for the resumption of diplomatic ties between the two countries. Russia undertook not to press any claims for war reparations, and Germany gave up her demands for compensation for the property of Germans in Russia that had been nationalized. Economic relations between the two countries were to be expanded.

The importance of Rapallo has been greatly exaggerated, both by its supporters and its critics. As one observer put it later, it was not an alliance nor an aggressive treaty, nor a non-aggression pact, nor even a declaration of neutrality. It was simply a political manifestation of the need for self-assertion on the part of two European powers which had been ostracized by the rest. As far as Germany was concerned, Rapallo simply demonstrated her ability to operate a foreign policy that was at least partly independent. If Russia used Weimar Germany to split the anti-Soviet front, those who shaped German foreign policy rightly assumed that their international bargaining position would improve if they became less dependent on the West. On the whole, there was a clear realization both in Moscow and Berlin of the limits of this anti-Versailles front; it was not in Russia or Germany, but in England and France that its significance was magnified. In the writings of historians it began to assume an importance it had never possessed. Rapallo became the symbol of a Russian-German alliance, just as Tauroggen had been more than a hundred years earlier, but it did not in itself constitute such an alliance. Had there been any such illusions at the time, they would have been dispersed by the Locarno Treaty three years after Rapallo, whereby England guaranteed Germany's western frontiers and, as Lord D'Abernon

* A great number of books on the subject of Rapallo were published after the Second World War, in both West and East Germany. There was also a truly staggering number of articles devoted to the subject on the occasion of the fortieth anniversary in April 1962; special historical conferences on 'Rapallo' were called in Moscow and East Berlin, etc. etc. See the bibliography at the end of this book.

put it, made it unlikely that Germany would in future need Russian help to fight off a French attack, thus giving Germany a feeling of security and detaching her from Russia. This, at any rate, was how the British saw it. The Russians, whose appraisal was not very different, said Germany was becoming a pawn in the anti-Soviet front headed by Great Britain. This was an alarmist view and a considerable exaggeration, because for Germany Locarno was mainly a means of safeguarding her position *vis-à-vis* France, and, indirectly, *vis-à-vis* France's allies in the East – Poland and Czechoslovakia. Just as Rapallo had not been the beginning of a grand alliance, so Locarno did not denote its end. Once Stresemann had successfully concluded his negotiations with the Western powers, he continued his talks with Soviet diplomats and these culminated in the Berlin Treaty of April 1926. This agreement was more specific than that of Rapallo, though it received far less publicity. Broadly speaking, it provided for German neutrality in the event of an attack on Russia, and vice versa.

What were the consequences of the Treaties of Rapallo and Berlin? Politically their impact was strictly limited. They made a great impression in the West; they awoke certain fears – but did little else. There was a clear threat that, if pressed too hard by the Western Allies, Germany might be driven into a political alliance with Moscow. During the twenties Germany could be of no political help to Russia, which remained cut off from the series of conferences, League of Nations meetings, and ministerial visits that enlivened the diplomatic scene; it is doubtful whether she suffered as a result. Once the Russian civil war had ended, Allied intervention in the Soviet Union had become extremely unlikely, despite the periodical alarms sounded in Moscow; so whether Germany remained neutral or not was of little importance in the circumstances. Nor, on the other hand, did Soviet support for Germany's stand against the Versailles Treaty, as was shown during the Ruhr crisis in 1923, have much effect either.

Of far greater importance were the military collaboration and the economic ties between the two countries. Contacts had been established before Rapallo between the commands of the two armies; under the agreement signed in July 1922 German officers set up training schools in Russia for the use of weapons (such as tanks and aircraft) which were banned in Germany by the provisions of the Versailles Treaty. In addition, the German armament industry established branches in the Soviet Union, German scientists were sent to Russia to do research into chemical warfare, and there was a constant exchange of staff officers.[2] The German army showed more enthusiasm in this co-operation than the navy, whose higher ranks preferred a British to a Soviet connection. General Seeckt, Chief of the Army Command in the early and middle twenties, was the leading protagonist of the pro-Russian orientation. This military collaboration, which lasted for ten years, was successfully kept secret. There were some indiscreet disclosures, mainly on the part of German pacifists and Social Democrats, but there was little that Paris and London could do. Soviet–German military co-operation continued after Seeckt's dismissal in 1926, and even Hitler's rise to power did not immediately put an end to it; it ceased only in September 1933. There is no doubt that both sides profited; German rearmament after 1933 would have taken considerably longer without the experience gained in Russia, especially by air force and tank officers, whilst the Russians, in their turn, gained technical experience from German armament engineers and staff instructors.[*] As Tukhachevsky said in 1933: 'The Reichswehr has been the teacher of the Red Army, and that will never be forgotten.'

Russia and Germany had been closely linked by trade ever since the development of modern means of transport made the large-scale exchange of goods possible. From 1865 until the First World War, Germany was Russia's best trading partner for both exports and imports. Germany exported coal, machinery, cotton goods, and many other commodities to Russia, and imported grain and timber. There is also no doubt that both Russians and Germans were deeply involved in the smuggling from Russia which, for several decades, was one of the most lucrative activities along the Polish border. Both countries had introduced a protective customs policy in the eighteen-seventies which caused trade between them to slacken off in the eighties, but from 1893 onwards more liberal policies prevailed, and between that year and the outbreak of the First World War, trade

---

[*] The great, and still growing, literature on German–Soviet military co-operation is discussed in F. L. Carsten, 'The Reichswehr and the Red Army, 1920–1933', *Survey*, October 1962, p. 114 *et seq.*, and Hans W. Gatzke, 'Russo-German military collaboration during the Weimar republic', *American Historical Review*, 1958. To this day there is no account of this aspect of Soviet–German collaboration in Soviet or East German historical literature, for reasons that are not difficult to divine. Yet the facts are not denied by Communist historians (see G. Rosenfeld, *op. cit.*, pp. 299–303), who have charged Western writers with sensationalist revelations intended to discredit Soviet foreign policy and to impute to it unworthy motives.

between the two quintupled. Russia competed with the United States in providing the highest imports into Germany, but she took only eight to ten per cent of German exports – considerably less than England and Austria. There were also substantial German investments in Russia, notably in the electrical industry and the production of railway equipment.

Economic relations between Germany and Russia were restored even before diplomatic relations after the war. A preliminary treaty was signed in May 1921, Krupp being one of the German firms most actively interested. Both countries benefited from a brisk exchange of goods, especially in the early thirties, yet in the end this trade did not live up to German expectations. In 1928 the Soviet Union took twenty-five per cent of her total imports from Germany; in 1932 this had risen to forty-seven per cent – as much as in 1914. These are imposing figures, but the total volume of Russian foreign trade at the time was small. The following table shows the percentage of Germany's exports that went to Russia:

1913	8·7
1928	3·3
1930	3·6
1931	8·0
1932	10·9

After 1933 German exports to Russia fell sharply, to recover again only in 1939–41, following the German-Soviet Treaty. The Germans took a great interest in increasing exports to Russia; among the first to exploit that market were Junkers, the German aircraft constructors, and many other leading German industrialists visited Russia in the late twenties and early thirties; there were trade fairs, exhibitions, and conferences, and some experts regarded Russia as a country of boundless prospects. But in reality there were distinct limitations. Germany was ready and keen to deliver goods, but unable to grant the long-term credit Russia needed. Russia was in urgent need of German imports, in particular of machinery, but handicapped by the slow growth of her ability to pay or to make satisfactory exchange arrangements. Despite a great deal of good will and energy, it took almost ten years for German exports to Russia to reach sizeable proportions. In the early thirties, sales to Russia were of some importance to certain branches of German heavy industry, particularly as the world economic crisis had hit German industry hard. Yet even in 1932, when the volume of German-Russian trade was at its highest, German exports to Russia were less than those to Holland.

The economic significance and political meaning of German-Russian trade relations during the Weimar republic were carefully studied, and there were even special periodicals devoted to the subject. But in fact, German exports to Russia during the Weimar period were smaller than in the years before the First World War – in terms of German trade – and in those days these exports were accepted as a natural phenomenon needing neither investigation nor particular encouragement.

There were no startling major developments in German-Soviet relations in the years following the signing of the Treaty of Berlin in 1926; a new pattern of economic and military collaboration had emerged, while political ties were growing markedly cooler. There was no sudden deterioration, though the last Chancellors of the Weimar Republic, such as Bruening or von Papen, were not exactly pro-Russian in their outlook. The simple but significant fact was that the reasons which had caused Germany and Russia to seek a *rapprochement* in the early twenties had largely ceased to operate. In 1921 Germany was politically ostracized, economically ruined, and militarily helpless; an alliance with Russia seemed the only way out, the only lever with which to bring about a revision of the Versailles Treaty. By 1931 the French had evacuated the Rhineland, reparations, already reduced, were about to be abolished altogether, there had been a German-French reconciliation under Stresemann and Briand, and Berlin could rely on London to thwart any scheme that might reinforce French power on the Continent. In these circumstances there was little that Germany could gain from Russia. The gradual emergence of a fairly strong 'Russian party' in Germany after 1929 did not exactly help improve relations between the two countries. The capitalist system was suffering from the shock of the economic crisis; there were millions of unemployed, and a large number of them began to look for their salvation to the country which seemed unaffected by the panic on Wall Street or the closing of the big banks. The bourgeois proponents of a German-Russian alliance such as Hoetzsch and von Seeckt had based their policy on the assumption that Germany was immune to Communist propaganda; this was now very much in doubt.

133

Although German policy did not become actively hostile to Russia, most German politicians simply lost interest in the subject; relations between the two countries stagnated during the last few years of the Weimar period, for the diminution of interest was reciprocal. In the early twenties a dissatisfied, have-not, and nearly ruined Germany seemed the only likely ally for a politically isolated Soviet Union. Ten years later the diplomatic position of the Soviet Union was comparatively normal; like Germany, Russia was no longer a pariah among nations. Stalin, who never kept all his eggs in one basket if he could help it, pressed for a non-aggression pact with France in 1931. There had been talks between the Soviet Union and Poland since 1927, although admittedly nothing much had come of them. It was a common distrust of France, and of France's East European ally Poland, that had drawn Germany and Russia together, and now that the reasons for their fears were by and large invalidated, a 'special relationship' between Moscow and Berlin became unnecessary. Russia ceased to appear, in German eyes, as a counter-force to the West, while Moscow now looked upon Germany simply as one of the countries with which the Russians wished only, as they were wont to say, to live in peace and to co-operate to their mutual advantage.

Within Weimar Germany the conflict of opinion concerning Russia frequently cut across party lines; there were pro- and anti-Russian factions in almost every camp. The Catholic Centre Party, by its very constitution and its ties with the Church, was of course implacably hostile to atheist Bolshevism; yet under Chancellor Wirth, a staunch Centre leader, relations with the Soviet Union were better than ever before or since. The Democratic and National Democratic parties (*Deutsche Volkspartei*) stood more or less for fulfilment of the Versailles Treaty and eventual reconciliation with the West. This did not prevent either Rathenau the Democrat or Stresemann of the *Volkspartei* from playing off the West against the East whenever possible. Even the Nazi Party had its pro-Russian wing, for all that Rosenberg could do to keep it pure. He had great difficulty with the 'National Bolsheviks', who combined a pro-Soviet orientation with an acceptance of some of the basic tenets of Leninism for German usage. Nor did the two largest parties – the *Deutschnationale* (the traditional right wing) and the Social Democrats – always run true to form. The conservatives of course were staunchly anti-socialist;

the best of all possible worlds for them had been Wilhelmian Germany, and any co-operation, let alone alliance with the revolutionaries from the East, might appear unthinkable. Yet there were a number of considerations dictating a more moderate attitude towards the Soviet Union. For instance, there were economic factors: German industry had to be rebuilt after the ravages of the war, and Russia was traditionally a major market for German products. There were military advantages; those who bewailed the loss of the German Army and stressed the need for rearmament realized that Russia, and only Russia, offered the ways and means of equipping the German Army with some of the weapons prohibited under the Versailles Treaty. Lastly, there were foreign political considerations. Germany's territorial structure was directly threatened by France (in the Ruhr) and by Poland (in Upper Silesia). From Russia there was no direct menace; on the contrary, Moscow was as suspicious of Polish intentions as was Berlin, and the Soviet Union had offered moral support, for what it was worth, at the time of the French occupation of the Ruhr.

In these circumstances influential sections of the right came out in favour of German-Soviet collaboration – some with far-reaching designs for its implementation, others in a more guarded way, aware of its inevitably temporary and limited nature. Those who favoured collaboration were often willing to give money to combat Bolshevik propaganda at home, but their anti-Communist zeal did not prevent leading German industrialists and bankers, such as Krupp, Stinnes, and Felix Deutsch (of the Electrical Trust) from doing business with the Soviets. The only German 'industrialist' usually mentioned in this context as an advocate of a war of intervention, Arnold Rechberg, belonged in fact to a family that had large interests in the Kali Syndicate – but Rechberg himself was never active in business and cannot be regarded as a 'representative of industry'.

Generals Ludendorff and Hoffmann were among the most prominent representatives of the anti-Russian line, but von Seeckt favoured close co-operation with the Red Army. And Seeckt was 'in' whilst Ludendorff and the other old officers had no say in German military policy under the Weimar Republic. Hugenberg, the leader of the Conservatives and owner of an influential press trust, took an intransigently anti-Russian line, whereas other conservative parliamentarians (such as Hoetzsch) did just the reverse. Senior officials in the Wilhelmstrasse (such as von Maltzan) and most German diplomats in Moscow were likewise partisans of a pro-Russian orientation; the very name of Brockdorff-Rantzau became a symbol for this policy. But although, during the early and middle twenties, the force of altered circumstances thus transformed some long-standing conservative attitudes, they had mostly reverted to type by the end of that decade. This was partly because Germany's political position had improved, but largely because the strengthening of the Soviet Union in the international field and of the German Communist Party on the domestic scene, made an alliance politically impossible.

Of all the major German parties, the Social Democrats were the most consistently hostile to the Soviet Union. They did not, of course, advocate a war of intervention, but neither did they see any point in Soviet–German collaboration. There were no captains of industry or generals among them who could be tempted by the economic or military fruits of such an alliance. They had distrusted the Russian extremists before 1917, and the sad fate of the Russian Social Democrats after 1917 and of the Menshevik Republic of Georgia did nothing to alter their view. They were under constant attack from the German Communists and the Comintern; 'traitors', 'capitalist lackeys', 'gangsters and hangmen' were some of the less offensive epithets used against them by the Communists. Gustav Hilger, who held a key position in the German embassy in Moscow for almost twenty years, wrote later that the Russian Communists' hatred of German Social Democrats was one of the most important forces shaping the relationship between Soviet Russia and Weimar Germany:

> 'This hatred was much deeper and more bitter than their feelings towards the bourgeoisie or the feudal reaction ... No wonder the Kremlin worked hard to prevent the establishment of a socialist government in Germany, an effort which was watched with satisfaction by some of the embassy personnel. In retrospect it seems really remarkable that Chicherin and Litvinov should have openly discussed with German diplomats the desirability of keeping the SPD out of office.'[8]

In Soviet eyes the Social Democrats, their chief rivals for the allegiance of the working class, were traitors to the proletariat and were responsible for the failure of the revolution of 1918–19. Only with the help of the Social Democrats was it possible to maintain bourgeois order. After 1928 the 'social-fascists' – as the Social Democrats were now called – were officially named by the Communists as their most dangerous enemy and the chief target of their attack.

The Social Democrats were slow to react; they were not a very dynamic party but they felt compelled to make a move when, for instance, their position in the trade unions was challenged. Their hostility towards the German Communists, whom they regarded as a destructive element in German politics, was transferred to the Soviet Union as the power behind them. Their foreign political orientation was pro-Western and they regarded good relations with England and France as the key to German foreign policy. They thought the Soviet political regime was as lacking in freedom as that of Tsarist Russia, if not more so, and that the transplantation of 'Bolshevist methods' into Europe would be the greatest evil that could befall the socialist movement. They followed the close and secret collaboration between the Red Army and the Reichswehr with distrust, convinced that no benefit to the German working class could come from it. The only leakage of information on this subject ever made in the Reichstag came, not surprisingly, from a Social Democratic deputy.

Needless to say, the German Communist Party tried by every means to promote friendly relations between the Soviet Union and Germany. It sponsored lectures, organized trips to Moscow by delegations, called mass meetings to protest against the threat of intervention, published periodicals and books, straining every nerve to win friends for the new Russia. Yet it antagonized more people than it attracted through these activities. All the German bourgeois publicists and politicians who wanted a *rapprochement* between Germany and the Soviet Union regarded (German) Communism as the principal obstacle in their way. Of course, they were told that the Comintern was an independent organization and that the Soviet state could not be held responsible for its activities, let alone the actions of its German section. But these arguments carried little weight. The German Communists stood not only for friendship with Russia, but also for a revolution in their own country; whereas the German friends of the Soviet Union who were not Communists wanted co-operation on the basis of non-intervention in each other's domestic affairs. Some of them went even farther and argued that fruitful collaboration was possible only if the German Communist Party was suppressed. In the mid-twenties, when the KPD had no influence, whatever it did or proclaimed could be ignored; but when

its numbers had grown and its influence spread, and the world economic blizzard was sweeping over Germany, its existence was an in-
superable impediment to any closer German–Soviet relations. Outside the working class the KPD made little impact, and even there its
effect was often negative.

Public opinion about Russia in Weimar Germany was sharply
divided, as was to be expected. It was not by any means influenced
only by the political parties; many other factors were at work, some
of which at least deserve a little attention. Not surprisingly, the
Christian churches were hostile to the Soviet Union; the persecution
of religious dignitaries and believers in Russia had antagonized them
from the beginning. Some of the large publishing houses and news
agencies of the right followed an extreme anti-Soviet line; a few
specialized in the diffusion of news items under the dateline 'Kovno'
– these were prefabricated by a group of forgers in Berlin. On the
other hand, the coverage by the big 'bourgeois' press was, on the
whole, objective; there was even a tendency to be ostentatiously un-
prejudiced in reporting and appraising what was often called an
interesting social experiment. Prominent Soviet figures such as Radek
were frequently invited to contribute to leading German newspapers,
but some of the German correspondents in Moscow, who had gone
there with much goodwill, returned with their enthusiasm damped
and published critical books. Among these were Paul Scheffer of the
Berliner Tageblatt and Theodor Siebert of the *Hamburger Fremden-
blatt*: while they had been in the Soviet capital their reports were not,
generally speaking, unfair.

The fate of the German minorities in Russia, more than a million
settlers in the Volga region and tens of thousands in the Black Sea
area, the Caucasus and Siberia, made little impact on public opinion
in the Reich. These regions had suffered in the revolution and the civil
war, and since their people were on the whole more prosperous than
their Russian neighbours, they were classified as *Kulaks* in the collectivization campaign of 1929–30. Many of them were deported,
others succeeded in emigrating; and the ties between those who
remained and their native country grew more tenuous until, in the
Hitler period, they were severed altogether. Some Volga Germans
who had returned to the Reich tried to enlist help for their compatriots who had remained, but without success; the Berlin government
could not very well interfere in what was a domestic Soviet problem.
Yet the documentary reports, the fictionalized accounts, and the eye-

witness stories about the fate of the Russian Germans did not pass unnoticed but created much resentment in Germany.*

However, the general climate of thought in Weimar Germany was by no means hostile towards the Soviet Union – at least not so far as the liberal press, the leading publishing houses, and the cultural centres were concerned. The right-wing *voelkisch* trend, which was fairly strong outside the big cities, bitterly opposed anything that smacked, however slightly, of *Kulturbolschewismus*. But among the liberal intelligentsia, which set the dominant fashion, there was tremendous interest in the new Russia. Everyone admired Eisenstein's *Battleship Potemkin* and Pudovkin's *Mother*; Goebbels, who had some understanding of these things, said that *Potemkin* was one of the greatest films of all time and that German movie-makers should learn from it. This they did; at any rate some German films of the late twenties and early thirties were clearly influenced by the Soviet cinema, quite apart from such productions as Pabst's *Love of Jeanne Ney* (based on Ehrenburg's book) and the many other films on 'Russian subjects'.

From the early twenties on, there was an unending stream of translations of Soviet authors, published not only by Communist or fellow-travelling publishing houses, but also by eminently respectable 'bourgeois' firms. The books of Isaac Babel (almost unknown in the West at the time), of Leonid Leonov and Konstantin Fedin, of Vsevolod Ivanov, Pilniak, and Sholokhov, were published in Germany within a year of their appearance in the Soviet Union. There was not a single successful Soviet novel in the twenties that did not come out in Germany within a very short time. Descriptions of the life of the young generation in Russia attracted particular attention. Books like *Shkid* or *The Diary of a Communist Schoolboy* were widely read, discussed, and admired. The left-wing intelligentsia in Weimar Germany were keenly interested in all avant-garde writing and art. In the late twenties, when the experimental period ended in Russia, this fascination lessened. By then, however, the new theme of social and economic reconstruction began to attract many people because of the appalling economic crisis. Similar interest was shown in the daring new plays from Moscow and in the way they were staged,

---

* The most widely read examples of this literature, Georg Loedsack's *Einsam kaempft das Wolgaland*, and Hans Harder's *Das Dorf an der Wolga*, were published after 1933. But there was already a whole literature on the subject before Hitler came to power.

as well as in the innovations in Soviet painting and music. A leading young poet, Johannes R. Becher, translated Maiakovsky into German. In some circles a trip to Moscow – a more adventurous operation then than it was to become later – became fashionable, and the number of travelogues and essays on the Russian cultural and political scene grew by leaps and bounds. There was an aura of dynamism and purpose about everything that emanated from Russia. True, the Communists had set up a dictatorship, their political attitude was far from liberal, and they committed many grievous mistakes from time to time, but at least they got things done. The sense of optimism and purpose was so refreshingly different from the unending debates of weak German parliaments and the irresolution of timid German governments. This attitude was very widespread, and not only among the German left. A writer like E. E. Dwinger, with his trilogy on the fate of a group of German soldiers during the civil war in Russia, was the idol of the right; he had fought in the White Armies (and ended up an honorary SS leader). Yet Dwinger was absolutely fascinated by Bolshevik Russia; he thought that the coming German revolution would be a synthesis between 'White and Red', and believed that the German Communists were better patriots than the bourgeois liberals and reactionaries. [4]

The German youth movements were similarly intrigued by events in Russia; on their excursions and around their camp fires they sang of Stalin and of the leaders of the White Armies with equal fervour. They showed a touching political naïveté, with their belief that Stalin and Admiral Kolchak were equally impressive manifestations of the mysterious Russian soul. They were dimly aware that some important changes had taken place in that great country to the east, but unable to understand the historical significance of the revolution. In this, admittedly, they were not alone. There were a number of German essayists who thought that a knowledge of Dostoevsky and perhaps a fleeting glance at Maxim Gorki were sufficient keys to the understanding of current developments in Russia. Some of these men were right-wingers (Moeller van den Bruck) and some were pacifists (Alons Paquet); others had developed elaborate pseudo-philosophical schools of their own (Count Keyserling). What they had in common was the conviction, formulated by a great Russian poet of the last century, that Russia could not be understood in terms of rationality: one had to believe in her. They trusted their intuition more than they studied Marxism.

During the First World War, Thomas Mann had expressed his great admiration for things Russian in a series of essays; in the twenties he returned to this theme in the famous encounter between the beautiful Russian Madame Chauchat and her shy lover, Hans Castorp, two residents on his Magic Mountain. 'Do you think we Germans are pedantic?' Castorp asks, and he gets the predictable answer, '*Mais c'est vrai. Ihr seid ein wenig bourgeois. Vous aimez l'ordre mieux que la liberté, toute l'Europe le sait.*' And again: '*Bourgeois, humaniste et poète – voilà l'Allemand complète, comme il faut.*' Many other writers were attracted by the Russian theme; Arnold Zweig provided a masterly picture of life on the Eastern Front during the First World War; Josef Ponten went even further back into history with his unfinished trilogy on the Volga Germans.

Among the members of the younger generation there were small but vociferous pro-Russian groups of 'nationalist revolutionaries', better known by the designation 'National-Bolsheviks'; their views and activities will be discussed in a different context. Some of their elders took up a similar position when it came to German foreign policy. Thus in 1933 General von Seeckt, the former Chief of Staff of the Reichswehr and still a figure of some importance, wrote, when Hitler had already come to power, that 'tremendous work had been done in the Soviet economy'. He continued to favour a German–Russian alliance, for if Germany discarded Russia from her political plans there was a real danger that the fatherland would again find itself fighting a war on two fronts, with the Poles advancing towards and reaching the Oder. 'So we appeal to German policy: Safeguard the rear.'[5] Seven years later Hitler thought he could safely disregard that warning.

The geo-politicians, headed by Professor Haushofer in Munich, are usually thought to have been the pace-makers of National Socialism, and in some respects the charge is justified, though their influence on Hitler has been greatly overrated. But in the Weimar Republic the geo-politicians' attitude was far from being anti-Russian. Mackinder, their great teacher, had taught them in 1919 that co-operation between Germany and Russia was a vital necessity. Some of the leaders of the school were inclined to pay little attention to developments in Russia up to the end of the twenties simply because they doubted whether Russia was still a great power. Others were quite willing to recognize the 'extraordinary intellectual gifts and capacities of the Soviet

141

leaders'.[6] After Hitler had come to power Oskar von Niedermayer, who had played an important rôle in the co-operation between the Reichswehr and the Red Army, wrote in a special supplement to the geo-politicians' journal that Soviet achievements in the field of national defence deserved the highest recognition; he thought that Germany should only welcome the peaceful reconstruction of the giant empire to the east: 'As Russia needs our political and technical help, so we need Russia's help and friendship in our struggle against Versailles.'[7] The geo-politicians proved themselves surprisingly adaptable in the Third Reich; they found suitable quotations to justify whatever foreign political decision was taken by Hitler. They participated in the anti-Soviet campaign of 1936–7 as a matter of course, they thought the reconciliation of 1939–40 an act of great wisdom and statesmanship, and, after June 21, 1941, they welcomed Hitler's decision to eliminate the Soviet menace and establish a new order in Eastern Europe. They trailed behind German foreign policy in the Third Reich, faithfully reflecting it, but never initiating it.

Nor would it be fair to accuse Weimar Germany's Russian experts of extreme hostility towards the Soviet Union, as some East German and East European publicists did after the Second World War, saying that during the Weimar period the German *Ostforscher* had systematically prepared the way for Hitlerite aggression both by propagating their views and by their subversive activities in Eastern Europe.[8] Yet the Nazis themselves had no such opinion of their alleged forerunners: one Nazi author writing in 1936 described the chief institution in this field, the 'German Society for the study of Eastern Europe', as a 'retreat for all Jewish-masonic-liberalist fellow-travellers and parlour Bolsheviks',[9] and said of its president, Professor Hoetzsch, that he had done all he could to play down the Bolshevik danger and to assist Communist infiltration, that he had helped the Comintern to conceal the misery of the German peasants in Russia and the horrors of forced collectivization.[10] These were not exactly friendly words for a society alleged to have paved the way for Hitler and his movement. The real state of affairs, which will be discussed in greater detail below, was rather more complicated. The study of Eastern Europe, and of Russia in particular, was more developed in Germany than in any other country at the time. There were four chairs for the study of Russia (Berlin, Koenigsberg, Breslau, and Leipzig), a very active association of research workers, and a number of periodicals dealing with the subject – and this at a time when Russian studies were almost non-existent in other parts of the world. Among Weimar Germany's leading Russian experts there were men of various political opinions, but there were no Russophobes in the Schiemann tradition. It was more usual to be anti-Polish than anti-Russian. The German Society for the Study of Eastern Europe arranged cultural exchanges (including meetings between German and Soviet historians), helped to promote trade between the two countries, and, generally speaking, endeavoured to maintain high standards of objectivity in its publications. In fact, they frequently leaned over backwards in their effort to find reasonable meaning in current developments in the Soviet Union. For years there was hardly a number of the periodical *Osteuropa* which did not have a major contribution by a Soviet author. And there were no fellow-travellers among these Russian experts; they simply believed that Germany had to accept the victory of Bolshevism in Russia with all its implications. If some maintained an attitude of reserve, others were fascinated by the subject of their study and sympathized with it as experts so often do. With the coming of the Third Reich German *Ostforschung* entered upon a new and less edifying era. Yet before the Third Reich Germany's Russian experts stood for collaboration between their country and the Soviet Union, in most cases because of their interest in a Russia whose addiction to Bolshevism was seen as a temporary aberration from the norm. Like some of his eminent contemporaries in the West, such as Bernard Pares and Samuel Harper, Hoetzsch knew a lot about Russian history but little about Marxism. In consequence, he exaggerated the factors of Russian tradition and underrated those of Communist ideology in Soviet policies. Even so, German Russian studies showed a far better knowledge of current developments in the Soviet Union than did those of any other country.

As the decade of the twenties drew to its close the world political constellation that had brought Russia and Germany together gradually changed, and their interests also began to diverge. Germany contracted new ties and obligations, and Russia, profoundly absorbed with internal affairs, could pursue no active foreign policy, and no longer expected much from any close commitment to Germany. Thus political relations cooled off during the late twenties, although military co-operation continued until 1933, and economic ties between the two reached their peak in the early thirties. This incongruity

between political and economic relations is an interesting phenomenon; a similar discrepancy had occurred in Wilhelmian Germany.*
Russia showed more interest in Republican Germany than in any
other country. In Germany, as in other Western countries, there was a
strong anti-Bolshevik current even before the rise of National
Socialism, but, unlike most other European countries, Germany had
also a large reservoir of goodwill. Nowhere else did Russia get a
fuller or more sympathetic hearing than in the German press, in the
output of its publishing houses, in the theatres, the cinemas, and the
concert halls.

* See Chapter 4. Only between 1939 and 1941 did a political *rapprochement*
coincide with large scale economic exchanges.

Chapter 8

HITLER AND RUSSIA 1923–33

IN NOVEMBER 1923 Hitler entered Landsberg prison; he remained there until his release in December 1924. To all practical intents and purposes his party had ceased to exist and it was perhaps as well for the Fuehrer that he had to withdraw from all political activity, for the general climate was not propitious. Inflation had come to an end, and after experiencing some severe shocks in her domestic and foreign affairs, Germany entered a period of relative calm and stability. For the time being, at any rate, this reduced the appeal that the extremist movements of both right and left had for the public. Stability was not to last and in retrospect the mid-twenties appear to have provided the Nazis with the necessary interlude in which to prepare themselves for the great onslaught on the Weimar Republic which took place towards the end of the decade. Hitler's stay in prison, almost as merry and certainly as comfortable as that described in Johann Strauss' famous operetta, provided him with a welcome opportunity to put some of his ideas in writing, thus giving National Socialism a doctrine of sorts. On foreign policy in particular National Socialism had been rather weak, frequently contradictory; Hitler must have felt an urgent need to give his movement some guidance in this field when, in 1926, he wrote the sections on a future German policy in the last part of *Mein Kampf*, and when, in 1928, he dictated his second book entirely devoted to foreign political questions, destined not to appear in print in his lifetime.* In these writings Hitler's views about Russia and Bolshevism were systematically developed for the first and last time; essentially, they did not undergo any major change throughout the rest of his life.

There is an infinite chasm between the German and the Russian 'racial soul', according to Hitler. 'Actually the Slavic Russian has

* It was published for the first time in 1961.

145

always felt this and has therefore always had an instinctive antipathy toward the German.'[1] The Russians greatly preferred the facile, superficial and more or less effeminate French way of life to the solid thoroughness, the cold logic and the severities of the German national character. Even educated Germans were altogether ignorant of the psyche of the Slavs. Hitler, on the other hand, was one of the few who understood this, because Rosenberg and Scheubner-Richter had told him. Slavdom lacked the ability to build a state. Since the days of Peter the Great the Germans (Baltic Germans, in particular) had constituted the skeleton and the brains of the Russian state; Russia was indebted to that little Germanic upper stratum not only for becoming a modern state but also 'for what little exists of her cultural value.'[2] The officer corps, too, was mostly non-Slav by descent.

Yet gradually the German upper stratum was suppressed, a racially pure Russian bourgeoisie emerged, and the new Russian intelligentsia was anti-German; it was a revolt against the autocratic, alien, former ruling class, but even more a protest of the Slavic national character against the German. Hence the impudent Panslavic agitation in the nineteenth century which helped to bring about the world war. As an afterthought Hitler adds that Germany should have given up its colonial dreams and allied itself with Britain against Russia.[3] The world war brought a further weakening of the Nordic elements in Russia; the last remains were extirpated by the Bolshevik revolution. Meanwhile, a new ruling class emerged in the Soviet Union – the Jews. With the help of the anti-German Russians the Jews had overthrown the Nordic element and, since the Russians lacked all organizational ability, they were now the undisputed masters of Russia. Many German bourgeois simpletons did not, of course, understand these deeper currents, or the fact that the Russian Revolution was a deep, instinctive process – the urge towards world domination by the Jewish people.[4]

If Germany wanted more *Lebensraum* in Europe it could be found only in Russia; the new Reich would have to follow in the steps of the Teutonic knights to obtain soil for the German peasant, to assure the daily bread for the nation. This meant drawing a line under the whole foreign political orientation of the pre-war era – the drive of the Germans towards the south and the west. 'Instead our eyes will be cast towards the East. For did not fate itself seem to give a sign; by delivering Russia to Bolshevism, it had deprived the Russian people of the intelligentsia which had so far guaranteed the existence of

146

Russia as a state. Up to then Russia had been a striking example of the state-creating activity of the German element among an inferior race.'[5] For centuries Russia had lived on that German nucleus, which was by now almost totally destroyed. The Russians on their own were incapable of throwing off the Jewish yoke, yet the Jews could not hold this big empire together in the long run. Russia was therefore ripe for disaster; the end of Jewish domination would be also the end of Russia as a state.[6] Fate had called the Germans to be witnesses of this gigantic catastrophe, but they were to be more than passive onlookers.

These sections of *Mein Kampf* were written in 1926; in his unpublished second book of 1928, Hitler was more cautious in his predictions. He still believed that the Jew would act as a ferment of decomposition in Russia but he also took into account the possibility that one day the Jewish character of the Bolshevist regime in Russia would disappear, making room for some form of National Communism. Hitler seemed quite certain in 1928 that the struggle between what he called the Panslav idea and the Bolshevist idea would end with the destruction of Jewry. But since the Panslavists were all anarchists, this new regime would be quite weak, a power vacuum, a source of perpetual unrest and insecurity.[7]

Some German right-wing politicians, including several prominent members of Hitler's own party, had been strongly in favour of a German–Russian alliance, in continuance of Bismarck's policy. They thought that such collaboration was desirable even with Russia as she was then, let alone with the future Russia in which (they predicted) the Russian nationalist element would prevail over the Jewish-internationalists. These views were anathema to Hitler and Rosenberg, who read the articles and speeches of the brothers Strasser, Goebbels, and Reventlow with growing indignation. Hitler devoted considerable time and space to a refutation of these advocates of an Eastern orientation in *Mein Kampf*. It seemed incomprehensible to him that a nationalist German could support an alliance that would carry the Bolshevik poison to Germany, suppress the national element in Germany, and establish the rule of Jewry there. He was willing to assume, for argument's sake, that the Soviet Union might undergo internal change and that the Jewish element would be crowded out by the Russian. 'In this case, to which many signs seem to point, it would be conceivable, to be sure, that West European capitalism would seriously take a stand against Russia. But then an alliance of

Germany with this (new) Russia would also be complete insanity.'[8] Hitler adduces both tactical arguments and principles to justify his position. An alliance between Russia and Germany could not be kept secret and it would be quite impossible to make military preparations that would not come to the knowledge of the other powers. This being so, there would be no time for Germany to re-arm herself sufficiently to prevent a collapse within the first twenty-four hours. France would not wait until Germany had built up its tank and air defences; Germany would almost automatically become a battlefield. Russia could not come to Germany's assistance, even if she wanted to do so; Russia would gain some time while the catastrophe broke over Germany. Russia had no common frontier with Germany; she would first have to overrun Polish territory – an unlikely move – and in any case, Russian help would arrive only when the German state no longer existed. The landing of Russian divisions was completely excluded so long as England and France had complete control of the Baltic. In brief, the outcome of an alliance between Germany and Russia would be the destruction of the former for the possible survival of the latter. Even if, by some miracle, this disaster did not take place, Germany would be involved in an alliance that ran contrary to her own vital interests for she could not gain more *Lebensraum* in south or west Europe.[9]

There was an even more basic factor which in Hitler's eyes precluded any alliance: a National-Communist Russia would be very anti-German. In *Mein Kampf*, designed for the widest circulation, Hitler had called Russia's rulers bloodstained, common criminals of bestial cruelty, liars, and cheats, pastmasters in robbery and plunder, parasites, scum of the earth, bloody oppressors, and the most cruel tyrants of all time – to quote only a few of the ornate epithets.[10] In his second book, on the other hand, which was meant for a smaller circle of readers, there is much less name calling. Hitler simply states: 'For the future an alliance of Germany with Russia has no sense for Germany, neither from the standpoint of sober expediency nor from that of human community. On the contrary, it is good fortune for the future that this development has taken place in just this way because thereby a spell has been broken which would have prevented us from seeking the goal of German foreign policy where it solely and exclusively lies: territory in the East.'[11]

There is a striking resemblance between Hitler's views on Russia and its future and the writings of the pre-war German Russophobes.

Hitler's opinions are to a large extent a rehash of ideas that had been expressed in the widely read articles of Paul Rohrbach a decade or two earlier: that Russia did not belong to the European family of nations, that she had no part in the heritage of the occident, that the Asian (Tatar and Mongol) element in her blood had prevailed over the higher strains, and that Russia had made no contribution to human civilization.[12] Long before Hitler, Rohrbach and several like-minded publicists had argued that Russia was the worst menace facing Germany and only a division of Russia would avert this danger and offer Germany a tremendous chance. For in the east, and only there, was there room for German colonization.[13] Rohrbach also wrote eloquently about Russian barbarism, but there was one important difference between him and the later-day Russophobes. Until 1917 the main opposition to Russia did not come from right-wing extremists. Rohrbach, for instance, was a liberal of sorts; the Pan-Germans very much disliked his liberal imperialism which contrasted with their own territorial aspirations. Theories that in retrospect appear to be racialist in character about Russian inferiority, were not at all uncommon among liberals and even left-wingers before 1917; the opposition to Tsarist autocracy not infrequently turned into a condemnation of all things Russian. Rosenberg and Hitler thus purloined both the terminology and the policies of German liberal imperialism.

To establish this ideological genealogy is of importance; Hitler's and Rosenberg's ideas on Eastern Europe were not some startling, new, unheard-of, development, altogether without precedent; their antecedents can easily be traced for at least two generations back. Yet it would be misleading to regard Hitler's and Rosenberg's doctrine as the culmination of German political doctrine on Eastern Europe, the logical and inescapable sequel in a long chain of thought. For the Lagardes and Constantin Frantzs, the Schiemanns and Rohrbachs have to be seen in the context of their own times, not those of a later age. Many Germans did indeed believe that their people were superior to the Slavs. There were very few nineteenth-century thinkers who believed that all peoples were equal; Marx and Engels, at any rate, were not among them, as we know from their comments on Panslavism and Russian history. Education was far more widely advanced in Western and Central than in Eastern Europe, and these feelings of superiority can easily be understood; who would have imagined at the time that the fruits of civilization would not prevent a German relapse into barbarity? If some Germans felt a mission in Eastern Europe, was this not similar to the colonial mission of British and French empire-builders? However, the Germans were dealing with a great European nation, temporarily retarded in its development; their missionary and colonizing schemes were bound to fail even before Western colonial power came to an end in Asia and Africa.

Rohrbach was one of the greatest travellers of his time, whereas Hitler had no such first-hand knowledge of the countries he wrote about. The enormous output of twaddle by people who were anything but men of the world, had always been a prominent feature of political discussion in Germany. The breadth and scope of their sweeping historical generalizations were usually in inverse ratio to their factual knowledge. People with little knowledge and experience outside their native country (sometimes their native city) thought it perfectly natural to develop the most elaborate theories about the past, the present, and the historical destiny of countries they had never visited, of peoples of which they had, at best, a second-hand knowledge. Hitler, who had never been east of the Oder or south of Vienna at the time he wrote *Mein Kampf*, who, for all we know, had never met a Russian in the flesh, was in this tradition of the German philistine *Kannegiesser* of the nineteenth century.

While Hitler was in prison the leaderless National Socialist movement split into several factions. Some Bavarian Nazis decided to follow a more radical left-wing line, mainly in order to attract Communists; there was some vague idea of a division of labour between the extremes. 'You hang the Jews, we'll hang the other capitalists,' some Communists are alleged to have replied.[14] But since this demagoguery alienated the lower middle class, which was, after all, the backbone of Nazism, the political line eventually was changed, and Communism again became a dangerous enemy. In the west of Germany, there was but little hope of attracting workers with the anti-leftist slogans that had been successful in Munich before 1923. The brothers Gregor and Otto Strasser, as well as young Dr Goebbels, who built up the Nazi Party in west Germany, decided on a much more radical approach, and one which led to open conflict within the Nazi movement and eventually to a showdown.

Dr Goebbels, a young agitator from the Rhineland, who was not yet widely known outside west Germany, argued that socialism was the *Weltanschauung* of the future and that class struggle was a fact which it was no use denying. Goebbels sharply rejected the accusations of the more conservative Nazis who had charged the 'young Turks' with Bolshevism, yet he saw nothing reprehensible in ideological and political contacts between left- and right-wing extremists. He developed his ideas in a number of newspaper articles subsequently published in a booklet significantly called *The Second Revolution*; they were in the form of letters directed to contemporaries – some real, others imaginary. In one such open letter, addressed to a Russian *emigré*, Iwan Wienurowski (who had already figured in a previous Goebbels novel), the young Nazi leader said:

'. . . we look towards Russia because it is the country most likely to take with us the road towards socialism. Because Russia is an ally which nature has given us against the devilish temptation and corruption of the West. We watch in bitter pain while so-called German statesmen destroy all bridges that lead towards Russia. Our pain is so strongly felt not because we love Bolshevism, but because alliance with a really nationalist and socialist Russia will strengthen our own national and socialist position and dignity.'[15]

Goebbels thought that the Russian peasant would defend his own land to the last breath (this was written long before collectivization). He said that he had not the slightest intention of joining the 'chorus of bourgeois liars and ignoramuses' who defamed Soviet Russia. Russia and Bolshevism were not facing a disaster; no Tsar had ever understood the Russian people as deeply as Lenin, who had given the peasant what he wanted most – freedom and property. Lenin had made the peasantry the real pillar of the new system; he had sacrificed Marx and given Russia its freedom. What was Bolshevist internationalism but Panslavism in its purest form?[16] Dr Goebbels was no less outspoken about the attitude of the extreme German right to the Russian *emigrés*; they pitied these co-sufferers whose situation was even worse than their own. They positively revelled in the atrocity stories spread by the Russian *emigrés*; they saw in them Russia's future – in a striking misjudgment of world historic trends, they collaborated with the *emigrés* in spreading the most primitive anti-Semitism.[17]

The anti-Bolshevism of the German right was suspect in Goebbels' eyes: the bourgeois were merely afraid of losing their property. National Socialism they regarded as their last hope and comfort against the menace of Bolshevism; for them Nazism was a sort of

Pinkertons, a private detective agency to guard their property by night.[18] Goebbels had only contempt for the 'primitive anti-Semitism' of the right. Anti-Semitism for him was the *beginning* of all political understanding, something self-evident. Yet the anti-Communist right-wingers preferred not to move on from that very first and elementary plank; instead, they raved in the most primitive manner against Jews and Jew-lovers, and thus glossed over the things for which not the Jews but the Germans – and above all the German right wing – were responsible. The Jewish question was much more complicated than the Rosenbergs and their friends pretended. The capitalist and the Bolshevik Jew had not really identical interests.[19]

These heretical views provoked much irritation in Munich. The polemic that ensued lasted throughout the autumn and early winter of 1925–6. Rosenberg reprinted one of Goebbels' 'letters' in the party's central newspaper, only to attack it sharply; it was an illusion to believe that Bolshevism could somehow develop towards National Communism in Russia. To idealize Lenin was politically extremely harmful, mere wishful thinking would not do in politics.

A few weeks after the Goebbels-Rosenberg controversy, the Locarno Pact was made public; it meant a reconciliation between Germany and France, and the recognition of existing frontiers in Western Europe; the entrance of Germany into the League of Nations was envisaged. Only the Russian question was left open, and the Russians, not unnaturally, regarded the pact as partly directed against them. Gregor Strasser, one of the most prominent Nazi leaders and head of the extremist wing, denounced the pact, as did many other German rightists, in an editorial in the *Voelkischer Beobachter*, with an additional radical slant: he emphatically rejected the plans of certain extremist groups to participate in a war of intervention against the Soviet Union. Without Germany all these plans were doomed to failure, but Germany's main aim was the struggle against the Versailles Peace Treaty; there was no room for a common front with France and England in these circumstances. Germany's place was at the side of the future Russia, the Indians and the Chinese as well as the other colonial peoples such as the Arabs and the Druzes. Soviet relations with Fascist Italy had shown that there could be co-operation in the foreign political field if each abstained from interfering in the domestic affairs of the other. There could be no doubt that Germany had many more interests in common with Russia than with the West.[20] In subsequent articles both Strasser and Goebbels reiterated their arguments in favour of an Eastern orientation. An alliance with Russia was desirable from every point of view; the destruction of Russia would mean that 'the dreams of a National Socialist Germany would have to be buried forever'.[21] Germany was tied to Russia by a common fate, since a socialist Germany should be the ally of Russia. Strasser added some biting remarks about the lack of political instinct of certain right wing organizations. Did they really think that England and France were interested in strengthening Germany? If not, why were they so enthusiastic about launching a crusade against Russia? An anti-Bolshevism, devoid of political sense, had been preached to the German youth for years and had permeated their hearts and minds; this could have disastrous consequences for Germany. If Communism constituted an obstacle to profit-making Western capitalism, what business was this of German patriots? Why did they unthinkingly swallow Western capitalist propaganda?[22]

All this was, of course, anathema to Hitler, who nevertheless did not personally intervene in the dispute at the time; only in the last sections of *Mein Kampf* did he answer the deviationists. The Russian problem was not the only bone of contention between him and the west German party leaders who, in addition to those already mentioned, included a great many who were subsequently to rise to important positions such as Robert Ley, Rust, Kerrl, Karl Kaufmann, etc. The Nazi movement was too small at the time to be able to afford a split and Hitler decided therefore to win over the opposition by clever tactical manoeuvring, thus splitting it. This he did at a leaders meeting in Bamberg in February 1926; Goebbels was the first to accept Hitler's leadership and to subordinate his own Eastern orientation to the pro-British and pro-Italian line propagated by the Fuehrer. The west German opposition collapsed.

Heretical views on Russia continued to be aired on the fringe of the Nazi Party for several years after 1926, especially among those who gravitated towards 'National Bolshevism'. Even Goebbels had an occasional relapse as in his rebuke to the conservatives in 1932–3, or at the Nuremberg party congress in 1936 when, in the middle of an otherwise staunch anti-Bolshevik speech, he commented on the background of the purges: it was widely believed, but mistaken to assume, that the Jews always agreed among themselves; Jews had killed Jews (in Russia) out of lust for power and the will to destruction.[23] However, the Nazi Party line on things Russian was fixed after 1926;

there could be differences of opinion as to the interpretation of current events – but not on essentials.

Hitler, Rosenberg, and their friends followed events in Eastern Europe after 1923 with somewhat diminished interest; after all, there was no prospect for an immediate overthrow of Bolshevism as many had hoped during and immediately after the civil war. Russia had re-emerged as an active factor in European and world politics that could not be ignored. Three problems above all preoccupied those Nazis who gave more than a passing thought to foreign political affairs. What was the meaning of Stalin's emergence as the new dictator? Could it be interpreted as the victory of the National Bolshevist faction over the Jewish internationalist elements? Subsequently the five year plan caused some discussion among National Socialists; perhaps there was something to be said for economic planning after all? And lastly there was the question whether Nazism should not support the centrifugal forces inside the Soviet Union (such as the Ukrainian nationalists) rather than the right wing Russian *emigrés.*

Nazi propaganda about Russia remained as mendacious as before. It was said that the body of the bishop of Voronezh had been cooked to make soup which the monks of a local monastery had been compelled by the Cheka to eat. It was said that a monument had been erected in Sviyazhsk to Judas Iscariot, that fifty to seventy per cent of the Communist leadership were syphilitics, and that Trotsky had been an informer for the Tsarist police; later he was said to have been the owner of a firm of furniture movers in Petrograd. Stalin, on the other hand, was described – by a Russian *emigré* at that – as a former stevedore in the harbour of Tiflis.[24] The level of political comment was of equal sophistication. Nemirovich-Danchenko announced in 1924 that the supreme power had been till then in the hands of the Slav Lenin, but now it had passed into the hands of the Jews, above all Trotsky.[25] Yet precisely because they stressed the racialist factor so much, the Nazis were bound to welcome, albeit reluctantly, Stalin's emergence as a dictator. Otto Strasser wrote that it was Stalin's historical task to liquidate Communism and bring the revolution to an end. Henceforth there would be no room in Russia for rootless, cynical Jews like Trotsky; Stalin was really a Russian nationalist who talked about internationalism only to keep up appearances.[26] Otto Strasser belonged to the extreme left wing of Nazism and his reaction was not surprising. More startling was the fact that even

154

Weltkampf, Rosenberg's house organ, discussed what it called Stalin's anti-Semitism; Schwarz-Bostunich wrote that it was impossible to describe Russia simply as a Jewish state – after all, Trotsky had been deposed while Kalinin, Rykov, and Stalin were on the way up. In 1930 Count Reventlow went one step farther: the rule of Jews in Russia had been broken, there were no more Jews in leading positions, hence the attacks by world Jewry on Soviet Russia.[27] This was all very well, but then the Nazis suddenly realized that if they persevered in these racial comments, they would soon have to change their whole approach to Communism and the Soviet Union. This, for a great variety of reasons, they simply could not do, and hence the decision to pursue their anti-Communist campaign regardless of what Stalin had done to his Jewish rivals.

Rosenberg gradually dissociated himself from Russian *emigré* politics after 1923. During Hitler's absence in Landsberg prison he was the nominal head of the party, though in fact he did not have the necessary authority to establish himself as leader. His intellectual interests, too, now took a different direction; these were the years during which he worked on his magnum opus, the *Mythus.* From time to time he continued to comment on Russian and Communist affairs,[28] but much less frequently. A certain shift in his orientation could also be detected; he became much less enthusiastic about the right wing Russian emigration, including the self-styled Fascists among them. Reviewing a book by the White General Zakharov,[29] Rosenberg did not accept the view of the author that the White movement was the very first manifestation of Fascism, that the motives which guided it were identical or comparable with Fascism elsewhere. This was a gross exaggeration, Rosenberg said; the White emigration lacked a central idea, for nobody now advocated a return to Tsarism. The White movement lived in its past; the logical conclusion soon to be drawn by Rosenberg was that it had no future. He had had contacts with Ukrainian nationalist leaders in Munich for a long time; now he switched to full support for them.

The liquidation of the Polish state was the basic aim of an active German foreign policy, Rosenberg wrote in 1928; an alliance between Kiev and Berlin (not Moscow and Berlin) was an absolute necessity. England, too, would be interested; had Bismarck not shown that English interests in India were easier to defend at the Russian–Polish border than in Afghanistan? Would not England be grateful to Germany for containing the power that constituted the main danger to its rule in India, and would she not in return take over the defence of Germany's frontier with France?[30]

Rosenberg could point to a tradition in German foreign policy that went back a fairly long time. A German–Ukrainian alliance had been advocated not only by Rohrbach and other Baltic political writers; one of Bismarck's confidants, Hartmann, had come up with a similar project. Even earlier, in 1854, Baron Bunsen, in a memorandum to the King of Prussia, had urged the end of the alliance with Russia and expatiated on the advantages of co-operation between Prussia and a new Black Sea power, namely the Ukraine. The Nazis now detected all kinds of fine qualities in their Ukrainian protégés, whose organization was said to have a Fascist basis.[31] In fact, it was a small right-wing group, radically anti-Semitic but very religious at the same time. It had no more sympathy with Nazi racialist teachings than had the Russian *emigrés*. This did not prevent the Nazis mobilizing support for this group headed by Hetman Poltavets-Ostranitsa, whose co-operation with the Hitler movement dates back to the days of Scheubner-Richter.[32] Poltavets-Ostranitsa received some money from Hitler, though the sum involved was apparently not great;[33] the Nazis were not, after all, ready to invest much in their ally. In 1933 they switched their support to another Ukrainian faction, the UVO, and Poltavets-Ostranitsa was sent for a while to a German prison.

By the late twenties both Hitler and Rosenberg realized that Bolshevism was there to stay in Russia. On the tenth anniversary of the revolution Rosenberg was willing to admit that there were two conflicting groups in Moscow, and that Stalin supported the small peasantry. But in the end Stalinists and Trotskyites would collaborate, as it was in their vital interest to do so.[34] Even in 1930, when the five year plan was already under way, Rosenberg was unwilling to admit that anything of importance would ever be achieved in Russia. Literally everything in Russia, including houses and factories, would fall into ruins unless American engineers took charge. Left on its own Russia would become, within a few decades, a great horde, most probably headed by a pure Mongol. Was it not ridiculous of certain German right-wingers to be enraptured by Soviet planning or to describe Stalin as one of the greatest statesmen of the age?[35] Rosenberg's chief aide, Schickedanz, was even more emphatic; the five year plan was bound to fail, he wrote early in 1931. Bolshevism was a system 'created of chaos'; the Russian people were in general incapable, and particularly unfit for technical enterprises and the natural sciences. The laziness of the Russian peasant would surely defeat Stalin.[36] Yet in the very same year warning voices were already heard in the Nazi camp. Count Reventlow was one of those who poked fun at false prophecies by the 'Russian experts' who had 'twice a year predicted Russia's impending disaster'. In an article entitled 'Danger in the East', he called the five year plan 'tremendous and gigantic' and said that if it succeeded it would be an event of decisive historic importance. The attraction of Communism for the dissatisfied masses in other countries would greatly increase; no capitalist system would be able to compete with Russian 'dumping'.[37] (Soviet 'dumping', which never materialized, played an important role at the time in Western political and economic writing.) In October 1932, when the economic crisis in the West had reached its peak, the official organ of the Nazis declared: 'The five year plan has ceased to be a theory. It has become a reality, a hateful reality, but one that must be taken into account.'[38] The relative success of the plan made a deep impression in these circles; its cost and the many unnecessary victims it demanded did not worry the Nazis; on the contrary, the 'Gewaltmensch Stalin' became for some of them almost an attractive figure. Yet it did not make them more friendly disposed towards Communism. They stressed in their propaganda now that the Soviet menace in the East had grown and that only a National Socialist Germany could successfully withstand the Bolshevik tide. National Socialism, they said, would defend Germany not for capitalism, which was bankrupt – it was certainly not worth while to shed one's blood for this. Germany would be saved only by an idea, a new organic social order – namely, National Socialism.[39]

How was Hitler himself affected by developments in Eastern Europe in the twenties and early thirties? Like Rosenberg he was against Rapallo which he regarded not as an economic treaty, nor an attempt to split the front of the Versailles powers; it was 'a recognition of the Moscow gangster government'.[40] Like Rosenberg, he thought it was a disgrace that the German ambassador had to convey congratulations to the mortal enemies of European culture on the tenth anniversary of the revolution.[41] Hitler's ideas about Russia had been fixed since he wrote the sections in *Mein Kampf* dealing with the subject, and since he was preoccupied during the twenties and early thirties with domestic German affairs, there was nothing to induce him to re-examine the question. Nevertheless, on some occasions it appeared that developments in the Soviet Union had left a trace on him. If he had talked contemptuously in 1922 about the 'chaos in Soviet-judaea', and about the impending dissolution of the Russian empire, his attitude in 1932 was quite different:

> 'A *Weltanschauung* has conquered a state, and emanating from this state it will slowly shatter the entire world and bring about its collapse. Bolshevism, if unchecked, will change the world as completely as Christianity did. Three hundred years from now it will no longer be said that it is merely a question of organizing production in a different way . . . If this movement continues to develop, Lenin, three hundred years from now, will be regarded not only as one of the revolutionaries of 1917, but as the founder of a new world doctrine, and he will be worshipped as much perhaps as Buddha.'[42]

These predictions must have been read with considerable satisfaction in Moscow; the prophecy about Lenin certainly came true much earlier. Nor was this an isolated statement. On another occasion Hitler was reported as having said:

> In any case, if European and American thinking remains in the future what it is now, then Bolshevism will slowly spread over Asia. A period of thirty or fifty years does not matter, since it is a question of a *Weltanschauung*. It was three hundred years after Christ before Christianity began to pervade all southern Europe, and seven hundred years before it also took hold in northern Europe. *Weltanschauungen* of such a basic nature can, even five hundred years after their establishment, prove their ability to conquer unless they are broken by the natural instinct of self-preservation of other peoples.[43]

Such statements betray an almost apocalyptic vision and suggest that Hitler substantially revised the image of inefficient Jewish Bolshevism as portrayed in *Mein Kampf*. Yet on closer inspection it is not at all clear whether Hitler did not deliberately exaggerate the danger of Bolshevism after 1931 in order to shock the German middle classes and induce them to support Nazism. After 1933 his anti-Bolshevism was a useful pretext for neutralizing Western Europe. Luedecke, one of Hitler's supporters and financial agents from the early years, wrote that Hitler told him that he had to make England

and France believe that Germany was the last bulwark against the red flood, for this was the only way to come through the 'danger period', to get rid of Versailles and re-arm.[44] We know from *Mein Kampf* that this fear loomed very prominently in Hilter's thinking; France would wage a preventive war before Germany had a chance to re-arm. There is no certainty that Hitler was really afraid of Bolshevism in the early thirties. If he was, it was no more than a passing phase, for we find very little of it remaining once he had come to power. The relative ease with which he had prevailed over his adversaries enormously strengthened his self-confidence. He was certain that he would defeat his external enemies in the same decisive fashion as he had defeated his domestic opponents in the battle for Germany. He came to believe that there was a historical law according to which this pattern was bound to recur: the Soviet Union was a somewhat bigger and better organized German Communist Party; the German Communists were a bitter and stubborn enemy, but Hitler had never regarded them as a serious rival in the contest for power.

Chapter 9

NAZI POLICY AND THE
SOVIET UNION 1933-8

WHEN HITLER came to power the whole world expected the new
Germany to pursue a sharply anti-Russian policy. Everybody remembered the frenzied speeches, the promises to smash Communism
– or as he often put it *Die Kommune* – once and forever. How often
had Hitler declared that Communism was the worst enemy of the
German people and that there could be no truck between him and
the Jewish tyrants and bloodsuckers in the Kremlin? *Mein Kampf*
had made Germany's intentions in Eastern Europe abundantly clear
to anyone able to read. But it seemed, as a German diplomat wrote of
the Nazis early in 1933 in a private letter, that 'their bark was worse
than their bite'. Communism in Germany was smashed but there was
no radical break in German–Russian relations on January 30, 1933,
nor in the first months thereafter. On the contrary, Hitler, precisely
because of his reputation as an anti-Russian fire-eater, in the beginning moved very cautiously. Nor was there any sudden, dramatic
shift in Soviet policy towards Germany. At the end of 1933 Molotov
declared that there was no reason for a change. No reason for change?
One knew that dictatorships had been capable of astonishing political
somersaults. But Germany and Russia were dictatorships of a novel
type in which doctrine played an important role; could they possibly
pursue a foreign policy entirely at variance with the doctrine they
preached for domestic consumption? These questions were to come
up again and again in the coming years. It was probably dimly realized by some that an eventual clash between an expanding Germany
and the Soviet Union was almost inevitable in the long run.

In a revealing statement before some high officials Hitler declared
that Russia would never forgive the Nazis for smashing Communism

at home. 'In our relations with Russia the liabilities have always out-weighed the profits.' Good German–Russian relations could not in practice be maintained for long; in the meantime tactical concessions should be made to prevent a sudden rupture.[1] On the other side both Litvinov and the less official and more outspoken Radek made it quite clear that they had no doubts about Germany's aggressive intentions. 'Of course,' said Radek, 'at present Germany is too weak to attack Russia.' But in case the Soviet Union became involved with Japan, was it not extremely likely that Nazi Germany would pounce on Poland – and then offer Poland compensation in the Soviet Ukraine? Neither Hitler nor Rosenberg had changed his ideas about Russia in any way – what was written in *Mein Kampf* (the famous chapter fourteen) was plainly the long-range policy of the Third Reich. For the time being the Nazis were too weak to carry out their policy and disseminated their ideas in pamphlets and newspaper articles instead.[2] Litvinov, whom the Germans believed to be the leader of the anti-German party in Moscow, stated that although the German Foreign Ministry may have wanted good relations, other forces in Germany were more powerful. As far as most Russian diplomats could see there was no doubt that Germany's new direc-tion was anti-Soviet. However, there were other voices in Moscow which induced the Germans to believe in the existence of 'two parties' behind Russia's attitude towards them. Enukidze assured the German envoy that Stalin and Molotov wanted to maintain friendly relations with Germany; they were said not to attribute un-due importance to the propagandistic excesses in Berlin. Krestinsky on another occasion said that it was not yet certain which direction would prevail in the Nazi Party – Rosenberg's rigid anti-Soviet line or a more constructive approach.[3]

And in 1933 both sides were preoccupied with more immediate problems; German rearmament had not really got under way and Stalin was immersed in economic problems and projects. The stage for a direct Soviet–German confrontation was not yet set.

Gustav Hilger, who watched German–Soviet relations from the German embassy in Moscow, relates that for many weeks in the spring of 1933 Hitler's policy towards Russia was vague, hesitant, and quite ambiguous. After an anti-Russian outburst in early March, Hitler made a declaration of readiness to maintain friendly relations to the advantage of both countries. The German diplo-mats in Moscow were certainly as much at sea as everyone else.

Dirksen in his first dispatch after the take-over told the Foreign Office that the Russians were mainly afraid of the conservative Hugenberg, whereas they had confidence in Neurath, Blomberg, and Schwerin-Krosigk. The Nazi Party was of course regarded as strongly anti-Soviet; had not its principal organ described Russia as Germany's greatest enemy?[4] In early March, Dirksen thought considerations of practical policy would compel the Russians to maintain friendly relations with Germany.[5] In a political report in early April he was still inclined to play down the incipient conflict; despite the fact that the National Socialists had become the government, and despite the ban on the Communists, a continuation of the previous policy was both possible and desirable in the view of those Soviet leaders who really mattered. To characterize that previous policy, Dirksen added in brackets the magic word 'Rapallo'.[6]

The German diplomats advised their Russian colleagues not to get unduly excited: having accepted governmental responsibilities the Nazis would pursue a different policy from the one proclaimed before – it was always like this, and it applied to all political parties.[7] That both the Communists and the National Socialists differed in some essential respects from traditional 'parties' did not at the moment occur to the German Foreign Office.

Throughout 1933 there were minor crises in German–Soviet relations; Soviet citizens were arrested and maltreated in the Reich; Soviet correspondents were excluded from the Reichstag fire trial; the personnel of Soviet trade agencies in Germany were harassed. The Germans on their side complained about hostile Soviet radio propaganda, inflammatory speeches and newspaper comment. These irritations, however, did not prevent prolific exchanges; when Hitler received Khinchuk, the new Soviet ambassador, in late April he told him that he wanted to put Soviet–German relations on a permanently friendly basis. He recalled that both states had common enemies, and therefore vital common interests.[8] Yet Moscow was not really impressed by words, and a few days later Dirksen again reported from the Soviet capital that the Soviet attitude towards Germany was 'anxious, mistrustful, uncertain'. This attitude went back to the summer of 1932 and the Lausanne conference, when von Papen, the then Reich Chancellor, had offered Herriot an anti-Soviet alliance. The Russians had then realized that unqualified opposition to the Treaty of Versailles – their policy for the past fourteen years – could no longer be pursued. Instead the argument that revision of the

Versailles Treaty meant war gained ground.[9] The anti-Russian fulminations of Alfred Rosenberg came up frequently in discussions between Litvinov and the German ambassador; Rosenberg's ties with Russian and, in particular, Ukrainian *emigré* leaders such as Konovalets and Poltavets clearly worried the Kremlin.[10] As a result the German Foreign Ministry urged that co-operation with the Russian *emigrés* should be discontinued, or at least managed more discreetly.

In their conversations with the Russians, German diplomats argued that it was inadmissible to bring up time and again, year after year, statements made by their politicians which were no longer valid. After all, even the *Voelkischer Beobachter* had taken a decidedly pro-Soviet attitude.[11] Even Alfred Rosenberg, arch-protagonist of anti-Bolshevism, declared solemnly that Germany was no more prejudiced against Russia than against any other power; he even stressed the need for German non-intervention in Russian domestic affairs.[12] There were other conciliatory gestures; Hugenberg, the veteran leader of the right-wing Conservative Party, had explained at the London Economic Conference that Germany wanted to annex the Ukraine, and he now got the sack. Hitler had been looking for an opportunity to get rid of this erstwhile rival. What is more, in May 1933 Hitler ratified the Berlin Treaty; his predecessors had hesitated to do this. A Berlin newspaper noted that Bruening had refused to renew the Rapallo policy, and that von Papen had been actively anti-Soviet. It also affirmed that Germany had reverted to a positive policy *vis-à-vis* Russia, only *after* Hitler had come to power.[13] Some other writers in the German press ridiculed the professional Russophobes and prophets of doom who for so many years had been predicting the immediate downfall of the Soviet regime. Even the *Voelkischer Beobachter* reprinted an article from a German military journal which gave a very favourable account of Soviet military strength and of the popular support for the Stalin regime. These sharply conflicting reports and comments show that the whole situation was extremely confused; Russo–German relations remained in a state of 'obscurity and cloudiness' as the German ambassador to Moscow put it in August 1933.[14] When he left Moscow three months later he concluded his final report with the words: 'The Rapallo chapter is closed.'[15]

On one day the German diplomats would tell one another that the Russians had decided in principle to join the Franco–Polish axis – the 'Little Entente' bloc – but on the next day there was usually a report that the Russians had not yet written off the Germans and there was still hope of collaboration. Hitler continued to assure the Soviet ambassador in Berlin of his goodwill, and Litvinov likewise reiterated in public speeches the wish for good relations with Germany, for 'nothing but good could result from such a relationship for both countries'. Behind the official declarations there was of course a great deal of uneasiness; according to one German report from Moscow in October 'anti-German excitement had become almost hysterical'; although the writer hastened to add that there was as yet no definite change of line towards Germany.[16] Privately the Soviet diplomats declared that there was no imminent danger of German attack; but since the Nazis had withdrawn from the League of Nations and the Disarmament Conference it was to be assumed that they would re-arm – and then their long-term plans would enter a critical stage.[17]

This was the reaction of most Soviet diplomats; the Red Army staff was on the whole more friendly. Voroshilov assured the Germans that 'military policy had always proved a stable and unifying bond in former crises' and the Russians wished this to continue.[18] Another Soviet military leader declared in September 1933 that the Rapallo Treaty was still the foundation of friendly political relations, and Tukhachevsky in November 1933 assured the Germans that the Red Army would never betray its co-operation with the Reichswehr to other powers. There was now, as before, 'the greatest sympathy in the Red Army for the Reichswehr, which had been the teacher of the Red Army in a difficult period – a fact that had not been forgotten and never would be'.[19] Yet despite all this talk about comradeship-in-arms, the Russians decided to close down the German military stations in the Soviet Union. These had existed there since the middle twenties, implementing the terms of co-operation between the Reichswehr and the Red Army. In June 1933 a German general, von Bockelberg, visited the Soviet Union and was, as German commanders had been on previous occasions, very well received. There were parades, receptions, and toasts, but in the middle of all this it was announced that the Russians had decided to close down the stations.[20]

The first twelve months of Hitler's rule thus brought growing uneasiness in German–Soviet relations, which had started to deteriorate about two years before the Nazis came to power. Friendly diplomatic declarations continued almost monotonously on both sides, and underlying these there was a genuine desire not to cause a radical change in the *status quo*. If the Germans complained about anti-Nazi propaganda disseminated by German Communists and others in Moscow, the Soviets complained about constant anti-Bolshevik attacks and exhibitions such as 'Brothers in Need' (Brueder in Not), drawing attention to the plight of the Volga Germans. Yet by and large German foreign policy in 1933 showed much less change than had been expected by many on the basis of Hitler's aggressive policy declarations prior to 1933. The only dramatic action was Germany's withdrawal from the League of Nations. The Nazis needed first to secure their foothold inside Germany and to build up the army to back their policy of expansion. For the time being their aggression was restrained by obvious military weakness. The year 1934 saw a further gradual deterioration. The Fuehrer on the first anniversary of his coming to power did again emphasize that despite the great differences in their ideologies Germany intended to cultivate good relations with the Soviet Union. But at the same time an agreement was signed with Poland, Germany's old enemy, and Stalin speaking at the Communist Party Congress then in session could not but wonder about Germany's intentions and express disquiet at the growth of revanchist and imperialist trends in Germany.

Dirksen, the German ambassador, had left Moscow in October 1933 and was replaced by Nadolny who was known to be an advocate of close relations with the Soviet Union. However, his suggestions for a change in the German attitude made no impression in Berlin; they were not in line with Nazi policy. Nadolny, in a series of memoranda, and in an interview with Hitler, noted the 'mountain of prejudice and mistrust' that would have to be overcome in Moscow where fears of the German *Drang nach Osten* had assumed nightmare proportions.[21] If Paris was worth a Mass, would not the decent treatment of M. Litvinov (whom Nadolny in the usual Nazi fashion persisted in calling 'Wallach') be a moderate price to pay for the collaboration of Soviet Russia? Really friendly relations were impossible, Nadolny agreed, but on the other hand Germany should not remain merely inactive, antagonize Russia, and allow herself to be encircled. Realistic co-operation and serious political discussion would be possible once the German Government refrained from direct attacks on the very existence of the Soviet state.[22] However, Berlin

165

thought much less highly of Russia's value as an ally. The instructions sent to the Moscow embassy said that the Russians, with their fear of German aggression, were hysterical; there was no point in trying to refute these allegations since a denial would not be believed anyway. Soviet co-operation should not be rejected outright, but there should be great reserve in dealing with the Russians. The German diplomats were asked, in effect, to do as little as possible.

Nadolny resigned after his policy suggestions had been rejected, a fact that was probably known in Moscow and added fresh substance to Russian suspicions. At some time during 1934 Moscow re-examined the world situation and came to a more acute realization of the dangers of a re-militarized Germany. A German envoy reported from the Soviet capital that the atmosphere was daily becoming more hostile; he added that this worked to the disadvantage of the Germans without causing any particular injury to the Russians, to whom it might even be acceptable as a domestic stimulant. Politically, Germany could no longer harm Russia, and trade with Germany was not vital to the Soviet Union.[23] When Schulenburg, Nadolny's successor, came to Moscow in October 1934 he immediately noted Russian anger towards Germany, but at the same time reported that the Russians were keeping a hand free.[24] Meanwhile the Russians had changed their man in Berlin, and Surits the new ambassador came to see Hitler in November 1934. Never before had an ambassadorial visit been so formal or the speeches so short.[25] When Surits met leading German officials a few days later he was told that the Russian fears were fantastic, and wholly unfounded. The Germans on the other hand had real cause for worry, because Moscow's anti-German attitude had been demonstrated in recent months on all international questions. This charge was not without foundation; Moscow's new approach was manifested when Russia joined the League of Nations which she had attacked and ridiculed for so many years. Shortly afterwards Mr Anthony Eden went to Moscow, and mutual assistance pacts were signed between Russia, France, and Czechoslovakia.

This Russian re-orientation was also reflected in the change of line that the Comintern adopted in 1935. Its new Popular Front policy meant that the Comintern was willing to ally itself with all anti-Nazi groups and parties except their rivals of the extreme left, regardless of their social constitution and class interests. This of course was a far cry from the 'third period', in which even collaboration with the left-wing socialists had been considered a mortal sin.

Moscow was nervous about German re-armament, for the Russian officers held their former teacher in the highest respect. Radek in 1934 had told a German journalist that Germany, if she wished, could have a stronger air force than France within three months.[26] The German military attaché reported in April 1935 that a general belief among Soviet officers was that Germany was rearming specifically to make war on the Russians. Previously the Russians had encouraged the Germans to disregard the military provisions of the Versailles Treaty and to again become a great power; now this attitude had been reversed.[27] There was a great deal of war talk in Moscow in the spring of 1935; the question being asked everywhere according to Schulenburg was 'will there really be war with Germany?'[28] Twardowski, his deputy, was told by Stern, an important Foreign Commissariat official, that Russo–German relations were deteriorating daily and would inevitably end in war.[29]

But even if Russia was nervous and distrustful, Stalin did not want any further deterioration in relations with Germany. The German diplomats always thought that Litvinov was the evil spirit, though Radek on one occasion put them right: 'You know what Litvinov represents. Over him there is a hard, cautious, distrustful man endowed with a firm will. Stalin does not know where he stands with Germany. He is uncertain. ...'[30] Stalin was disappointed by the French; the Laval Pact once signed did not amount to much; anyway his character and policy were such that he always preferred to back more than one horse. He commissioned Kandelaki, officially head of a trade delegation, to discuss with leading German economists and businessmen what prospects there might be for improving relations between the two countries. As a good Marxist Stalin apparently thought that Schacht, the Minister of Economics, was a man of great political influence in the Third Reich. Kandelaki saw Schacht first in the spring or early summer of 1935 and reported back to Stalin; at a second meeting he brought up the question of political negotiations but did not get any response from Schacht, who said that the Foreign Ministry would have to see to that.[31] The matter did not end there, for Surits and his deputy, Bessonov, took the question up with various German Foreign Ministry officials in December 1935. Speaking privately, Bessonov suggested that the Berlin Treaty should be supplemented by a bilateral non-aggression pact between Germany and Russia.[32] Surits likewise pressed for strengthening economic relations, closer political ties and even the development of cultural and social connections. The Germans formed the impression that he had strict instructions to do everything in his power to bring about at least an external improvement in mutual relations.[33] There were other straws in the wind. Schulenburg reported from Moscow that Litvinov at the November 7 celebrations had proposed a toast 'to the re-birth of our friendship'.[34] Tuchachevsky when seeing off Twardowski, a departing German official, reiterated once again that different ideologies need not be an obstacle to German–Soviet co-operation.[35] The German reaction was invariably one of studied reserve: there were very difficult questions, the diplomats said, one would have to proceed very cautiously in tackling them. The Nazis had already realized that with extreme anti-Bolshevism they were on to a good thing as far as the rest of the world was concerned. Germany as a 'bulwark against Bolshevism' would get much more consideration than Germany demanding the revision of her frontiers in the name of historical justice and whatnot. Hitler, apparently in answer to these Soviet feelers (about which only a handful of people knew at the time), declared early in 1936 that any contacts with the Soviets were out of the question. A year before the decision had already been taken to step up the anti-Bolshevik campaign which reached its climax in 1936–7; the violent speeches at the Nuremberg party congress in September 1935 were an unmistakable sign.

Hitler in 1933 had many preoccupations more urgent than his relations with Russia. This is undoubtedly the explanation of the confused state of affairs that prevailed in German–Soviet relations for at least two years after the Nazis had come to power. Hitler's long-term plan included German expansion in the East and the German domination of Europe. But in 1933–4 Germany was not yet strong enough to carry out an aggressive foreign policy. German–Soviet relations gradually deteriorated during these years, but neither side wanted a sudden break. In 1935 Hitler seems to have realized that a major anti-Soviet propaganda campaign would pay dividends in other parts of the world while hardly affecting German–Soviet exchanges, which by that time were reduced to an absolute minimum. Stalin on the other hand understood somewhat belatedly that the new Germany was a serious menace to Russia, but his distrust of the

Western powers made it unlikely that the Soviet Union would join an anti-German alliance, even if, which was uncertain, the Western powers consistently pursued such a policy. Moscow did retaliate in kind to the attacks made in German propaganda; but this did not prevent Stalin from putting out feelers with a view to improving relations between the two countries even at the height of the tenson in 1936-7. Nothing came of these approaches; in addition Stalin was then very much absorbed in domestic affairs such as the purges and the trials.

Much of the German anti-Soviet propaganda campaign of the middle thirties was planned and carried out by Goebbels' Propaganda Ministry and its special agency, the Anti-Komintern – a subject discussed in some detail elsewhere in this study. The German press and radio were not satisfied with publishing the highly damaging admissions of the Soviet newspapers on alleged internal sabotage, betrayal and mass espionage. In addition they broadcast the most fantastic inventions, calculated to make the flesh of all good Germans creep; the downfall of the Soviet regime was only a matter of weeks, if not days, it was announced; in Magnitogorsk general moral dissolution had reached unprecedented depths.[36] The German public was told that the very words 'father', 'mother', 'son', 'daughter', 'brother', and 'sister' had been banned by decree, but incest was permitted.[37] The first standard works of Nazi anti-Soviet literature appeared, such as Fehst's work on Jews in the Soviet leadership (1934) and Adamheit's book *Red Army, Red World Revolution, Red Imperialism* (1935). Hitler himself officially declared that Bolshevism and National Socialism were divided by an unbridgeable abyss; four hundred party members had been killed and forty-three thousand wounded by the Bolsheviks in the struggle for Germany.[38] The figures were greatly exaggerated; nor did he mention the number of Communists killed by the Nazis. For some years to come Hitler was to bring up these statistics whenever he dealt with German–Soviet relations.

In 1936 German re-armament was far from being completed, but it had progressed to such an extent that Hitler was able to pursue a more active foreign policy. The risks he now took became increasingly greater; the re-militarization of the Rhineland; intervention in the Spanish civil war and ultimately the conquest of Austria and Czechoslovakia. In 1936-7 the anti-Soviet propaganda campaign also reached its climax. Since Hitler had not the slightest intention of attacking Russia at that time, it remains to be asked what his motives were in engaging in a campaign which largely preoccupied German domestic and foreign policy, ostensibly at least, and began to slacken only in 1938. Various explanations could be put forward. Every totalitarian regime needs an enemy. In this specific instance it was the very enemy against whom the Nazis had been fulminating for many years prior to 1933. But at the time it was a tactical question rather than a matter of principle; the Soviet Union had drawn closer to the Western European powers during the middle thirties, but Hitler guessed correctly that there was still a considerable residue of anti-Soviet feeling and a great deal of uneasiness in the West. By playing on the French and British *haute bourgeoisie's* fears of the Bolshevik menace he hoped to establish himself as Europe's saviour against the 'common enemy', or at least to neutralize the effect of Germany's aggressive policy. In a famous remark already quoted, Hitler had said that he needed the anti-Soviet policy mainly for Western consumption to help him over the critical period when German rearmament was not yet complete and there was still some danger of a preventive war by the French. We have no reason to doubt his word. The Anti-Comintern Pact with Japan (November 1936) and Italy (November 1937) was ultimately directed more against the Western Allies than against Russia. At the same time it provided a good line to strengthen the hold of Nazism in Germany. 1936 and 1937 moreover were the years of the purges and trials in Moscow and nobody knew what would happen next in the Soviet capital; Soviet prestige abroad was low and the Russian armed forces were disorganized by the arrest and execution of most of their commanders. In these circumstances Russia's position seemed very much weakened, and a political campaign against that country not particularly hazardous.

Hitler told a foreign correspondent in September 1935 that Germany was the bulwark of the West against Bolshevism.[39] This theme was to recur many times in 1936 and 1937. He had saved not only Germany but also England from the danger of Bolshevism. Hitler was sarcastic about the British politicians and leader writers who refused to recognize the world revolutionary mission of Bolshevism; this was about as significant as if a fifteenth-century Viennese humanist had refused to recognize the intention of the Mohammedans to extend their influence in Europe.[40]

Hitler's New Year message in 1936 contained a violent attack on the Soviet Union. Soon afterwards he announced that any close contact with the Russians was out of the question. Bolshevism was a malignant poison, and Hitler did not want his own people contaminated by it. He demanded from every German workman that he should have no contact with these international mischief-makers. The German worker would never see him (Hitler) clinking glasses or rubbing shoulders with the Bolsheviks. Moreover, any further formal connections with the present Bolshevik Russia would be completely worthless for Germany; was it not ridiculous to think of National Socialist Germany ever agreeing to accept assistance from the Bolshevik state? Yet politics make strange bed-fellows; three years later Hitler and Ribbentrop were clinking glasses and rubbing shoulders with the Russians.

The annual party rallies in Nuremberg were devoted to the struggle against Bolshevism. Alfred Rosenberg, the pioneer, had started the series in 1935 with a long speech on 'Bolshevism as the action of an alien race'.[41] He recapitulated the old arguments of the twenties about the rebellion of a racial underworld, the parallels with ancient times, the new military menace of Bolshevism and the identity of Zionism and Bolshevism. Yet Rosenberg was an indifferent speaker and always fairly predictable on the subject of Russia. When Hitler and Goebbels tackled the subject in 1936 the sparks really began to fly. 'From the very first hour of our political thinking we have waged war against this world menace with utter fearlessness.' Thus Goebbels, who ten years before had raved about the great Russo–German alliance. But now he found nothing at all to admire in Russia; only in one field were the Bolshevists past masters – in the field of negative propaganda, of insolent lying and hypocrisy.[42] It must indeed have been galling for the little Doktor to be permanently exposed to competition from the comrades in the East.

The verbal onslaught was relatively unimportant, but in Hitler's speech there were more ominous references to German plans with regard to the Ukraine, the Urals and Siberia; to the natural wealth of these regions and Germany's mission to exploit them. What was behind these threats? Hitler was then in no position to attack the Soviet Union; insofar as he had a detailed plan of action, it implied quite a different time table. The main intention was to impress Britain, France and perhaps the United States with the idea that Germany's territorial ambitions lay in the East. True, Hitler had talked to Polish diplomats about the desirability of a common anti-Russian front; so had several other Nazi leaders. But nobody took this very seriously at the time, for Hitler was clearly not yet prepared for any major military action. Nor did the Anti-Comintern Pact mean much in practice, apart from an exchange of information about Communist activities and a rather vague promise that in the event of an unprovoked attack, or the threat of attack by Russia upon either power, the other would refrain from taking measures that might improve the situation of the USSR. This was certainly not a substantial political or military alliance as events were soon to prove.

1936 was the year of anti-Bolshevik speeches rather than action. The propaganda inside Germany was stepped up. Many new books and periodicals were devoted to Russia and Bolshevism, and the newspapers were flooded with articles on the subject. There were study conferences and meetings of experts. The Anti-Komintern publishing departments, such as the Nibelungen publishing house (not a well-chosen name for such an enterprise) worked at top pressure. The upheaval in Spain gave a much needed impetus to the campaign; all the enemies of National Socialism were now branded as Russian agents and Bolsheviks, right-wing Austrian leaders like Schuschnigg as well as Dr Benes in Prague, not to mention Mr Winston Churchill and all non-appeasers in France. The League of Nations was said to be a Soviet institution ('Hinter Genf steht Moskau').

Early in 1938 Hitler stated yet again that Soviet Russia was the one state with which 'we have not sought to establish good relations, nor do we wish to enter into close relations . . . More than ever do we see in Bolshevism the incarnation of humanity's destructive elements.'[43] Yet as the Austrian crisis, and later the Czech crisis came to a head the Russian theme became less and less important; the Soviet Union all but disappeared from speeches and official pronouncements. There were hardly any contacts at all between Russia and Germany, even on international occasions. Russia had been represented at the Nyon conference during the Spanish civil war, but it was not invited to Munich, and played no conspicuous part in any of the diplomatic moves during or after the Czech crisis. Even economic exchanges came to a complete standstill during the early months of 1938; for the existing treaty, which came to an end on December 31, 1937, was not renewed until several months later. Cultural relations of course were non-existent, and the problems relating to the few hundred Germans arrested in Russia (whose national status was dubious) and their counterparts in Germany were handled at consular level. There was a German ambassador in Moscow, and a Soviet envoy in Berlin writing their weekly or monthly reports but so far as German foreign policy was concerned Russia had virtually ceased to exist by the beginning of 1938. The Soviet Union was at that time in a state of isolation, partly voluntary, partly enforced. A real change in the situation was to come only after Munich.

Thus far we have found little to say about economic relations between Russia and Germany, in a discussion mainly devoted to political and propagandistic warfare. In totalitarian states economic considerations are virtually always subordinated to political intentions. If exchanges between Germany and Russia deteriorated after 1933 this merely reflected the growing political tension. The year 1932 had been the high water mark in trade between the two countries; in 1935 German exports to the Soviet Union dropped to a mere seven per cent of what they were three years earlier. The import and export figures really speak for themselves.

GERMAN–SOVIET FOREIGN TRADE AS PERCENTAGE OF TOTAL GERMAN
FOREIGN TRADE

Year	Imports from Russia	Exports to Russia
1932	5.8	10.9
1933	4.6	5.8
1934	4.7	1.5
1935	5.2	0.9
1936	2.2	2.7
1937	1.2	2.0
1938	0.9	0.6
1939	0.6	0.6
1940	c. 11.0	c. 7.0

German imports from Russia remained more or less steady till 1935, but fell sharply after that date. They increased again in the year of the Soviet–German Treaty. German exports to Russia on the other hand fell sharply from 1935, although there was a temporary recovery in 1936 and 1937. There were some half-hearted attempts on both sides to maintain trade relations despite political differences. One leading German economic journal wrote that one should distinguish in politics between shifting moods and permanent interests. 'As far as economic interests are concerned, nothing has altered the fact that no other countries complement each other in such a natural way as Germany and Russia.'[44] Soviet initiatives were even more ambitious. Kandelaki, head of the economic mission in Berlin (a man believed to enjoy Stalin's confidence) wanted not only to negotiate more extensive economic exchanges, but also suggested to Schacht a general normalization of relations. The suggestion was passed on to Hitler who displayed no interest.

Trade between the two countries would probably have fallen during this period anyway since Germany lacked foreign valuta and put its foreign trade more and more on a basis of barter. Both countries were now rearming at full speed; Germany wanted to buy raw materials from Russia for military purposes, which Moscow did not always want to supply, and Germany displayed a similar unwillingness when the Russians showed an interest in submarines and other military material. Russia's economic relations with the outside world had been extended in the thirties and she now had much less need for Germany as a market or as a buyer. In Wilhelmian Germany and during the Weimar period, economic exchanges had been affected only to a limited extent by foreign policy: the situation in the totalitarian era was very different indeed.

German–Soviet relations between 1933 and 1938 are in some ways an unrewarding subject of study, extremely complex and plagued with apparent contradictions and inconsistencies. If some aspects are highly revealing, others are very misleading, for diplomats in a totalitarian regime are little more than glorified errand-boys and certainly not the most reliable guides to the real intentions of their masters. Neither Hitler nor Stalin trusted his diplomats; in both Nazi Germany and the Soviet Union the Ministers of Foreign Affairs – with one exception – never belonged to the 'inner circle'. The one exception, Molotov, proves the rule, for what was Molotov if not Stalin's most faithful hatchet man? Neither Chicherin, Litvinov, Vyshinsky, or Gromyko were members of the Politburo; among the Germans, von Neurath was a complete outsider, and Rosenberg and Ribbentrop were at best on the fringe of Hitler's entourage. We have reason to believe that Stalin often did exactly the opposite of what his diplomats advised him. Hitler considered his own Foreign Ministry completely useless, and his diplomats, with a very few exceptions, as a worthless bunch of lawyers – in his eyes the worst one could say about any human beings. Diplomats were people who cut out newspaper articles and pasted them together. Hitler not only refused to listen to their advice; he even boasted of never telling them his own intentions and ideas. Under these conditions, a study of the diplomatic notes of the period is of limited interest. It shows what German diplomats thought, or frequently, what they thought would be well-received in the Wilhelmstrasse. But it sheds very little light on Hitler's thoughts. Even the instructions sent out from Berlin to the embassies abroad were merely glosses on the decisions already taken by the Fuehrer. About what induced Hitler to take certain decisions the diplomatic documents are rarely illuminating.

From the diplomatic files it could not be guessed that the confrontation between National Socialism and Bolshevism was the first historical occasion on which two totalitarian regimes faced each other. The Italian case was not a precedent. Mussolini's Italy never blossomed into full totalitarianism; moreover, Italy was not really a world power although some people in Rome and elsewhere had illusions on the subject. Between Germany and Italy there were only minor causes of friction – nothing that would have impelled either country into taking sides against the other in a global conflict. Soviet–German relations were a very different proposition; even if the Soviet Union had not been the spearhead of a world-wide revolutionary movement, the clash would have been in the long run inevitable in view of Hitler's plans for expansion into Eastern Europe.

Chapter 10

ANTI-KOMINTERN

NAZI POLITICAL WARFARE against the Soviet Union was mainly carried out by an agency that attracted considerable notoriety at the time. In retrospect there is no doubt that the Anti-Komintern helped Stalin far more than it harmed him. The fact that Hitler and Goebbels were the chief sponsors of anti-Bolshevism automatically generated sympathy, or at least understanding, for the Soviet Union and the Communist parties, especially in the years 1935–8, even though in 1939 it appeared that Soviet anti-Fascism and Nazi anti-Bolshevism did not constitute an insurmountable obstacle to temporary collaboration between the two regimes. No attempt has been made so far to analyse the Anti-Komintern and its place in Nazi policy; such an analysis shows that in this, as in so many other fields, the Nazis' professed aims and their real intentions were by no means always identical. Just as the Anti-Comintern Pact was not primarily directed against the USSR – Japan, after all, never joined Germany in its war against the Soviet Union – the true aim of the Anti-Komintern was not to denounce the Soviet Union but to gain support in the West for Nazi policy. Fortunately for the historian, the Nazis in the Anti-Komintern were cynically frank in their correspondence and inter-office memos. If Rosenberg and a few other ideologists took their Russophobia seriously those who launched and ran the Anti-Komintern had very different views.[1]

The clash between National Socialism and Communism, one of the most fateful in recent European history, never produced a serious ideological confrontation. The few Nazis who had read Marx or Lenin were professional economists or philosophers, none of them high in the party hierarchy. The Nazi Party itself was not an ideological movement in the traditional sense; whatever doctrines it proclaimed were believed to be self-evident, not a matter for reflection, investigation, or learned comment. It strenuously denied that Marxism was a *Weltanschauung*. Hitler and Rosenberg had decided, once and forever, that Communism was the revolt of the underlings; a racial, not an ideological movement. Ideological discussions with Marxists, they said, were not merely senseless and absurd but positively harmful; it would imply that National Socialists accepted the Communists as more or less equal partners; that the Communists had an ideology which deserved to be taken seriously; what was important was to analyse the true (racial) sources of Communism. As a Communist one could win an argument simply by proving that one's ideas conformed to those of Marx, Lenin, or Stalin. As a Nazi any connection with Marx or Marxism was *a priori* evil, for Marx had been born a Jew.

There was little mention of Marxism or Bolshevism in Nazi literature or speeches before they came to power in 1933.[2] When the terms were used it was with considerable flexibility; 'Marxism' more often than not stood for German Social Democracy, and 'Bolshevism' could be applied to anything, from modern art to a conservative writer who happened to have incurred Nazi displeasure. Such anti-Bolshevik or anti-Soviet propaganda as was produced at this time, and there was surprisingly little, was the work of the local Nazi propaganda machines in working-class regions like the Ruhr.[3] It was taken for granted that the middle classes – particularly the lower middle classes – were firmly anti-Communist.

When the Nazis took over there were few people within the party with the necessary qualifications to direct anti-Bolshevik propaganda. Rosenberg, his deputy Schickedanz, and Georg Leibbrandt (a Russian-German, like most of the Nazi Russian experts), the head of the Eastern department of the Nazi foreign political office, were busy with other tasks, such as supervising Nazi ideological training. They viewed with increasing distrust the activities of the various state and party agencies in the Russian field, and occasionally tried to sabotage their efforts. The latter replied in kind.

From the early days of the Nazi regime to its very end the various factions with a vested interest in Russia and Bolshevism fought each other tooth and nail. Apart from the 'academic' *Ostforschung*, there were at least half a dozen different institutions with interests in research and propaganda in the Russian sphere. The foreign ministry and the army (Abwehr) had their own advisers and contact men. They also had far more money than the rest, which was a source of much envy. The SS and its security service, the SD, joined the field comparatively late, but soon made themselves felt. The propaganda ministry was the sponsor and controller of the Anti-Komintern, and, to make a complicated situation even more confused, Dr Goebbels decided that his anti-Soviet experts should be split into two groups. One was officially part of his ministry (Section II/4) under Eberhart Taubert; the other was ostensibly an autonomous organization under Adolf Ehrt, called the 'Anti-Komintern'. In fact it was part of Dr Taubert's section.[4]

Dr Adolf Ehrt had been the secretary of a diffuse and inactive association of German anti-Communist groups which came into existence in the early thirties. Yet another *Volksdeutscher* who had been born in Russia, his chief claim to distinction was a little book on the history of the Mennonites, a religious sect among the German settlers in Russia. His organization had originally been sponsored by the Press section of the German Protestant church, the Catholic Institute for Research into Bolshevism and Atheism, and the Russian Scientific Institute in Berlin. Later sponsors included the Catholic *Pro Deo* group, the Association of German Refugees from Russia, and the Nazi Institute for the study of the Jewish Question.* From the Nazi standpoint this list of sponsors was not very promising; church influence was too prominent; the Berlin Russian Institute was said to have been supported by Jews and freemasons. The collaboration of the churches was not undesirable in the early years, 'since they gave the publications of the Anti-Komintern an aura of respectability; later they were squeezed out', Taubert, the guiding spirit behind it, wrote ten years later.[5] Worst of all was the fact that Dr Ehrt was a lapsed Nazi. He had joined the party in 1932 but left it again shortly afterwards, because, he said, of pressure from the churches; he thought he would be able to fight more effectively for Nazi ideals from outside the party. This, at least, was his version, but his enemies were not slow to cite excerpts from his writings in 1932 in which he had bitterly attacked some aspects of Nazism, particularly

* Among its publications were *Bewaffneter Aufstand* (1933) which provoked a Soviet diplomatic protest, since it contained details about Soviet help to an alleged Communist-planned take-over in Germany. Other books include Ehrt and Schweickerts, *Entfesselung der Unterwelt*, dealing mainly with Communist front organizations, Dr Cramer's (one of Ehrt's pen names) *Notbuch der russischen Christenheit*, and Professor Iljin's *Welt vor dem Abgrund*, a symposium by members of the Russian Scientific Institute in Berlin. This institute was subsequently closed by the Gestapo and Professor Iljin settled in Paris.

Rosenberg's doctrine and the anti-Christian trend in the Hitler movement. Rosenberg's men were quick to seize the opportunity of attacking Ehrt and what they considered the shortcomings of the propaganda ministry. Dr Goebbels retaliated by forbidding his staff to have any communication with Leibbrandt, head of the Eastern section in Rosenberg's office.[6] At times it seemed as if the enemy of which all the Nazi agencies wrote and talked was not in Moscow, but in the rival government or party office. Indeed, the only common interest Goebbels and Rosenberg had at that time was a purge of German *Ostforschung* from all nefarious Marxist, liberal, Jewish, and masonic influences; this was begun in 1935.

In Germany, Professor Otto Hoetzsch and East European studies were more or less synonymous in the public mind, for the editor of *Osteuropa* – the journal of the German Society for the study of Eastern Europe – was by far the most active and influential of German experts on the USSR. Unlike most professors, he combined academic teaching with a political career, journalism, and much public speaking. As a pro-Russian conservative he had little sympathy for Hitler's movement and none at all for the anti-Russian ideology of the Nazis. Klaus Mehnert, his assistant, who had made a name for himself with a well-received book on the younger generation in Russia, was at that time a sympathizer of Otto Strasser's 'Black Front'. Members of the Society, and contributors to its journal, included Jews, and what the Nazis loosely called liberals. Yet Professor Hoetzsch, like most German intellectuals, found in 1933 that there was no point in actively resisting 'the national revival', as he called it in one of his writings.[7] The Jewish and liberal collaborators were gradually dropped, but otherwise the character of the Society and the journal changed little after January 1933. Hoetzsch and his colleagues made ritual obeisance to the new regime, observing that in the new Reich German Eastern policy would be of even greater importance than before. But they were not to escape so lightly. Their activities had long been an irritant to the Nazis in charge of anti-Bolshevik propaganda, who felt that the time was now ripe for getting rid of these 'crypto-Communists' permanently. The attack was launched on various levels. A junior employee of the Anti-Komintern denounced the Society to the Gestapo as a hotbed of pro-Bolshevik activity.[8] At the same time Dr Greife, Ehrt's assistant, protested in a letter to the Dean of Berlin University against the fact that a Jew of

Polish origin called Heller had, under the aegis of Professor Hoetzsch, written a dissertation on the fate of the Jews in the Soviet Union. This, thought Dr Greife, was an outrage: What was a Jew doing in a German university in this year of grace 1935? And why was he allowed to produce anti-Nazi propaganda? For his thesis, that the condition of the Jews in Russia was unenviable, was in direct contradiction to the Nazi thesis that Russia was a Jewish state. The Dean apologized to the young Nazi activist and told him that he had refrained from conferring a doctorate on Mr Heller. But the damage had been done, and Professor Hoetzsch had to resign soon afterwards both from the University and the Osteuropa Association. He was also ousted from the journal. Mehnert had earlier retreated to Moscow, where he was working as a correspondent for various German newspapers. His reports from the Soviet capital were, however, considered too friendly; had not *Bolshevik* once quoted him as an admirer of Soviet achievements?[9] In the correspondence of the Anti-Komintern he figured as 'the notorious Communist Mehnert'. (Dr Mehnert eventually went to the United States, and later to Honolulu and Shanghai; his subsequent activities are outside the scope of the present book.)

The chief culprits among the old *Ostforscher* had been dispatched by means of backroom intrigues and administrative measures. It only remained to discredit them morally and ideologically. Dr Greife volunteered for this task, too, with the backing of the Nazi Party and the police. The result was a short book published in 1936,[10] in which he surveyed the field of Soviet studies in Germany, and reached the sad conclusion that in almost all German universities the liberal tradition still persisted; Marxism was studied as an economic doctrine and Bolshevism as a social experiment, the only exception being the 'anti-Marxist' seminary at the *Hochschule für Politik*. Greife reiterated stock Nazi statements about Russia and Communism, and ridiculed those experts who welcomed the Soviet retreat from Communism. The methods of Soviet rule might change, he wrote, but it remained the rule of an alien race. A liberal expert who did not realize the importance of race theory, for whom the Jewish race did not exist, was a figure of fun; a Don Quixote tilting against windmills, unable to recognize the real enemy. German Soviet studies were the legitimate offspring of Weimar. Their exponents were almost all liberals; some were Marxists; the Jewish question was taboo for them. But they were not complete innocents; a man like

Hoetzsch had known all about the Bolshevik menace and the Comintern threat and played them down. Had he not written that Soviet achievements did not threaten Germany? But Hoetzsch was not the only culprit. There were others who had done much harm; the 'German Stalinists' for instance. These had been greatly impressed by the swing to militarist discipline in the Soviet Union; they welcomed centralized economic planning and saw in it the Russian version of the Nazi *Fuehrerprinzip*. These misguided souls failed to realize that the brutal dictatorship of an alien race could never be equated with a sacred German principle. Some of them had even suggested that the patriotic fever in Russia was inspired by the Nazi Revolution in Germany, which of course was blasphemy.[11]

Nor did Greife approve of the theologians among the experts (such as Berdiaev, Waldemar Gurian, Fedor Stepun), who, for all their hostility to atheistic Bolshevism, still refused to accept the Nazi creed. There was a real danger that the enemies of Nazism would use the work of these 'Soviet experts' to attack Hitler's Germany. The only valuable and realistic works on Bolshevism and the Soviet Union had been produced by convinced Nazis. They, and only they, saw the world as it really was; only they had a real grasp of political factors; they were interested not in the economic, but in the racial structure of the Soviet regime. Who were these National Socialist experts who had – as another contemporary writer put it – not only defeated the liberals ideologically, but also produced better scientific work?[12] The list was very short; it included Ehrt's pamphlets, Hermann Fehst's *Jews in the Soviet Union*, and the work of 'K. Michael', who wrote on economic topics (the pen-name concealed a Georgian *emigré* named Akhmeteli). No wonder Greife reached the conclusion that the state of German *Ostforschung* after the national revolution of 1933 remained unsatisfactory.

The young Nazi expert was not alone in his anxiety. Himmler, together with the Gestapo intellectuals, was also concerned about the dangerous currents in certain German intellectual circles. There was Ernst Niekisch, preaching a synthesis of Potsdam and Moscow, who maintained that the Prussian state only came into being as the result of the mixture of German and Slavic blood.* Other misguided souls had found many similarities between German and Russian agrarian

---

* The genetic ties between the Prussian spirit and Bolshevism was not, as commonly believed, a discovery of Niekisch. The first to comment about it in some detail was Otto Bauer in his *Bolschewismus und Sozialdemokratie* (1920).

Communism, regarded the Elbe as Germany's real frontier, and wanted to get rid of Western and Southern Germany as unnecessary encumbrances and strongholds of alien influences.*

It was not until 1938 that the purge was completed. Part of the Breslau East European Institute had been transferred to the SD, which had established its own research institution near Berlin, the Wannsee Institut. This was headed by Akhmeteli, alias K. Michael. A new generation of experts had emerged; the Seraphims, von Mendes, and Maurachs, who were more at home in the new climate. The *Osteuropa* publishing house brought out a symposium on Russia, edited by Bolko von Richthofen, a fanatical anti-Semite, which compared not unfavourably with *Der Stuermer*.[13] The leading newspaper of the Nazi party announced that *Osteuropa* was compulsory reading for everybody interested in East European affairs.

Peace, however, still did not reign among the various institutions and agencies dealing with Russian affairs. *Osteuropa*, even under its new editorship, remained incomparably more detached and objective than the publications issued by the underlings of Goebbels and Rosenberg, who continued to attack each other in their inter-office memos as 'Communist stooges'.[14] The so-called 'liberals and freemasons' of the German Foreign Ministry, and the 'reactionaries' of the Reichswehr, such as Tippelskirch, still continued their activities, and professors of the old school, such as Laubert in Breslau, sabotaged the efforts of the new experts. Dr Taubert, writing a few months before the Nazi defeat, recalled that it had been very easy to get rid of Professor Hoetzsch, but the other 'pro-Russian elements' proved harder nuts to crack. Among these he mentions Colonel Niedermayer, who had influential supporters in Rudolf Hess and Blomberg, the Minister of War.[15]

The Anti-Komintern idea played an important rôle in Nazi foreign propaganda, yet the organization behind its activities was weak. Not one leading figure in the Nazi regime showed particular interest in its activities. The official head of the Anti-Komintern, Dr Adolf Ehrt, certainly did not pull much weight in the Third Reich, nor indeed in his own office; real power was in the hands of Dr Taubert. Ehrt was

* These and other deviationists are discussed in an internal document published in June 1935, *Der Reichsfuehrer SS Sonderbericht. Zersetzung der nationalsozialistischen Grundwerte im deutschsprachigen Schrifttum seit 1933*. One of the few existing copies is in the Wiener Library, London.

assisted by a number of young specialists, such as Rudolf Kommoss and Karl Baumboeck (in charge of press affairs), Bockhoff (legal affairs), Karl August Stuckenberg (colonial affairs). His office produced a periodical (*Contra-Komintern*) and a great many books, chiefly in its own publishing house, the Nibelungen Verlag. It arranged study circles, exhibitions, film shows, and even international anti-Communist conferences. Some of its pamphlets were circulated in millions of copies. Yet all this was merely the visible fraction of the iceberg; the submerged, but incomparably more important, section was located in Goebbels' propaganda ministry.

Goebbels' closest collaborators, Haegert and Taubert, had envisaged the establishment of an Anti-Komintern even before the Nazis came to power. In October 1932, we learn from an internal report:

a proposal was brought forward to unite the anti-Communist associations under the leadership of the NSDAP. The necessity to replenish the party treasury, which had become much depleted, played a certain part in this context (*wobei die Ueberlegung mitspielte die arg zusammengeschmolzenen Kampffonds der Partei aufzufuellen*).[16]

It could hardly have been put more plainly. Nothing came of the plan at the time, but Taubert took it up again after Hitler came to power. In the autumn of 1933 an organization called the Anti-Komintern was officially registered, the idea of its sponsors being that neither the state nor the Nazi Party could, for diplomatic reasons, take an open stand against the Soviet Union. A similar dilemma had been solved in Moscow by disclaiming any responsibility for the Comintern; why should the Nazis not play the same game, and set up an 'independent', semi-private organization for which they could disclaim all responsibility? Dr Taubert, writing more than ten years later, was satisfied with his own creation; its very name seemed well chosen, because it could be easily remembered.

The functions of the Anti-Komintern were never clearly defined; was it to influence public opinion in Germany, or to act mainly as a clearing-house for governments and police departments in various European countries? Even in Rosenberg's office it was for a time believed that no German agents were involved in the Anti-Komintern.[17] According to its secretary, the Anti-Komintern had 'only *one* assignment; the struggle against Judaeo-Bolshevism.'[18] Yet its real aim was to win friends and support for Nazi Germany. When Ribbentrop met the secretary of the Anti-Komintern for the first time his only thought was: 'Your activity against the Comintern will make us many friends abroad.' He was not interested, as Dr Ehrt notes, in the content of its propaganda; he did not even believe Anti-Komintern propaganda about starvation in the Soviet Union. Ribbentrop had never specialized in Russian or Communist affairs. But even the experts from Amt Osten seemed to regard the Anti-Komintern's pro-Nazi propaganda as of even greater importance than its avowed aim: 'through anti-Communist propaganda the interests of National-Socialist Germany should be promoted, the Nazi revolution and the measures against the Jews be justified'.

In the middle and late thirties Stalin's Russia itself, with its purges and trials, supplied the most effective anti-Bolshevik propaganda. Many people outside Germany realized this, but very few were willing to join an organization sponsored by the Nazis. Nazism, not to mention its many other abhorred features, believed in the superiority of the German race, and with this basic belief in racial exclusiveness and the inferiority of all other peoples, no genuine international co-operation was possible.

The Anti-Komintern sought its contacts primarily in right-wing and clerical circles in the Western world. But clergymen in France and other countries, however anti-Communist, looked with disfavour on the anti-Catholic measures taken by the Nazis. The Anti-Komintern had a fairly sizeable office in Holland supplying the provincial Press with material; it had contacts (according to its own reports) with some officers of the Swedish General Staff and some obscure organizations in Greece and Belgium.* According to the same reports, the Anti-Komintern provided material for speeches by Prime Ministers de Valera of Eire, Tsaldaris of Greece, Motta of Switzerland, and Bennett of Canada, while the Archbishop of Athens 'was contacted through his niece Mrs Karaiskalis', for whatever that was worth. Some of this was idle boasting, other claims may

* Some of the internal monthly reports of activities have been preserved in T 81/11, 14. These records are, however, rather vague. 'Contact has been established with X in Poland' means more often than not that X was sent some magazine. If, for instance, a visit by Mr William Shirer to the Anti-Komintern office is recorded, this means, indubitably, that Shirer, a good journalist, wanted to find out about its activities, not that he sympathized with it. . . . Some of the foreign contacts of the Anti-Komintern were apparently British intelligence agents.

be true. On the whole, the activities of the Anti-Komintern on the international scene were thoroughly inept, in striking contrast to the extravagant claims of its sponsors. If the Comintern brought together erstwhile professional revolutionaries turned bureaucrat, the Anti-Komintern convened motley assemblies of retired Austrian colonels, Polish priests, and Japanese counter-spies, who, whatever their other qualities, had an exceedingly limited political intelligence and were quite incapable of understanding Bolshevism, let alone of combating it. These men were clearly quite unprepared for an ideological confrontation with Communism: all they could do was to adopt resolutions about the necessity of stamping it out by force.[19] As the Gestapo engaged in these activities, their assistance was in any case hardly needed.

The attempt to find a common ideological denominator for the Anti-Komintern, however vague, ended in failure. Ehrt, and behind him Taubert, tried their best by giving anti-Semitic slogans pride of place and equating Bolshevism with world Jewry. This, however, was no great help as far as Germany's two main partners in the Anti-Comintern Pact were concerned, Italy and Japan, where the Jewish problem was of no importance at all. Nor did anti-Semitic propaganda have any relevance in Spain, the focus of the battle between 'Bolshevism' and 'Fascism' in the middle thirties. Nor was the Jewish issue of any significance in connection with the advance of Communism in colonial countries. Asia in particular was a trial to the Anti-Komintern, which in its publications had frequently denounced 'Asian Bolshevism'; after the pact with Japan all this had to be changed.

Confusion reigned not only on ideological issues; there was general organizational muddle as well. The whole Anti-Komintern had been founded as a provisional body, a preparatory committee for a first world congress that was to establish a real world organization.* A world conference was never held. The Anti-Komintern had a Scandinavian secretary-general, Niels von Bahr (who had replaced Ehrt), yet secretly it was manipulated as a German government office (as Dr Taubert put it in his charming bureaucratic language: 'im geheimen aber als deutsche Dienststelle gesteuert wurde'). The

---

* Contra-Komintern announced for three years in its sub-title that it was the organ of the preparatory committee for the Anti-Communist World Conference. This sub-title was dropped only in August 1939, but August 1939 was the last issue of Contra-Komintern.

Nazi leaders did not think very highly of Anti-Komintern activities, and were unwilling to invest large sums of money in the venture. It had to make do with a very small staff and never had sufficient technical means at its disposal; it needed, for instance, a big radio station to compete with the foreign broadcasts from Radio Moscow, yet was quite unsuccessful in its attempts to set up a radio station of its own.[20] When an Anti-Komintern Congress was planned in 1937, Hitler ordered that it should not take place in Germany and that no German Government agency should participate; Himmler suggested Danzig as a place for this convention.[21]

So much for the overt activities of Anti-Komintern. The more important initiatives came from the submerged part of the organization at the Propaganda ministry. Russia and the Comintern were simply used as a bogy by these wire pullers in Goebbels' ministry to enlist sympathy for the Third Reich, to extort concessions to Nazi foreign policy, and ultimately as a means to gain supremacy in Europe. These aims were stressed time and again with refreshing if cynical frankness.

The first great propaganda drive concerned the effects of collectivization in the Volga German region, and the decision of the Soviet government to export grain despite the famine. The facts were basically correct, and an international relief campaign for the starving met with much sympathy. It was not realized at the time that the Nazis were wholly indifferent to the fate of the Germans in Russia; they used the campaign to break down the 'Chinese Wall' between Nazi Germany and Western public opinion: so far, they admitted, Nazi propaganda had been rejected by the world press – now there was a chance of a breakthrough:

> With the help of the charitable relief action, in which the churchmen of two confessions let themselves be used as marionettes by our propaganda, this Chinese Wall was breached. A particularly gifted agent, who worked for us, Ewald Amende, secretary-general of the Congress of European Nationalists, succeeded in persuading the Archbishop of Canterbury that the situation (in Russia) was indeed as painted by the 'Brüder in Not' committee ... The Archbishop of Canterbury later realized whose work he had done, and declared sadly that he had been used as a fig-leaf by the Nazi propaganda ministry.[22]

The sponsors of the Anti-Komintern were ambitious men. Taubert

thought it could be used to give Germany the leadership of a powerful band of forces embracing the whole world ('*die Fuehrung einer
gewaltigen weltumspannenden Kraeftegruppe gewinnen*'), and offered
the Nazis a moral formula to embellish power politics ('*eine moral-
ische Formel zur Verbraemung des machtpolitischen Zusammenge-
hens*'). To that end it intervened in all major crises of the thirties with
a varying degree of success. It tried to assist Germany to regain the
Saar through its agents in Switzerland and the help of the local
clergy, and by denouncing France as the ally of atheistic Russia. The
ease with which the religious dignitaries were taken in caused great
hilarity in Dr Goebbels' office:

> It was one of the unforgettable anecdotes of the Anti-Komintern
> that even the little priests in Saarbruecken never suspected for
> whom they were working.[23]

When Germany reoccupied the Rhineland in 1936 the Anti-Komintern provided some of the ideological justification, as it had done
during the visit of Lord Simon and Anthony Eden to Berlin the
previous year. On that occasion, Taubert reports, Hitler used anti-
Bolshevik arguments to stress the need for German rearmament, but
Mr Eden was not taken in. Whereupon it was decided to put even
more stress in future on emphasizing the Soviet military danger.

The Anti-Komintern took an interest in Spain: 'Dr Taubert was
the first to intervene in Spain. A very clever agent was sent to Franco
via Portugal, and served as Franco's first propaganda adviser.' Franco
was advised to use the anti-Bolshevik card in his fight against the
Republicans. In 1938, the Anti-Komintern devised the label 'The aircraft carrier of Bolshevism in Central Europe' to describe Czechoslovakia during the crisis.

Dr Taubert claims that German foreign policy in the mid-thirties
was not made by the foreign ministry but by the Propaganda
ministry or, to be precise, by the Anti-Komintern. Hitler, according
to this version, took from Dr Taubert the idea of making anti-
Bolshevism the central issue at the Nuremberg rally in 1935. The
decisive impulse in the direction of German foreign policy ('*entschei-
dende Richtgebung der deutschen Politik*') came from the propaganda
ministry, not the foreign ministry. It is indeed true that Hitler decided
in 1935 to adopt a sharp anti-Russian line, and it has been established
that the Anti-Komintern supplied the material for some of the key
speeches in Nuremberg. Yet to look for a causal link between Dr

Taubert's brilliant ideas and Hitler's political decisions is very far-fetched; Hitler was not in need of any prompting or persuasion; he had realized years before that he would have to play the anti-Bolshevik trump card during the dangerous years, when German rearmament was still in progress and the danger still existed of a preventive war by France.*

To return to the more prosaic activities of the overt branch of the Anti-Komintern: for domestic consumption it published a number of books on Communism and the Soviet Union, prominent among them the recollections of German and other Communists. Maria Reese, a former Communist Reichstag deputy and a friend of Clara Zetkin, returned to Germany after the Saar plebiscite, and in a comparatively moderate report related that she had been disappointed by what she saw in the emigration.[24] A more violent affair was Kajetan Klug's report on the Soviet labour camps. The author, a left-wing Austrian socialist, had fled to Russia after the suppression of his party in Vienna in 1934. The most substantial and influential work of this kind was Karl Albrecht's *Der Verratene Sozialismus*, which went through many editions. The author, who had been a deputy people's commissar, left Russia in the middle thirties and after a short, and apparently painless, sojourn in a German prison, began to work for the Anti-Komintern. Another series put out by the Nibelungen publishing house presented the recollections of Russians who had left the Soviet Union at various dates, some of them quite recently. Among them were Unishevsky and Kravets, both pilots; Butenko, the former Soviet ambassador to Rumania; Nikolaiev, who reported on the condition of the peasants in the Soviet Union, and Goryanova, who told the life story of a Russian engineer.[25] These books differed greatly in quality. Some had obviously been concocted or rewritten in the Anti-Komintern offices and were full of lies or exaggerations, or simply horror stories. Others, such as Maria Reese's book, had the ring of truth. Some of these books and pamphlets were distributed in hundreds of thousands of copies,† but their propaganda impact was apparently limited; the narratives were usually repetitive and boring. Having

* Hitler admitted this to Luedecke in so many words.
† For instance Laubenheimer's *UDSSR* (*Und Du Siehst die Sowjets Richtig*), one of Greife's pamphlets on forced labour in the USSR, had a circulation of 1·5 million; most of this literature was not sold but given away.

read one, hardly anyone wanted to repeat the experience. Moreover, they said no more than could be found in the daily newspapers; there was no attempt to analyse or understand Communist and Bolshevik policy on a more sophisticated level. The few attempts that were made in this direction by Dr Ehrt and his associates were pitiable.* The most interesting publications of the Anti-Komintern were translations from foreign languages, such as Sir Samuel Hoare's *The Fourth Seal.*†

The journal *Contra-Komintern* was badly edited, attracted few readers, and made no political impact whatsoever. Occasionally it spread confusion by presenting a version of some specific event which differed from that given in other Nazi journals. If the *Weltdienst*, for instance, asserted that the March revolution of 1917 had been organized and carried out by the freemason, Sir George Buchanan (the British ambassador in St Petersburg), *Contra-Komintern* had nothing but praise for Sir George, and published articles written by his daughter, complete with a photograph.

From the Nazi point of view the activities of the Anti-Komintern were not a conspicuous success, and at many points it overlapped with other government and party agencies. Yet bureaucratic institutions, once established, have remarkable staying power, and but for the Nazi-Soviet Pact of 1939 the flow of publications would probably have continued without interruption. But in view of the *rapprochement* with Moscow, the Nibelungen output dwindled after 1938 and was discontinued altogether in August 1939. When war broke out, the Anti-Komintern was clearly considered non-essential. Its personnel were dismissed, and even some of its leading officials had to join the army.[26] Only a skeleton staff was maintained. The *Contra-Komintern* changed both name and function; it became a periodical devoted, as its subtitle said, to the struggle against the Western plutocracies.‡ The situation changed in the Spring of 1941, when the

* For instance Bockhoff's *Voelkerrecht gegen Bolschewismus* (1938), or Greife's *Die Klassenkampfpolitik der Sowjetregierung* (1936).

† Dr Taubert hailed it as a great triumph that Sir Samuel Hoare gave permission for a German translation to the Anti-Komintern.

‡ The subsequent fate of some of the major *dramatis personae* should be noted briefly: Ehrt, who had been the nominal head of the Anti-Komintern, disappeared from the political scene in the late thirties. Dr Taubert, who was the guiding spirit behind it, remained with Dr Goebbels up to the very end. In the middle fifties he reappeared as the deputy head of a self-styled anti-Communist organization in West Germany, but had to resign when his past caught up with him. In Soviet publications, including even novels, he is frequently mentioned as one of the most

propaganda preliminaries for the attack on the Soviet Union were started. After the invasion the Anti-Komintern brought out a *Red Book*[27] and a few other publications. But after June 22, 1941, anti-Soviet propaganda became the main Nazi theme; its planning and execution could no longer be left to a mere sub-department of the propaganda ministry.

When the Anti-Komintern was closed down in September 1939, all German anti-Soviet propaganda ceased. The general press had already received a directive from Goebbels in late May 1939, banning polemics against the Soviet Union; on June 24 a second, even more emphatic, directive followed: 'The Soviet Union is in no circumstances to be attacked.'[28] A few days later comment on world Bolshevism was also forbidden. The periodical of the Anti-Komintern was apparently the only exception, perhaps on the assumption that hardly anyone was reading it anyway. On August 26 instructions came that the re-establishment of German–Soviet friendship was to be emphasized. The word 'Russia' could be used when referring to the Soviet Union. And above all: 'The approach should be warm and sympathetic.'[29] German political commentators did their best. The SS weekly reminded its readers that Russia had twice in her history saved Prussia; in 1762, and again in 1812. The Tsarist Empire had been rotten through and through, whereas the Soviet Union was incomparably stronger, based on very different principles. If this was the approach of the *Schwarze Korps*, no wonder that the less orthodox Nazi writers were even warmer and more sympathetic in the tenor of their comments. No wonder, too, that the experts of Rosenberg's Eastern office were greatly disturbed about what they considered 'indecent deviations' and 'a general confusion of the German Press'. 'Should we give up all our anti-Moscow armoury?', one of them asked plaintively.[30] Until then they had competed with the Anti-Komintern on a modest scale, publishing books and booklets, and financing and

---

influential men in West German and NATO politics. If the Russians should indeed take Dr Taubert seriously, this throws an interesting light on the critical faculties of his antagonists in Moscow. Dr Leibbrandt, who was in charge of the corresponding department in Rosenberg's office, fell a victim to an SS intrigue in June 1943, and spent the latter part of the war in the German navy. He was charged as a war criminal in 1950, but the charges against him were dismissed by a German court; after a few difficult years he found employment as a representative of a major industrial firm in Bonn. Judging the situation more realistically than Dr Taubert, he found the post-war climate uncongenial to a political career.

directing the Berlin Russian language newspaper *Novoe Slovo*, under an editor with the unlikely name of Despotuli. As late as early August they had sent to the party publishing house in Munich a manuscript written by a Mr Roedel and entitled *Eastern Ideology and Bolshevism*. It was intended as a crushing blow to those misguided Germans who had advocated a Russian–German alliance. The book could not have come at a worse moment, for the Fuehrer had decided months before in favour of just such an alliance. The Amt Osten was thoroughly inept at interpreting the international situation. It should have seen the writing on the wall nine months before, when it had prepared a series of anti-Bolshevik talks for the German broadcasting service. At the very last moment, after all the manuscripts were ready, Dr Taubert stepped in and announced that Hitler himself had given an order that all anti-Bolshevik propaganda was to be discontinued in order 'not to weaken the effect of the anti-Jewish propaganda'.[31] However much they disliked it, the experts from Amt Osten had to discontinue their publications in August 1939, and to be content with internal memos about the activities of the Comintern – not very numerous or important at that time. All the good work done in the years before 1938 seemed to have been in vain. In June 1940 Franz Eher, working in the Nazi central publishing house, enquired whether the unsold copies of the various anti-Bolshevik books and pamphlets could be destroyed. After some hesitation Rosenberg refused to give permission;[32] he hoped that one day there would be a fresh demand for this literature.

What were the ideological innovations of the Anti-Komintern and Nazi *Ostforschung*? Some of these writers saw as their main task the popularization of Alfred Rosenberg's theories about the origins of Bolshevism, Russian history, and similar topics. Others published articles and books in which they demonstrated that the new 'national wave' in the Soviet Union, which began in the middle thirties, was a mere tactical manoeuvre without deeper significance. Lastly, a series of books and articles attempted to demonstrate that, broadly speaking, all Bolsheviks were Jews, and all Jews were Bolsheviks.

The popularization of Rosenberg's view was, naturally, the preserve of his own office, the Amt Osten of the Nazi Party foreign political office. Leibbrandt argued that the ideas of liberalism, humanism, and democracy had emerged from the Mediterranean *Voelkerchaos*. This in its turn had given birth to parasitic 'Near-Eastern

Marxism'. Much of it was the fault of the Russian character; Byzantium had left a tradition of slave morality in which there was no place for such things as honour, heroism, or liberty. Dostoevsky's heroes were all criminals and idiots – certainly this was not pure coincidence. The Russians lived in perpetual discord; plagued by discontent and self-torment. Russia, in brief, was an Asian monster with a thin outer skin of European varnish (as Napoleon and Pilsudski had claimed before). It was a 'frozen corpse which would stink horribly once it began to thaw'.[33]

These trite views were presented in pseudo-scientific language as an exercise in the history of cultural traditions and ideas. Occasionally Leibbrandt stepped down from these (comparatively) rarefied heights of quasi-philosophical discussion and engaged in the fabrication of crude forgeries: if Rosenberg, his master, had commented on the *Protocols of the Elders of Zion*, the disciple wrote about the *Protocols of the Poale Zion*,[34] describing in lurid language the alleged convention of a left-wing socialist group in the Ukraine in March 1919 as yet another conspiracy for world conquest. In so far as they referred to verifiable historical facts, Leibbrandt's writings were replete with elementary errors;* he was clearly ill-equipped for the task he had set himself, which demanded at least a basic knowledge of Communism and Russian history. Some of the authors of the series of pamphlets he published did have this factual knowledge,† but on the whole it made a very slight impact; the demand for this kind of literature was limited, and publishers had difficulties in selling even small editions.

Other Nazi institutions had their doubts about Rosenberg's philosophy of history; it was not openly attacked until much later, but was on the whole ignored. Goebbels' lieutenants argued, probably correctly, that very few people had any interest at all in amateurish comments on the Russian 'racial soul', while many were interested in what was actually happening in the Soviet Union. Many outside observers were surprised by the patriotic fervour of Soviet policy in the middle thirties – by the rehabilitation of so many national heroes of the past, the restoration of 'Homeland' and 'Soviet people' as central values in Soviet life; by the reforms in education and family legislation, and last but not least, by the reintroduction in the army of

* For instance, Marx's year of birth is given as 1788.
† For instance: Otto Keil (i.e. Otto Schiller), *Der Bauer in der Sowjet Union*, or Paul Schmitz-Kairo, *Moskau und die islamische Welt.*

the traditional ranks. Some German writers argued that the Russian element was again prevailing in the Soviet Union; that life was stronger than impractical theories; that Stalin was a *Russian* revolutionary and patriot who had no desire for world revolution, and that, generally speaking, what happened in the Soviet Union had little in common with the theories of Karl Marx.[35] Others even thought to discern important parallels between recent developments in Russia and Germany; had not the *Fuehrerprinzip* prevailed in both countries?

The backroom boys of the Anti-Komintern were set to work to counter these dangerous interpretations: 'We reject most emphatically any attempt to draw parallels between Bolshevism and National Socialism.'[36] The only purpose of the new Soviet patriotism was to enlist the peoples of the Soviet Union in the cause of world revolution by misuse of national, patriotic feelings. It was a change, of course, carried out with typically Jewish lack of scruple. The evolution of Bolshevism towards a national state was impossible for the simple reason that Russia was a Jewish state and a Jew could not evolve into an Aryan.[37]

If Nazism made any original contribution to this field of study, it was the identification of world Jewry and Bolshevism; a dogma it repeated time and again on every level of sophistication from the quasi-scientific to the most vulgar. From the factual angle it was an uphill struggle; true, a fairly large percentage of the early Bolshevik leaders had been Jewish by origin. But what the Nazis chose to ignore was the inconvenient fact that these Jewish Bolsheviks had turned against their own religion and people and wanted nothing to do with them; and that the percentage of Jews in anti-Bolshevik political parties – such as the Mensheviks – was even higher. They also ignored the fact that even within the Bolshevik party leadership the participation of Jews had begun to decrease in the middle twenties, and had become quite insignificant after the big purges of the late thirties; Kaganovich was in fact the only Communist of Jewish origin left in the supreme party leadership.*

All this had to be ignored by the Nazi writers in their endeavours to show that 'Soviet Judaea' was still the bulwark of the Elders of Zion. To prove that point a whole literature came into being; books that consisted mainly of long lists of names and photographs which

---

* Another favourite Nazi thesis was the argument that Zionism and Bolshevism were one and the same thing. In fact, Zionism was persecuted as a counter-revolutionary movement in the Soviet Union.

purported to show that all those listed were Jews.[38] An enormous amount of energy was invested, though it was not always clear to what purpose; for even if it was shown that a certain typist at the Tass office in Moscow was a Jew, what did this prove? Much of course was outright forgery. Fehst, lecturer at the German Academy of Politics, maintained that Lenin was of Jewish origin (his grandfather Blank having been a baptized Jew), so were Krasin and Kollontai (who came from old Russian aristocratic families), Manuilski, Safarov (who was an Armenian), Unschlicht (who was of Latvian origin), Lashevich, Petrovsky, and even Tomsky, who, he said, 'passes as a Russian with a mixture of some Jewish blood'. But Tomsky's looks were very suspicious, and in Professor Guenther's textbook on race his picture appeared with the caption 'Near-Eastern race'. Fehst argued that Stalin had taken an anti-Semitic line in his struggle against the opposition, or had at any rate tolerated the growth of anti-Semitic tendencies; but this had been a mere tactical manoeuvre.[39] After Fehst had finished with the Soviet Union there were few non-Jewish citizens left; everybody with a non-Russian name, regardless whether of Armenian, Latvian, or German origin, was automatically described as a Jew – and many good old Russian names fell into the same category. After so much spadework had been done, little scope remained for Mr Kommoss, who succeeded nevertheless in attributing to Stalin a Jewish wife. Among other Russians who were hebraised by Kommoss were the composer Shostakovich, and the political leaders Shvernik and Gorkin; Beria and Marshal Blucher looked like Jews, and Kerensky became at least half a Jew. Kommoss even claimed that the Red Army commanders Rataitchak and Mustafin were Jews, which was no mean feat, since the former was so obviously a Latvian, and the latter a Tatar or Azerbaidjani. Kommoss also maintained that Stalin had played on anti-Semitism in his struggle against the opposition; but this changed at once after his victory when he switched to support the Kaganovich clique.[40]

The Anti-Komintern propaganda embodied a great many contradictions. At one and the same time the Bolshevik system was described as utterly inefficient, bankrupt, devoid of order, discipline, and organization, while the Red Army was described as the most formidable menace to the rest of the world. The Nazi propagandists were well aware that some of their slogans could backfire: it was pointed out in the instructions given to party speakers that to working-class audiences the world revolutionary mission should not be given undue emphasis, for this could be a source of encouragement to some circles and evoke feelings of class solidarity.[41] It is striking to what an extent considerations that had nothing to do with Russia or Bolshevism were of decisive importance; nor was any secret made of them. It was stated, for instance, in the secret instructions that those German economic circles which complained about high taxation might well benefit from speeches about the terror in the Soviet Union, the destruction of the family, etc. Or elsewhere: the shortage of foodstuffs in Germany and the complaints about alleged abuses by the party apparatus (in Germany) would appear as mere bagatelles when compared with the situation in Russia. The anti-Bolshevik campaign of the Third Reich was certainly not launched solely to distract attention from shortcomings at home, but it is far too often forgotten that these domestic considerations played a very important role indeed.

This raises another question: to what extent did the sponsors of the Anti-Komintern believe their own propaganda? There seems to be a clear division. Those around Rosenberg in the Foreign Political Office of the Nazi Party had no doubts about it. The German Foreign Ministry and the experts of the Wehrmacht had their doubts about the Anti-Komintern propaganda and activities, but did nothing about it, apart from making a few critical remarks from time to time. A perusal of the top secret monthly bulletins of the SD about the situation in Russia shows that they were far more concerned with the political and economic realities of Soviet power than with the theories of Rosenberg's office or the slogans emanating from the propaganda ministry.[42] Yet the real sponsors in the Propaganda Ministry were cynics, and there is much evidence that they regarded their extreme anti-Bolshevism as little more than a gimmick; they were technicians of the big lie, who in different circumstances would have undoubtedly been quite willing to offer their services to other bidders.

Chapter 11

NAZISM IN THE SOVIET MIRROR

BEHIND THE SCREEN of demagogic speeches and slogans, what was Nazism really like? Vsevolod Vishnevsky, the Soviet writer, suggested an answer in a play written about thirty years ago, *The Battle in the West*. In this, Schigaida (the Nazi leader) and Hirsch (the big industrialist) talk, in the hearing of others, about patriotism and *weltanschauung*, but once they are alone the following dialogue takes place:

Schigaida: Now we had better stop talking for the benefit of the masses. No more fools present. ...
Hirsch: Yes, the blockheads have gone. Let's talk. How much? (takes a cheque book from his pocket).

A few years later Bertold Brecht described in *Arturo Ui* the rise of Nazism as he saw it. Arturo Ui, the leader of a small gang in Chicago, runs a protection racket among the local greengrocers. He and his cronies, Roma (Roehm), Givola (Goebbels) and Giri (Goering) offer their services to the cauliflower trade and after a short while establish complete mastery. Arturo Ui, in a long monologue, relates how he had started his career fourteen years before when he was unemployed in the Bronx. With him there were seven good lads with nothing to their name, but all firmly intent, like himself, on 'cutting their piece of meat out of any cow that the good God had made'.

Arturo Ui is a complicated character who cajoles and terrorizes the businessmen; at the same time, he is more independent than Schigaida, a mere employee of the capitalists. Vishnevsky had written his play for working-class audiences whereas Brecht, as he stated in his notes, had attempted 'to explain Hitler's rise to the capitalists by placing him in a milieu that was familiar to them'. Both Vishnevsky and Brecht agreed that Fascism had emerged as the result of a

196

deal between the Nazis and the capitalists and that all the Nazis wanted was to get into the big money.

One of the strangest aspects of the confrontation of Communism and Fascism was the intense, but almost entirely unsuccessful, endeavour by each side to understand the other. The Nazi image of Bolshevism – Russian, German, or any other – had the advantage of simplicity: Communism was the revolt of the criminal underworld against the Aryan race and all its values. This theory hardly made sense in Rome, and certainly not in Tokyo, but it sufficed for Germany. In a way, National Socialism was not an ideological movement, and the finer points of doctrine did not really matter in the eyes of its leaders or its followers.

The Soviet image of Fascism, on the other hand, is a matter of far greater complexity. Mere intuition or mythology would not do; what the Communists needed was a *scientific* theory of Fascism. This was not a purely academic exercise. If, in the nineteen-twenties, the Fascist question had been one of many confronting the Communist International, it became in the thirties, after Hitler's victory in Germany, the most important problem facing the Comintern and Soviet foreign policy.

For many years Communist leaders and ideologists tried to analyse Fascism. Was it a conservative-reactionary movement of the extreme right? Or did it perhaps contain some revolutionary elements? What class did it serve, what was its social composition? From the first Fascism was a source of exasperation to the Communists because it was so totally unlike their own movement. Fascist doctrine was ill defined; the whim of the Fuehrer was of greater importance than any point in the programme. In their speeches Hitler and Mussolini quoted hardly any figures and mentioned few facts; they had no general theoretical conception of things (or so it seemed to the Communists), instead there was a direct, unbridled appeal to passions which the Communist leadership found unintelligible and ridiculous. Karl Radek, probably the most intelligent Soviet observer, wrote a biographical sketch of Hitler in 1932, in which he noted with some surprise that the Nazi leader was a backwoodsman, whose speeches contained no serious political or social analysis whatever. The nationalist demagogy appeared to him similarly ineffectual. Hitler fulminated at the corrupting influence of French literature and praised the Edda, but the German *petit bourgeois* knew nothing about the one and did not care about the other.[1] Radek had known the

German political scene in 1910 and in 1919–20; Hitler was unlike anything he had seen at that time. It did not occur to Radek, or to any other Communist at the time, that there were various keys to success in politics, and that a mass movement need not necessarily base itself on a detailed programme and an elaborate political and social analysis. Radek, in a way, did an injustice to the political acumen of the Fascists; they were not great theoreticians but they knew instinctively who were their enemies. The Communists, curiously enough, were much less astute in judging the situation. Wherever Fascist or pro-Fascist regimes came to power in Europe between 1923 and 1933, in Italy and Bulgaria, in Finland, Poland, or Germany, the Communists went to great lengths to stress that though Fascism was of course an enemy, it was by no means the chief enemy of the working class and the Communist party. The rude awakening invariably came a few months, sometimes a few years, later.

Fascism in the nineteen-twenties and thirties was frequently misinterpreted; it is only since the Second World War that a clearer conception has prevailed. The reasons for these misjudgments are not difficult to explain in retrospect. Fascism was, after all, a novel phenomenon on the European political scene (a fact that escaped many observers for a considerable time); its very dynamism – so often emphasized by its leaders – its elusive, amorphous character made it difficult to analyse. It was even more difficult to predict its future course of action, since its leaders were not clear about this themselves. Certainly the Communists were not the only people to be wrong about Fascism, and once they realized that they had been mistaken they were second to none in their resistance to it, provided the interests of the Soviet state did not force them into a different position. Many liberals and Social Democrats had illusions about Fascism and the possibility of appeasing it or incorporating it in the parliamentary framework. Yet they learned by bitter experience, even though they were ill prepared for active resistance to a totalitarian regime. The Communists were in a far better position to offer resistance in view of their much tighter organization and their experience of acting in conditions of illegality. They were believers in a holy cause, not just men and women who put their trust in the force of reason and self-evident truths. Instinctively they may have known that Fascism was the main enemy, but it did not fit into their traditional political scheme; for instance, there was no provision (within the framework of Marxism-Leninism) for nationalist passions as a major political factor in the industrialized world.

For many years the Communists stubbornly refused to admit any difference in principle between 'bourgeois' parliamentary democracy and a Fascist dictatorship. Since there were no major economic or social differences between these two regimes, how could there possibly be a radical political difference? Not until the middle thirties did the realization dawn that the difference was one of life or death for the European Communist parties, their leaders and militants. Between 1935 and 1945, except for the break in 1939–41, European Communism regarded Fascism as the main enemy and subordinated everything else to the struggle against it. The brave fight by thousands of nameless militants in Germany's and Italy's darkest hour, a fight that seemed at times without hope, will remain one of the brightest pages in the annals of world Communism. Yet during that period, and even after 1945, there have been only some modifications and no basic readjustment of the Communist appraisal of Fascism. Even then Fascism was not considered a regime qualitatively different from democracy; what mattered was not the inhumanity of Fascism, but Hitler's anti-Soviet foreign policy.

In the great clash between Fascism and Communism in Europe both sides thus misjudged the character of the enemy in all essential respects. The Nazis did not waver in their belief that Communism was the Judaeo-masonic revolt of a racial underworld, while the Communists persisted in regarding Fascism as the praetorian guard of monopoly capitalism. It would have been high comedy but for the hecatombs of victims.

Fascism in Italy

In the early days the Italian Communists, the first to come into direct contact with Fascism, regarded Mussolini's *squadri* as a group of terrorists, desperadoes, declassed military adventurers, a *'fenomeno di militarismo primitivo'*. The Communists were at the time preoccupied with events in the Italian socialist camp, and were not paying much attention to the Fascist campaign; with one or two exceptions (Gramsci) they seriously underrated its importance and its chances of success. Subsequently much of the blame was put on Bordiga, the leader of the Communist Party at that time, but in fact the confusion about Fascism was fairly universal, not only among the Italian

199

leadership but also in Moscow. The *fasci di combattimento* were thought to be a weapon in the hands of the large landowners, from which the industrial and commercial bourgeoisie dissociated itself, for was not Fascism something in the nature of a 'black Bolshevism'?[2] A book published in Moscow after Mussolini had assumed power stressed the revolutionary significance of the Fascists;[3] another early Comintern publication defined the Hitler movement as it appeared in 1922–3, as a party with a pronounced '*petit-bourgeois* revolutionary' programme.[4]

Commenting on a pamphlet by Karl Radek, a Comintern publicist wrote in 1923 that Fascism was a movement not of the bourgeoisie but of the broad popular masses whose basic economic interests were hostile to the exploiting and impoverishing policy of the bourgeoisie. Fascism was the enemy of the revolutionary working class – but not because of historically irreconcilable class contradictions.

Whether they were revolutionary in character or the running dogs of the large landowners, the Fascists were certainly never considered potential allies of the Communists. The fourth Comintern Congress (December 1922) had compared them with the Russian White Guards (the experiences of the Russian civil war were still vivid). It was noted, too, that the Fascists did not confine themselves to repressive measures; unlike Kolchak and Wrangel, they also made use of social demagogy and were, therefore, more dangerous rivals. But this certainly did not mean that the Communists should join the Social Democrats and liberals in a common anti-Fascist front. One day before Mussolini became prime minister the Italian Communist Party published a manifesto in which the workers were urged not to support either the government or the Fascist forces, but to act against both enemies. A few days later a leading Communist spokesman commented on the Fascist victory in a way that was to become familiar in years to come: no great changes had taken place, neither a revolution, nor even a *coup d'état* had occurred; the class situation in Italy was unchanged, the existing state of affairs had merely been legalized.[5] The official party journal added: 'The parliamentary farce will continue in a different form.' Togliatti was to write years later: 'We cannot read this article now without smiling.' It must have been a bitter smile.[6] The basic assumption underlying this attitude was that there were but two camps in the world, the Communists and the rest, and that the differences between the various systems used by the bourgeoisie to suppress the working class were relatively unimportant. Looking back in 1928, Togliatti argued that this thesis had been correct (seen in a wide historical perspective), but it certainly was not helpful from a tactical point of view. It led the Communists into underestimating the danger of Fascism, into denying the danger of a Fascist *coup*, and, generally speaking, into equating 'capitalism' and 'fascism'. Since one capitalist was as bad as another what point was there in singling out the Fascists for special attack?

Zinoviev, in a speech in Moscow at the time of the march on Rome, was inclined to take it rather lightly; viewed historically, he said, what had happened in Italy was a comedy. Radek was one of the few to take a gloomier view. He regarded the Fascist victory as the most serious setback to the Communist movement since the war.

Slowly it emerged that Radek was right. The Italian Communists in the following years had much time to ponder the reasons for their defeat. Bordiga argued that appearances had been deceptive, Fascism was not a middle-class movement but was sponsored and led by the strong conservative bourgeoisie.[7] Gramsci and Togliatti (Ercoli), his rivals for party leadership, devoted much time and effort to tracing the specific Italian roots of Fascism.[8] Some of their observations were considerably shrewder and more realistic than the Comintern pronouncements both before and after; they pointed out, for instance, that it was quite wrong to define every reactionary, terrorist regime as 'Fascist'.[9] Fascism was not merely a reactionary-capitalist movement, it was also the revolt of the rural and urban lower middle class against the powers that be.

Such insights found no echo in Moscow. The Soviet leaders put all the blame for the victory of Fascism on the socialist betrayal, some even predicted that Social Democrats and Fascists would soon make common cause. In Moscow both Bukharin and Stalin argued that Fascism and social democracy were twins, two sides of the same instrument of capitalist dictatorship. 'Social democracy is objectively the moderate wing of fascism.'[10] Thus a general policy had been outlined for many years to come.

What is Fascism?

The term 'Fascism' has been indiscriminately used for a long time not only in political propaganda, where anything goes, but also on the level of serious political analysis. A great many people have been termed Fascists by their political opponents on various occasions: Trotsky, the Pope, Greek kings, Austrian chancellors, Polish marshals, Latin American adventurers, and, of course, Stalin himself.

Purists will argue, on the other hand, that it is doubtful whether the term 'Fascism' ought to be applied to any movement or state other than Italy. There was, of course, much common ground between Hitler and Mussolini, and not only Communists have been reluctant to use the term 'National Socialist' when dealing with the Hitler movement and the Third Reich. But all generalizations about Fascism are to some extent misleading; they tend to disregard some very essential differences between Italian Fascism and Nazism.[11]

To overcome these difficulties some writers have suggested that one should differentiate between left-wing, right-wing, and 'centre' Fascism. There is something to be said for this exercise, but it is not certain whether it will help us very much. So-called left-wing Fascism may be closer in inspiration to left-wing parties than to right-wing Fascism which is the extreme fringe of traditional conservatism. There is no 'ideal type' Fascism that can serve as a yardstick for all Fascist movements. One could regard Italian Fascism as the norm, and German National Socialism as a deviation or aberration arising from specifically German historical circumstances. It would be equally justified to consider Italian Fascism as a half-way house on the way to a full totalitarian state. Mussolini, after all, had to coexist with both the Church and the Monarchy. Totalitarianism prevailed in Germany only during the late years of the Third Reich. If there are, nevertheless, weighty arguments for describing both Germany and Italy as Fascist, the term ought to be used only with circumspection in regard to other parties and countries. The custom prevailed in Europe (in the nineteen-twenties and thirties) of designating as Fascist all governments that had their opponents shot; since many governments at the time engaged in this pastime there was a whole crop of Fascisms. If such a government, in addition to applying repressive measures, also used a certain amount of social demagogy, there was no doubt at all about its 'Fascist character'. In reality, many of these regimes were simply military dictatorships or authoritarian governments which were trying (mostly with very little success) to become more streamlined and to gain a 'mass basis'.

The warnings of some Italian Communist leaders that it was misleading to call all repressive political regimes Fascist were not heeded in Moscow. At one time or another Soviet leaders and the Comintern discovered Fascism in most parts of the globe. Trotsky used the term both with regard to Léon Daudet in France and to the situation in Bulgaria; there was much talk about 'agrarian Fascism' and even about 'exotic Fascism'.[12] It should be added, in fairness, that this confusion about the real character of Fascism was by no means confined to the Communists.

This loose talk betrayed a great deal of ideological inconsistency. If one regarded Fascism (as the Communists did after 1924) as the weapon of monopoly (or finance) capitalism, how could one possibly talk about 'agrarian Fascism' or about Fascism in Eastern Europe, the Balkans, in Asia, or Latin America?

In the twenties little thought was given in Moscow to a 'scientific explanation' of Fascism. In its post-mortem on Italy the Comintern said that Fascism was the punishment of the proletariat for failing to continue the revolution begun in Russia; Fascism, as Palme Dutt then put it, was the child of (Social Democratic) reformism. Fascism arose where a powerful working-class movement reached a stage of growth which inevitably raised revolutionary issues, yet was held back from revolutionary action by the Social Democratic leaders.[13] What was the class character of Fascism? According to the fashionable version at that time, in its early phase it brought together the rootless in every stratum; at a period of revolutionary ferment, Fascism even flirted with proletarian demands. But as the acute economic crisis passed, the Fascists went over to the bourgeoisie.

According to the same version, Fascism originally included revolutionary tendencies directed against capitalism and the bourgeois state, but gradually it had become a counter-revolutionary force.[14]

Some steps were taken to combat Fascism. An anti-Fascist manifesto was published and one of the first 'front' organizations was established – the International Committee for Action against the War Danger and Fascism, led by Henri Barbusse and Clara Zetkin. But this organization was not very active; there were normal political and economic relations between Russia and Italy and an officially sponsored anti-Fascist campaign might have had unwelcome consequences.

Fascism, in brief, was an enemy. But it was by no means the worst, or the most dangerous enemy. If the Italian Communists drew some lessons from their defeat, their comrades elsewhere did not benefit from this; whenever a crisis occurred in the nineteen-twenties the Communists with an uncanny instinct continued to take the wrong position. This is not the place for a detailed discussion of events in Bulgaria in 1923 or Poland in 1926. Suffice it to say that in June 1923 the left-wing peasant party government in Sofia was overthrown by a military clique with strong pro-Fascist inclinations. Instead of actively resisting this pro-Fascist *coup*, the local Communist leaders (including Georgi Dimitrov) welcomed it with 'a certain amount of relief', called on the masses to abstain from armed struggle and 'not to pull the chestnuts out of the fire for their own exploiters and oppressors'.[15] It remains to be added that Moscow disagreed with the stand taken by the local comrades and compelled them to change their policy. But the Bulgarian mistake was not an isolated episode, nor was it entirely fortuitous.

In May 1926 the Polish Communists faced a rather similar situation; the democratically elected government of Wincenti Witos, the peasant leader, was overthrown by Pilsudski. Polish Communists thought Pilsudski was the lesser evil and they called for a united front against the 'Fascist government of Witos'. In the general strike declared by Polish Communists and socialists all trains were stopped – only Pilsudski's troops were let through.[16] Moscow was again very angry, mainly, perhaps, because Pilsudski was a sworn enemy of the Soviet Union, but its sharp criticism did not prevent similar 'mistakes' by local Communist parties in later years.

It is highly unlikely that a different stand taken by the Bulgarian or the Polish Communists would have decisively influenced the course of events in these countries; the Communists were weak, particularly in Poland. However, the reaction of these Communist parties was certainly of great symptomatic interest. As far as Fascist or pro-Fascist parties were concerned, they were no more able to identify them than a man who is colour blind can tell the difference between red, green, and blue.

Germany

In 1922 Moscow learned of a local radical group in Bavaria led by one Adolf Hitler; for some time it was to be at a loss to judge its significance. National Socialism was in those days a provincial Bavarian affair; since the Communists were weak in Munich, there were few direct clashes between the two parties and certainly no major confrontation. The early Nazi Party was thought to be a '*petit bourgeois* revolutionary group', which 'owed much of its success to the justified indignation of the German middle classes against the mutilation of Germany by the Versailles Treaty'.[17] The struggle of the Nazis (according to this source) was primarily directed against the Social Democrats, and only incidentally against Germany's enemies.[18] Hitler's ideological antics were not taken very seriously; after the failure of his *putsch* he was called a megalomaniac philistine (*grössenwahnsinnig gewordener Spiessbuerger*)[19] who had stolen much of his programme from the left. Hitler was thought to be a somewhat comic figure, certainly not a dangerous opponent, though leading Soviet and German Communists were quite aware of the potentially explosive effect of national slogans in a defeated country. At the time Radek thought the strong emphasis on national demands in Germany was as revolutionary as the demand for national independence in a colony; the German nation was in the gravest danger and only the German proletariat could save it.[20] The short flirtation between Communists and some right-wing German extremists in 1923 is well known and need not be retold here; Hitler nowhere entered the picture.

Towards the end of 1923 the immediate post-war German crisis was nearing its end; the inflation was over, the Communists had not succeeded in making any significant advance, and Hitler too had failed in his attempt to gain power in Munich. The defeat of the Nazi movement was explained in Moscow as the result of an internal quarrel. The argument was very ingenious and rather confused; Hitler had received money from both French and German heavy industry. But since France merely wanted him for his nuisance value, it would never put up with a strong German Fascist Government which could constitute a real danger. German heavy industry had also stopped its subsidies; as a result Hitler had decided to 'go it alone' – and had failed.[21] Hitler was now expendable; since the Communist danger had passed the ruling classes no longer needed him. In future his party, if it continued to exist at all, would undoubtedly become more radical.

Most Russian and German Communists now thought that they had fought against a mere chimera. The big capitalists and the middle class which supported them had easily prevailed over Hitler; nobody was taking the Nazis seriously any more.[22] There were a few dissenting voices arguing that this was a mistaken and potentially dangerous attitude, that there was no reason to be less watchful *vis-à-vis* the danger of the *voelkisch* and Fascist movement, even if it had suffered a set-back.[23] ('*Voelkisch*', incidentally, was translated into Russian as '*narodnicheski*', surely a very inept rendering, for the Nazis did not have much in common with the Russian populists of the eighteen eighties.) Nobody paid much attention to these Cassandras. When the editors of the *Large Soviet Encyclopedia* summarized their views on Hitler and Nazism in the late twenties, they left no doubt about the way things in Germany were going – the National Socialist movement had lost its importance for the bourgeoisie and Hitler had ceased to play a significant rôle.[24] Encyclopedias, unfortunately, take longer to prepare and publish than newspapers; when the volume appeared in print the Nazi Party had once again reappeared as a major political factor on the German political scene.

'*Social Fascism*'

In July 1928, when the leaders of the Communist International met for their sixth and longest Congress ever, the danger of Nazism seemed a long way off. The one German delegate who so much as mentioned it, said that the Fascist movement in Germany was not really an important factor in terms of political power.[25] Yet Fascism figured very prominently at this Congress and in its resolutions – not the movement of Mussolini or Hitler but 'social Fascism', as represented by the Social Democratic and labour parties of Europe. The strategy then adopted was to be followed for almost seven years. It was based on the assumption that the capitalist world was about to enter a new (third) period of revolutionary crisis. The first revolutionary post-war period had given way to economic and political stabilization all over Europe and the United States. However, this prosperity was nearing its end; for the new revolutionary situation a new revolutionary policy would be needed.

The prediction of a new economic crisis was justified by subsequent events; Communists, to be sure, had made similar predictions every other year and it could be argued that sooner or later their prophecies were bound to come true. This does not detract from the fact that the Communists confidently predicted the world economic crisis almost a year before its first signs could be detected and at a time when few other observers were likely to agree with them. They were mistaken not in their economic prognosis but in their political predictions, namely, in assuming that, in the coming revolutionary crisis, an extremist policy would bring them victory.

As a result 'social Fascism' was declared the main enemy – a blatant case of political misjudgment if ever there was one. Even thirty-five years later the historian finds it difficult to understand the reasons that induced people who were no novices in politics to pursue a strategy that completely isolated them and greatly helped Fascism in its victory in Germany and elsewhere.

The adoption of the 'social Fascism' line originated in Moscow, like everything else in the Comintern at that time. Stalin, who had emerged then as the sole leader in the Kremlin, had stated in 1924 that Fascism and social democracy were twins. Not that Stalin alone should be blamed; one does not know of any opposition to this policy at a time when criticism was still possible. Outside Russia, too, there were not many dissenters – the Social Democrats were, after all, the Communists' main rivals in their struggle for leadership of the working class. Everywhere, in France, England, and, above all, in Germany, they blocked the way. Were not the German Social Democrats responsible for the failure of the German Revolution in 1919? Had they not preferred to collaborate with right-wing army leaders rather than Spartacus? Had they not declared that they hated revolution like sin? Had they not betrayed the legacy of Marxism? Did they not bear responsibility for the murder of Liebknecht and Rosa Luxemburg, the leaders of the extreme left in Germany? In the German trade unions and other working class organizations the Communists clashed time and time again with the Social Democrats; the Nazis were not serious competitors, at least not during the early days: they got their support from different social strata.

The Russians, too, found it much easier to co-operate with 'bourgeois' and right-wing personalities in Weimar Germany than with the Social Democrats, who were not willing to forgive the Bolsheviks the suppression of Russian social democracy after 1917. There was much military collaboration between Soviet Russia and Weimar Germany in the nineteen twenties, and since it was in direct violation of the Treaty of Versailles, it was kept strictly secret. The right-wing German Army commanders could be relied upon to keep confidences, but the leading Social Democrats were uneasy about it and on occasion did not hesitate to reveal some facts about what seemed to them an unholy alliance. All this made the Soviet leaders very angry indeed, and undoubtably added fuel to the campaign against 'social Fascism'.

There were some dissenters; Togliatti, for one, who argued that even if there were close ideological and organizational ties between

Fascism and social democracy, there was a basic difference between the two;[26] but the Italian leader soon had to renounce such heretical opinions. Those who refused to recant were branded as traitors and excluded from the world Communist movement.

To summarize again, official Communist policy was that social democracy was in the process of becoming a Fascist Party and that it was the main enemy of Communism. This theme was laboured in countless books, speeches, articles, and slogans. Social democracy in Germany was the most active factor of fascization; it was 'socialism in theory, Fascism in practice' (Thaelmann – the German Communist chief).[27] Bela Kun, former leader of the Hungarian Communists and now a leading figure in the Comintern, maintained that even the victory of Fascism would not stop the fascization of social democracy.[28] The Russian comrades were equally outspoken. Even Radek, who should have known better, argued that the idea of a common front with social democracy was simply ridiculous since the Social Democrats were 'growing' into a front with the Nazis.[29] Georg Lukacs, the noted literary historian and Marxist philosopher, who was still permitted to write about political subjects at that time, was not less emphatic: 'As servants of monopoly capitalism, Fascism and social democracy have an inner link' ('*gehoeren innerlich zusammen*').[30] Kuusinen, another leading Comintern thinker, believed he had discovered similar developments not only in Europe but also in America, where the socialists and the American Federation of Labor helped Roosevelt to carry out what were, in fact, Fascist economic measures.[31] In Czechoslovakia, too, Fascism had allegedly been introduced under Masaryk and Benes – about the only democrats left in Eastern Europe – and local Communists were upbraided for not fighting it and, in general, for underrating the seriousness of the situation. Manuilsky, yet another Comintern lumen, thought one of the cardinal sins of the Social Democrats was their deliberate attempt to deceive the masses by proclaiming that Fascism was the chief enemy.[32]

Eventually, as the Nazi danger grew nearer, the party members were told that the defeat of the Social Democrats was the precondition for victory over Fascism. Without the rout of the major socialist parties, no Communist victory was possible.[33]

What did this mean in practice? The 'social Fascists' had to be chased from their jobs in the industrial plants, the employment exchanges, and even the apprentice schools and the kindergarten. Had not delegates at the sixth Comintern Congress announced that the solution of the conflict between the Social Democrats and the Communists would eventually be decided by arms?[34] It also meant, for example, Communist participation with the Nazis in the referendum against the Prussian Social-Democratic Government; politically such a decision was sheer lunacy, but in terms of the prevailing general line it made perfect sense. If the Social Democrats (so the argument ran) were introducing Fascism step by step, they obviously had to be stopped. If the Social Democrats were indeed (as Kuusinen had declared) the chief agents of the world bourgeoisie in the preparations for a new world war against the Soviet Union – the sooner they were crushed the better. Their defeat would leave the way free for the Communists to lead the working class in the coming decisive struggles. The emergence of Nazism as the strongest political force in Germany did to some extent shake the confidence of the Russian and German Communists in their policy; if Communist militants were set upon and killed, as often happened after 1930, there could be no doubt about the identity of the attackers. Yet the shock was not sufficient to induce them to change their policy; there were constant appeals for a united front with the Social Democrats against Nazism, but it was to be a united front from below, against the Social-Democratic leadership. Any such offer was unrealistic, and the Communists must have known it. Perhaps they wanted to reassure the growing number of fellow travellers and well-wishers who pointed out the fatal consequences of their policy. Even Hitler's ascent to power did not cause a basic change in approach; Moscow and the German Communists denied the existence of any essential difference between Nazism and Social Democracy, even after January 30, 1933. Heckert, the German Communist leader, wrote a few days later that 'social Fascism' had now finally become a conscious tool of the Fascist counter-revolution.[35]

Such attacks about the 'fascization of Social Democracy' continued to appear throughout 1933, though German Social Democracy, together with German Communism, had already ceased to exist.[36] Even in the spring of 1934, when thousands of Hitler's political enemies had already been killed in concentration camps, the *Communist International* continued to publish manifestos that 'a break with Social Democracy was the prerequisite to prevent Fascism and to overthrow the Fascist dictatorship'.[37] Only in the summer of 1934 was a reappraisal carried out in Moscow. The fatal consequences of the campaign against the Social Democrats were realized and the grosser attacks were discontinued. But even then there was considerable reluctance to admit that Social Democracy and Fascism were not really the same thing. New and ingenious explanations were made; the author of one of the very few books on Nazi doctrine ever published in the Soviet Union compared Social Democracy and Hitlerism to two horses of different race and colour who were yet pulling in the same trace. They were indeed different, they *had* to be different and to quarrel; the outward show of a basic conflict between them was the most important asset of the bourgeoisie which was calling the tune.[38] Palme Dutt, the British Communist theoretician, put it in a very similar way: The aims of Social Democracy and Fascism were the same, they differed only in their methods.[39]

A more detailed analysis shows certain minor fluctuations. Between summer 1930 and April 1931 the Communists in Germany showed more awareness of the Nazi danger than in the period after that – not because the danger of Nazism had decreased in 1931, but because the Comintern had intervened. In October 1932, on the other hand, German Communists were again criticized by Moscow – this time for ignoring the Nazi danger altogether.[40] These ups and downs are undoubtedly of great significance for the historian of that period and ought to be studied in detail.* What matters in this context is that basically the political line did not change during the whole period. Of the Communists' many enemies, Social Democracy was thought to be the worst.

* What Russian and German Communists wrote and said at the time for the record can be fully documented. There is no such full picture about their internal discussions at top level, possible doubts and reservations about their attitude to Nazism. The Comintern archives are of course not open to inspection but a great amount of material has recently been made available in the declassified German records at the World War II Records Division, at the National Archives in Washington. This includes very substantial files of correspondence, internal circular letters, minutes of meetings, etc., of the Central Committee of the German Communist Party, referring both to the period 1930–3 and to Communist activities in the Third Reich. Incomplete as they are, they throw new light on the Communist attitude towards Social Democracy, their appraisal of Nazism, their activities as an illegal party, the 'popular front campaign', their reaction to the non-aggression pact of 1939 and to many other important issues. Of particular interest are the internal Communist bulletins about enemy activities ('*Mitteilungen über gegnerische Parteien*', '*Information–aus der NSDAP*'. etc.) published in 1931–2. I refer specifically to files such as EAP 173-b-16-05/114–466. They also include much source material about the activities of other European Communist parties in the nineteen-thirties, and of various socialist and anti-Nazi groups. This indispensable material has provided much of the general background to the present study, though I have only infrequently given specific quotations.

The End of the Weimar Republic

In the Germany of 1928, the Weimar Republic seemed relatively prosperous and stable and nothing appeared less likely than a major crisis. In the 1928 elections the Social Democrats polled almost one third of the votes, the Communists ten per cent and the National Socialists a mere 2·6 per cent of the total. The Social Democrats formed a government and their chances of providing sound, if uninspired, leadership seemed excellent. Yet they had been in power for only a few months when the economic crisis overtook them. The number of unemployed, two millions in the winter of 1928–9, showed a steady rise, and the Reich was in serious financial trouble. During this period of strain it became apparent how shaky were the roots of the democratic institutions; the Social Democrats and the centre parties were unable to cope with the crisis, and the radical and anti-democratic movements made quick progress. Eventually the coalition between the Social Democrats and their allies of the centre broke up and a right-wing catholic leader, Dr Bruening, took over in March 1930. In the next general election, in September of that year, there was a sudden startling reversal of the traditional political pattern. The Social Democrats, held responsible for Germany's domestic failures and accused of pursuing a policy of 'fulfilment' towards those powers who had imposed the Versailles Treaty on Germany, received only a quarter of the total vote. The Communists made some slight progress but, far more decisive, the Nazis, an insignificant sect only two years before, now emerged as the second strongest party in Germany with more than twenty-two per cent of the total vote.

This, in brief, was the general background of the German crisis. Nobody was prepared for it – with the single exception of Hitler and his friends who were quick to adapt themselves to the new situation. The Communists, on the other hand, who had predicted the crisis, showed far less ability in this respect.

Stalin was preoccupied on the home front in 1930 and had little time for foreign political issues, except the most important ones. Those responsible for Soviet foreign policy were not unduly perturbed at first by the turn of events in Germany. We do not know what Soviet diplomats in Germany reported home, and we shall not know for a long time; from the German documents it would appear that Hitler and the Nazi Party were hardly ever discussed in conversations between German and Soviet diplomats in 1930 and 1931. As far as the planners of Soviet foreign policy were concerned, the normal-to-good relations between the two countries were to continue. They certainly did not regret the fall of the Social Democratic Government in 1930, for the Social Democrats had always been an awkward partner from the Soviet point of view. German diplomats failed to explain to their Soviet colleagues that *Vorwaerts* (the organ of the Social Democrats) was not the mouthpiece of the German Government and that its attacks on Bolshevism should not be taken as an authoritative expression of government policy.

Later on, Soviet diplomats began to pay some attention to the Nazi movement; Hitler's *Mein Kampf* was read and the Nazi press followed by Soviet observers. Litvinov once complained about the *Angriff*, Goebbels' mouthpiece, but this was in 1932 when the Nazis had already emerged as the strongest party in Germany.[41] Soviet public figures, such as Lunacharsky (who visited Germany in 1931–2) or Krestinsky, discounted the possibility of a Fascist victory in Germany; the Nazis had won some popularity through their anti-French demagogy, but the majority would not support Hitler.[42] There were some articles in the Soviet press by Radek and other observers of the German scene, but with very few exceptions they showed little understanding of the situation. By and large, scant attention was paid to the phenomenon of 'national Fascism', as the Nazi Party was called, to distinguish it from the Social Democrats – the 'social Fascists'. For a Soviet reader who wanted to know about Hitler and his supporters there was not a single book on the subject. All he had to go on were some speeches by the Comintern leaders, like Manuilsky, Pyatnitsky, Kuusinen, or Knorin, who had emerged as experts on Germany. These men did not actually belong to the front rank of Soviet leaders, but they had a professional stake in German affairs. None of them showed much interest in the rise of 'national Fascism'. Strangest of all was the lack of awareness among those most directly concerned, the German Communist leaders such as Thaelmann, the Hamburg worker, and his supporters. Little guidance or comment could be elicited from them.

In June 1929, the German Communists had met for their twelfth (and last) party congress in Weimar Germany; there was a long programmatic address by Thaelmann and more speeches by other leaders; on Hitler and his movement there was not a word, apart from random remarks by regional delegates who said that Communists should not neglect to discuss the situation with Nazi workers. The working class was sympathetic towards a dictatorship.[43] There were indications early in 1930 that the German Communists were somewhat perturbed by the intensified Nazi activities and their successes in local elections. The slogan that had been given out – 'Beat the Fascists wherever you meet them' (*'Schlagt die Faschisten wo ihr sie trefft'*), was withdrawn; the fight against Fascism should be stepped up, but the Communists ought to differentiate between the Nazi leaders and their working-class followers who would doubtless turn their backs on the Nazis soon.

German Communists were not, however, impressed by the great Nazi successes in the 1930 elections. September 14, 1930, was the zenith of the Nazi movement, *Rote Fahne* wrote the day after, and from now on it would weaken and decline. One year later Thaelmann still maintained that September 14, 1930, had been Hitler's greatest day. He advised the Comintern not to overrate the Fascist danger; the Nazi movement, he maintained, was in process of disintegration. Other Communist leaders, such as Muenzenberg, were less sanguine and demanded that the 'greatest attention' should be paid to National Socialism.[45]

The German Communists realized that to compete with the Nazis they had to put stress on nationalist themes in their propaganda. In 1930 they adopted a new programme ('for the national and social liberation of the German people'), in which they declared, *inter alia*, their unswerving opposition to the Versailles Peace Treaty which, they said, had enslaved the German people. Slogans alone, however, would not do the trick; the Nazis could always outdo, in nationalist demagogy, a party that identified itself so closely with a foreign power.

If there was no real attempt to analyse and understand Nazism, the label 'Fascist' was freely bandied about. Thaelmann had announced in the Reichstag in February 1930 that Fascism was already in power in Germany – this at a time when the Social Democrats still headed the government.[46] More than a year later he said that Fascism would not come to Germany with Hitler – it was there already. This was by no means Thaelmann's private foible; the general feeling in his party was that the danger looming from the right-wing and Catholic parties, from Hindenburg and Bruening, was as big, if not bigger, than the Nazi menace. The Nazi Party, according to this reasoning, was only one wing, and not necessarily the most dangerous one, of the Fascist movement in Germany.[47]

When the Social Democratic government was followed by a coalition of the Catholics, with some of the right-of-centre parties, both Russian and German Communists had no doubt that this government was already 'Fascist in its kernel' (Radek).[48] The only issue to decide was whether it was already a fully fledged Fascist government or a government that was gradually to establish the Fascist dictatorship in Germany. On these issues there were protracted discussions that might have continued forever had not the Bruening government in its turn given way (in May 1932) to a more right-wing cabinet. This created certain problems for those who had already argued before that the Bruening government had been Fascist. No difference was made between the Nazi, the centre parties and the right-wing, conservative groups. Since they all had the same class interests, what major political conflicts could there be between them?

Karl Radek

Mention has already been made of Karl Radek, undoubtedly the most intelligent Communist commentator on international affairs at the time. An early supporter of Lenin, he had lived in Germany before the First World War. After having been exiled as a member of the Soviet party opposition in 1927 he had recanted and was re-employed as a star commentator in the Soviet press. There is some doubt whether his writing still influenced Soviet policies, but he was certainly given more latitude than any other Soviet political writer at the time. For that reason, if for no other, his comments remain of interest.

Radek became interested in the Nazi movement in 1930–1 and wrote a substantial essay on Hitler and his party in January 1932.[49] Hitler was a hireling of monopoly capitalism, of this there was no doubt. But like a typical Praetorian chief he was trying to haggle about the price for his services. In the early days he had been the leader of a *petit bourgeois* movement which burst like a bubble after the capitalists no longer needed him. The lower middle class was still with Hitler, but he had attracted other strata as well. The typical *petit bourgeois*, Radek wrote, likes to boast, not to fight; Hitler's storm troopers had therefore to be enlisted from the *lumpenproletariat*. The Nazi Party differed from the other bourgeois parties by its strong emphasis on military organization.

According to Radek, both British and French monopoly capitalists were sympathetic to Hitler's social policy, but as a representative of

214

German monopoly capitalism the Fuehrer could not very well be pro-French. He wanted to come to power legally – on this point Radek was more correct than Trotsky. The class character of the German Government would not change in any way with Hitler's ascent to power. For the Communists, however, it would mean merciless persecution – on this, too, Radek saw more clearly than most of his comrades.

Hitler's attacks on Social Democracy, Radek thought, were mere demagogy; they were his rivals for the goodwill of the big capitalists: Hitler wanted to be the *only* representative of finance capital. As for Bruening, Radek, never at a loss for trenchant phrases, maintained that he was a 'Fascist whom the Fascist party was fighting'. Radek undoubtedly had grave misgivings about the Nazi Party, but he did not really expect a Nazi victory; in a great country like Germany, how could a party triumph that had no serious political, social, or economic programme, but merely a ridiculous nationalistic mystique! Radek's understanding of the real driving forces in European politics in the thirties was, after all, quite limited; or, to be precise, it was strictly circumscribed by a doctrine into which Nazism did not fit. In one of his longer essays written in 1932 he relates with indignation a little incident that happened at the Social Democratic party conference that year. Eckstein, one of the speakers of the party left-wing (he subsequently founded his own group, the SAP), asked in what way the present (Bruening) government differed from a Fascist government. One of the majority leaders, Wels apparently, answered that under present circumstances he (Eckstein) could oppose the government, under Hitler he would find himself in prison.[50] Radek was at his most ironic: what a ridiculous answer, what an open admission of bankruptcy, what an expression of willingness on the part of the Social Democrats to co-operate in the execution of a Fascist policy!

Eighteen months later Eckstein was killed by the storm troopers, one of the first victims of the Nazis.

1932

When 1932 dawned, the fabric of republican Germany was in a state of disintegration. Six million unemployed in the streets and the rapidly worsening economic situation compelled the quickly changing minority governments to cut unemployment benefits and other social services. In March Hitler got more than thirteen million votes in the elections for *Reichspraesident*; a democratic majority was now impossible since National Socialists and Communists together had a majority. The shortlived governments ruled by emergency orders and decrees. The Social Democrats and the centre parties showed utter helplessness *vis-à-vis* the rising Nazi tide; they seemed to be paralysed by fear. Frequent elections only made the atmosphere more feverish; German democracy was clearly in its death throes.

In Moscow and among the Communist leaders in Berlin there were now high hopes as to the probable outcome of what was clearly, according to all the textbooks, a revolutionary situation. Nazism was still regarded as a transitory phenomenon; nothing would be more fatal than an opportunist exaggeration of its importance (Thaelmann wrote at the beginning of 1932), nothing more ridiculous than creating a panic, as the Social Democrats did. The SPD was still the main pillar of the German bourgeoisie, as it had been formerly.[51] Departing for a moment from their unflagging antagonism to the SPD, the KPD called (at the last moment, it is true) for a general strike against the deposition of the Social Democratic government in Prussia in July 1932; to this there was no response. After that, the proposals for a 'united front from below' were renewed – with the Social Democratic masses against the Social Democratic leaders and under Communist leadership. Some Communists thought that the Fascist menace had now reached dangerous proportions and that a major setback for the socialists also threatened German Communism. These were the views of a few dissidents, the general consensus of opinion being that the overthrow of the Prussian Social Democratic Government was a very good thing; Fascism, after all, could only be defeated after Social Democracy had been smashed. Was the prospect of a Fascist government so terrible after all, would it not also depend, as Thaelmann put it, on the toleration of the working class?[52]

Meanwhile, Hitler's triumphant advance continued. In the election of July 1932 his movement polled thirty-eight per cent of the total, emerging as far the biggest party. Moscow was not worried, or at least pretended not to be. The German Communist Party had also increased its vote: if the Nazi advance had been incomparably bigger, what did that matter? Only riff-raff supported the Nazis, whereas the Communists had the support of class-conscious workers. There was a basic difference in quality.

To discuss the situation in Germany, yet another plenum (the twelfth of the Communist International) was convened in Moscow in August 1932. It decided once again that the main blow (*'glavny udar'*) should be directed against Social Democracy. Manuilski thought it highly unlikely that the German bourgeoisie would hand over power to Hitler, because he was obviously incapable of saving German capitalism;[53] he was merely needed as a counterweight against the rapidly growing Communist Party. Even Radek, a more astute observer of the German scene than the Comintern spokesmen, agreed. The real masters of Germany (the *Reichswehr* and the *Herrenklub*) would not surrender power to Hitler, for they did not want to weaken Social Democracy too much.[54] Soviet diplomats in Berlin seemed far more concerned about Papen's foreign policy than about the growth of the Hitler movement and the danger of a Nazi dictatorship. They feared Papen's pro-French and anti-Soviet policy and expected a radical turn for the worse in Soviet–German relations. There is no way of knowing whether they, too, believed in the official version of the ripening revolutionary crisis and that German Communism was about to launch a mighty counter-offensive.

For a moment it appeared as if this optimism might be justified; in the elections of November 1932, the Nazis lost two million votes, the Communists made a further advance and got almost seventeen per cent of the poll. Kuusinen announced in Moscow that Nazism was in process of disintegration. Knorin thought that Hitler's strength lay in his demagogy, and demagogy alone was not enough to establish a dictatorship. Radek alone put in a word of warning: the decline of the Nazis should not be overrated; the well-to-do had dropped out, but the party had preserved its mass basis.[55] The German Communists were jubilant; the leaders of the KPD saw in their advance the justification of their policy, including such recent actions as the Berlin transport strike which they had organized together with the Nazis against the decision of the trade union. At last they were on the offensive; the masses had begun to understand that 'chauvinism would not destroy the Versailles Treaty'.[56]

Nobody could be quite sure during these months about the party line *vis-à-vis* the Social Democrats. Pyatnitsky complained that some members had overdone anti-Social-Democratic propaganda; the impression had been created that the Communist Party actually preferred Hitler to Social Democracy. It is difficult to see how such an impression could have been avoided, in view of the continued campaign against the Social Democrats and the assertion that the task of the party remained as before, to direct the chief blow against Social Democracy.[57] Confusion reigned.

Trotsky

Amongst the veterans of the Communist movement there were a few who fully realized the insanity of the official line on Fascism and Germany. The most prominent among them was Trotsky, at that time an exile on the Turkish island of Prinkipo. In a steady stream of articles and pamphlets between 1929 and 1933 Trotsky commented on the situation in Germany. Though he had no first-hand information about events there, his comments and predictions were much less misguided than the official Comintern line.

In former years Trotsky had revealed no particular interest in Fascism. His *obiter dicta* in the twenties do not betray any deeper understanding; in 1924, for instance, he had reasoned that Fascism could not possibly last. It was merely an instrument of the bourgeoisie to be used in extreme situations; if the bourgeoisie remained in power (as in Germany in 1923) it would discard fascism, 'for the bourgeoisie could not coexist for long with a Fascist regime, just as the proletariat could not live for years in a state of armed insurrection'.[58] Menshevism would gradually replace Fascism – this was Trotsky's prognosis at the time. Nor did he show prophetic gifts when he wrote in 1930 that the most important objective conditions for a proletarian revolution were then in existence in Germany.[59]

It is not certain to what extent Trotsky merely paid lip service to such revolutionary formulations; had he been less optimistic the Stalinists would have found it easy to attack him. Trotsky had realized from the start that the whole Comintern 'third period' policy was mistaken and that the Communist parties of central Europe, far from taking the offensive, would have to follow a defensive line in co-operation with the Social Democrats. By 1931 he had understood that Hitler was far more likely than Thaelmann to benefit from the crisis. The Comintern regarded the Hitler movement as a 'belated reaction of the bourgeoisie to the crisis of the twenties', whereas Trotsky noted, quite correctly, that Nazism, far from being a 'belated reaction', was in a very strong starting position on the eve of a new crisis.[60] He thundered time and time again against equating Bruening with Hitler. 'The wiseacres who claim that they see no difference between Bruening and Hitler are in fact stating that it makes no difference whether our organizations exist or whether they are already destroyed.'[61]

Of more immediate interest in this context than Trotsky's tactical advice to German Communism is his appraisal of the Nazi movement. This he described as the party of the *petit bourgeois* running amok, the movement of counter-revolutionary despair, supported by the 'human dust', the *Kleinbuerger*. Fascism came to power as the party of the *petite bourgeoisie*, and as a ruling party it shed all its socialist demagogy and became the most merciless dictatorship of monopoly capitalism.

Trotsky's appraisal of the character of the Nazi Party was not very different from that of the Comintern – or, for that matter, of Marx's description of the social basis of Louis Bonaparte in 1851. He seriously underrated the impact of nationalist mystique in Germany, and his judgment of the power and the internal cohesion of both working class and *petite bourgeoisie* was seriously distorted by his political sympathies. He had no real conception of the mainsprings of Nazism's successes and of its hold over so many millions. He realized far more clearly than Stalin, Thaelmann, or the Comintern chiefs that it was suicidal to declare (as they did): let Hitler come to power, we are not afraid of him; he will soon go bankrupt and then it will be our day. He understood that the victory of Nazism would mean a decisive setback for Communism in Europe, the destruction of the German Communist Party, and, ultimately, war against the Soviet Union.

Trotsky felt instinctively that Nazism meant something far more explosive than one could conclude from the premises of traditional socio-economic rationalizations – that it was a relapse into barbarism. He was unable to explain the fascination Nazism exerted, not only on the 'human dust' but on a great party of the German people, the enthusiasm and fanaticism it inspired. Phrases about counter-revolutionary despair were quite inadequate to explain these phenomena. Trotsky, however, realized that, once established in power, the Nazis would be exceedingly difficult to dislodge; it had, after all, taken historic earthquakes and a war to overthrow Louis Napoleon.

Trotsky had no clear concept of the essentially new elements in Nazism; Hitler appeared to him an arch-reactionary, a super-Wrangel; it was very difficult, apparently, to dispense with the terminology of the Russian revolution. He thought that, once in power, Fascism would become bureaucratic in character and thus grow into a regular police dictatorship;[61] the idea of a totalitarian state no doubt appeared meaningless to him. Yet he sensed the impending disaster – hence the incongruity between his orthodox Marxist–Leninist class analysis and the great concern, indeed alarm, in his predictions.

The Comintern, needless to say, sharply condemned what it called the criminal theories of an utterly bankrupt Fascist. Such denunciations make Trotsky's comments appear in retrospect more farsighted than they really were. The more extravagant claims subsequently made by some of Trotsky's pupils are not really justified. Trotsky called for an anti-Fascist united front but was he really willing and able to co-operate with the Social Democratic leaders? He equated democracy with capitalism and had chided the Social Democrats for many years for defending democracy. His whole conception was shaped by the course of the Russian Revolution of 1917; it so happened that the German situation in 1932 differed in most essential aspects. His ideological equipment enabled him to analyse and understand the socio-economic trends behind Hitler's rise to power, but Nazism was not only, and not mainly, a socio-economic trend.

The Last Weeks

Nazism passed through a serious political and financial crisis in the winter of 1932–3, but confusion and defeatism were even more pronounced in the camp of its opponents. The conservative von Papen government, which had no parliamentary support whatever, gave way in early December to a cabinet led by General Schleicher, who tried by means of a series of highly ingenious but wholly ineffective political manoeuvres to isolate Hitler. Eventually Schleicher himself fell victim to an intrigue of conservative politicians who reached an understanding with Hitler in early January. Hitler became chancellor on a day that was to be remembered for many years.

The general turmoil had by now infected the Comintern and the German Communist leadership. Outwardly the general line did not change; there was a strange equanimity in most official announcements, as if it was in the Communist interest that Hitler should seize power. *Pravda* authoritatively stated that even extreme Fascist terror would merely bring about a sharpening of the class struggle and the growth of the German Communist Party: this argument was not dropped even after Hitler had taken over. 'Hitler's rise to power hastens the revolutionary crisis.'[63]

At the same time, however, doubts were voiced whether the capitalists would agree to give Hitler any power before he had purged his party of its quasi-socialist traits.[64] According to the official party line, any common action with the Social Democrats (let alone with non-socialist opponents of Hitler) was still out of the question, but some of the regional Communist organizations, if not the party executive, showed that they now regarded Hitler as the main danger; there were agreements on the local level and even joint demonstrations.[65] By this time the Communists were as much on the defensive as the Social Democrats and it is extremely doubtful whether even common action by the two working-class parties would have prevented Hitler's rise to power at this late stage.

January 30 took the Communist leadership by surprise; Soviet press comment showed that Schleicher and his backers were thought to be far stronger than they really were. Knorin, the Comintern German expert, assured the *Pravda* staff on January 30 that it was foolish to assume that the German bourgeoisie would give up even the slightest part of its powers to Hitler. The possibility of a coup by the SA was even less likely; the *Reichswehr* would in no circumstances put up with a Hitler dictatorship.[66] In a letter written during the Nazi era, Torgler, one of the former leaders of the German Communist Party, reported that when he asked Thaelmann to declare a state of special preparedness in the party on January 29, Thaelmann replied: 'You are mad. The bourgeoisie won't let Hitler anywhere near power. Let's go to Lichtenberg to play skittles.'[67] That all the warning signs should have been so blatantly disregarded is clear evidence of the mistaken interpretation of Nazism generally held at the time.

If one form of Fascist dictatorship was already in existence in Germany, the worst that could possibly happen was the emergence of a different variety. There was also an unwavering belief in the omnipotence of the finance and monopoly capitalists; they, and only they, were making and breaking chancellors and governments. The idea that Nazism could have a political momentum of its own, that it could perhaps even play off the great capitalists against each other for its own ends, does not seem to have occurred to any one influential figure in Communist politics at that time.

Or perhaps it did, but it certainly did not find expression in official manifestos, editorials, or the party policy at that time. It is only fair to add that there was all along considerable covert opposition in the

Communist Party of Germany and other European countries to the campaign against 'social Fascism' and the whole 'third period' concept. From internal evidence one gathers that there was on occasion a more realistic appraisal of the Nazi danger than one would surmise on the basis of the study of the official documents. In a speech at KPD headquarters on December 18, 1932, one of the party's leading figures told some fifty of his colleagues that it was far too early to rejoice at Hitler's setback, that Germany was moving towards Fascism at a frantic pace (*in rasendem Tempo*), that the party would probably be made illegal, and that despite the seriousness of the situation many comrades were displaying a frivolous attitude in their preparations for illegality. This attitude was apparently widespread, and it was not quite accidental.[68]

The Dawn of the Third Reich

It is a disconcerting fact that the political judgment even of highly intelligent people is so frequently clouded by wishful thinking. Marx thought that Louis Bonaparte was a bad joke who had come to power with the help of vagabonds, ex-jailbirds, discharged soldiers, swindlers, mountebanks, pickpockets, brothel keepers, rag pickers, organ grinders, etc. (The impressive full list appears in the *Eighteenth Brumaire*.) Engels was convinced that Napoleon III was the most insignificant man in the world and that his adventure could not possibly last. Lassalle likewise believed that it would last 'a very, very short while'; never had he seen a 'greater inability to think in a man'. The only realistic appraisal of the situation came from an entirely unpolitical person, namely, Lassalle's lady friend, Countess Hatzfeld who, in a letter to Marx, not only expressed the fear that the new regime would last for years but, even more surprisingly, analysed the roots of the illusions of her more sophisticated contemporaries. She wrote that they were blinded by their wishful thinking.

There was no thinker on the left of the calibre of a Marx, an Engels, or a Lassalle in 1933, but wishful thinking was just as widespread as in their era. The first Soviet reaction was to call Hitler's success 'very doubtful indeed'; the new government was merely an instrument in the hands of monopoly capitalism, which had kept all the key economic positions in the new cabinet; Hugenberg, a leading industrialist, had been made Economics Minister.[69] This was quite true, and yet utterly irrelevant. In a revolutionary situation it is the key positions alone that matter. Hitler seemed to have a firmer grasp of the realities of power than Lenin's pupils.

Even Radek, who provided the first detailed Soviet comments, continued to believe that January 30, 1933, was merely a further stage in the process of fascization of Germany. (This was the title of his article in *Bolshevik*; later he had second thoughts, and he preferred not to include this essay in a collection of his articles on German affairs.) The monopolists, Radek wrote, still had doubts and hesitations about Hitler; the fact that they had retained all the economic key positions in his government seemed to him of great political significance. Hitler's main problem, according to Radek, was the narrow social basis of his regime; fifteen million German workers could put up much more effective resistance than the Italian proletariat had been able to muster against Mussolini. The Communist Party could be made illegal, but a movement that represented six million voters could not possibly disappear unless Hitler wanted to terrorize the whole working class.[70] This appeared quite unthinkable to Radek.

After the immediate shock of Hitler's accession to power the German Communists appealed on January 30 to the Social Democrats and the trade union leaders, calling for a general strike. Yet, at the very same time, they renewed their bitter attacks on the Social Democrats. How could they refrain from attacking the party that had 'just completed its transformation from social chauvinism to being a conscious weapon of the Fascist dictatorship'?[71]

Meanwhile, Hitler dissolved the German parliament; on February 27, after the Reichstag fire, the Communist Party was made illegal; its property was seized and thousands of its members were arrested. This in itself did not induce the Comintern to change its line: Communist parties, after all, had been through bad times in other countries and there had been persecution and arrests in Russia shortly before the revolution of 1917. According to the official version, the end of the rule of capitalism was very near; the urgent task of the German Communists was now to prepare their October revolution. The Fascist dictatorship was bound to fail in view of its inner contradictions and the objective difficulties facing it; then the Communists would take over.[72] The fact that political parties were banned was not an unmitigated disaster either; from now on only two parties would be left and there would be a direct confrontation between

National Socialism, the party of monopoly capitalism, and Communism, the party of proletarian revolution.

A few weeks later, in Moscow, Fritz Heckert, one of the German party leaders, was asked to give a full report to the Comintern executive about events in Germany. Heckert was almost aggressively optimistic: the bourgeoisie had declared open civil war on the proletariat; decisive battles were near. As a result of the Social Democratic betrayal, the Communists could not carry out a political mass strike on January 30. Thus, Social Democracy had openly passed into the Fascist camp. Never had the moral prestige of German Communism stood so high in the working class; the rumours about the destruction of the KPD were merely the idle talk of philistines and morons. Nobody could destroy a workers' party unless it destroyed itself by pursuing a wrong policy. The situation in Germany was quite different from that in Italy eleven years earlier: Mussolini had come to power at the beginning of an era of capitalist stabilization, whereas German Fascism had triumphed at the end of such a period. Moreover, Communism and the working classes were so much stronger in Germany than in Italy. Even the arrest of several thousand militants could not affect a party with five million voters. Such a belief could be held only by a charlatan or a clown.[73] After listening to this and similar reports, the Comintern executive unanimously passed a resolution stating that the political line of the German Communist Party under Thaelmann had been absolutely correct.[74]

The Russians React

Brave talk and unanimous resolutions could not hide for long the harsh fact that the largest and most respected Communist Party outside the Soviet Union had disappeared, almost overnight, without trace.[75] The German disaster shocked Moscow and it did eventually, albeit with considerable delay, bring about changes in Soviet foreign policy and the strategy of the Comintern. In 1934 the Soviet Union joined the League of Nations (which Nazi Germany had just left), there was a pact with France and the beginning of the 'Popular Front' line. But these changes were not caused by a radical re-examination of the character of Fascism. Rather they were the Soviet reaction to the growing danger of war.

This was made quite clear by Stalin who had refrained (and was to refrain for a long time to come), from any comment on Hitler and the Third Reich. At the Seventeenth Soviet Party Congress in January 1934 Stalin declared that 'of course, we are far from enthusiastic about the Fascist regime in Germany'. Yet he added that Fascism was not really the issue, 'Fascism in Italy has not prevented the USSR from maintaining the best of relations with that country'. The real point was that Germany's foreign policy had changed, that even before Hitler had come to power, and particularly after that, there had been a fight between the old policy (of *rapprochement* with Russia) and the new hostile approach, which recalled the policy of the Kaiser, and the occupation of the Ukraine and the Baltic countries in 1918–19. The supporters of the new policy such as Hugenberg [*sic*] and Rosenberg had gained supremacy.[76]

Germany's foreign policy was of far greater significance to Stalin than its internal affairs, since Russia needed peace. He himself was preoccupied with the five year plan and later with the purges. He had never thought much of the Communist parties outside Russia; he did not trust his own comrades, let alone foreign Communists. At the same time there is no good reason, and certainly no evidence, to assume that Stalin wanted the destruction of German Communism because he was afraid of a Communist Germany as a second centre of world Communism. If Hitler's advent to power had any effect on him it was an indirect one; the growing stress on the *fuehrerprinzip* in the Soviet Union, the return to national traditions which had long been neglected or completely negated. How much these developments owed to the triumph of National Socialism is debatable, for many of them were bound to come anyway once Stalin had committed himself to build 'socialism in one country'.

This lack of reaction to the events in Germany provoked much pained surprise in left-wing circles in Europe. Most of the world's press had denounced the anti-Jewish pogroms, while the Soviet press had only published the bare facts without comment. When four Communist militants were executed in Altona in August 1933 the Soviet newspapers reported 'bourgeois' protests from Western Europe, but there were no protests from those parties which had so emphatically denounced the Sacco and Vanzetti trial and had demanded the release of Tom Mooney and the Scottsboro boys.

Soviet readers must have asked themselves why capitalists should protest against the murder of Communists while they themselves abstained.[77] Nor was it merely a matter of refraining from press comment. The Soviet Union refused to have anything to do with an economic boycott of Germany; instead the renewal of the non-aggression treaty of 1926 was ratified. No Soviet citizen emerged in 1933 to join Einstein, Rolland, and many Western intellectuals in a protest against Nazism. Nor was there any help offered to Jewish refugees though not long before a Jewish autonomous republic, Biro Bidjan, had been founded in the RSFSR, with much fanfare.

Those who justified this policy had of course their own reasons, but how valid were they? It was said that an economic boycott would be ineffectual, which proved to be an accurate forecast. It was argued that protests in newspapers had no effect; this was a curious contention, because it certainly had never before stopped the Soviet press from protesting against many crimes, real or alleged, committed in the capitalist world. It was argued that the Soviet Union could not afford unfriendly gestures *vis-à-vis* Germany which would endanger its freedom of movement. 'The French would know that we would be compelled to adopt a pro-French policy and they would pay less for our friendship.'[78] Decisive in Stalin's eyes were probably other considerations – the fact that the Soviet Union was threatened by Japan in the East, and it would be unwise to involve Russia in any complications in Europe. Besides, the country was ill prepared for a military contest, though this argument, too, is hardly convincing, for Nazi Germany before rearmament was seriously under way was even less ready for a war than the Soviet Union.

Perhaps from Stalin's point of view it was a waiting game. Nobody, after all, knew how the Nazi experiment would turn out. It is unlikely that Stalin assumed that the Nazis' anti-Communism was a passing phase, although he may well have nursed illusions as to the feasibility of 'peaceful coexistence', of relations similar to those prevailing with Italy.

As the Nazi attacks on the Soviet Union became more bitter and far more frequent during the latter half of 1934, the policy of restraint was discontinued, and the Soviet press and radio answered in kind.

Radek Again

But in 1933 there was no serious attempt among the Communist parties and in the Soviet Union to understand and analyse what had happened in the centre of Europe. Karl Radek, who has been mentioned before, was almost the only Soviet commentator to probe deeper in his comments on the current German scene; his voice, too, was soon to be silenced forever. He still thought Nazi doctrine, in particular on economic affairs, absolutely mad, but there was method in this madness.[79] Nazism, he wrote, was a dynamic and powerful movement; Hitler was not a mere adventurer, he deserved to be taken seriously.

Radek was willing to admit, if indirectly, that Fascism was a new phenomenon; loose talk about Fascism all over the globe had merely succeeded in obscuring the issue. Fascism was not merely the dictatorial bureaucratic rule of extreme reactionary circles; its existence was possible only in highly developed countries. Neither brutal terror nor demagogy in themselves were synonymous with Fascism; it was not correct, for instance, to speak about Bulgarian or Hungarian Fascism. Even the *Stahlhelm*, the extreme reactionary German ex-servicemen's organization, had not really been Fascist. On the basis of the same reasoning, Radek reached the conclusion that the Japanese regime was Fascist despite the existence of so many mediaeval feudal remnants.[80]

Such comment was much in advance of the time; when these lines were written, the Comintern was still persevering in its struggle against 'social Fascism'. Radek, however, had little patience with Comintern shibboleths; he displayed remarkable foresight in some of his predictions. He noted that Hitler was systematically creating the tools for expansion, but that the emergence of a big anti-Soviet bloc was unlikely. Even in the face of imminent revolution the capitalist states would not make a common front, since the differences between them were too many and too great. British attempts to channel German and Japanese aggression against the USSR would fail; it was childish to assume that such a scheme could possibly succeed – it would cost Poland its national existence and all French positions would be severely hit. In the Far East the United States would be affected.[81] These lines, written in late 1933, were remarkably prophetic. Radek thought that Hitler threatened not only world Communism but most European countries, and that all should unite and fight him. He could not say this overtly, but it was the conclusion emerging from his writings. The German diplomats who had for many years been accustomed, perhaps not always rightly, to consider Radek Moscow's most important political oracle, continued to report back his commentaries. But nobody else seemed to take much notice.

Ernst Henri

Radek enjoyed more freedom than other Soviet journalists, but whether he had much influence in the Kremlin is doubtful. More indicative of the level of Communist interpretation of Nazism were the books of 'Ernst Henri', a Soviet political commentator who enjoyed great success in the thirties in both the Soviet Union and Western Europe. He was first introduced by the London *New Statesman* as a German refugee who had exceptional sources of information. In the foreword to one of his books, Henri announced that he had not been inspired by any quarter and that he had no connections with either official or unofficial circles in any country.[82] His real identity was disclosed only in 1962 in the Soviet press.

Much of Henri's writing is devoted to predictions about the future war ('The Italian Army before it joins up with the German Army at Lake Constance will immediately be attacked in the flank by the united Czech and Yugoslav forces and perhaps the Rumanian troops, etc.').[83] Henri's political observations are of greater interest. According to him, Fritz Thyssen, the Ruhr magnate, not Adolf Hitler, was the prime mover of German Fascism. He was the 'inspiration', the 'brain of the whole system', the 'driving force behind it'. Thyssen had given Hitler orders to launch a grandiose offensive in world politics. He had also instigated the 'Brown International'.[84] Hitler was a hesitant man, a 'Fabius Cunctator'; he represented the moderate legitimate wing in world Fascism, in contrast to Goering (the 'Bonapartists'), Mussolini, and Mosley, who were its left wing.[85] Such insights abound in Henri's books. The idea that Hitler and Mussolini were puppets of Thyssen was, of course, ridiculous. Henri had the additional misfortune of singling out as the 'real prime mover' a man who, among all the leading German industrialists, was perhaps the dimmest – Hitler would no more have needed his political advice than that of his valet. In 1939 Thyssen broke with Hitler and went into exile; his property was confiscated, the 'inspiration and the brain of the Nazi system' disappeared without trace. After the Nazi conquest of France, Thyssen ended up in a concentration camp.

One of the most interesting features of the case of Ernst Henri is that his version of events found believers not only among the Communists but among other circles as well. A leading British weekly called Henri's book 'probably the best work on the Third Reich that has appeared in English'. His statements were almost everywhere supplemented by documents, names, dates, and figures – 'a profound, thorough exposition of what the Nazis really are'. Bertrand Russell added: 'Extraordinarily interesting and valuable.'[86] In the Soviet Union, Ernst Henri's books serve to this day as source books on the history of the Third Reich.

In fact, his books fulfilled a function similar to that of the *Protocols* after the First World War. In both cases there had been a major political disaster that could not be explained in traditional political terms, and many people were looking for the hidden hand; the conspiracy theory of history therefore enjoyed considerable popularity. Henri – to give a few more illustrations – described in detail how the June 1934 blood purge (the murder of Roehm and his friends) had really been engineered by the German Chemical Trust (I. G. Farben). He maintained that the Nazi anti-Jewish propaganda was mere make-believe; nothing at all would happen to the Jewish monopoly capitalists; had not Jewish finance capital provided the main support for Mussolini (and Mosley)?

According to Henri, Mussolini was Toeplitz' puppet, just as Hitler was Thyssen's.[87] From the German underground movements Henri had reassuring news. 'Thirteen million revolutionary socialists were thirsting for revenge, willing to rise at the first recoil of the Nazi regime.' He also reported that following Hitler's rise to power the circulation of *Rote Fahne*, the German Communist organ, had risen from seventy thousand to three hundred thousand. The only point on which Henri proved to be right was his prediction that Hitler would one day attack Russia; but there was no German *emigré* publication at the time to dispute this.

This sensationalist farrago of unconnected facts and figures and sheer fantasy found many believers at the time; in its way it was symptomatic of the lack of understanding of the real character of Nazism, even among the most dedicated anti-Fascists.

Belated Insights: the Popular Front

By December 1933 Hitler's power in Germany was absolute. All political parties other than the NSDAP had been dissolved the summer before, and a law had made the formation of new parties illegal. The free trade unions and all other organizations that were not Nazi-sponsored or controlled had ceased to exist. In the new Reichstag Hitler's party had a majority of 92 per cent, but the Reichstag itself was no longer of any importance. The enemies of the regime who had not succeeded in escaping in time had been killed or were in prison or concentration camps. German economic and cultural life had been 'co-ordinated' (*gleichgeschaltet*) – to use one of the favourite expressions of those days.

In December 1933 the executive of the Communist International convened in Moscow to consider once again the situation in Germany. It produced a definition of Fascism which has remained in the Communist political dictionary to this day – that Fascism is the open terrorist dictatorship of the most reactionary, most chauvinist and most imperialist elements of finance capital, that it tries to secure a mass basis for monopoly capitalism among the *petite bourgeoisie*, appealing to the peasantry, artisans, office employees, and particularly to the *déclassé* elements in the big cities.

Other than this, nothing seemed to have changed in the fantasy world of the Comintern. The *Theses* and *Resolutions* stated that the revolutionary crisis was growing daily, and the Social Democrats deliberately deceiving the workers by arguing that there was a difference in principle between the democratic countries and the countries of Fascist dictatorship. There was no such contrast. All bourgeois parties (including Social Democrats) were rapidly becoming Fascist, though there might be disagreements between them as to the forms and methods of fascization.[88]

There were some veiled suggestions that recent events had not passed entirely unnoticed. The Nazi government was denounced as the chief instigator of war in Europe. It was realized, Manuilsky said, that the world economic crisis had not become more acute but that, on the contrary, there had been a certain revival of economic life in some capitalist countries. Moreover, the crisis had not been an unmixed blessing from the Communist point of view, for 'the elements of Fascism and war had matured more rapidly than the elements of revolutionary crisis'.[89] This may not appear sensational news eleven months after Hitler's seizure of power but for the Comintern it was a startling admission. In future Communists were to be on the alert against the setting up of any more Fascist dictatorships; together with other groups they should lead an indefatigable struggle for every particle of liberty. This did not quite tally with what the *Resolutions* said about all non-Communist parties becoming rapidly Fascist; individual parties and members were left to make sense out of these conflicting statements.

When it came to the discussion of the situation inside Germany (initiated by Wilhelm Pieck) the divorce from reality was palpable. In October 1933 the exiled Politburo of the German party had noted a 'new upsurge of the revolutionary mass movement' in Germany: Pieck developed this theme in great detail, with many fantastic reports about the alleged activities of the illegal Communist Party; mass strikes, demonstrations, etc., 'at every moment hundreds of thousands of members were willing to follow its call'.[90] The Social Democrats' assertion that the German working class had suffered a heavy defeat was a stupid and wicked lie. The prospects of Nazism in Germany were much worse than those of Fascism in Italy, because Germany was a more industrialized country and had a far stronger working class and Communist Party. One had heard it all before, but now it made even less sense than in the past. Nazi propaganda was to be countered by a call to establish a Soviet Germany. At the same time, the Hitler government was blamed for not representing Germany's national interests in a forceful manner. 'Our slogans are: Down with the Hitler government, the government of reparations, the policy of fulfilment (*Erfuellungspolitik*), and of the Versailles enslavement.'[91]

It would be tedious to repeat in detail the various appeals, manifestos and resolutions issued by the German Communist leadership during 1934, about the great revolutionary upsurges in Germany, about the necessity of destroying Social Democracy as a precondition of the victory over Nazism. The impression created was that inside Germany a bitter struggle was going on, that the Nazis were not the masters of the situation and that the outcome of the struggle was by no means decided. All this must have appeared bitter irony to the few Communists inside Germany who had not broken with the party and who had somehow escaped arrest.[92] The exiled German Communist leaders were now generals without an army and as far as they were concerned the fantasies about imaginary successes could have continued indefinitely. The position of the Soviet leaders was different; they had to co-exist with Nazi Germany, they felt directly menaced, and they had, in consequence, to adjust their political strategy to realities. At the beginning of the year *Pravda* had found some 'objectively' progressive features in Fascism; it certainly was a dangerous enemy, but at the same time it was acting as a pacemaker of revolution.[93]

In late June 1934, Hitler had some of his potential rivals killed, including most of the SA leaders. This purge was interpreted in Moscow as the 'liquidation of the *petit bourgeois* elements by the monopolists'.[94] The Nazi regime had been greatly weakened, even Hitler could not now be sure whether he would remain in power for another hundred days. This was, at any rate, the propagandists' version.

At about the same time, in the middle of 1934, the attitude to Nazism was subjected in Moscow to a thorough re-examination. As a result, the Comintern pendulum swung all the way from an ultra-leftist sectarian policy to an 'ultra-right' course, according to which collaboration with all the enemies of the Nazi regime, without distinction of class or political conviction, was made mandatory. The majority of German Communist leaders accepted this new policy only after considerable prodding on the part of the Russian party and the Comintern, but in January 1935 they, too, were persuaded to adopt and represent loyally the new popular front policy.

The change was dramatic and quite abrupt. It had been realized that Nazism was there to stay, for some years at any rate, and that it constituted a major danger against which the Soviet Union had to be defended. It was also understood that the old policy of sectarian isolation had ended in failure and defeat; the new strategy seemed far more promising for the future growth of Communist political influence outside Russia. The old version of Fascism as the open and brutal dictatorship of monopoly (or finance) capitalism did not have to be modified. On the contrary, it could easily be adapted to the new popular front policy. For if Germany was indeed run by, or on behalf of, the monopoly capitalists, everybody who did not belong to that group was a potential ally, and since the number of monopoly capitalists was exceedingly small, 99·99 per cent of the German people were potential allies. This included not only yesterday's 'social Fascists' but also Catholics, middle-class nationalists, and even members of the Nazi Party and the storm troops to whom many appeals and manifestos were addressed.

In this new strategy, at least for the time being, there were no antagonistic classes. It was not even necessary to overthrow the capitalist order in Germany. Nazism could be defeated if only the rest of the people would make common cause against the three thousand millionaires who were the guilty men. As one such appeal put it: 'The three thousand millionaires have already once been responsible for Germany's defeat. The three thousand millionaires are again interested in a new war, because they profit from rearmament to the tune of billions. The three thousand millionaires play one part of the people off against another, because this safeguards their profits and their rule.' All this could be changed if only the millions would rise against that tiny group of three thousand evil men.[95]

The popular front strategy was undoubtedly a more suitable and realistic answer to the Nazi challenge than the previous policy. However, the old confusion about the identity of the enemy still prevailed. If the Social Democrats had been the greater danger in 1932, Schacht and Thyssen replaced them in 1935. True, the results were less fatal than the attacks on 'Social Fascism', because at least they did not split the anti-Nazi front; but the ambiguities, the inability to understand the character of Fascism, remained a source of danger. Four years later, at the time of the Soviet-German non-aggression pact, when both sides had to engage in ideological disarmament, the Communists could again adapt their old thesis to the new strategy without much difficulty. Since monopoly capitalism, not Fascism, was the main enemy, and since monopoly capitalists were in power both in Germany and Italy and in the western democracies, why should the Soviet Union support one imperialist camp against the other?

In 1935, temporarily at least, everything was to be subordinated to the anti-Fascist struggle. The seventh Comintern Congress engaged in a veritable orgy of self-criticism. It was argued that basically the Communists, and not the Social Democrats, had been right all along. However, the moment it came to a discussion of details there was not much self-congratulation. The policy of class against class was wrong. Sectarian mistakes had been committed. It had been harmful to call the social democrat workers 'little Zoergiebels' (the name of the Social Democratic police chief in Berlin). It had been a mistake to attack the Social Democratic trade unions and the Social Democratic government as 'Fascist'. The Bruening government should not have been called a Fascist dictatorship. The Communists had failed to make a serious study of Italian and Polish Fascism. They had the absolutely false conception that all bourgeois parties were Fascist, and that it was unseemly for Communists to defend the remnants of bourgeois democracy. They had underestimated the national question.[96] And so it went on.

There were even some genuine attempts to explain the mass appeal of National Socialism: Nazism had been successful because it appealed demagogically to the most urgent needs and demands of the people. It had played on their better sentiments as well as their prejudices. The irrational element in politics had been underrated; many comrades had believed that such a lunatic ideology would never gain influence among the masses.[97] Some attempts were made to analyse the weaknesses of Fascism. Fascism was designed to overcome the disharmonies and antagonisms within the bourgeois camp, but in fact it made them more acute; the policy of autarky undermined the economic life of Germany, and it had a negative effect on the economic relations between the various capitalist countries. Above all, there was the realization, repeated in countless appeals and speeches, that 'Fascism is war'.

Few outside observers of the German scene would have disagreed with this prognosis, yet their warnings were not heeded; the belief that Hitler could be restrained or appeased was still generally accepted among the ruling circles of Britain, France and many other countries. Whatever the basis of the assumption, Communist reasoning was for once correct.

Russia Studies Nazism

German-Soviet relations entered their most decisive phase in 1935. From that year until 1938 the propaganda warfare was conducted unremittingly. It was followed by an attempt, in 1938 and during the first half of 1939, to ignore each other. The two years of 'positive neutrality' led, in June 1941, to four years of bitter fighting.

Over these ten years German Fascism was the main enemy between 1935–8, but after Munich the situation became more confused, and after the non-aggression pact the anti-Fascist theme was very much played down or disappeared altogether, to reappear, with a vengeance, after June 22, 1941. The defence of the Soviet Union was the supreme consideration both for the Comintern (not much in evidence after 1935) and for the various Communist parties. On the doctrinal level there was no rethinking on the subject of Fascism after 1935; Nazi Germany was a major foreign political problem for the Soviet Union, but nobody lost much sleep trying to provide a Marxist-Leninist explanation of the Fascist phenomenon. Soviet experts closely followed developments in all parts of the world and freely commented on them; there was nothing too insignificant to escape their notice, whether it was the then largely non-existent revolutionary movement in distant countries or minor fluctuations in world trade. There was one exception – German Fascism. During the whole decade of this great contest there was no attempt above the level of current political comment to tackle the subject. Not a single history of Nazism or the Third Reich was produced, nor any other general work on Nazi foreign or domestic policy, such as appeared by the hundred in the rest of the world. A Soviet student of international affairs who wanted to know about Nazism, its origins and development, had but a single book at his disposal – Konrad Heiden's *History of National Socialism*, which appeared in Russian in 1935. Written by a 'bourgeois liberal', it could hardly replace authoritative Marxist-Leninist guidance on the subject.*

This unwillingness to deal with a subject of such vital political importance was surely not fortuitous. Could it be argued that since Communism had long ago found a formula to explain Fascism (the rule of monopoly capitalism) no further research was necessary? This was hardly convincing; it should, on the contrary, have acted as a spur to further and more detailed study. True enough, conditions in Stalin's Russia were hardly conducive to the study of international affairs or politics in general. Any writer on these topics, however cautiously he moved, was likely to find himself in sudden and possibly serious trouble. But had Stalin wanted such studies, they would have been published anyway. He did not want any discussion of a subject that was bound to raise disturbing questions; however emphatically Soviet writers might denounce Fascism, there would be uncomfortable parallels, and how could they possibly fail to compare it with other dictatorships? Reading about the *fuehrerprinzip* in Germany, for instance, what Soviet citizen could help thinking about the 'cult of the individual' nearer home?

* On current developments there were two collections of essays – *Germanski fashizm u vlasti* (edited by Varga and others in 1934) and *O fashistskoi Diktature v Germanii* (Partizdat, 1939), a few books on specialized economic or legal subjects such as F. Manfred on German civil law (1936), Sidorov on the German middle classes (1936), Faingar on problems of German industry (1934), Segal on Nazi agrarian policy (1938), N. N. Liubimov on the finances of Fascist states, Dvorkin on the economic programme of Nazism (1933). In addition there was one single attempt to tackle Nazi doctrine *Protiv fashistskoi falsifikatsii istorii* (1939), translations of Ernst Henri's books, and a few more brochures by Varga. During the war a number of pamphlets were published; almost all of them dealt with German imperialism, past and present, not with fascism.

Whenever Stalin had to face a new problem for which there was no prescription in the Leninist canon, he was not deeply perturbed by considerations of doctrinal consistency. This emerged, *inter alia*, in his attitude towards Nazism. In 1935 the Comintern still professed to believe in the success of a revolt by the anti-Nazi forces inside Germany. Florin, at the seventh Comintern congress, had solemnly declared that 'we Communists must root out the Social Democratic theory, which is widely held in Germany, that Fascism can only be overthrown by war and with external aid'.[98] Stalin had no such illusions; he always respected the strong. Hitler's Germany was by then a major factor in world politics, and was continuing to grow stronger. Stalin was impressed by German military strength and German economic growth; German industrial output (Stalin told the Eighteenth Communist Party congress in spring 1939) had grown by sixty per cent in four years. These figures hardly betrayed economic or any other weakness; admittedly, hidden behind them was the story of German rearmament. Stalin presumably had no doubts about the aggressive designs of German Fascism. He seemed convinced that it might be possible to deflect Hitler from his '*Drang nach Osten*', in the same way as certain western politicians thought that Hitler could be appeased by diverting him towards the East. Early in 1939 Stalin saw a good chance of success. The Germans (he announced) had cruelly disappointed European and American politicians by turning to the West and demanding colonies instead of marching farther East.[99] The non-aggression pact of August 1939 was based on the assumption that there was not much to choose between the various imperialist robbers, basically they were all alike. The best interests of the Soviet Union demanded 'positive neutrality' towards Germany. Stalin apparently thought that this uneasy peace would last; after the German attack the first Soviet reaction was a complaint about the German 'betrayal'! Since Hitler did not have the reputation of a man who kept his word, while credulity was not Stalin's outstanding characteristic, this reaction is the more difficult to understand; or did Stalin believe that there ought to be a certain solidarity among dictators? Once the war had broken out, there was no time to deal with finer ideological issues. The pretence of the popular-front period, that National Socialism was the rule of three thousand monopoly capitalists, was immediately dropped. 'The enemy is cruel and implacable,' Stalin said in one of his early war speeches;[100] and 'the enemy', from now on, was every single German.

236

If the Germans wanted a war of extermination (Stalin said), they would get it, and from now on every single German who had set his invading foot on Soviet soil would be destroyed.[101] There was a general surge of nationalist feeling, committees and periodicals sponsoring the Slav cause were founded and frequent reference was made to the age-old struggle against the aggressive German. The contemporary literature proved that all the great Russian classical writers had been anti-German; even Hegel, Feuerbach and the German classical philosophers suffered an eclipse (as they had done during the First World War). The propagandists argued that the only good Germans were those below the face of the earth. True, Stalin once observed that it would be ludicrous to identify Hitler's clique with the German people, or with the German state. The experience of history indicated that Hitlers come and go, but the German people and the German state remain.[102] This dictum was to be frequently repeated in East Germany after the war, but at the time it passed almost unnoticed in Russia. It did not make a great deal of difference to the Red Army whether the German guns were manned by sons of workers or monopoly capitalists. Only when victory was already in sight were the more outspoken anti-German propagandists curbed. Russia, according to the generally accepted version, was fighting a patriotic war against a ruthless invader; Nazi intentions were interpreted in terms of traditional German expansionism. Nobody gave much thought at the time to the specific character of the invader, his political and socio-economic system. For the overwhelming majority of those involved, the war was a struggle between Russia and Germany, not between Fascism and Communism.

The Post-mortem

When the Second World War was over and Hitlerism had been destroyed, the question was asked by many millions all over the world: how could it have happened? This interest was reflected in a great many publications on such subjects as Eichmann and the concentration camps. On the more scholarly level there were hundreds of books and booklets examining various aspects of Nazi rule in Germany and Europe. Since the end of the Second World War whole libraries have been written on these topics, not only in Germany, the country most directly affected, but in all European countries and in America. There was one exception, the Soviet Union, the country that had suffered more than any other from the Nazi invasion. Hitler literally disappeared from the Soviet political dictionary; the *Politicheskii Slovar* of 1958 has entries on Jan Hus and Marshal Govorov (a Soviet artillery commander in the Second World War), but none on Adolf Hitler. The *Small Soviet Encyclopaedia* contains a short entry on Hitler, Adolf – it is half as long as the one on Remarque, Erich Maria; in the three volume *Diplomatic Dictionary* (1960–3) the reader finds all he needs about Motta, the Swiss president in the nineteen forties, but nothing at all about Hitler. While Stalin lived there were several accounts published of partisan warfare and similar themes, but Nazi Germany was an unmentionable subject. No attempt was made to analyse the character of Fascism, no books were published on the Nazi Party, or on the history of the Third Reich and its aggression and expansion. Soviet spokesmen were often very bitter about their western ex-allies who, they claimed, did not adhere to the policy of the Nuremberg trials. But when the indictment and the evidence of the Nuremberg trials were brought out in 1946 in a series of huge volumes, the Soviet Government alone did not publish these documents, the most massive record of Nazi crimes. After Stalin's death second thoughts prevailed, and with eleven years' delay, the first volume of an abridged series of Nuremberg documents was published.

If the blackout on recent German history was almost total until 1953, the situation changed somewhat around 1960. Yet even now (1964) there is no Soviet history or sociological study of the Nazi Party, no systematic attempt to describe and analyse the rise of Fascism. (The only study so far in which a modest attempt in this direction has been made appeared under the perhaps intentionally misleading title *The Bourgeois State in the Period Between 1918 and 1939*.)[103] Even now there is no biography of Hitler, let alone of any other leading figure of German or world Fascism; nor is there any comprehensive account of German rule in occupied Russia during the war. In a seven-hundred-page history of modern Germany, published in 1961, the author fails to mention that Hitler was an anti-Semite and that the Nazis killed six million Jews; he does say, however, that *Mein Kampf* 'called for the destruction of twenty million Slavs'.[104] Even in this post-Stalinist literature there is much confusion about Nazi doctrine in the very few pages that are usually devoted to this topic.[105] Anti-Semitism is explained solely in terms of economic interest: the Nazis persecuted the Jews in order to corrupt the German *petite bourgeoisie* by the 'Aryanization' of Jewish property; about eight to ten million Germans benefited financially from this policy. Thus the Fascist dictatorship gained its mass basis.

This new explanation is not much better than the 1930 version, according to which the Nazis merely hated the Jewish proletariat, whereas the rich Jews would be permitted to stay and prosper in the Third Reich. Nor does one obtain from this literature any new details about the financial backers of Nazism, the ties between Hitler, the banks and heavy industry. Strictly speaking, there is some new material; this purports to show that Hitler was the tool not only of German monopoly capitalism but also of Wall Street, that the Nazis' rise to power was engineered by Kuhn, Loeb, and Co. of Wall Street and their (non-existent) German representative Sidney Warburg.[106] Even this innovation, however, is not really new. It first appeared in a book by a Dutchman, published in 1933. The author had been convicted of forgery, and his sensational assertions were disproved, but this apparently carried little weight with those who continued to quote him thirty years later.

The one available Soviet study of Fascism defends the old monopoly capitalism theory against its bourgeois and Social-Democratic detractors. Fascism, according to the authors, is a 'bourgeois, anti-democratic *coup d'état* (*gosudarstvennyi povorot*), carried out in the interests of the most reactionary circles of monopoly capitalism with the aim of establishing an open terrorist dictatorship'.[107] The reader is also told that a Fascist takeover is more than a mere change from one bourgeois government to another, but this bold statement is at once put into proper perspective: a Fascist coup is merely a change in the *form* of bourgeois dictatorship. Parliamentary democracy, in other words, is one form of bourgeois dictatorship, Fascism another. The authors prefer not to touch such topics as totalitarianism, or the German 'cult of personality'. Some of this may simply be the outcome of the fact that Nazism, as a subject of study, did not exist until very recently in the Soviet Union. Soviet writers have so far not made extensive use of the enormous mass of Nazi documents available in the West, and to a lesser degree in the East. It is obviously impossible to write an authoritative study at this date without using the most essential source material.*

* These sources are used to a far larger extent in East Germany. There the main interest is devoted to the activities of Communists in the Third Reich; there is no East German history of the Third Reich, no study of the Nazi Party, no biography of Hitler. There are countless books on Adenauer and his regime.

239

However, lack of curiosity or lack of knowledge is the least likely explanation of this riddle. Nor were Soviet historians so shocked or Soviet readers so squeamish that works on Fascism could not be written and published. The real reason is that the Nazi era is part of the *unbewaeltigte Vergangenheit*, the past that has not yet been mastered. That Hitlerism could not be studied under Stalin needs no explanation. Yet even in the post-Stalin period many of these difficulties persist. A historical account of German rule in occupied Russia would have to deal with the painful phenomenon of collaboration. A book on the 'final solution' – none being in existence so far – would give rise to questions about the Jewish problem in the Soviet Union. It could not provide a satisfactory answer from a doctrinal point of view; for what direct material interest had the German monopolists in exterminating six million Jews? A study of Nazi cultural policies is impossible without a discussion of the general problem of cultural freedom in a dictatorship. An investigation into the structure of the totalitarian state would raise many awkward questions, so would studies of the German secret police, and its political influence in the Third Reich. A dictatorship, in brief, is not the ideal place in which to study another dictatorship, however great the differences between them. It is admittedly doubtful whether the Soviet appraisal of Fascism would have undergone great change had Soviet historians been permitted to make a close study of the subject. Since no rethinking on the subject has taken place, the attitudes and the definitions of the thirties have simply been taken over. The chapter is by no means closed; a future generation of Soviet students will probably tackle the subject assiduously. But since the topic is so intimately connected with internal developments in the Soviet Union, and since such a revival of interest is bound to end in the discarding of old and untenable formulas, it may be unrealistic to expect a decisive change in the near future.

Fascism and the Monopolists

The study of politics has been defined as the examination of who gets what, when, and how; it is only legitimate to ask who supported Nazism and who benefited from it. It is, in fact, an absolutely essential question for the understanding of this phenomenon. Today it is incomparably easier to provide an answer than it was in the nineteen-thirties. Not only is Fascist rule a thing of the past, but many essential facts have also come to light which make more definite conclusions possible.

To recapitulate very briefly; according to the standard Communist definition, Fascism is the open terrorist dictatorship of the most reactionary, chauvinistic, and imperialist elements of monopoly capitalism. This version, which has not basically changed over the last thirty years, states that a Fascist dictatorship became necessary because of the growing threat of proletarian revolution, and because monopoly capitalism proved unable to maintain its rule by traditional means. It argues that Fascism was a mass movement, which based itself largely on the *petite bourgeoisie*, and even on those sections of the working class and the peasantry who, as a result of continued economic crises, were not aware of their own class interests and fell easy prey to social and national demagogy. Fascism requires the support of the masses before it can assume power, but its historical role does not consist of representing the interests of the *petite bourgeoisie* (let alone the working class). Once in power, Fascism shows its real face as the tool of finance capitalism.

So much for the Communist definition of Fascism. If this version were correct, and if it were able to provide a realistic and satisfactory explanation of such a complicated phenomenon as Fascism, Communist doctrine would have much to recommend it. If, on the other hand, it is wrong, it would throw serious doubt on its claims to be the only truly scientific method of explaining the modern world.

It has been established beyond any shadow of doubt that some leading German and Italian industrialists did support the Fascist movements in their countries from an early date. It can further be shown, without particular difficulty, that heavy industry and banking in both Germany and Italy benefited from the economic policy followed by Mussolini and Hitler, and that they collaborated closely with the dictators. Despite all the socialist demagogy, the Fascist regimes in Italy and Germany acted as props to the existing social order, removed any socialist or Communist pressure, and made the industrialists' profits secure.

Among Hitler's earliest backers was Fritz Thyssen, head of one of the biggest Ruhr enterprises and, from about 1929, Emil Kirdorf, the Nestor of German heavy industry. In September 1931 Hitler met a group of German industrial tycoons; there were more such meetings in early 1932. By that time the Nazi Party also had the moral (if not financial) support of the renowned Dr Schacht. From about 1930 or 1931 Hitler received an annual subsidy of about two million marks (then about £100,000) from heavy industry.[108] These contributions, needless to say, increased substantially after January 30, 1933. In Italy there was a similar process. Leading financiers, such as Volpe, were among Mussolini's earliest backers, and in October 1922, the *Confindustria*, the association of Italian industrialists, warmly welcomed the establishment of the Mussolini government. That German industry benefited from Hitler's regime, its counterpart in Italy profited from the Fascist dictatorship is proven; the statistics of steel production and industrial profits between 1933 and 1938 are more convincing than some recent attempts to whitewash German industry.[109]

Many leading industrialists joined the Nazi Party or even got high, albeit honorary, posts in the SS. Some profited from German rearmament, all enjoyed the political and social stability imposed by the dictatorship and the absence of strikes. During the war some leading concerns used slave labour. While heavy industry loyally collaborated with the regime, the banks and the big landowners also had few grounds for complaint in the Third Reich. These are incontrovertible facts, but our concern here is the politics and not the economics of the Third Reich. It remains to be asked whether the financial help given to Hitler before 1933 was in any way decisive for his political triumph. Did Hitler in his domestic and foreign policy represent the interests of 'monopoly capitalism', or to put it more bluntly, was his policy dictated by the Krupps, the Thyssens, and the German chemical trust?

The Nazi Party received financial help from highly placed well-wishers almost from the very beginning, but its backers were a small minority in the world of German industry and finance. Even after 1930 the Nazis received only a fraction of the money the conservatives and the centre parties received. As late as 1932, the majority of German industrialists supported the *Volkspartei*, and in the presidential contest of that year they backed Hindenburg rather than Hitler. The finances of the Nazi Party reached their nadir during the very last months before Hitler became Chancellor.[110] There is an interesting parallel with Italy for, shortly before the march on Rome, Mussolini had been told by Olivetti, the representative of the Italian industrialists, that no more help could be expected. The evidence that has come to light shows that the leaders of the German chemical trust, such as Duisberg and Bosch, or Siemens of the electrical trust,

242

opposed Hitler, and that even Krupp, who became a most loyal collaborator in the Third Reich, refused to support Hitler as late as January 1933.[111]

German industry did not 'make' Hitler, nor was its support decisive for the triumph of the Nazi Party; it jumped on the Nazi bandwaggon after January 30, 1933. Similarly, Italian industry joined Fascism after it had become a dominant political factor. As Robert Michels put it at the time, 'das Grosskapital ist terziaer dazugewachsen'.[112] In November 1932 an attempt was made by Schacht, Voegler and von Schroeder to collect signatures among their fellow industrialists and bankers for an appeal to be sent to Hindenburg demanding the appointment of Hitler as Chancellor. Quite a few of those approached were willing to oblige, but many important names (including Krupp) were missing.[113] Commenting on this campaign, Schacht wrote Hitler that German heavy industry had earned its name; it was 'heavy of movement', could not easily take a decision. The memorandum probably had a certain effect on Hindenburg, but at most it was only one of the factors that induced him and his advisers to invite Hitler to form a government. His own personal affairs (the *Osthilfe* scandal) and von Papen's intrigues were far more decisive.

After Hitler had become Chancellor, the attitude of German industry changed rapidly. Almost without exception the captains of industry did all they could to ingratiate themselves with the new masters, in an attempt to hide the fact that they had not always supported them. They entertained the new bosses, sent them valuable presents, and in their speeches had the most fulsome praise for Nazism and the Fuehrer. During the Hitler era militant anti-Nazis were found among the working class, and less frequently among the intellectuals and the middle classes – these men and women were willing to risk life and property in the struggle against the dictatorship. There was dissent but no active resistance among the industrialists; the only one who had sufficient courage to dissociate himself openly was, ironically enough, Hitler's earliest backer, Fritz Thyssen.

The record of leading German industrialists in the Third Reich is a bad one, and this judgment is not affected by the recognition that Nazism had a great deal of support among all classes of German society. Yet it is not the record of German industry that is under discussion but the question of its political influence on the Nazi regime. There is no evidence that the 'monopoly capitalists' were able to influence Hitler's policy at any stage in any decisive way. They had no grand strategy of their own, let alone the will and the inner cohesion to press it. The regime had granted great favours to some of them[114] and they reciprocated with loyal service. They were only too willing to profit from Hitler's political and strategic conquests, but nobody had ever asked them whether they wanted a war and how it would affect their profits. Their real political status emerges even more clearly if we consider one of the more damaging episodes in their collaboration with the Nazi regime – the 'Circle of friends of Heinrich Himmler'. This was a group of about thirty senior German bankers and industrialists (and about fifteen leading state officials), who met about once a month, were told about the activities of the SS, and on one or two occasions were taken to visit a concentration camp. The circle paid for its privileges. In 1943, they contributed more than a million marks which were handed to Himmler, to be used at his own discretion.[115]

What were the privileges for which 'Himmler's friends' were permitted to pay one million marks a year? They did receive occasional orders, including the contract for the Zyklon poison gas used in the extermination camps, and it is likely that the German chemical trust obtained some of the slave labour employed in its East European factories through these connections. Above all, these captains of industry wanted to make an impressive display of sycophancy. Ohlendorf, one of the highest SS leaders, said in his evidence at Nuremberg: 'They wanted to have a direct pipeline to Himmler in case of any emergency'; e.g. should the Gestapo make trouble at their factories. In other words, omnipotent German monopoly capitalism was paying Danegeld, some form of protection money, for the privilege of not being molested by the political police. Their ancestors undoubtedly paid similar tribute to the local robber knight who made the roads unsafe.

Konrad Heiden, the first historian of National Socialism, once wrote that 'according to a well-known myth, Krupp, Thyssen, and Voegler had made National Socialism', adding, 'clearly a small child's version of world history' ('*wie sich der kleine Moritz die Weltgeschichte vorstellt*').[116] He was perhaps not sufficiently aware that children's versions can persist; if they are politically useful, they may endure for a long time.

Economic and political power

Some of these mistaken interpretations of Fascism had their origin in false definitions or insufficient factual knowledge; others went much deeper. It was factually wrong, for instance, to attribute decisive political importance to finance capital. The banks had had their heyday before the First World War; afterwards they never really recovered the lost ground. The generalizations about 'monopoly capitalism' were very often misleading. The Communists (and not only they) attributed to the leaders of German industry, heavy industry in particular, farsightedness, diabolical cunning, and above all a unity of purpose which they never had. The German captains of industry of that period were, with very few exceptions, almost the exact opposite – very limited and shortsighted men, not at all daring, but rather spineless. Their self-confidence had disappeared in the great economic crisis; they only wanted to be left alone. To attribute grand political concepts and Macchiavellian strategies to these knights of the sad countenance was a pathetic misreading of political realities.

There was no unity of purpose in these circles. The interests of the big landowners clashed with those of industry. There were basic conflicts of interest even within heavy industry. The many firms which had a large stake in foreign trade did not want a government that would antagonize foreign countries. Forty-three per cent of German machine industry exports went to the Soviet Union in 1932; it is little wonder that German heavy industry became increasingly interested in this market. A representative delegation, with Kloeckner at its head, went to Moscow in 1932 against the advice of the German Foreign Ministry.[117]

If the Nazis had some backing in sections of the German coal and steel industry in 1932, it came mainly (as Hallgarten has emphasized) from the managers of big anonymous enterprises, who received high salaries but had no personal stake in their firms. On the other hand, the privately owned family concerns, such as Krupp, Kloeckner, or Reusch, feared the 'economic radicalism' of the Nazi Party.[118]

The German economy was as split and as disunited as the rest of the country, but were not the ruling classes, at least, united in their desire to save the social order, threatened by a big revolutionary wave? According to the Communist version, the 'dictatorship of the bourgeoisie' was in mortal danger, both in Italy in 1922, and in

245

Germany ten years later. The capitalists therefore decided to adopt Fascism in a last desperate attempt to stem the revolutionary tide. In fact, Mussolini came to power two years after the 'socialist threat' had passed (there never was a Communist menace in Italy).[119] Nor was there a 'revolutionary situation' in Germany in 1933 – except perhaps in the imagination of the Communists, who had in the last elections displaced the Catholic *Zentrum* as the third strongest party in the country. The Nazis were, however, twice as strong, and, as it soon appeared, better organized. If the Communists misjudged the situation, and thought it conducive to revolutionary action, this was a tactical error, albeit a major one. The reasons for their inability to understand the character of Nazism went much deeper. These were, in a way, inevitable because they were part and parcel of their ideological equipment on which all Communist socio-political thinking was based. Their position was similar to that of a bacteriologist who gets wrong results in his research because he has used a faulty microscope or the wrong lenses. They tried to explain Fascism by analysing its character solely in terms of class interests. They even had an answer for the disconcerting fact that the great majority of the members of a Fascist Party apparently voted and acted *against* their class interest. This was a case of mistaken interest. Soon enough the Nazi leadership would show its real face, and then its working class and *petit bourgeois* supporters would drop out.

Class interests, needless to say, were indeed involved in the growth of the Nazi Party, but an analysis on these lines could not account for the great wave of nationalist passion on whose crest Hitler and his party rode to power. This was a political fact of the first magnitude that could not possibly be explained in terms of even mistaken class interest; its ideological sources (including the race theory) went far back into German history. All this was impatiently dismissed by the Communists as being unimportant. It was, in fact, of the very greatest relevance for the understanding of the Nazi party and the policy of the Third Reich – even if it did not fit into the Marxist-Leninist scheme. In Communist eyes the Nazi mystique was of no consequence, since it was part of a 'superstructure' that was conditioned by, and dependent on, the 'material base', as taught in the textbooks of historical materialism. They thought, accordingly, that it was quite impossible for the 'superstructure' to detach itself from its 'material base', that it could follow an independent course and perhaps even make the 'material base' serve its purposes.

This reveals the central failing of Communist ideologists, *viz.* their inability to appreciate the importance of political power. When they argued that the monopoly capitalists were the true masters of Germany, or that Thyssen was Hitler's real boss, they were arguing from one of their basic doctrinal tenets, that economics determine politics. They maintained that, since the factories had not been nationalized, and since the owners still got enormous profits, the social system was still capitalist; and the capitalists, as everyone knew, were the masters of capitalist society. In fact, things had never been so simple, and in the totalitarian state the relationship between political and economic power was exactly the opposite of what the Communists thought it was: the state made the economy subservient to its own non-economic purposes (such as war or aggression). This baffled all orthodox Marxists. Some Communists refused to see the problem, while others tried, often very ingeniously, to find an explanation. The first to tackle the problem squarely was Rudolf Hilferding, who had been, before the First World War, one of the leading Marxist thinkers and to whom Lenin owed much in his work on imperialism. Hilferding, then a refugee in France, realized that fairly often in history, major trends had their origin in military or political action that could not be explained in economic terms. On the contrary, such action had often decisively influenced the development of the economy. He mentioned specifically the conquest by the Germans of the West Roman empire, and the advance of the Arabs in the seventh and eighth centuries along the coast of the Mediterranean. These conquests caused the destruction of cities, the ruin of trade, and ultimately the end of the feudal system. In other words, force (*Gewalt*, as Hilferding put it) had been the decisive factor. *Gewalt*, however, was blind – one could not foresee its results in terms of Marxian 'historical necessity'. At most, one could talk of a 'chance', as Max Weber had done.[120]

In recent European history, particularly after 1914, the state had steadily increased its power, and had developed a momentum of its own. This development was contrary to Communist doctrine, in which there was no room for an independent rôle for the state, for its only function was as a tool of the ruling classes. Some more independent Marxists talked about *étatisme* and there were many discussions as to whether Germany under Hitler was still a capitalist country, and Russia under Stalin a socialist one. In strictly legal terms Russia was, of course, a socialist country (because the means of

247

production had been nationalized) and Germany was capitalist (because they had not been), but there was also a growing realization that the question of legal relationships was not the most relevant one in a totalitarian state; what really mattered was political power. In Nazi Germany the political leaders gave the orders. The factory owners continued to receive profits and dividends, though in the later stages of totalitarianism they lost the free use of their means of production, just as the workers lost the right to dispose of their labour. They all became parts of a centrally-controlled economy which was geared to the political purposes of the regime. Hilferding stated: 'The totalitarian power lives by the economy, but not for the economy, or even for the class ruling the economy . . .'

The acceptance of these facts would have been tantamount to a major revision of Marxism-Leninism, and to jettisoning some of its basic tenets.

Theories on Fascism

Whatever Soviet and Communist speakers did, said, or wrote about the subject of Fascism ought to be seen in the context of the time. If Communist adherence to an untenable doctrine seems indefensible twenty years after the destruction of the Fascist regimes, some of the mistakes they committed in the twenties and thirties were no worse than the blunders of other parties and leaders. Sympathy with Fascism in certain circles in England and France quite apart, there was a great deal of confusion and very little understanding of Fascism in the camp that, broadly speaking, should be defined as anti-Fascist. The German liberals and Social Democrats nurtured legalistic illusions about the Nazi movement that were totally unwarranted; their policies were often short-sighted and sometimes cowardly. As a result of their failure to destroy effectively the power of the old ruling classes in the 1918 revolution, the Social Democrats, in particular, carry part of the responsibility for the conditions that made Hitler's rise to power possible.

After 1933 there was a proliferation of theories about Hitler, Nazism, and the Third Reich. It was maintained by some that this phenomenon was totally inexplicable, the irrational creation and the responsibility of a single man. Others saw it as a logical, indeed inevitable stage in German history. The Communist version which expounded the guilt of 'monopoly capitalism' found supporters for some time, even among some Social Democrats and liberals, such as Georg Bernhard.[121] There are strong traces of it in Franz Neumann's *Behemoth* with its theory of 'totalitarian monopoly capitalism'; Neumann maintained that it was significant that some of the most powerful figures in the National-Socialist hierarchy were prominent bankers[122] – an observation that was factually incorrect, and, in any case, misleading.

Of considerable interest were the discussions about the character of Nazism among the socialist *emigrés* from Germany and Austria. Many of them shared the feeling that the catastrophe had happened because Social Democracy had not been radical and militant enough, and in these circles there was a revival of Marxist thought. The attempts of Otto Bauer, Paul Sering, or Arthur Rosenberg – to mention only the most important of them – to explain Fascism ought to be noted in this context.[123] Their writings showed more imagination and a greater readiness to face realities than the official Communist version. Otto Bauer, for instance, thought that capitalism had been forced to surrender much of its power to a movement which it feared; the Fascist terror threatened it no less than it did the workers; yet, once Fascism was in power, the ruling classes soon succeeded without great difficulty in making the new regime a tool of their class interests. Thus even these more sophisticated attempts at explanation were sterile or, at best, incomplete, in view of their one-sided concentration on economic factors. The right-wing Social Democrats were hardly the peers of their left-wing comrades in critical intelligence and ingenuity. Yet the historian finds, somewhat to his surprise, that they proved to be nearer the truth when they maintained that Germany, under Hitler, was no longer a class state in terms of Marxist theory, and that Germany was not ruled by a class that could be defined in accordance with the traditional categories, but by a bureaucratic-military caste which regarded it as the purpose of the state to mobilize the whole people for war.[124] The accuracy of this definition can be disputed but there is no doubt that it was nearer the mark than the other contemporary theories of Fascism. Within the confines of traditional Marxist doctrine there was simply no answer to the problem.

Re-reading the contemporary comments and predictions about Nazism thirty years later, one finds that the statements of party executives, and the writings of most political thinkers of renown have not stood the test of time as well as the essays of some litterateurs[125] or the books of a conservative ex-Nazi like Hermann Rauschning. To understand Germany in 1933, either an intimate knowledge of the Nazi mind or a great amount of imagination was needed. Less relevant was the ability to analyse the statistics of the profits of the German steel industry.

I assume that a future historian, summarizing events during the second quarter of the twentieth century, will conclude that Fascism was a particularly ruthless and aggressive form of dictatorship. Anti-socialist and anti-democratic in inspiration, it based its doctrine on racial or national superiority. Owing to the great technical advances in the means of control and mass communication, Fascism was able to establish a regime of total rule. In attempting to explain the success of National Socialism, the historian will undoubtedly refer to a great many factors and trends, such as the political and economic consequences of the Versailles Treaty – a subject which has not been a fashionable topic of study in our time. He will devote much attention to Germany's arrested development as a nation in the nineteenth century, to the fact that it had not experienced a successful liberal-democratic revolution, to the deep roots of authoritarianism and militarism, and to Pan-German and racialist thought in recent German history. He will stress lack of moderation as a very pronounced feature of the German national character. Few will emerge entirely free from guilt or blame for the rise of Hitler. Many are guilty of having actively collaborated with the Nazis, others of not having actively opposed them, when resistance was still possible.

My intention has been neither to explain Fascism nor to try to apportion blame for Hitler's rise to power.[126] Nor was it to judge Communist policy *vis-à-vis* Hitler, though some such judgment became inevitable in the course of the narrative. I was mainly concerned with their image of Nazism. Judgment on their actions, as distinct from their doctrinal pronouncements, would have to take into account a great many additional factors. Their disastrous attacks on the Social Democrats, branding them the 'main enemy', would be on one side of the balance, while the staunch anti-Fascism, the self-sacrifice and heroism of individual Communists in the Third Reich would be on the other. At present, extravagant claims are made for the German Communists by Soviet and East German writers and speakers; their policy is described as having always been correct in most essential points, and they are represented as having been the only consistent fighters against Nazism, the bearers of a near monopoly of resistance to Hitler both before 1933 and after.* Such fantastic assertions usually provoke non-Communists into doubting Communist anti-Fascism altogether – a reaction that should be resisted.

The subject of our investigation has been of more limited scope. We have tried to establish how leading Communists in the Soviet Union and Germany viewed Fascism, how they explained it, and where and why their political analysis went wrong. It is to a large extent a study in profound misunderstanding. But history is what men make it and it is affected by misunderstandings as much as by insights. In fact, a clear understanding of the issues involved is by no means a guarantee of political success, unless it is backed by belief in one's own cause and the readiness to fight for it, which may be one of the reasons why those on the side of the angels have not always prevailed.

* Klaus Mammach writes that the KPD has the historical merit of having been the only party that ever realized – and at an early date at that – that finance capitalism intended to establish a Fascist dictatorship. 'Therefore it carried out a policy which aimed at preventing the Fascist dictatorship in order to save the nation from barbarism and war'. The author concludes: 'this is the historical truth'. '*Ueber die Wende der KPD zum Kampf gegen den Faschismus*', in *Beitraege zur Geschichte der deutschen Arbeiterbewegung*, 4, 1963, p. 674.

Chapter 12

DAYS OF WRATH 1939–63

IN RECENT DECADES German-Soviet relations have followed, on the whole, the Aristotelian prescripts for Greek tragedies, with each new stage arising out of what preceded it as its necessary consequence. Greek tragedy, as well as Soviet-German relations, had also the *peripeteia*, the sudden, startling reversal, which had not been expected by the spectator, and their *anagnorismos*, the revelation, at a critical moment, of a close relationship unsuspected (to follow a classical definition) 'until some dreadful deed was done or about to be done, or events had reached an *impasse*'.

Few doubted in 1937 that the Soviet Union and Nazi Germany were on a collision course; even fewer foresaw the complicated, tortuous prelude to the great contest in the East. None could then have foreseen the far reaching consequences. The division of Germany and its disappearance as a great power led to a situation somewhat similar to the state of affairs after 1918; then, as after 1945, Germany ceased to play a central role in Soviet foreign political thinking, which came to concentrate on the powers west of Germany. In the twenties Germany had been Russia's one potential ally; after the Second World War it was the country most hostile to the Soviet Union in Europe. Above all, the dimensions had changed. After the First World War the young Soviet regime had to struggle for its very survival; after 1945 the Soviet sphere of influence had been advanced far into the centre of Europe, and it was stronger than the rest of the continent taken together. Although in 1945 Germany ceased to be a world power and a threat to the Soviet Union, the problem of Soviet-German relations has continued to preoccupy chancelleries, general staffs, and public opinion all over the globe. It has remained one of the burning issues of our time to which no early, certainly no easy, solution is in sight.

252

Great storms dispel the clouds, but they do not necessarily create good visibility. The main landmarks in Soviet-German relations in recent decades, the non-aggression pact of 1939, Hitler's decision to invade Russia in 1941, the division of Germany and Russia's post-war policy in Central Europe remain almost as hotly contested as they were at the time. Hitler, as he repeatedly stated, wanted war while he and the Duce were still young and energetic and before the rearmament of Germany's potential enemies had made too much progress. He needed the war because his aim was not merely to gain *Lebensraum* for the German nation; German hegemony in Europe would not be secure until all potential enemies were destroyed. He knew, as did all students of the First World War, amateur or professional, that Germany's cardinal mistake had been to wage war on two fronts. Hitler did not want to repeat that mistake; hence his efforts in 1939 to neutralize the Soviet Union.

Whether the original initiative for the non-aggression pact came from Hitler or Stalin will remain a bone of contention between historians in East and West for some time to come. There is unanimity about the Soviet Union's disgust with Western policy before and after Munich. Stalin thought that there was apparently no limit to the willingness of France and England to appease the Fascist dictators; as a result, the Soviet Union found itself shut out from the deliberations about the 'New Order' in Europe. There was no immediate danger that England and France would gang up with Hitler against Russia (though Soviet spokesmen from time to time professed to believe in such intrigues), but the possibility that the Western powers might, under certain conditions, give Hitler a free hand in Eastern Europe could not altogether be excluded. Soviet policy under Stalin, despite the fiery Comintern manifestos, had never been one of burning bridges; Bismarck advised his successors to keep open the wire to St Petersburg; Stalin's emissaries in Berlin continued to put out feelers for a possible improvement in Russian-German relations even at the time of greatest tension, in 1936 and 1937. At the Soviet Communist party congress in March 1939, Stalin called for the restoration of good neighbourly relations with Germany; this call did not pass unnoticed in Germany where the anti-Soviet propaganda was almost at once toned down. However, Hitler was still distrustful, afraid of double-dealing by the Russians, and suspected deception or provocation.

Litvinov's dismissal in May 1939 helped to reassure the Germans, and so did the continued moves of the Soviet diplomats in Berlin.

The initiative for a *rapprochement* in spring 1939 almost certainly came from the Russians, but, once negotiations had started, the Germans wanted to proceed much faster and considerably farther than the Russians. In early August, German pressure for the early conclusion of a pact became very insistent indeed. Stalin tried to procrastinate – he would have preferred to keep his hands free, playing off the Germans against the British and the French. Stalin's aim was to keep Russia out of a European war, and he would have preferred not to commit himself to too close co-operation with one side. That the talks between Soviet and Western military delegations had not made progress was not his fault. Britain and France manoeuvred themselves into an impossible position. The Western military emissaries had no real authority and no Western foreign minister was sent to Moscow in that fateful summer. Soviet insistence on the right in certain circumstances to move its troops into Poland and Rumania, and perhaps other Eastern European countries as well, was logical and natural; Voroshilov was right in stressing that a military alliance without that proviso was meaningless. Yet England and France could not make Warsaw accept this condition, short of revoking their alliance with Poland. A military alliance would, of course, have made Eastern Europe a Soviet sphere of influence, for it would have left it to Stalin to decide when an aggression had taken place; he would have been entitled to come to the help of any neighbouring country with or without its agreement. Muddled as Western policy was, it did not wish to give Stalin what it refused to concede to Hitler.

Many realized in 1939 that there was no future for Eastern European independence between the German hammer and the Soviet anvil, and that the East European governments were not free of blame. Instead of co-operating with each other, they had engaged in a free-for-all which left them disunited and an easy prey to their stronger neighbours. There is no certainty that Stalin had wanted a military alliance with the Western powers, just as there is no guarantee that the Soviet Union would have really come to Czechoslovakia's assistance if challenged to do so at the time of Munich. There is no way of knowing, for the Western governments made no attempt to compel Stalin to show his cards.

'Now I have them in my pocket,' was Hitler's comment when he was told of the signing of the non-aggression pact with the Soviet Union.

Would Hitler have attacked Poland without such backing? He would not have given up his designs, of course, but he might have postponed the campaign, or decided to destroy Poland piecemeal, like Czecho-slovakia. Hitler's madness was usually in his ultimate aims, not in the execution of the various stages. Until the later stages of the war when there was nothing more to lose, the risks he took were calculated. He would not have dared to challenge an Anglo-French-Russian coali-tion in the summer of 1939, but what if the Soviet Union had made it clear that it would stay neutral, while refusing to sign a treaty with Germany? Could this neutrality have been maintained? The Nazi conquest of Poland would soon have led to a military alliance be-tween London, Paris, and Moscow, all equally threatened by this further extension of Hitler's sphere of influence. It is, perhaps, too much to say that the key to war or peace was in Stalin's hands; since the Nazi regime was geared to aggression, war was inevitable within one or two years. Nazi power could have been destroyed only in a war; whether its destruction was bound to have taken six years, and claim tens of millions of victims, is a different question.

According to the official Soviet version which, incidentally, has not changed to this day, Stalin followed, in the existing circumstances, the only course open to him. Had he not signed the non-aggression treaty (it is still argued), war between Russia and Germany would have been inevitable in the very next weeks. The Soviet Union was admittedly just then in an unfavourable position – fighting a minor war against the Japanese in the East and without much hope of sup-port in Europe from France, England or the United States. By signing a treaty with Hitler, Stalin gained not only territory which was stra-tegically important, but also time to rearm, and he made certain that Russia would not be without allies when the Nazis invaded. This, in very brief, is the Communist case; it is not quite complete, since Soviet historians never mention the existence of the secret protocol about the division of Eastern Europe, which was of far greater signi-ficance than the non-aggression pact.

It is a stronger case than commonly assumed in the West, and not only because Stalin won the war and Hitler lost it. Certainly there is no point in blaming Stalin because his interests happened not to be identical with those of France and Britain, or because some people had taken Soviet professions of anti-Fascism a bit too literally during the popular front period. Co-operation with the Nazi regime did some harm to the world Communist movement, but no lasting damage was caused in terms of power politics. Communist and extreme left-wing critics of Stalin are on weak ground: if they had moral or ideological scruples they had joined the wrong party in the first place. It is somewhat surprising that the German-Soviet pact should have become, and remained, the centre of so much acrimonious debate in these circles. Seen in historic perspective, a far stronger case for Stalin's policy could be made on this occasion than on most others, which does not mean that the policy he followed was the best from the Soviet point of view. The assumption, to begin with, that Hitler would have attacked the Soviet Union in September 1939 had not Stalin signed the treaty[1] is certainly false. We now know that the German Army was in no way prepared to attack the Soviet Union in 1939, there was not even a blueprint for such a campaign. However, assuming that the army had been ready, the order to attack would not have been given with winter only a few weeks ahead. The earliest date for the campaign would have been late May 1940, and this would have been feasible only if French and Polish resistance had already been broken. Stalin gained, at most, a year and some territory; Nazi Germany acquired in the meantime not only military experience but many valuable resources. According to all the evidence available, Nazi industrial and military power grew much faster between August 1939 and June 1941 than did Soviet power. If the Soviet Army was better prepared in June 1941 than it was twenty-one months before, the initial superiority of the German Army had increased even more. The following figures do not leave much room for argument: if the industrial labour force of Nazi Germany was roughly ten millions by the end of 1937; on the eve of the invasion of Russia it numbered, with the satellites and the occupied countries, twenty-eight millions. Production of coal rose from 250 to 400 million tons; steel output rose by more than fifty per cent and, perhaps most important, the output of crude oil rose from one million to more than seven million tons. It is more than doubtful whether, with the fuel resources at his disposal in 1939, Hitler would have been able to engage in a major war of more than a few weeks duration. It was a calculated risk Stalin took, but, as events showed, an unnecessary and very costly one for the Soviet Union.

When the German invasion came, the Soviet Union found itself politically less isolated than in 1939. There was no longer a danger of a Japanese attack, and Western help was given almost immediately. Stalin's basic idea had been to keep the Soviet Union out of the war as long as possible. He assumed that Nazi Germany would be involved in a protracted struggle against the Western Allies, that both sides would gradually exhaust their strength and that consequently the position of the Soviet Union and the Communist parties in the post-war world would be very strong. He underrated German military power and the breathing spell was therefore much shorter than he had expected. If the Soviet Union received immediate Western assistance, it owed it less to Stalin's foresight than to Hitler's successes. The Western powers had to help the Soviet Union because by themselves they could not defeat Germany. There were some voices in the West suggesting that the Russians and Germans should be left to fight it out among themselves (just as Stalin had hoped to profit from a protracted war between Hitler and the West), but neither in official circles nor among the public was there support for such a policy.

The German-Soviet Pact

The possibility that the devil could be made honest by act of parliament was discussed by sixteenth-century writers as amusing, though not very likely. Their scepticism was justified, but they could not foresee that a total state, unimpeded by parliament, with absolute control of all means of communication, would be capable of even more considerable feats.

German-Soviet relations in autumn 1939 provide a perfect illustration of how even the most abrupt switches can be engineered without undue difficulty. 'We had the task of converting to a completely reverse opinion those whom we had originally made into fanatical opponents of Russia,' Hitler said later. 'Fortunately the spirit of party solidarity held firm.' The attacks on Judaeo-Bolshevism were discontinued, instead there appeared editorials celebrating traditional Russian-German friendship. It had been a bitter decision for the Fuehrer which tested his self-restraint. 'The most humiliating thing I ever did'; but Hitler is not really the most reliable witness. While the alliance lasted, in 1939-40, he found a great many redeeming features in it. Ciano was told that Russia had given up its world revolutionary aims, and that, by and large, the Russian-nationalist trend had prevailed under Stalin over the Jewish-internationalist element. He never made a secret of his conviction that treaties would be kept only so long as they were profitable. Up to the fall of France, the alliance was extremely profitable from Hitler's point of view, but after the summer of 1940, German interests became more and more involved in the Balkans where they were bound to clash with the Soviet Union. Stalin made very great efforts to please Hitler – by supplying to Germany raw materials which were of vital importance, by withdrawing recognition from the governments of countries which had been conquered by the Nazis, and in many other demonstrative ways. Yet the *raison d'être* of the pact as far as the Germans were concerned, had disappeared, and no concession would satisfy Hitler.

In the Soviet Union the manipulation of public opinion was no less intensive and radical after August 1939; the anti-Fascist literature and the speeches were discontinued, and Molotov told his compatriots after the destruction of Poland that the new alliance had been 'cemented with blood'. Since the propaganda machine in a totalitarian state is nothing if not thorough, regardless of what message it carries, it proved very efficient in keeping from the Soviet public the truth about the inhuman character of Nazism and its aggressive designs *vis-à-vis* Eastern Europe, with the result that psychologically the Soviet Union was almost totally unprepared in June 1941. This was another risk Stalin took. In an alliance between two dictatorships any critical, let alone hostile, comment is received as a major act of bad faith, an expression of official policy. Stalin had yet another worry which did not beset Hitler – the policy of the Comintern, and in particular of the European Communist parties. The Comintern, to be sure, had not been very active since 1936, but the European Communist parties continued to exist though by 1939 most were illegal. They had to be given clear instructions – it was not enough to tell them to lie low for the time being, a course which many of them would have undoubtedly preferred after the shock of the Molotov–Ribbentrop pact, 'Down with the Imperialist war!' was the watchword – and remained so until June 22, 1941.

After the attack on the Soviet Union, not only the slogans changed, but also the writing of history. Nowadays it is claimed that the Communist parties of Europe were the main anti-Fascist resistance force from the very beginning of the war. In this contention the Communists find support, paradoxically, in certain Nazi statements published after June 1941, for the Nazis, for obvious reasons, wanted to justify their attack and pointed, among other things, to alleged anti-German activities by various European Communist parties.[2] It is true that in the Balkans, with the growing tension between Russia and Germany in spring 1941, certain Communist parties became more outspoken in their condemnation of Nazi aggression. We do not know whether they were cut off from Moscow or whether they had been secretly encouraged by the Comintern. By and large, however, the policy of revolutionary defeatism remained the basic policy until the very day of the German attack on Russia.

The Decision to Attack

The German–Soviet Pact lasted twenty-one months; during the first half of this period, which ended with the fall of France, there were no major signs of discord. Hitler did not seem worried by the gains Stalin had made, which included two thirds of Poland, the three Baltic republics, Bessarabia, parts of Finnish Karelia and the Bukovina. Unknown to most, the turning point in Soviet–German relations came shortly after the fall of France. On July 21, 1940, Field Marshal von Brauchitsch received the order to prepare a plan of attack on the Soviet Union; subsequently the plan became known under the name of 'Barbarossa'.

Hitler's decision to attack the Soviet Union has been the subject of some controversy. It has been argued that although a plan to attack Russia was prepared as early as July 1940, this did not mean that an irrevocable decision to launch a military campaign had already been taken – blueprints for the conquest of various parts of the world were in existence. Such a decision, it is suggested, was definitely made only several months later, probably under the influence of growing Soviet pressure in the Balkans, especially in Rumania. It has also been asked whether Hitler's decision was determined mainly by military or political considerations. It has also been suggested that Hitler's campaign was, after all, only a war of prevention for sooner or later Stalin would have attacked Nazi Germany.

Whether the decision to attack was taken in July 1940 or a few months later is not really a very important problem, though some have read great significance into the timing. Does it really matter whether Hitler made up his mind immediately after the fall of France, to which most of the evidence points, or only after he had realized that Stalin was not willing to participate in his schemes for the establishment of a new order (under German leadership) in South-east Europe?

Hitler regarded the Soviet Union both as a political and as a military threat; there could be no clear dividing line. He attacked the Soviet Union not because of anything the Russians had done after August 1939, but because of what they were – a strong military power headed by a leader and a party who remained potential enemies despite all the mutual assurances of good will and peace. One consideration was the intention to destroy 'England's last ally on the Continent'. True, there was much talk about the mortal danger facing the German nation from the East, and about a new Hun invasion, but this came only after Hitler had realized that he had underrated Soviet military strength. According to his own words, other Nazi leaders, such as Goering, had belittled Russia even more, assuming that the campaign for Moscow would be a walkover. The longer the war continued, the more Hitler concentrated on Russia; this now overshadowed the fact that the original intention had largely been to defeat England. Since Hitler thought that England could not be directly attacked, he intended to isolate it by destroying its only remaining potential ally in Europe. He may have overrated British ability to resist a large scale invasion in 1940–1, just as he underrated the difficulties in the East, but all the evidence shows that he based his decisions on such an appraisal, mistaken or not. The suggestion that the German attack on the Soviet Union was a 'self-defensive offensive', that the Red Army had already been mobilized, that Germany was menaced by the Soviet air fleet, that, in brief, Stalin had provoked the attack, is an interesting one, but the known facts do not sustain it. This version is based on Hitler's speeches after June 22, 1941, in which he used to argue that 'only now do we know how enormous the danger was, by what a narrow margin (*haarscharf*) Germany and the whole of Europe had escaped disaster.' He seems to have come to believe his own lies, but then Hitler always had a propensity for auto-suggestion. In his *Table Talk* he mentions some of the facts which influenced him in his decision to invade the Soviet Union, such as the news that one single Soviet factory produced more tanks than the whole of German industry. The thesis of the preventive war has been taken up by some German writers since the war. That the Soviet Union concentrated on heavy armaments is undisputed fact, but Hitler exaggerated its output in order to make his victory over the 'already defeated enemy' even more spectacular. No serious military expert now maintains that the Red Army was ready for an offensive in 1941. There was no operational plan, no concentration of troops; Soviet material was inferior and the training of the units was insufficient. Not only was Stalin not 'ready for any eventuality', meaning offensive action, there was even no clear defensive plan. The work on fortifications in the territories acquired after 1939 had proceeded at a very leisurely pace. When Hitler told his old comrades in a speech in Munich in November 1941 that in the middle of June of that year it had appeared as if a 'Russian attack was only a matter of a few days', this was his customary way of justifying his decision. His ambassador in Moscow had repeatedly assured him that Stalin wanted to prevent a war at almost any price. Stalin had given orders to the Red Army to use only a minimum of force in case of local German attacks and he had instructed his ministers to continue to supply Germany with manganese, chrome, crude oil, and other raw materials of the greatest importance, even though the Germans had, in effect, stopped paying. He demonstrated on many occasions, above all in the critical months of May and June 1941, that he wanted to appease Hitler. In a famous Tass bulletin published a few days before the actual attack he emphatically denied the 'senseless and provocative rumours' of an imminent German attack.

Stalin had heard from many quarters about the impending invasion; by early June 1941 millions of Germans knew about it, or at any rate guessed it, thousands of others in different parts of Europe and even America knew it for a fact. Yet Stalin, like many other paranoiacs, had a peculiar knack for ignoring real dangers, concentrating instead on imaginary ones. Since everyone seemed to agree that a German offensive was about to be launched, this must have appeared to him as a gigantic plot to deceive him, and to sow distrust between his country and Nazi Germany.

The German attack came in the form of an attempt, by now familiar, to destroy an enemy in a lightning campaign. For once it did not work; the distances involved were so much greater, the climatic conditions so much worse, the enemy forces so much more numerous, and their resources apparently unlimited.

What if Hitler had waited for a few years, if he had permitted Stalin to rearm on a large scale? Would not Moscow then have pressed its claims in the Balkans and the Middle East, would it not have led to war anyway? Stalin was one of the most cautious of men in foreign politics; he would make war against a small country like Finland to gain a local advantage, but a major military power he would attack only if he was certain of decisive superiority, and in this he resembled some other modern strategists. Such crushing superiority, however, he was not likely to gain for many years to come.

Both National Socialism and Soviet Communism were expansive by nature, but Soviet Communism with its enormous underdeveloped resources was, unlike Nazi Germany, under no pressure to attack its neighbours. The Soviet Union would expand, as it did in 1939–41 and again after 1945, if it met no, or little, resistance.

Hitler lacked Stalin's conviction that time worked in his favour, hence his strategy of uninterrupted aggression. It is difficult to say how much of this can be attributed to the regime, and how much to the personality of the Fuehrer. The combination of Fascism with German militarism, the feelings of hurt national pride, the resentment about Versailles, produced a highly explosive mixture. Yet without Hitler it would not have been the same. More than any leader of his time, more even than Stalin, he made a personal impact on the policy of his country. There were other Nazi leaders as relentless and as devoid of moral scruples, but they had not his authority, his self-confidence or his madness. Nazi Germany under Goering would have engaged in aggression against its weaker neighbours, but it would not deliberately have provoked a world war, and it would certainly not have engaged in plans as ambitious as Hitler's. Hitler's rôle in history shows how, in certain conditions, an individual can influence the course of events for decades to come. For that reason it is a meaningless question to ask what would have happened had Hitler not attacked the Soviet Union in 1941. Since he was Hitler, he had to attack.

Germany Invades Russia

The easy victories during the first year of the war had immensely strengthened Hitler's self-confidence. He now came to believe in his omnipotence – no task was too difficult for the brave German Army under his leadership of genius. In comparison with some of his contemporaries he was, indeed, a military genius. But he knew no measure and no moderation: what had before been a daring gamble became now a mad disregard of military, economic, and political realities. Hitler decided to invade Russia before the other war fronts had been liquidated, and he showed even less concern about America's entry into the war than had Ludendorff in 1917. Thus Germany's doom was sealed well before June 22, 1941.

Hitler's strategy in Russia has been criticized on many grounds: his plans were always too ambitious, instead of trying to force a decision in one major direction he dispersed his troops. It is elementary strategy to be stronger than the enemy in the decisive place at the right time. Hitler managed just at that moment to be weaker than his foes – in front of Moscow in October 1941 and before Stalingrad the following summer. His strategy was rigid, strongly influenced by considerations of prestige rather than sober military calculation. He was incapable of learning from mistakes, whereas the Russians, after their initial setbacks, were quick to correct their errors. Whilst he used to drive his troops and their commanders to unresting effort, he hesitated unaccountably on important occasions and missed major chances. His attitude to the peoples of the Soviet Union, about which more presently, was bound to turn the overwhelming majority into implacable enemies, and to strengthen immensely the Red Army's will to resist. However, the war could not have been won by Germany, even if Hitler and his generals had made no mistakes at all, unless it is assumed that the Red Army was led by unmitigated fools, that it consisted of cowards, and that Stalinism would crumble following the slightest setback. Industrially, the Soviet Union of 1940 was much more advanced than Tsarist Russia in 1914. True, progress was not nearly so great as the propagandists would have had the world believe. If Russia in 1914 had produced, roughly, as much as France, its output in 1940 was more or less the same as Britain's – somewhat higher in steel, lower in coal. With the important exception of crude oil, it was inferior in essential respects to Germany, Soviet industry was to a much higher degree geared to the production of military equipment than that of any other country in the world. Hitler, with his sovereign disdain for economics, had not made serious preparations for a lengthy war; Germany shifted to a totalitarian war economy only in 1943, while the Soviet Union had been concentrating on armaments for years. Nazi Germany, to give but one illustration, produced at the time of the invasion only six hundred tanks per month, which was not even enough to replace armoured vehicles that had been damaged or destroyed – let alone supply new units.

The Nazi Army never enjoyed numerical superiority, even if one includes the satellite divisions which, with the exception of the Finnish, were of doubtful value. The Russians had twice as many aircraft and their superiority in tanks was almost threefold. If Hitler subsequently complained that he had not known about these 'gigantic preparations' this was, at best, only partly true. He had hoped to prevail over the Russians owing to the element of surprise and by superior quality. True enough, many Soviet aircraft and tanks proved to be inferior, and an alarmingly high proportion was destroyed or captured by the Germans during the very first days of the war. By the time the German armies were bogged down in front of Moscow and Leningrad in autumn 1941, however, they too had lost much of their equipment; what they retained was paralysed by the elements. The Soviet Army lost millions of men during the very first weeks after the invasion, but as the war continued it found it much easier to mobilize new units than did Germany, a country with half its population. The loss of a considerable part of European Russia, including the industrial regions of the Ukraine, was an unmitigated disaster, but it was not a mortal blow. Under the second and third five year plans new industries had been established in the eastern part of the Soviet Union and many factories from the occupied areas had been evacuated in time. On the other hand, the German logistic problems became almost insoluble with the advance of the Wehrmacht – the Germans found conditions very different from those they had encountered in Denmark, France, or even Yugoslavia; nor did it help if they cursed Russian inefficiency for not building enough roads and railways to secure steady German supplies.

The Soviet regime had grave weaknesses which, at a time of crisis, became glaring. There was a great deal of disaffection among the population; even the reception of the Wehrmacht was at first not unfriendly. Not, of course, that Hitler would have won the war if only the Wehrmacht's public relations had functioned more effectively, or if he had consented to make use of Russian volunteers in his 'crusade against Bolshevism'. The Nazi aim was to destroy Russia and to enslave its people, and no clever little stratagems could have made the Russians forget this stark fact. Hitler acted in accordance with his self-imposed mission; he was quite incapable of conducting any other kind of war.

By late autumn 1941 it was clear that the purpose of the campaign, to destroy Soviet power, had failed; if the *Blitzkrieg* had not succeeded, a long drawn out war was certainly beyond Germany's capacity. The events of summer 1942 merely confirmed this – even if the Germans made further advances up to Stalingrad and the slopes of the Caucasus. They were no longer able to keep their spoils; the element of surprise was now missing. It was the turning point of the war, after which the initiative passed to the Russians. All that the Wehrmacht was capable of was counter-offensives on a local scale, and by the end of 1943 the orderly retreat became a rout.

The fighting power of the Red Army had been underrated in the nineteen-thirties and the events of the first war months tended to confirm this mistaken impression. It had been forgotten that the Russian Army, even under the miserable leadership of Archdukes and Tsarist generals, had been a formidable military force, despite the lack of ammunition and other supplies. The impact of the purges on the Red Army, on the other hand, had been grossly exaggerated. A great many Soviet officers had perished between 1936 and 1939, but the inference drawn, that their removal had paralysed the Red Army, was quite wrong. There is apparently much scope for amateurs in war: both the German and the Soviet military forces were directed by dictators who had no strategic training; further down, lieutenants made meteor-like careers and eventually commanded regiments or even divisions. The Second World War has shown that, technical units apart, there had been an artificial nimbus around military leadership; the qualifications needed to direct whole armies were much fewer and far more widespread than was generally assumed.

From a military point of view, the first three or four months of the war were the most critical for the Soviets. After that the initial shock and chaos were overcome, new units were mobilized and trained, the evacuated factories provided fresh supplies and substantial allied help began to arrive. Troops and civilians alike continued to suffer tremendous hardships, but there was no imminent danger of defeat and disintegration. It is difficult to understand what induced Hitler and his aides to expect that the Soviet will to resist would crack within the first months of the war. It ought to have been clear from the outset that the German Army would neither be able to administer a decisive blow at the centre nor to cut off the rest of the country from the centre. True, the German Army could deliver severe blows, but none of them fatal; the Soviet Union had the resources and the totalitarian state provided the means to continue resistance indefinitely. If the Wehrmacht continued to fight to the bitter end, until it was completely destroyed and the Nazi leadership killed, there is every reason to assume that Soviet resistance would have continued from centres east, had Leningrad, Moscow, and Stalingrad fallen. The Germans found it difficult to accept that the *Untermenschen* were driven not only by fear of Stalin's commissars and the NKVD, but by tenacity, genuine patriotism (of which the Nazis thought they had a monopoly) and growing hatred of the Germans. In more ways than one they were better equipped than the Germans to suffer hardship; Stalin's Russia had been a good training ground.

The first fifteen months were a sombre period for the Russian Armies, but as the German advance came to a halt, Soviet self-confidence grew. For sheer stamina, they were more than a match for the Germans; after overcoming the initial chaos, their organization improved rapidly and they showed great ability to adapt themselves to modern warfare. The Germans complained that General Winter, not the Russians, had defeated them both in 1941 and in 1942, yet the same climate prevailed on both sides of the front, and it did not prevent major Soviet offensives in 1942 and the following years.

When Germany's position in the East became critical, excuses were readily found. The eastern hordes were countless, Germany had to fight on two fronts and was outnumbered by three or four to one in the East. The arrogant belief in German superiority gradually turned into black despair. There is much self-pity in post-war German military writing, as if the German high command had to blame anyone but itself for being outnumbered – and for having attacked in the first place.

The war had begun with one of the usual Hitlerian performances in the Reichstag on June 22, 1941; the last scenes were played out in the immediate vicinity, thus preserving belatedly the Aristotelian unity of place. Two Soviet soldiers hoisted their flag on the Reichstag building hardly a stone's throw from the bunker where Hitler had just committed suicide. In his testament he had announced that the German people did not really deserve to exist, the nation had proved itself weak, it had not been worthy of its Fuehrer; the future belonged to the stronger nation in the East. There was no Wagnerian finale to a campaign begun with so much fanfare; Hagen had always been Hitler's idol, but he was to end his days like Alberich: all he left behind was a terrible curse.

Victories and Defeat

Soon after the invasion in 1941 Hitler announced that this was no ordinary war: 'The German soldier opposes an enemy who, I must admit, does not consist of human beings, but of animals, of beasts.'[3] In Western and Northern Europe the German Army had, occasional lapses apart, not strayed from the international conventions of warfare. The occupation regimes subsequently set up, with their mass executions of hostages and other terrorist acts, saw the introduction of Nazi methods of government into the occupied countries. In Eastern Europe, the trail of blood and destruction left behind by the German forces was on a greater scale than anything the world had witnessed for centuries. The German Army, contrary to military tradition and international law, killed some of its prisoners; the 'Commissars decree' stated that political officers should be killed 'at the latest' in the prisoner of war transit camps. There was worse to come; as the army advanced it was replaced by SS units and *Einsatzkommandos*, who systematically murdered millions of people. The occupation authorities meanwhile engaged in large scale pillage and in rounding up slave labour for work in Germany. The relationship between Germans and Russians in the occupied areas was one between master and serf; throughout the occupation the natives had to provide raw material and cheap labour for German industry and agriculture. Ultimately they would have been expelled or exterminated, for Russia and the Ukraine were to be settled after the war by colonists from Germany.

The general policy was to encourage dissension, schism, and splits; since no native intelligentsia would be needed, higher education was discontinued. German propaganda continued to fulminate against the monstrous crimes of Bolshevism, but in their actions the German occupation authorities showed themselves only too willing to pursue the very policies they so continuously denounced. How much ink was spilled by the Nazi press about that inhuman institution, the Kolkhoz; yet faced with the need to supply grain to Germany, the occupiers found the Kolkhoz a very useful instrument to get what they wanted; they strictly banned all dangerous experimenting such as dissolving the Kolkhoz and returning the land to the peasants.

There was no clear concept as to Russia's political future. Rosenberg had been asked to work out a blueprint in early 1941. He proposed the establishment of a truncated Greater Muscovy gravitating towards Siberia, an 'independent' Greater Ukraine, a Baltic protectorate and a Caucasian Federation. But nobody paid much attention to Rosenberg's fantasies; in the end military or economic expediency would prevail – or simply the whim of the Fuehrer and the inclinations of other Nazi leaders. If Rosenberg and a few likeminded spirits at least envisaged certain attempts to win over part of the population in the East and to give them, under strict German supervision, some pretence of political independence, Hitler, Himmler, and other prominent Nazi leaders were utterly opposed to any such experiments with *Untermenschen* who were in any case incapable of managing their own affairs. True, they thought more highly of Estonians than of Lithuanians, and they preferred Azerbaidjanis to Georgians and Armenians, but they had not the slightest intention to give them even satellite status, or to enlist them in the military struggle against the Soviet Union. The man who had branded the peoples of the Soviet Union as sub-human could not possibly accept their help (as some of his advisers had suggested) except in the most lowly capacity as unskilled workers and, towards the end of the war, in a small number of military units. He simply did not trust the Slavs and always recalled the Slav units in the Austro-Hungarian Army in the First World War, which had changed sides at the first opportunity.

It was a matter of indifference to Hitler that his policy in Russia was bound to antagonize the maximum number of people in the shortest possible time. Germany had already won a decisive victory; what did the thoughts and attitudes of a defeated people matter? His outlook did not change even after the tide had turned. Up to Stalingrad German propaganda had reflected feelings of superiority; thereafter it played on German fears. When Germany invaded Russia, Hitler had rejected as gross impertinence the thesis proclaimed by some French newspapers that Germany was fulfilling a 'European mission' in attacking the Soviet Union. Germany, he said, was fulfilling nobody's mission but her own. After Stalingrad the idea of a European dam against Asian Bolshevism appeared as one of the main themes in German propaganda. Nazi Germany, in the words of a famous brochure, distributed in hundreds of thousands of copies at the time, was protecting western civilization against the new Huns, against the *Untermensch* who had risen to conquer the world. A Soviet victory would be the triumph of all instincts of bestial frenzy, night would descend on Europe, western civilization would cease to exist.

Nazi propaganda about the sub-human Russian helped to a certain extent to stiffen German resistance; it also expressed, in an exaggerated way, the impressions of many Germans who had been to Russia during the war. What they had seen was thought to justify, as it were, the anti-Bolshevik propaganda with which they had been fed. There was abject poverty, especially in the Russian countryside, general backwardness and, above all, disorder and dirt, the absence of which, to many Germans, had always seemed the truest, if not the only, measure of culture. If living conditions in the Soviet Union had been bad before the war, the general dislocation following the invasion and the policy of the German occupation authorities caused further deterioration and degradation. It seemed indeed, as Goebbels wrote in *Das Reich*, that 'realities in the Soviet Union made Nazi propaganda turn pale.'[4] To the Germans it was a major riddle that an army raised in this land could fight back with such stubbornness and even fanaticism; it could not be explained only by reference to the fear of the bloodthirsty, omnipotent 'commissar'; it was even less explicable that such an inferior race should be able, after the initial major reverses, to defeat German bravery, organization and leadership.

Even if only a minority of German soldiers were actively engaged in crimes against humanity, there were few who did not know about the millions of Russians, Jews and other civilians who had been murdered, and about the villages and towns which had been ransacked and destroyed. Was it not natural to expect that the Russians, once they reached Germany, would behave in a similar way? If Germany had tried to reduce Russia to a state of slavery, would not the Russians do the same after their victory? These fears did not totally eradicate the German sense of superiority. The Russians, it was argued, had merely copied western techniques, and they were not really capable of any sustained creative effort. The Germans had been defeated by sheer numbers – and of course by the Western Allies who had stabbed them in the back while they were defending European civilization in the East. The impression made on German soldiers in Russia during the war had a far more lasting and widespread influence on the German image of Russia than the writings of Rosenberg and the speeches of Goebbels and all their underlings.

The impact of the war on the Russian attitude towards Germany and things German was not less far reaching. At first many Russians had thought (like Lieutenant Gavrilov in Sholokhov's *Science of Hate*) that it would be a war like any other war; cruel, full of hardships, but not essentially different from other ordeals. They had known the Germans, after all, in the First World War when they had occupied a considerable part of European Russia; they had been neither better nor worse than other occupiers. The Russians had known many thousands of Germans between the wars. These had been civilized people and very competent in whatever they did; perhaps not

269

very sympathetic, but certainly not inhuman. The Russians were thus ill prepared for what was about to happen. The official reaction was predictable: there was a general patriotic upsurge, all the national heroes of Russia were enlisted, and great play was made of traditional Russian enmity to all things German. This kind of propaganda produced some strange results, as it had during the First World War. One of its consequences was the debunking of classical German philosophy (including Hegel and Feuerbach, excluding only Marx). This was on the intellectual level. The ordinary Russians, who did not care about Hegel and Marx, reacted violently too. As they learned of the murder and the destruction in the occupied areas, a wave of indignation, turning into hate, swept the country. Ehrenburg, perhaps the most widely read author at the time, wrote that this war was unlike any previous war. For the first time the Russians were facing not human beings, but evil and vile creatures, savages, equipped with all the most recent technical achievements, who had transformed the killing of babies into a matter of political philosophy. Aleksei Tolstoy wrote: 'Kill the beast, this is your holy duty.' The more extreme anti-German propaganda was stopped a few months before the end of the war, but the Soviet units in Germany showed during the first weeks of the occupation that they were not in a forgiving mood. These fairly widespread incidents naturally did not make the Germans fear the Russians any less, but they cannot possibly be compared with the German crimes in Russia, not only in view of the number of those murdered in Poland and Russia, and not only because the Russians were the aggrieved party.

If the Germans were perplexed by the striking disparity between Russian poverty and backwardness on one hand, and Soviet military power on the other, the Russians were no less mystified by the stark contrast between German inhumanity and the high living standards, even in a destroyed Germany. This, at any rate, was what impressed the common soldier most. The intellectuals faced another riddle: they could not understand how a civilized, *kulturny* people who had given birth to Goethe, Schiller, and Heine, to Bach and Beethoven, to Marx and Engels, had fallen to such depths. Germans and Russians had seriously misjudged each other – the Germans by assuming that deplorable sanitary habits showed grave deficiencies of character, the Russians by naïvely thinking that high living standards were a guarantee of civilized behaviour. Violent as the Russian hate was, it died down fairly quickly; the Russians remained resentful and suspicious but they are, on the whole, bad haters. Considering the enormity of the German crime in Russia, the Russians forgot rather quickly. It did help, of course, that Germany had ceased to be a major power.

Until well after Stalingrad, Stalin had no clear concept of what to do with post-war Germany, not, of course, because he opposed Soviet expansion into Central Europe, but because the fate of Russia was still in the balance and there were many more urgent problems to solve. A 'German National Committee' was set up in Moscow under Communist leadership, consisting mainly of German prisoners who had 'seen the light'. This was largely a propaganda tactic calculated to weaken the enemy's morale, not part of a great master plan for the future of Germany. Not until the Red Army was approaching Germany's frontiers and the Allies had invaded France did the future of Germany become a major problem in Soviet eyes. Even so, it was not the overriding international issue. From what we know of Stalin's conversations with Western statesmen he wavered between killing off the German general staff and the dismemberment of Germany into a number of small states, and giving Germany more power than the Western Allies wanted it to have at that time. On the whole he favoured the division of Germany, as he first told Eden in 1941, and as he stated with great emphasis at Yalta. Stalin, in his way, was more farsighted than the Western Allies, certainly more than Roosevelt and Truman, realizing that the main problem of the post-war period would not be Soviet–German, but Soviet–American, relations. Above all, he wanted to fortify his position in Eastern Europe. Germany, it was then already apparent, would be divided into a Western and an Eastern sphere of influence. Stalin may or may not have realized that mastery over Germany meant hegemony over Europe, but he was not yet ready for such a test of strength; like all cautious people, he preferred to do one thing at a time.

Finis Germaniae?

With the defeat, Germany ceased to be an active factor in world politics, but what gradually became known as the German question continued to be given the highest priority by politicians and diplomats. It was now a quarrel between the powers over Germany; what the Germans themselves thought or did was only of very limited interest. Not long before Germany had challenged the whole world;

271

after her defeat, the views of the governments of the newly independent Asian and African states became of greater importance than the opinions of those who had only a short time before tried to dictate their will to the whole world.

It had been agreed in 1944 that Germany would be divided into four military occupation areas; its ultimate future was to be settled at a peace conference. A formal decision to dismember Germany was never taken and all the occupying powers, including the Soviet Union, remained bound to the continued existence of a German state with Berlin as its capital. The gradual division of Germany came about as the result of the growing conflict between East and West, not in consequence of some deliberate decision.

This was well nigh inevitable, for Germany was the major prize of the Second World War and of the cold war; it was not a minor country whose neutrality would have been tolerated by the major powers. The end of the war signified the breakup of the alliance; the common interest uniting the Soviet Union and the West was the necessity to defeat Hitler. Once this aim had been achieved the alliance lost its *raison d'être*. Some well meaning observers think it was all a tragic misunderstanding based on suspicions and that, with a minimum of good will, all the difficulties could have been overcome. The exact opposite is true; the conflict arose because the two sides came to understand each other only too well. The Soviet Union had political aims in Europe and other parts of the world of which it had never made a secret, but they were quite incompatible with Western interests. By 1945 the British leaders had strong misgivings, only the Americans seemed blissfully unaware of the realities of the postwar world, making large concessions to the Russians and assuming an equal amount of goodwill on the other side. Their awakening was rude, and they reacted the more violently, after having realized that they had been duped.

But is it really fair to blame the Russians? Stalin, after all, had never promised to make East Europe safe for Western democracy. In the last resort, Americans had mainly themselves to blame for the unrealistic picture that they had formed about Soviet policies and intentions. In retrospect it seems probable that the struggle for Germany would have taken a less sharp form had not America shown so much gullibility in 1945. If, for instance, orders had been given by the Allied armies not to delay their march on Berlin, there would have been no Berlin problem. If the Western Allies had given up their claims on Berlin altogether but had instead kept their positions on the Elbe, there would not have been a Berlin problem either, nor, most probably, a DDR, for what remained of Germany east of the Elbe was not large enough to form the nucleus of a state. These are the advantages of hindsight; but quite a few statesmen, Churchill for instance, realized the dangers at the time. Had American demobilization not been carried out with such haste, disregarding the political situation, the United States would have been spared much trouble and awkward commitments in the post-war world. The Russians cannot really be accused of showing bad faith. Both sides had undertaken to do everything in their zone of occupation to make Germany a democratic state. The Russians stuck to the bargain and proceeded to carry out democratic reforms as they understood them; their ideal was, of course, Stalinist Russia, and not the America of Roosevelt and Truman.

Nothing is easier than to criticize Western, and in particular American, policy on Germany between 1944 and 1947. This is frequently done in German quarters and though substantially correct it seems somehow misplaced. Germans too often forget that but for Nazi aggression there would not have been a German problem. Had the West shown more foresight in 1945 the area of conflict could have been narrowed, but a showdown over Germany, a protracted struggle, could not have been avoided.

Soviet policy in Germany pursued several incompatible aims at one and the same time. The large scale dismantling of industry in the Soviet zone which continued almost up to Stalin's death, could be regarded as a legitimate form of reparation for the immense damage done in Russia, yet such a policy fatally weakened the Eastern zone in the political struggle for Germany. It shows that too much consistency and perspicacity should not be read into Soviet policy in Germany. Broadly speaking there was, from the beginning, only one aim, namely, to make the Soviet position in Germany as strong as possible. It was by no means readily obvious in the early post-war period in what way that aim could best be achieved. Conditions were very much in a state of flux and even in the late forties the dilemma facing Moscow was far from clear. By fortifying their position in the eastern quarter of Germany they effectively lost any possibility of neutralizing the rest of Germany; in fact, they drove West Germany into joining NATO. Was the certainty of a small Soviet Germany not preferable to uncertain prospects? Would not a united Germany soon become too powerful to be amenable to Soviet pressure? What course of action, short of world war, would have been open to the Soviet Union had a united Germany founded on the basis of neutrality between West and East, and uncommitted to any power bloc, subsequently decided to join the West? Both Stalin and Khrushchev continued to pursue two policies at the same time, that of the Bolshevization of East Germany and that of neutralizing the whole of Germany; but there was less and less conviction that these aims could be combined, and in 1959 Khrushchev publicly lectured German workers about the advantages accruing to them from the division of their country.

Fourteen years earlier there were no such certainties in Soviet, or anybody else's eyes. Germany had reached the zero point of its history; its cities in ashes, its industry destroyed, communications interrupted and administration in collapse. It was a country not only without work, food, and shelter but, above all, without hope. Large parts of pre-1937 Germany had been lost to Poland and Russia, millions of refugees from the east and south-east were streaming into densely populated Western Germany. German self-confidence had suffered a seemingly fatal shock, the enormity of the crimes that had been committed had not even remotely been realized. There was no doubt about the completeness of the destruction that had been caused; in those days an independent and prosperous Germany was not a distant dream – it seemed a chimera.

In this 'year one', the German Communists stood a good chance of gaining a dominant position. This, at any rate, is what Stalin seems to have thought, and what he had been told by the German Communist leaders. Their reasoning was simple: German Communism had been a strong and growing force before Hitler and they had been the third strongest party after the Nazis and Social Democrats. The Nazi Party had disappeared, while the whole nationalist camp and the entire bourgeoisie had deeply compromised themselves in the Third Reich; they would be held responsible for all the misery. Nor were the Social Democrats a serious rival; their organization had been completely destroyed by the Nazis. Most of their leaders had been elderly men in 1933; support had come mainly from the powerful trade unions. These figures had died or disappeared and their party and trade unions were not likely to re-emerge in post-war Germany. 'German reformism' had developed in the nineteenth century in very specific historical conditions which no longer existed. Surely there

274

could be no right-wing 'revisionist' labour movement amid the poverty and chaos of post-war Germany? The Communist Party, on the other hand, had considerable prestige. It had warned the German people all along, it had fought actively in the most difficult conditions of illegality, and above all, unlike all other parties, it had the men and the means to resume activities at once. Ulbricht and other German Communist leaders had arrived in Berlin from Moscow even before the fighting was over. They had soon enlisted a few thousand Communist militants who had survived the Third Reich – a small number perhaps, but more than any other party could muster at the time. Above all, it had the unlimited support of the Soviet Union; no other German party had such assistance by an occupying power at that time, or indeed at any time thereafter. The German Communists entered the race in 1945 not with just a head start; it seemed, they had the race all to themselves. Yet only a year later it became apparent that something had gone seriously wrong. With all this massive support the most the Communists ever got in free elections in any part of Germany was twenty per cent of the poll (in Berlin in October 1946). They came in third on that occasion, polling less than half as much as the Social Democrats – this in a city in which they had been the strongest single party before 1933. The election results in West Germany, including the industrial areas such as the Ruhr, where the Communists had been very strong before 1933, were even more disappointing. These setbacks to a considerable extent determined Soviet and Communist tactics in the years to come. Not that they had expected to introduce Communism by act of parliament, but they had hoped that in Germany, as in Czechoslovakia, it might be possible to keep the pretence of parliamentary democracy. These setbacks, together with the electoral reverses which the Communists suffered at the same time in Austria and Hungary, strengthened the Kremlin's belief that the time for tougher, non-parliamentary action had come.

The reasons for the Communist defeat were manifold. Their identification with one of the occupying powers gave them great advantages, but politically it was a major liability. It made the party appear a mere puppet, and it was held responsible for all Soviet actions in Germany. After twelve years of tyranny, many Germans resented being pushed around again; the shotgun marriage between Social Democrats and Communists in the Eastern Zone was a major warning. The Communists, though a small minority, had managed to get all the key positions in Berlin and in the Eastern Zone, which did not make them very popular there either. The combined effect was to thwart any Communist or Soviet advances from below. The election results of 1946 doomed German unity, for they convinced the Soviet Union and the German Communists that in their lifetime they would not again be able to afford free elections and that the whole of Germany was too big a morsel for them to swallow at once.

The Split

Both the Soviet Union and the Western powers had envisaged a lengthy period of military occupation of Germany, without, it seems, any awareness of the obligations involved in administering and policing Germany, in directing and carrying the responsibility for its economic development, in prosecuting the war criminals, purging the state apparatus from Nazi elements and re-educating the German people. Faced with the prospect of permanently employing tens of thousands of their own nationals, civilians and soldiers, in administering Germany and of injecting unlimited amounts of money to keep the German economy going, the Western powers soon reached the conclusion that a greater amount of political responsibility ought to be given to Germans, that the dismantling of industries should be restricted to war industries and that efforts should be made to make Germany economically independent. This process was hastened by developments on the international scene and by 1947 it had become established Western policy. To make an efficient economic policy possible the British and American zones of occupation were united and the French followed suit in 1949. In May 1949 an all-German Government came into being, with its seat in Bonn. Four years after the capitulation, almost to the day, Germany had again achieved a large measure of independence. Events in the Eastern zone followed a similar pattern. A 'People's Congress', a pre-governmental body, was convened in Berlin in December 1947. This became, in March 1948, the *Volksrat* which prepared, *inter alia*, the constitution of the *Deutsche Demokratische Republik* which was proclaimed in October 1949.

German rearmament, too, got under way much earlier than had been expected or wished. After the outbreak of the Korean War the Western powers decided that it was dangerous for Germany to remain in a military vacuum; the *General Vertrag* of 1952 and the Paris treaties of 1954 provided for a German contribution to NATO. In this way a German Army was again built. In 1962 the strength of the *Bundeswehr* was 360,000 men. In East Germany the mobilization of para-military units began on a small scale in 1948 and their number eventually reached 100,000. Some 300,000 more men were enlisted in 'battle units' – a militia designed to deal mainly with potential 'internal enemies'.

With the outbreak of the cold war, the division of Germany became an established fact. It is impossible to point to any single event which made it final; the Prague coup, the Berlin blockade and the elimination of the non-Communist parties and their leaders in Eastern Europe all hastened it. Western policy was almost entirely defensive, usually reacting to a Soviet move; it hardly ever developed an initiative of its own. Whenever pushed too hard the West resisted, but its occasional memoranda and diplomatic proposals did not reflect anything like a long term strategy. If the Soviet Union had forced the gradual emergence of two separate German states, it also displayed more initiative, certainly during the early period, on the issue of German unity. The proposal for a peace treaty with Germany in March 1952 was perhaps the most famous move in that direction. This blueprint for a neutral but united and armed Germany was not given the attention it deserved in West Germany or by the Western Allies, and, as a result, in later years there was some talk of the 'great opportunity missed in 1952'. This is almost certainly an exaggeration.

The Soviet intention in 1952, and after, was to slow down German political, economic, and military integration with the West. This, it was thought, could be achieved by using the bait of German unity. Yet for the great majority of Germans it was more important to live in freedom than in unity; there was no escaping the thorny problem of free elections. Whether such elections should precede reunification or follow it might be debatable, but nobody doubted that free elections would result in the overwhelming defeat of Communism, not only in the West but probably even more so in East Germany. The Russians put forward various demands and conditions for a united Germany, some of them eminently sensible, such as educational and agrarian reform. However, there was no way to guarantee constitutionally, or in any other way, the perpetuation of Communist rule in East Germany. Since there is no evidence that Moscow ever seriously considered dispensing with the Ulbricht regime, the declarations about German unity are unlikely to have been genuine.

After Stalin's death some Russian leaders may have played with the idea of reconstructing the political regime in East Germany, but if so they were a minority and their suggestions were not accepted, if indeed they ever existed in a practical form. Had there been any substance behind the 1952 proposals they would have been renewed at some later date in a different form. But they never turned up again; instead there were vague peace plans or projects for a German confederation which left all the really decisive issues open. These were mere propaganda moves, which in the end nobody bothered to discuss. More serious was the Rapacki plan which, after 1958, became the subject of much debate. This proposed military disengagement and a neutral zone free of nuclear weapons in Central Europe; its motives and intentions were mainly strategic, not political. The Soviet and East German Governments have not altogether given up championing German unity, for these topics still figure prominently in editorials and propaganda slogans, but German unity is no longer regarded as a practical policy – for the time being and for many years to come. At most, the Communists seem willing to have a fresh look at it after the consolidation of Communist rule in East Germany and/or a possible change in the overall balance of power. But both these aims seem to be so elusive – always seemingly around the corner, yet never quite attainable.

Thus the fronts in Germany were frozen. However, there was Berlin, the one major exception. In many ways it had been the focus of the German question for years; after 1958 it also became one of the most sensitive zones in West–East relations. Legally there were few doubts about the merits of the case; according to the wartime agreements the whole of Berlin, including the Eastern part of the city, was to be under four power occupation; no one-sided action by any occupying power (such as a Soviet peace treaty with East Germany) could therefore change its status in international law. But when major powers confront each other in a trial of strength, international law counts for little; also, the Western powers had, over the years, permitted many of their rights to be whittled away. Those who had originally decided in 1944 that Berlin should be the fifth military occupation zone had forgotten to make provision for Western access to the former German capital. A clear-cut territorial division of Germany would have been the most practical solution. In 1945 Berlin could have been exchanged against Thuringia or Saxony. This chance was missed; Berlin, which was to have been the symbol of Allied unity, became instead the symbol of Allied disunity, a true mirror of West–East relations and of the state of the world. No agreement is in sight, short of Western or Eastern surrender; it is not at all certain that the ingenious proposals that have been made, such as internationalization, would really work, or whether they would at best mean a postponement of the conflict. To solve the Berlin issue it may be necessary to go back to 1945 and to reopen the whole question of German unity; this is clearly impossible in the prevailing political climate. A possible alternative is that some unforeseen developments will bring about a general lessening of tension which, with the passing of time, will make a solution possible.

East Germany

East Germany, officially called the DDR, or the 'Zone', in derogatory West German parlance, emerged after the war as one of the less agreeable Soviet satellites. It was comparatively easy to find redeeming features and encouraging trends in Poland and Hungary, even in Czechoslovakia, and of course in the Soviet Union. Not so in East Germany which, with the sole exception of Albania, remained the most rigid of all Communist regimes. This may seem surprising, for on the surface things have not gone too badly since the abortive revolt in 1953. Under Stalin, East Germany was somehow spared major excesses such as show trials and mass executions, though there were a great many purges and arrests both before and after 1953. Economically the country did not fare badly, especially if one considers the grave handicaps under which it had to labour, such as the dismantling of entire industries. In spite of this, between 1950 and 1958 industrial output doubled, and the seven year plan ending in 1965 provides for a further increase of one hundred and eighty per cent. The German worker likes a job well done, regardless of the political regime. While there is no reason to take at face value the periodical boasting about catching up with and overtaking the West Germans, East Germany has indeed done better than most other Communist regimes. There have been difficulties in agriculture, but no more than in other Communist countries. The political position of the German Communists in 1945 was considerably stronger than that of their comrades in Poland or Rumania.

In the cultural field, too, the East German regime had the support of some writers, scientists and philosophers of world renown, very much in contrast to the situation in other East European countries.

Yet all these assets were not enough to make the regime politically viable, let alone attractive. In contrast to Bulgaria for example it did not have that minimum of active popular support (variously estimated at between five and ten per cent) which is necessary to rule a country without constant recourse to terror. As in Poland, there was a deep division between the people and those in power, but unlike Gomulka, Ulbricht and his colleagues were not willing to compromise with the people. The task of the East German leaders was admittedly more difficult than that of any other Communist regime in Europe. They had to compete with the other part of Germany, the Bundesrepublik, more populous and richer in resources, with its 'economic miracle' and its so much higher living standards. With all its shortcomings, West Germany was also an infinitely freer country. Up to 1961, three million East Germans had fled to the West; there is no knowing how many more would have escaped had they known that the Wall would go up.

The Wall stopped the exodus and it helped the consolidation of the regime. At the same time it was a major admission of defeat; Communist Germany had lost the peaceful competition. Not only had it failed to make any headway, it had to call off the contest for fear of being routed. There was still the hope that the young generation, suitably educated and indoctrinated, would provide better human material, but in this respect, too, the achievements of the regime were at best doubtful.

The post-Stalin thaw was barely felt in East Berlin. There, even Soviet films could not be shown and Soviet novels could not be published because they were considered dangerously liberal. Ulbricht, after all, was fighting in the front line of the Cold War – not for him the luxury of de-Stalinization. What antagonized most outside observers was the shrill tone and the glaring mendacity of the propaganda, in comparison with which the tenor of Soviet newspapers was one of calm and statesmanlike moderation. The regime had some achievements to its credit: de-Nazification had been far more thorough than in West Germany, and it had also carried out some long overdue social reforms. Yet it succeeded in making even its positive measures appear detestable; what was the purpose of de-Nazification, if the new propagandists were almost as misleading as Goebbels?

Partly it was a question of personalities; East Germany was not very lucky in its new masters. Allowances have of course to be made; 'objectively' these new leaders faced a most difficult task. No other

Communist regime in Europe was so exposed to centrifugal forces, so open to constant comparison with the West. Their dilemma was almost insoluble; they could gain popular support only by following a more liberal policy, but they could not afford liberalization because their popular support was insufficient.

In retrospect it is somewhat ironical that East Germany should have emerged as the most intransigent of all the East European regimes. When this party resumed its activities immediately after the end of the war, it had taken great pains to avoid the sectarian mistakes of the pre-Hitler period. In its first manifesto there was no mention of Marx, Lenin, or Stalin, of Communism or socialism. Instead it said that the Soviet way would not do for Germany because conditions were so radically different.

Up to about 1960, East Germany had no more independence in foreign policy than any other Soviet-sponsored regime. The Sino-Soviet split presented the various states and parties with a variety of choices, whether they wanted this or not. The East Germans found themselves firmly in the pro-Russian camp, which confounded some observers; would it not have been more natural for Ulbricht to ally himself with those who advocated a tougher line *vis-à-vis* the West and who had rejected de-Stalinization as so much sentimental nonsense? However, the East German choice was dictated by political, military, and economic realities. Apart from the intense desire to 'liquidate the Berlin anomaly', the Ulbricht regime had not really much in common with the revolutionary fervour and the implied racialism of the Chinese. With the spread of polycentrism, all Communist regimes and parties have become more national in character; East Germany has been no exception. Historical and cultural traditions and national peculiarities have been of growing importance. Ulbricht's regime has been the German contribution to the cause of world Communism.

Bonn is not Weimar

Whoever had expected a radical new beginning in West Germany after the war was bound to be disappointed. Germany's astonishing economic resurrection after the currency reform of 1949 was not matched by anything like a moral or political rebirth of the German nation. Many active supporters of Nazism soon reappeared in the middle echelons of power, sometimes even in key positions. The general feeling was one of self satisfaction, conservative trends re-asserted themselves; in some ways the *Bunderepublik* resembled Wilhelmian Germany far more than its immediate predecessors. It was not at all easy to define the character of the new state and the new society that had emerged; Bonn was not Weimar and it certainly was not Potsdam – was it perhaps the belated emancipation of the middle classes which somehow had not been completed in the last century?

Nations, like individuals, are unable to jump over their own shadows; there is nothing more difficult than making a radical break with the past. The Germans had to start somewhere in 1945; it was probably unrealistic to expect that they would take a distant date in their own history (such as 1848) as a fresh starting point, leaving out the century in between. If many expectations have not been fulfilled and if Germany has not exactly become a model society, there is no denying that important changes have taken place. It is perhaps too early to say that German democracy has grown firm roots; there have been occasional disquieting manifestations of the old spirit. There was much authoritarianism, regarded by some as the sinister harbinger of a new tyranny, while others saw it as inevitable in a transition period. How could one reasonably expect a model democracy among a people that had not been educated to live in freedom? The old ideals of national glory and of an expansionist foreign policy persisted in some quarters, but on the whole German foreign policy has been remarkably free of them. Instead, a new European spirit has taken hold, especially among the younger generation, and the Bonn government has made determined efforts to live in peace and friendship with most of its neighbours.

The new Germany faced a wall of distrust and suspicion in both West and East. Much of this was only natural in view of the recent past, but some stemmed apparently from less creditable motives. It was strange, for instance, to hear and read from foreign politicians and newspapers comments on Adenauer and his regime that were much harsher than anything one had heard at the time about Hitler and his Reich. Sinister intentions were frequently imputed to the new Germany such as that it was trying to regain mastery over Europe. Of such ambitions the new Germany was almost certainly innocent; a truncated Germany cannot aspire to great power status in the atomic age. These facts of life were fully realized in a satisfied country that was mainly interested in maintaining and extending its *Wirtschaftswunder*; military adventures it was willing to leave to others. It had become a materialistic society; according to its critics it was devoid of spiritual values, but neither aggressive nor expansionist in character. It was, in brief, equidistant from Goethe's Weimar and Frederic II's Potsdam.

The attitude of the *Bundesrepublik* towards the Soviet Union and the other East European countries was one of fear and resentment; this was common to both government and public. Under the settlement imposed by the Russians, the Germans lost their Eastern provinces to Poland and the Soviet Union, the Russian occupation zone remained a Soviet satellite, and the very existence of the *Bundesrepublik* was threatened. If there was some remorse about the murder of millions of Jews and a willingness to make material amends, there were no guilt feelings with regard to Russians, Poles, and Czechs. The Jews had been murdered in cold blood, so the reasoning ran, while the East European nations had been enemies in the war, and they had retaliated, expelling millions of Germans from their homes, robbing all and killing some in the process. If Germany had misbehaved, the account now seemed settled in German eyes.

If the East German attitude towards the West was more unfriendly than that of other Eastern bloc countries, West German views about the Soviet Union were certainly more hostile than those of any other European nation. West Germany was in the forefront of the Cold War; for many years it bore the brunt of Soviet political and propaganda warfare. In addition, the very existence of the Ulbricht regime had a detrimental influence and clouded West Germany's political thinking. Communism for the Germans meant, first and foremost, the 'Zone'; since West Germans were almost exclusively preoccupied with affairs in the other part of the fatherland, the more promising developments in the Soviet Union and other Communist countries after Stalin's death too often escaped their view. The DDR also had a strong indirect impact on German domestic politics; it helped the Christian Democrats to keep the Social Democrats out of power. If the regime operated in East Germany was socialism, or anything remotely connected with it, many West Germans were going to keep clear of a party which also professed socialist beliefs, albeit very different in inspiration.

German policy under Adenauer was to ignore, as far as possible, the Soviet Union and the other Communist regimes in East Europe. In the German government and the foreign ministry there were few people who had any intimate knowledge of Eastern Europe, and their views were not heeded. Adenauer knew little and cared less about the world beyond the Elbe; he had been told that the Soviet Union was so poor that it would go bankrupt one of these days. He advocated an inflexibly tough policy towards Russia, and showed no interest in diplomatic negotiations and summit meetings. This was the only possible line to take at the height of the Cold War, but after 1953 a slightly milder climate prevailed, and Adenauer's unyielding attitude became the source of some dissension with his allies. He continued to resist demands for a more active German policy in Eastern Europe; the idea of a *rapprochement* with the Soviet Union seemed to him not merely a chimera, but altogether most undesirable. If there was any thinking on these lines it came not so much from the extreme left, whose influence was extremely small anyway, but from right-wing circles who resented what they regarded as undue dependence on the Western Allies, who remembered Rapallo, and who thought that an agreement with Russia would make Germany again independent and, perhaps, one day restore her great power status. Certain business interests who wanted to regain their traditional markets in Eastern Europe also advocated closer ties, but on the whole these groups remained uninfluential.

Almost until the end of the Adenauer era Germany's Russian policy remained one of *immobilisme*. Under the Hallstein doctrine Bonn would not maintain diplomatic relations with any country which recognized the DDR. The only exception was the Soviet Union itself, but though Bonn had begun to deviate from the doctrine it continued to be a serious obstacle to German policy in the East. Only towards the very end of Adenauer's rule were some determined efforts made to establish closer relations with some East European countries. It was then realized that if West Germany wanted to isolate the DDR, it could not afford to neglect contacts with the countries beyond.

There were, however, narrow limits to a German initiative in Eastern Europe. Any real reconciliation would involve the recognition of the Oder–Neisse line, of the permanent loss of Silesia, East Prussia, and other formerly German regions. Yet East European statesmen had made it quite clear that even a formal German renunciation would not make a decisive change in their eyes. If that was the case, it was asked in Bonn, why engage in futile demonstrations? Nor was there any real hope that closer contacts with the East would help to restore German unity, the great magic slogan in West German politics, on which all parties agreed. Those who favoured a closer relationship with the Soviet Union argued that Moscow continued to hold the key to German unity, that without its agreement there was no hope at all for reunification. This was correct, but gradually the Germans came to realize that they could have unity only on terms that none of them were willing to accept; unity in freedom remained an aim that simply was not to be realized in their time. Meanwhile the Wall went up, and despite occasional friendly gestures, Soviet and East European propaganda about German revanchism, neo-Nazism and militarism went on relentlessly. In these circumstances West German policy-makers were reduced to contemplating certain long term strategies in Eastern Europe; for the time being there was little outside the field of trade that could be done.

There had been no direct conflict of interests between Germany and Russia either before the First or before the Second World War – what there had been was a clash of aspirations, of great power ambitions, of ideologies. Russia had never really coveted German territory. Annexations had figured in the thinking of both the Kaiser and, to a far larger degree, Hitler, but neither in 1914 nor in 1941 had this been the main issue. The situation after the Second World War was totally different: as the result of Hitler's policy Germany was cut into two with the Russians permanently established in its former capital. Thus the scope of Russo–German relations after 1945 was narrowly circumscribed.

Soviet Fears and Ambitions

Soviet policy towards West Germany in the post-war period has followed at one and the same time various, often incompatible, aims. For several years after its establishment, Moscow refused to recognize the German Federal Republic, preferring not to call it by its proper name; for the Soviet press it was 'the puppet Bonn regime', Adenauer the 'so-called chancellor'.[5] Yet when it was realized in the middle fifties that the *Bundesrepublik* was there to stay and that it had made considerable political and economic progress, the Soviet Union was not only eager to establish diplomatic relations, but consented to repatriate a fairly large number of German prisoners of war and thousands of civilians. Soviet propaganda oscillated between dire warnings about the consequences of West German rearmament and, admittedly less frequently, reflections about the advantages of Russian–German collaboration. Moscow was not averse to invoking German national traditions if they had been Russophil. *Turnvater* Jahn, for instance, the founder of the German gymnasts movement, or E. M. Arndt, had been held in high esteem in the Third Reich as 'precursors of National Socialism'; nor did their reputation suffer after 1945, for had they not been early champions of German–Russian friendship? When the German National Committee published a newspaper in Moscow during the Second World War, it was framed in the black–white–red colours of Wilhelmian Germany – not the black–red–gold of 1848 or the Weimar Republic. Such attempts to attract support from nationalist elements alternated with violent campaigns against West German political and military leaders and, generally speaking, against everybody who, for one reason or another, had provoked Soviet displeasure. Willy Brandt, mayor of West Berlin, whose resistance record was as good as, if not better than, that of most Communists, thus became a Gestapo spy in the Soviet press; a well-known scholar and military expert, who went to America as a young Jewish refugee, was described as a member of the Hitler Youth.

One of the aims of the Soviet propaganda against the alleged spread of neo-Nazism was to sow doubts about the character of the new Germany among its Western Allies. The Soviet leaders knew that there was no such danger, but they had been surprised and perhaps slightly disturbed by the German economic come-back. Russia was, of course, much stronger now; if before the Second World War Soviet industry had lagged behind German, it had overtaken both Germanies in the fifties. Even so, Germany's recovery was astonishing; its economy had suffered not less than that of the Soviet Union. Germany received foreign help but probably much less than the Soviet Union had received after the war by means of reparations, etc. Explaining the German 'miracle' in terms of millionaires waxing rich by exploiting the workers would not do, for the fact had to be faced that the exploited German worker had again attained, fifteen years after the end of the war, a standard of living considerably higher than that of the Soviet worker. This could not fail to impress the Russians who in recent decades had come more and more to regard economic performance as the yardstick of political achievement.

In the military field, Soviet feelings were equally at variance. In the overall military balance of the nineteen sixties, even a rearmed

West Germany did not matter; Soviet superiority was so absolute that the talk about a German menace had ceased to make sense. Soviet spokesmen emphasized this more than once: if two world wars had brought the German nation to the brink of the abyss, a third would destroy it altogether. Yet at the same time other Soviet spokesmen made it appear as if the *Bundeswehr* – after all, only a shadow of the old *Wehrmacht* – was the greatest danger to world peace and that German revanchists, neo-Nazis and 'ultras', pursuing their traditional *Drang nach Osten*, were actively preparing a new invasion. This picture contrasted so much with realities that it made many Westerners assume that this was but another attempt to sow discord in the Western camp. For if the military power of the new Germany was insignificant in comparison with the Soviet Union, it was not inconsiderable by European standards; it could reawaken old suspicions about German ambitions. Such considerations un-doubtedly played a part in Soviet thinking, yet there was also a genuine fear and distrust. The events of 1941 had been a real shock for the Russians; the German armies had, after all, reached Stalin-grad and had almost entered Moscow. Many million Russians had been killed and untold destruction had been wrought. Less than twenty years later the new German Army was commanded in large part by the very same generals who had won their spurs in Hitler's *Wehrmacht*. It was not really surprising that after the traumatic experience of the early years of the Second World War, Soviet thinking should be influenced by old fears as much as by new reali-ties. In this thinking, not only the present strength of the *Bundes-wehr* mattered, but also various imaginary possibilities: what if the Germans set their heart on reconquering their lost eastern territories – alone or with the help of their NATO allies? It was sheer fantasy now, but these had been very real fears in the not-too-distant past. The massive heritage of hate and fear was not a mere phantom – it would not fade at the crowing of the cock.

Chapter 13

STALIN AND HITLER

GREAT MEN, taken up in any way – surely we know this at least since Carlyle – are profitable company: we can hardly contemplate them without gaining something. Yet how to define greatness?

'Of course, history alone can show how important this or that public man has been.'

It was Stalin who said this. But history, we are told, usually passes final judgments only after people cease to care; meanwhile each generation does its revaluing according to its political lights. To forecast how 'this or that public man' is likely to fare in the judgment of coming generations amounts to predicting the course of politics of the next century. Communists will hardly ever agree with non-Communists about the rôle of Stalin; even among the former, differences of opinion will persist as to whether the late 'father of the people' did more harm than good, or whether in that so-called last analysis he was 'a progressive force' after all. Such fluctuations in the posthumous fortunes of historical figures can persist for a long time. Up till the middle thirties Soviet historians took a dim view of the activities of Ivan IV ('the Terrible') who, they said, had been in a state close to mental illness. In the heyday of Stalinism (for obvious reasons) there was an entire reappraisal and Ivan became one of the great heroes of Russian history – cruel by necessity, yet wise in his decisions. After Stalin's death, the Tsar was at once downgraded, cautiously at first, but recently in a more sweeping way. Ivan IV has been dead for close on four hundred years; Jenghiz Khan has not been with us for even longer, and yet, as we recently learned to our surprise, Marxists cannot agree as to his place in history (some, in Mongolia and Peking, think he played a progressive rôle; those in Moscow disagree emphatically).

Such shifts and reversals in historical appraisal are bound to be far more abrupt in a dictatorship, but of course they do happen elsewhere: the historiography of the French Revolution and of Napoleon is an obvious example. Is it not extremely likely that rival historians of the future will champion Stalin against Trotsky, and vice versa, re-enacting the whole drama, in the same way that Aulard saw Danton as the hero of the revolution, while Mathiez held it to be Robespierre? The Michelet school already seems to be behind us — those who (as Pieter Geyl argues) described the terror but did not allow the radiant beauty of their dreams to be darkened by what they had so keenly observed. If patriotism and 'loyalty to the revolution' was the decisive criteria then, the 'strengthening of Soviet power' became the test in a later age. Since Stalin did not reintroduce private ownership of the means of production, he could scarcely escape remaining progressive whatever he did. Had fifty million people perished in the process instead of five or ten, would 'quantity' then have become a new quality? The dialectic doesn't tell us.

Yet there are good reasons for thinking that Stalin will fare worse than the heroes of the French revolution. 'Public men', to use his own phrase, are, after all, appraised in the context of their times. Some of Ivan's actions were deplorable, but then his age was not exactly a model of enlightenment. Stalin, on the other hand, will be judged as a twentieth-century ruler, not as a sixteenth-century despot — and against this background historians cannot fail to note the relapse into barbarity. It is surprising (and somewhat illogical) that those historians who believe that the golden progressive age is ahead of us should have any doubts about this, for a more civilized time is likely to judge Stalinism even more harshly than our own. Especially to Communist historians of the future, Stalin will be a major embarrassment. They may even do him some injustice, for the comparatively sane beginnings of a public figure in history are usually overshadowed by later wilder, more dramatic events. Who but a few readers of Suetonius remember that Caligula was universally welcomed as a moderate leader when he came to power and promised to restore the rule of law suspended under Tiberius? And who recalls that Napoleon was first hailed as the leader most likely to restore peace to France?

If history rarely passes unanimous judgments, still each generation of historians feels obliged to take a stand. Both Burke and Paine have survived as major commentators on the French Revolution despite their passionate engagement. I wonder whether today's relativist and wait-and-see historians will fare so well. Mr E. H. Carr has said that 'to us Hitler, at the moment, seems a bad man, but will they think Hitler a bad man in a hundred years' time or will they think the German society of the thirties bad? . . .' Most of us think that Hitler *was* 'a bad man' and that German society was in something less than good shape. It is possible that a hundred years from now some misguided people will put *all* the blame on German society; according to some evidence, this may even happen much earlier. Yet what concern is this of ours? Has the effort to anticipate the judgment of posterity ever really produced great works of historiography? Politically the suspension of moral standards is disastrous. It should be fairly obvious by now that the believers in 'historical necessity' bear at least some responsibility for the rise of Hitler and Stalin; a great many more people would have resisted the dictatorship had it not been said to be irresistible, had they not been captives of some notion of a 'wave of the future' or an 'historic process'.

We are, of course, all anti-Stalinists nowadays. The friends or relatives of many of his victims are still alive; in Russia the authorities have really only just begun to permit them to give expression to their feelings. It may take years before the anti-Stalin wave reaches its peak. Yet in a few decades the sufferings will have receded into the past and one can foresee with some certainty a revisionist school of historians who will reassess Stalin in historical perspective without emotional involvement. Who can believe that he will ever again be proclaimed as 'one of the geniuses of world history'? Stalin dominated a greater stage and his actions had an impact on many more people than had either Cromwell or Napoleon: which makes him very important indeed. Everything done by the ruler of two hundred million people is important, however cruel, however stupid. It is apparently exceedingly difficult to ruin a big country, and only Hitler seems to have succeeded, but then it is too early to say whether his was a lasting success, and anyway Germany was too small to qualify as a super-power by twentieth-century standards. Any President of the United States after 1914 (even Hoover, even Eisenhower), any ruler of Russia after 1880, any leader of China since 1930, must figure prominently in future history books.

Stalin, as the hero and villain of the totalitarian age, will probably be compared not with Napoleon or Robespierre but with his most outstanding contemporary, namely, Adolf Hitler. This, curiously enough, may be the best way of salvaging part of his reputation. Hitler suffered from delusions; he thought he could rule the world as the leader of a people of seventy million and with a doctrine of racial exclusivity which made collaboration with other peoples impossible. With all his political recollections of the First World War and the attempt (in *Mein Kampf*) to draw conclusions and lessons, he had no real understanding of the realities of power in the world. Economics he chose to ignore completely, for they bored him; this, of course, doomed him from the very beginning. Having won mastery over Germany, he thought that the struggle for Europe, and ultimately for the world, would be a repeat performance. Stalin, the realist, was far more aware of the limitations of his country and of the international Communist movement – his Marxist studies stood him in good stead here. Not only was he by nature a far more cautious man with stronger nerves, but he had also been taught that economics were of vital importance. He might attack Finland, but he would never have provoked a war against several countries whose combined potential was so much superior to his own. Hitler had grandiose, if rather nebulous, plans for the future, but he was certainly much more given to flights of fantasy than Stalin, who stayed much closer to the ground and therefore prevailed in the end.

Within the framework of their own movements, Hitler was undoubtedly the more important and the more gifted leader. Without Hitler, National Socialism, as we know it, would not have come to power. The extreme right might have won in 1933, but a Germany led by a Goering (not to mention one of the lesser figures) would have been a very different proposition. When Stalin came to power, the course of the Russian Revolution was already set. After 1921 there was no serious attempt at military intervention; Bolshevism would have remained in power with or without Stalin.

Hitler had many of the qualities of a political leader that Stalin lacked. A powerful speaker who had a magnetic effect on his audience, he absolutely dominated his subordinates by force of personality, and exuded the charisma of a leader of men, or at any rate of one possessed. If any important decision was to be taken, even the very highest Nazi leaders such as Goering, Goebbels, or Himmler counted for nothing, as they freely admitted. Up to the very end of the war they never questioned the authority of the Fuehrer, following him blindly, assuming that the Fuehrer knew best and that he was always right.

Stalin, on the other hand, was almost anti-charismatic. He was, at best, an indifferent speaker; both dictators were bad writers and they probably knew it. By 1941 many ordinary Russians had come to believe in Stalin in almost the same way as millions of Germans believed in Hitler. Thousands of Russian soldiers went into battle *za rodinu, za Stalina*. And yet it was not quite the same; there had been nothing spontaneous about the Stalin cult in the Soviet Union. A massive and very deliberate promotion campaign had propagated the image of a great, wise, and good leader who was larger than life. Millions of Russians had ultimately come to accept this image just as millions of people in the capitalist world have been persuaded of the excellence of some soap or baking powder, following a relentless promotion campaign. The Russians accepted this image because it answered the need for a father figure, a guide for the perplexed, a living symbol of the fatherland. But it was more a feeling of dependence than of fanatical belief; at the time of the worst excesses it was often said 'If only Stalin knew . . .', and after his death (according to an official announcement) there was a fear of panic in Moscow. Millions of Russians wept and many others asked: 'How shall we live without him?' Great is the power of modern mass media.

The Hitler cult was far more spontaneous. Those around the Fuehrer worshipped him and really believed in his prophetic gifts, while Stalin was surrounded by people, most of whom, as it subsequently emerged, had merely feared him. Stalin had come to power by organizational scheming and plotting, and ruled by means of an elaborate apparatus. Never accepted by the Old Bolsheviks, he liquidated them almost without exception, and there were recurrent purges because he could never feel quite certain of the loyalty of his closest assistants. Hitler, on the other hand, had no reason to be afraid of his old *Parteigenossen*, of whom he did not think very highly anyway. With the exception of June 1934, there were no major purges in the Third Reich – Goebbels, Goering, Himmler remained with the Fuehrer to the end of the war.

With Hitler, as his biographer wrote, one is uncomfortably aware of never being far from the realm of the irrational. He was a considerable actor; his famous attacks of sudden and violent rage were not artificial but he exploited them with consummate skill. In the later years, especially during the war, when things were not going so well, he lost his self-control with increasing frequency. There is no unanimity even now about his intellectual capacity, and even more important, about the genuineness of his beliefs. To some extent he was really convinced that providence had chosen him, and there was no limit to his self-confidence. Sometimes, however, in a small circle or with a close confidant, he was quite cynical, and it emerged that he did not believe in many of the things he proclaimed in public. The question of Hitler's real beliefs is, therefore, almost unanswerable. Some were genuine, others were not, and he was also given to a great deal of auto-suggestion. He gradually came to believe in some of his own lies, just as he gradually persuaded himself that everything he touched would succeed. Hitler was a man of wide, if superficial interests, of above average intelligence and intuition, and an extraordinary memory. His memory, above all, confounded his assistants and even the experts, time and time again, and led many of them to believe that he was both an original thinker and a great authority on a variety of subjects.

Yet a comparison suggests that Stalin was more ideally suited for the control of a totalitarian state. His critics have made great play with his intellectual shortcomings. That he was not a great thinker needs hardly to be emphasized today (though the distance between him and the other Old Bolsheviks was perhaps less than some wish us to believe). In this, as in most other respects, he was mediocre. But an intellectual at the helm might not have lasted long; in difficult situations he might have wavered, for there were so many aspects to be considered, so many eventualities to be taken into account. Stalin's mind was a simple one; there were a number of basic truths which he had learned at an early age, and these were all that mattered for his purpose. Surely he understood them better than his rivals did: that only power mattered and that all the rest was idle talk – that the *cadres* decide everything – that heavy industry was more decisive than light industry – and so on. His very limitations were an enormous advantage: they made it easier for him to act. That he frequently took wrong decisions did not greatly matter – somebody else would be paying for them in any case.

Both Hitler and Stalin regarded themselves as indispensable; they would have found much common ground in their distrust and contempt of the people; nor was there much to choose between their views about such things as justice or truth. Hitler could afford to be cynically frank in his infrequent utterances about these subjects, whereas Stalin had to be described in official and unofficial writings as modest, sincere, truthful, and deeply devoted to the masses. Hitler

293

fancied himself to be a kind man, basically; whereas Stalin (according to the official literature) was merciless towards the enemies of the party but a paragon of humanity and solicitude in every other respect. Hitler acted and reacted quickly without much self-control; Stalin was unhurried in his decisions. Stalin will be judged by rational criteria to a far greater extent than Hitler; yet what appeared to some of his contemporaries titanic achievements may appear to future historians as so much sound and fury. History is usually more willing to forgive cruelty (even senseless cruelty) than hypocrisy; surely Stalin was one of history's great hypocrites.

He shared with Hitler a great capacity for sustained work, though he was more painstaking, pedantic, plodding, and therefore better suited to direct a gigantic bureaucracy. Hitler was bored by the minute organizational work in which Stalin found obvious satisfaction. As strategists they were apparently equally gifted (which means that they understood no more about military science than possibly one or two million others). If they proved to be right on occasion against the advice of their generals, this reflects the quality of the judgments of professional soldiers. It is almost comical how easily myths are created – and believed. Stalin's best-known western biographer describes his image as a strategist: 'A prodigy of patience, tenacity, and vigilance, almost omnipresent, almost omniscient.' On another occasion: 'He displayed extraordinary willpower, tenacity, and coolheadedness.' One should compare this with what is now said and written on the subject in Russia by those who ought to know.

Hitler's ideas of the *Blitzkrieg*, it could be argued, proved very successful in the West – but disastrous in Russia. Stalin, in his military decisions as in his foreign policy, for many years mainly reacted to outside challenges; domestic affairs had for him absolute priority during the thirties. Once he had decided to 'build socialism in one country' he was more or less on his own: nothing that Marx, and very little that Lenin, had written was of much help in the transformation of Soviet society. Hitler's position was much easier; he never envisaged radical social change; economics and domestic affairs were of little interest to him; his party never had a clear social and economic programme. Yet is it really correct to say that German economy 'stagnated' under Hitler? In fact it made considerable progress (in comparison with the low of 1932–3), even if the rate of growth was much smaller than that in the Soviet Union; it was bound to be smaller in a country that was already fully industrialized. Once the worst of the world crisis was over the German economy would have improved anyway – but so would the Soviet economy after 1929 under any sensible leadership. Much of the German industrial production was geared to armament (though far less than is commonly assumed). It is one of the major riddles of the Third Reich that Hitler did not prepare more efficiently for his great war. Some historians now say that he did not 'really' want a war. I tend to believe that his ignorance of all things economic was a decisive factor.

Stalin's real and lasting merit (or so it is often said) was the industrialization of Russia. He realized that it was a race against time, that Russia would again be overwhelmed as it had been so often in its past, unless it emerged as a strong industrial power within a decade or so. And so it did – there was 'the tremendous advance in heavy industry in the thirties'; the Red Army was 'strong and fully prepared' when the great test came in 1941 and the Nazi menace was defeated. Russia became 'the strongest industrial and political power in Europe' – all this owing to the man in the Kremlin who relentlessly pursued his aims, regardless of all obstacles and difficulties. This amounts, surely, to the most persuasive plea that can be made for Stalin. Yet this version has already received some bad knocks, and in the years to come not much of it is likely to survive.

The First World War, the Revolution, and the Civil War had interrupted Russia's industrialization. By the time the ravages had healed, in the late twenties, the stage was set for rapid industrialization – under any leadership. It was merely a question of the rate of growth; Five-Year-Plans were not Stalin's invention. Soviet industrial output between 1928 and 1940 might have only been doubled rather than quadrupled under a less brutal regime, but it is more than doubtful whether this would have had a fatal effect on Russia's ability to resist the German invasion. Stalin's mistakes and failures weigh heavily in the balance: the dislocation in industry and the weakening of the army caused by the purges, the widespread disaffection of the population caused by the forced collectivization (which even Soviet authors are beginning to admit was 'a mistake' as carried out), and Stalin's refusal to believe in, and to prepare his forces for, a Nazi attack when all the world knew it would come in spring 1941. When all the mistakes are added up, not much remains of the myth of the great leader who foresaw so much. That the terrible reverses during the first part of the war were unnecessary is now maintained by all Soviet authors; Russia, after all, was neither Denmark nor Holland, and a *Blitzkrieg* could not have worked. She had been a formidable military power even under the not-so-efficient leadership of the Tsars; her armies – with the advantage of vast numbers and territory – had defeated greater military geniuses than Hitler. The question whether, at such a high price, Stalin was 'necessary' for the Communists has been debated in some detail. Necessity has been the tyrant's plea since time immemorial. Stalin's decision to achieve a high rate of industrial growth by holding down consumption and wages and by concentrating on high investment rates and the production of goods that cannot be consumed was dictated not by economic but by political considerations. Such a policy could be pursued only by a dictatorship, and (as an economic historian has recently emphasized) it provided a government with a social function and a justification for its existence:

'. . . a policy of rapid increases in the levels of consumption may in the short run bridge the political difficulties, but in the long run is likely to create troublesome problems. Plentiful supplies of consumers' goods produce a climate of relaxation among the populace which is not congenial to dictatorships. Once the stress and strain have been reduced, the problem of political liberty is almost bound to arise. . . .' (Alexander Gerschenkron: *Economic Backwardness in Historical Perspective*, 1962.)

Necessary or not, the social impact of Stalinism on the Russians was far more lasting than Hitler's on the Germans. So was its impact on Soviet intellectual life. Isaac Deutscher concludes his biography of Stalin with an impressive comparison of intellectual life in the Third Reich and in Stalinist Russia. Hitler, we learn, ruined German cultural life; Stalin on the other hand gave a tremendous impetus to Russian intellectual life by sending the whole nation to school. 'Its (Germany's) medical men were turned into specialists on the racialist purity of blood and into assassins of those whose blood was deemed impure . . .' The level of German medicine suffered from the exodus of the Jews, and several hundred German physicians committed unspeakable crimes against humanity. Yet ninety-nine per cent of German physicians went about their jobs as they had before and as they have since, as did Soviet physicians under Stalin, doing some good and some harm (inventing, incidentally, the sulphonamides and making a few other discoveries).

Mr Deutscher also stated that 'Stalin has not, like Hitler, forbidden the new generation to read and study the classics of their own literature whose ideological outlook does not accord with his.' Closer investigation shows that much of Dostoevsky, some of Tolstoy, Leskov, Pisemsky, and others, was either not published at all under Stalin, or in small editions for specialists; other classics were carefully edited. Hitler banned the works of Heine and other Jews; no other German classics, with the exception of Lessing's *Nathan der Weise*, were banned. Nazism, being less ideological in character, took less interest in cultural affairs; it had not time in half a dozen years to ripen into full totalitarianism. In order to survive (with some notable exceptions) it sufficed not to be anti-Nazi; in the Soviet Union a far greater measure of active participation and affirmation was needed. This is, I think, an important point that has not been given sufficient attention. The glaring exceptions in Nazi Germany were in architecture, painting, and sculpture. Here there is a curious parallelism with Stalin's Russia; for all dictators apparently have a weakness for monumental buildings, statues, and portraits. Psychoanalysis was banned in Nazi Germany (as in Russia) and it became difficult to do serious work in biology in either country.

In comparing the state of literature in Nazi Germany and in Stalin's Russia one finds some striking differences. Many German writers compromised themselves by signing political manifestos and, by and large, nothing of great importance was written in the era of the Third Reich. Yet there was no pressure on German writers to describe in their poems Hitler's boyhood in Braunau, or in their novels his military exploits as an NCO in the First World War. Their works were mainly an ineffectual kind of escapism. With the exceptions of an exceedingly small group who had a special commission to do so, they did not deal with the history of the Nazi Party in their works. In the Soviet Union the 'cult of personality' was incomparably more pervasive; the Leonidzes and Pogodins, the Pavlenkos and Virtas, the Alexei Tolstoys and Surkovs devoted poems, plays, and novels to the leader. Yet not only the hacks created such literature; the greatest contemporary writers made their contributions too – Leonid Leonov (*Slovo o Pervom deputate*) for instance, Konstantin Fedin (*Uncommon Summer*), and Sholokhov (*Virgin Soil Upturned*). So did many who are now in the forefront of the battle for a more liberal course in Soviet literature – Alexander Tvardovsky (in *Strana Muravia*), Margarita Aliger, and Konstantin Simonov. Even the writers of children's literature made their contribution. Re-reading what Soviet writers wrote on the occasion of Stalin's seventieth birthday in December 1949 is a painful experience. It has since been argued that 'the cult of the individual' was indeed very harmful but that, nevertheless, some great works were produced even in that dark period. The underlying idea is that one could delete the scenes or anecdotes where Stalin is introduced just as an entry could be omitted from an encyclopaedia. This may be so in a very few cases where the Stalin episodes were quite obviously added more or less artificially to a poem or novel (perhaps after some outside prodding). Yet by and large such surgery is quite impracticable. The books and poems and plays did not merely express fulsome praise for the leader; they were permeated with the spirit of the epoch. According to one of the proverbs which Chairman Khrushchev liked to quote, a little gall suffices to spoil a barrel of honey. The situation in other fields – whether we take the cinema in the early fifties or philosophy or political economy – was not very different. The intellectual impact of Stalinism was not less lasting than its social results; the Soviet Union will have to bear the consequences for a long time to come.

If Hitler was evil, the element of calculated cruelty was much smaller in Stalin. To equate the Nazi extermination camps and Stalin's labour camps betrays a lack of knowledge, or imagination, or both. Stalin was evil 'from necessity' (the ideological argument ran); he used terrible means to reach a humanist ideal; he killed in the name of liberty and for a better future. All this may not have made a noticeable difference to his victims, but it did in fact put certain limitations in his way – limitations which Hitler, for obvious reasons, never faced. It is debatable whether, and to what degree, Stalin still believed in the future ideal society towards the close of his life; or whether, as far as he was concerned, the means had become the ends themselves. The belief appears now to have been naïve, and naïveté in politics (as Stalin observed in one of his articles in 1917) 'borders on the criminal'. There is one important mitigating circumstance – Hitler's tyranny was entirely of his own making; Stalin's dictatorship was very much in line with his own character and style, yet the ground was largely prepared by historical circumstances – Tsarist *samoderzhavie* and the kind of regime established by Lenin in 1917 with its built-in tendency towards autocracy. The following year Rosa Luxemburg predicted accurately how it would all end – and at that time there was no Stalin in sight.

Seventeen thousand historians in the Soviet Union (according to the figures of October 1961) – and add to that a handful outside Russia – face then a difficult dilemma: how to explain the phenomenon of Stalinism in terms of Marxian historical materialism? Engels wrote that whether in a particular country at any particular time a particular individual emerged was 'pure accident', but if that man were removed the demand for a substitute would immediately arise and the substitute would be found *tout bien que mal*. Plekhanov, the 'father of Russian Marxism' who wrote the classic work about the rôle of the individual in history, was even more emphatic:

> 'It has long been observed that the great talents appear everywhere, whenever the social conditions favourable to their development exist. This means that every man of talent who becomes a social force is the product of social relations. ... A great man is great not because his personal qualities give individual features to great historical events, but because he possessed qualities which make him most capable of serving the great social needs of the time ...'

What social and political conditions existed in Russia in the twenties that favoured the appearance of Stalin and Stalinism? What social relations produced Stalin – and what qualities did he possess that made him 'most capable of serving the great social needs of the time'? These are admittedly difficult, not to say awkward, questions, and it is not surprising that we have not yet had a Marxist explanation from Russia. Since it is rather unlikely that Soviet historians will find Marxism completely satisfactory on the rôle of the hero in history, they will inevitably have to play down the rôle of Stalin. Perhaps he was not so important after all? In the most recent Russian historical works Stalin is not mentioned (or quoted) at all, even where for obvious reasons he should figure quite prominently. Instead, such circumlocutions as the 'Leadership of the party' (*Rukovodstvo KPSS*) are used; this is somewhat threadbare for it is not exactly a secret that one man constituted the leadership of the party for many years. Such sleight of hand will not serve very well on the stage of history. The Russians, with very few exceptions, suffered a great deal under Stalin. One can, perhaps, make Trotsky an 'unperson' but not Stalin; it would be inhuman and, incidentally, ineffective to belittle Stalinism. Since the Russians are very human and desperately eager to 'rehabilitate' their past, the present leadership has been steering a middle course – from the release of the Kremlin doctors in April 1953 to the publication of *Ivan Denisovich* in November 1962.

Broadly speaking, four periods can be discerned in the process of de-Stalinization. The first began almost immediately after the death of the dictator in March, 1953; the purges were discontinued, the leadership re-organized, some secret police chiefs were removed. In this period Ilya Ehrenburg wrote his novel *The Thaw*. There was as yet no open criticism of Stalin, but his name was mentioned less often in public speeches, the press, on the radio, and in scholarly publications. Some of the Old Bolsheviks were now rehabilitated, albeit posthumously. Publicity was given to these rehabilitations only after the famous twentieth party congress in February, 1956, which constitutes the beginning of the second phase of de-Stalinization. This congress proclaimed the consolidation of 'socialist legality' and the return to 'Leninist norms of inner-party democracy'. The official party history (the famous *Short Course*) was criticized for the first time. The highlight of this congress, Khrushchev's famous speech on February 25 (the text of which became known several weeks later) was a most effective debunking of Stalin all along the line. Yet it was a *secret* speech and has not been made public in the Soviet bloc to this very day. The Soviet leaders preferred to move with great caution. ('We had to tell the people the truth,' Khrushchev said later.) Word got round, nevertheless, and the second wave of de-Stalinization reached its peak in the summer of 1956 with a great debate among the Communist parties. The moment it appeared that the reaction might get out of hand, instructions were given to apply the brakes – as the Central Committee's resolution of June 30, 1956 (on the 'cult of personality'), and *Pravda* editorials (to the effect that Stalin's terrorism was necessary) bear witness. In these circumstances there was strictly limited scope for an intellectual ferment that found expression in a number of anthologies, novels, and poems. Even the most famous novel of the period, Vladimir Dudintsev's *Not by Bread Alone*, was not really directed against Stalin and Stalinism but merely against certain negative features in the society and a certain type of leader (Drozdov). Yet once the immovable controls had been removed, the borderline between what was permissible and what was taboo was no longer quite clear. A kind of no-man's-land came into being and some courageous men dared occasional forays – and beat their retreat when they sensed that the cross-fire was too dangerous.

The old leadership (the Molotovs and the Kaganovichs) warned against sweeping de-Stalinization; they were willing at most to criticize specific aspects of the Stalin epoch, but they refused to damn Stalin himself – both because they did not believe in the new-fangled methods of leadership and because they had been so deeply involved personally. Once de-Stalinization really got under way, where would it all end? Would it not cause (as did 'de-Nazification') an unending chain of mutual recriminations and purges? Khrushchev, and Mikoyan too, had been members of the Politburo under Stalin, yet they intended to carry de-Stalinization further than the diehards; for them, and for the younger generation of leaders, this was a necessity in order to win the freedom essential for carrying out a policy that differed in some essential respects from Stalinism. Such revisions could only be made once they had dissociated themselves clearly from the legacy of the past.

After the diehards had been excluded from the party leadership, the stage was set for yet another step forward, which came at the twenty-second congress of the CPSU in October 1961. This time there were public speeches about the horrors of the Stalin era, ranging from a somewhat perfunctory statement by Mikhail Suslov to the touching spiritualist account of Madame Lazurkina about Lenin's visitations and what he had told her about Stalin. This congress, like the one five years earlier, provoked heated discussions in the Communist camp. Again it appeared at one stage that the reaction would be too violent. Again, as in summer 1956, the limits of 'the thaw' had to be stressed. Yet in contrast to 1956, fresh impetus was given to the anti-Stalin campaign by the publication of a number of literary works such as Evtushenko's *Stalin's Heirs* in October, 1962, and the first books in a new genre hitherto known only in the West – the labour camp literature. This brings us to the fourth stage – or has de-Stalinization now become a continuing and paramount part of the revolution from above?

It is too soon to say. We are more certain about the limits of this movement for the time being. Everything Stalin did after 1935 can (in fact *must*) now be criticized in Russia; it is freely admitted that he committed 'political mistakes' in 1917 and 1923–4, that collectivization was unduly 'harsh'. Yet he is almost exclusively denounced only for what he did to his own supporters, the men and women who were willing to follow him almost blindly. He has not been taken to task for what he did to the opposition in the party (let alone to those

301

outside it). Evidently Trotsky, Zinoviev, Kamenev, as well as Bukharin and Tomsky, still remain political adversaries of the CPSU of 1964. True, they are no longer 'criminals', 'enemies of the people', 'German or Japanese spies', admissions that were made rather grudgingly, and so far implicitly. It seems fairly likely that within a few years the right-wing deviationists will be partly rehabilitated (rumours to that effect seem to have been premature). If they committed political mistakes, did not Stalin? The left-wing opposition of the twenties presents greater difficulties to Khrushchevian historiography, and no solution seems to be in sight. Yet all these are tactical problems, so to speak; the basic issues have not yet been faced.

According to the currently valid version, Stalinism was *not* inherent in Leninism, was *not* its natural and logical successor, but merely an aberration, a form of degeneration. The structure of Soviet society remained sound, economic reconstruction continued, and foreign policy was 'progressive', even during the darkest years. Some have compared – wrongly I believe – Stalin to Napoleon spreading the achievements of the French Revolution. (It is an inept comparison anyway. Do Soviet historians regard Napoleon's invasion of Russia as a progressive event? Did not Napoleon's aggression produce an anti-liberal, chauvinist reaction all over Europe? Did not Stalin do serious, perhaps lasting, harm to the Communist cause?) Real problems are not so easily solved. Those who maintain that 'it cannot happen again' are apparently willing to rely on the subjective factor of human goodwill (surely a very un-Marxist view) unless one insists that Russia has already made the jump 'from necessity to freedom' and that the laws of historical materialism have therefore ceased to function. It would be most in line with Marxism if they argued that Stalin was a regrettable necessity but that the phenomenon cannot possibly recur since Soviet society has now reached a 'higher stage' of social development and that therefore there is no longer a conceivable 'objective need' for a Stalin. It is doubtful, though, whether such an answer will satisfy even the determinists. A high degree of economic development is not a guarantee against tyranny, and dictators often have an unfortunate tendency to appear without reference to 'objective need'.

The general trend in Russia, as far as internal party life and government is concerned, is now 'back to the 1920s'. Admittedly, the twenties are greatly preferable to the thirties and forties; yet this was the decade that proved so conducive to the growth of Stalinism. If Stalinism was some form of aberration on the part of the ruler, was it not made possible by a parallel process among his subjects?

Ludwig Quidde, in his study on Caligula, notes that specific Caesarean madness is 'the product of conditions which develop from the moral degeneracy of monarchic peoples, or, at any rate, their upper classes'. Omit 'monarchic', and is this not a fairly accurate description of modern forms of dictatorship? Has Soviet society basically changed? Have new checks and balances come into being to bar the way of a new dictator? Despite notable changes in the Soviet Union during the last decade, the answer is still negative. Political power is still in the hands of a very few people; the rest have no way of influencing political decisions. Robert Rozhdestvensky says in a recent poem:

> 'We say no longer
> that somebody thinks for us
> because we know now how this ends . . .'

Independent thought may at some future date produce independent action; for the time being the independent thinker has to trust the good intentions of his rulers. The most that can be said is that, as in the twenties, various developments are possible – both towards the perpetuation of tyranny and towards a greater measure of liberty and even democracy.

Relative optimists (among them the present writer) may add that with the Stalinist experience behind us all, historical prospects could only be for the better. Some optimism is based on the agreeable assumption, hitherto unproven, that a totalitarian state may in time 'wither away' or may in time somehow normalize itself. But it has not happened yet. (Kemalist Turkey is hardly a suitable parallel.) Something approaching a public opinion may again develop in Russia in the course of years. An opposition outside the state party is extremely unlikely, but factions inside the party may gradually emerge and be recognized as a normal development, not as a deviation. Instead of a multi-party, there would at least be a multifaction system. If there is polycentrism within the Communist camp, why should there not be a similar development within the parties? But this, too, could happen only on the basis of mutual tolerance which at present is certainly not the norm.

These are the political problems of the Soviet Union of the sixties and, with luck, of the seventies and eighties. Whatever their outcome, they are hardly likely to influence our appraisal of Stalin very much.

What did Stalin accomplish? Above all, a rate of growth somewhere between twelve and fourteen per cent during the thirties. In terms of economic efficiency Stalin was a success – he did deliver the goods, or at least some of them. Against this, on the debit side, there has been untold suffering and millions of victims (during and after the collectivization campaign, the purges, and the early stages of the war). Politically and culturally Russia was a monumental wasteland.

Asian poets have compared Stalin to a 'mountain eagle'; some future historians may come to regard him as an ass in lion's skin.* Does this sound preposterous today? Can it be that the gigantic image of the man, the legend of the all-powerful father of the peoples has loomed too large for a whole generation? I feel it is too easily forgotten how almost any image of almost any person can be fabricated in a totalitarian state. How much will remain of Stalin's iron will, his steely nerves, his tenacity, once the archives are opened and real demythologization begins? There still is a widespread belief that extraordinary (if not superhuman) qualities are needed to reach the top in a dictatorship. Yet the essential qualities – the will to power, self-confidence, and single-mindedness – are not that uncommon. Historic luck seems to be much more important. Stalin was very lucky indeed.

---

* Brecht, writing, of course, about Hitler once discussed the question whether it was permissible to expose to ridicule great political criminals, alive or dead. 'Even the common people, it is said, are sensitive about the subject because they were involved in the crimes; those who survive will not be inclined or able to laugh.' Brecht made these two points: 'They are, above all, not great political criminals, but perpetrators of great political crimes, which is something quite different.' He also noted that if 'the failure of Hitler's enterprises did not make him a fool, the size of his undertakings did not make him a great man' (Bert Brecht: *Stücke*, Vol. 9, pp. 369–70). There is a natural temptation for historians to be affected in their judgment by the dimensions of the historical scene.

Chapter 14

RUSSIA, GERMANY AND THE FUTURE

MUCH OF THE DRAMA of history is concentrated in the relations between certain nations, while between others there have been but few events of great significance, or major surprises. A British or a French Rip van Winkle awakening in 1965 after a century's sleep would probably find much that was familiar in the relations between the two countries, whether he was a diplomat, a newspaperman, or an ordinary citizen. Britain and France had never misunderstood each other as Germans and Russians had done; or perhaps one should say that each side had reconciled itself to never truly understanding the other. Few people in Paris or London have believed in a mission to redeem a sinful and degenerate world, nor have there been any territorial issues between them in Europe.

Between Germany and Russia, on the other hand, there have been not only two world wars but momentous historical changes. True, Germany has twice been at war with France and Britain; many Germans thought that France was decadent and Britain perfidious. Yet the confrontation between Germany and Russia was different in kind, for it involved both German fears of Russia and feelings of superiority towards the Slavs. After 1933 this became a collision between Fascism and Communism. It was not really a clash between two hostile races or cultures. Racially, there is a strong Slavic element in the Germans, especially in Prussia; on the other hand, men of German origin have played a conspicuous part in the Pan-slavic movement in Russia and elsewhere in Eastern Europe. Culturally, the two nations were for many years nearer to each other than to any other country; if Germany in the nineteenth century was the main exporter of philosophical and political ideas to Russia, then

305

after 1917 a part of the German public began to look to Russia for inspiration. There had always been a strong Russian party in Germany, and Germany never lacked friends in Russia. With Hitler in power all this changed and war became inevitable; but only the most fervid believers in historical determinism think that the First World War could not have been averted.

The First World War brought Bolshevism to power in the Soviet Union and, with some delay, gave the victory to National Socialism. The aims of Communism are known: its advocates have made no secret of them and its opponents have not been silent either. But it is not easy to summarize its achievements and its function in historical perspective; Russia is now in a post-revolutionary phase, but the revolutionary impulses have not altogether disappeared. Soviet Communism set out to build a new and better world on the ruins of capitalist society. Yet it soon appeared that many evils that had been thought specific to capitalism had deeper roots and were of a more universal character; oppression of man by man certainly did not end in Russia in 1917. Nor has Communism succeeded, as many hoped it would, in putting an end to national antagonism and rivalries. The Soviet system has remarkable economic achievements to its credit and there is a possibility that it may develop in some respects a more efficient and rational production system than the rest of the world. But is it any nearer to the just and free society of the future that has been the ultimate aim? Even if there should be a gradual transformation of the totalitarian regime into a relatively enlightened authoritarian state, would this justify its cost in human suffering and sacrifice? Was a higher rate of economic growth worth the more intense degree of repression – or will growing economic wealth bring about, more or less automatically, more freedom? These are some of the questions that remain unanswered; only the doctrinaire or the uncritical enthusiast can feel as confident about the prospects of political freedom in Russia as about the future of Soviet heavy industry.

It is easier to pass judgment on Nazism because it belongs to the past. The neo-Nazi groups in Germany and elsewhere, ugly survivals of a horrible past, are utterly impotent and have no chance of a political comeback. There have been cruel tyrannies before Nazism and outside Germany (and there may be more to come in other parts of the world). Yet these were not Nazi in character; Nazism was something very specific, not just another right-wing dictatorship. It came into being in particular conditions and at a certain time. These have gone, and taken Nazism with them. To say this is not to advocate complacency or a lessening of that eternal vigilance which is said to be the price of liberty. But vigilance in the wrong direction is not a virtue, and brutal and inhuman dictatorships, if they should recur, will certainly not owe their inspiration to the nineteen-thirties, or appear on the political scene as a repeat performance of National Socialism.

An analysis of the character of Nazism has its difficulties because so many imponderable factors are involved, because of the irrational character of its doctrine – in so far as there was one – and because so much depended on the will of the leader. It is, in a way, more difficult to generalize about Fascism than about Communism, because Fascism was above all a nationalist movement, greatly differing from country to country; national exclusivity, after all, was one of its main tenets. While its aims were very different from those of Communism, its methods frequently were similar or even identical; and in a totalitarian state the dividing line between aims and methods is not an obvious one. Methods not only affect the aims, they have a tendency to replace them. Nazism had most of its following among the middle classes, especially the lower middle classes, while Communism sought its support among the industrial workers. Not the masses, however, shaped the policy of either movement, but the leaders; these were the uprooted from all classes, who took orders from none.

Could Nazism have changed in character? It is tempting to imagine – now that we know the world has been spared it – what would have occurred had Hitler won the war in Europe, or had it ended in a stalemate and had he died shortly thereafter. According to the Russian proverb, only the grave will cure the hunchback. The removal of Hitler before the war might have changed the course of history; after the outbreak of war, it would have been too late to undo what had been done. By then Germany was too heavily saddled with the responsibility for its crimes. Nazism had been a malignant growth from the very beginning and by 1939 it had spread too far for any cure but radical surgery.

If there was little or no chance that Nazism could have changed, there is a chance that Western Communism will, for it is in the main tradition of European civilization, a heresy perhaps, or a utopia, but corresponding to some deep-seated traditional aspirations. Even the most inhuman Stalinist actions had to be justified by humanist arguments. Since Stalin's death, Russia has again become conscious of its Western heritage; Russians are at great pains now to stress that, regardless of political and social differences, their country is part of the mainstream of Europe's cultural life. For a Russian there is no greater insult now than the argument that Russia has belonged to Asia all along. It is an encouraging development and one should not be unduly worried by the critics of Euro-centrism.

In 1950 few people had much hope that totalitarianism would disappear in Russia in the foreseeable future. Even now, we know only that totalitarian regimes have been defeated in war, and that none has been overthrown from within, and it is difficult to imagine how exactly such a transformation would take place. Those who hope for liberalization as a necessary result of rising living standards are probably mistaken, as were the apostles of enlightenment in the eighteenth century, who expected that the gradual spread of education and knowledge would mean the end of barbarism. There is room for guarded optimism only. A new generation in the Soviet Union may do away with those vested interests which want to perpetuate the totalitarian state. The break-up of the monolithic camp of world Communism may indirectly hasten this process, but nobody knows how this will happen nor, indeed, is it a foregone conclusion that it will.

The fate of Russia and Germany in the twentieth century has largely been shaped by two men, Hitler and Stalin. There were traditions in German history which made Hitler's rise possible; he could not have succeeded without the spadework of many others before and with him. Much of Stalin's policy was rooted in Russia's past and in a political system which others had established. Stalin, in contrast to Hitler, did not destroy his country; on the contrary, he led it to victory and made it more powerful than ever before. Yet future historians may find that the relapse into barbarism under his rule did lasting harm to both the Soviet Union and the world Communist movement.

Post-Hitlerian Germany is not only divided, and thus much less powerful; it is also a very different country. The lights that went out in 1939 have not gone on again. Not the lights in the Düsseldorf and Frankfurt shopping districts, which are shining more brightly than ever; but Germany and Central Europe before Hitler had been one of the political and cultural centres of the world. A political eclipse would have taken place anyway, and there was much in the old

Europe that was neither splendid nor worthy of emulaton – just as medieval Christian Europe was not as good and glorious as Novalis imagined. But it was the cultural centre of the world, it has gone, and it has not found a successor.

A cultural centre is established not merely by physical discoveries, political theories, great music, and literature – it is this and much more. The loss will be felt even more in years to come; at present America as well as Russia and much of the rest of the world subsist culturally and ideologically on what was created, broadly speaking, in nineteenth-century Europe; this sustenance may not last much longer. As the old Europe ceased to exist, the dream of a new one has reappeared. But can a Europe without Russia, without Poland and Hungary and Czechoslovakia, and with Germany split in two, ever be much more than an economic and military convenience? The political obstacles to the development of such a 'new Europe' appear overwhelming; close co-operation between countries of radically different political, social, and economic systems seems impossible. If the chances for German reunification are practically non-existent, how can one even imagine a wider European union?

One day, sooner perhaps than we think, a new generation will arise in Germany and Russia, free of prejudice and hate, but more than walls and barbed wire entanglements will have to be dismantled; a very great deal of good will and understanding will be needed to make a fresh beginning in Central and Eastern Europe. Human nature being what it is, and sovereign states behaving as they do, perhaps this is too much to expect. Perhaps totalitarian regimes are incapable of transforming themselves into freer societies. Perhaps there will be atomic war. But it is neither comforting nor wise always to anticipate the worst. Nor should one underrate the astonishing capacity of men to change, and to change their ideas and institutions too. In both West and East national character and cultural tradition have been strong divisive factors, but it may be too early to write off the centripetal forces of Europe. Not the Europe of the Six or of the Seven, not perhaps any empirical Europe, but the somewhat nebulous and yet immensely attractive idea of a common tradition, and perhaps a common future at some distant date.

Meanwhile, both Germans and Russians are strongly tempted to let the dead past bury its dead. There is a natural inclination not to reopen old wounds – and there are vested interests to give warning against the unhealthy habit and the dangerous consequences of rummaging in the dark alleys of a sinister past that is better forgotten. Yet the question of crime and punishment has always preoccupied the unquiet spirits in Germany and Russia. Theirs is not mere curiosity; they understand by now that there can be no better future without a full realization and acknowledgment of what really happened in the past. A few individuals may be able to evade justice, but nations cannot escape responsibility. In the Soviet Union only a strictly limited and controlled measure of rethinking has been permitted on the awkward subject of the 'cult of the individual'. Politically the problem is more difficult in Russia than in Germany because there has been no radical break with that dark period of Soviet history; psychologically it should be much easier in the end, for the Soviet people, for they themselves were the main victim, not foreigners.

It will take a long time to forget Stalin, and a much longer time to get away from Hitler. In Germany the past remains unmastered by all but a few. The German catastrophe would have been easier for Greek tragedians or medieval theologians to understand than for modern man. The Greeks understood sin as the consequence of *hubris*, the disregard of the rights of others; *hubris* resulted in *ate*, a state of moral blindness in which the evil appeared good. True, German history does not begin with Hitler and it certainly does not end with him. But Germany had to pay a heavy price and it may have to continue to do so for a long time to come. One day, one hopes, the walls will disappear and there will be free movement over the borders; Germans and Slavs may be able to work together again in freedom and without fear. Old and famous cities may re-emerge in a new glory as centres of a new civilization in which nations share their achievements and bury their rivalries.

Today all this seems very unreal, a vision at best, possibly no more than an *ignis fatuus*. This study has dealt with some of the darkest pages in history; such a preoccupation encourages a sombre view of the future. Yet history is not all crime, folly, and the eager pursuit of phantoms. There is a possibility that the future can be one of a more civilized form of human coexistence than any we have known in the past.

APPENDIX

THE HIDDEN HAND - A BRITISH
CONTRIBUTION

THE IMPACT OF the *Protocols* was not restricted to Germany; the spade work for their dissemination in Western Europe had been done by a small group of British correspondents in Russia who had taken a violent dislike to the revolution. The most prominent among them were Robert Wilton, representative of *The Times*, and Victor Marsden, correspondent of the *Morning Post*; several others published their memoirs or political comments after their return to Britain at about the same time.* Their writings influenced public opinion, the politicians, and even the novelists of the day.

Their opposition was by no means restricted to the Communists; some of them had greeted the democratic revolution of March 1917 with equal hostility. The Petrograd journalists, among whom there were no Communists at the time, had protested against the reports of Mr Wilton as early as summer 1917, and the editor of the London *Daily News* wrote at the time that the 'howling dervishes' of the Northcliffe papers (above all the *Morning Post*) had fed their readers with slanderous ridicule of Kerensky: 'This mad dervishism does not represent the real mind of the country towards the revolution (of March 1917) but it does represent much that is most powerful in the country.'[1]

Few people, least of all professional political observers, remain neutral at a time of revolution and civil war; some of the foreign correspondents in Russia threw in their lot with the Bolsheviks or, at any rate, became fellow-travellers. Others, on the contrary, sympathized with the extreme right. To say that this coloured their

* Such as, for instance, George Pitt-Rivers, *The World Significance of the Russian Revolution* (Oxford 1920).

311

reports would be an understatement; what appeared in the British press at the time was, with some notable exceptions, merely grotesque (the report about the nationalization of women in the *Daily Telegraph* being a famous example). Robert Wilton of *The Times* had been brought up in Russia and knew the country quite well; he had, as a civilian, participated in the battle of Baranovichi and gained the highest Russian distinction for valour, the St George Cross. He was utterly oblivious of the fact that the Tsarist regime had, through its folly and weakness, made a revolution inevitable; *plus tsariste que le Tsar*, he hated the revolutionaries, democrats and Communists alike. They were all criminals in German pay. He tried to prove in his writings that the Russian people had nothing at all to do with a revolution inspired and carried out by foreign (German–Jewish) invaders. Typical of this kind of political information was a report that 'Sovietdom had consecrated Judas Iscariot as one of its three main heroes to whom a monument had been dedicated'.[2] Presumably *The Times* owed its sponsorship of the *Protocols* to the same correspondent: on May 8, 1920, it carried a long article ('The Jewish Peril') in which it expressed the opinion that the *Protocols* deserved to be taken very seriously; it was apparently a genuine document written by Jews for Jews, which could not be shrugged off. What had the Jews to say in reply to these terrible and scandalous revelations?*

The *Morning Post* elaborated on the same theme at even greater length, in a series of seventeen articles based largely on the *Protocols*. It tried to prove, as Mr H. A. Gwynne, the editor of the paper, put it, that 'there has been for centuries a hidden conspiracy, chiefly Jewish, whose objects have been, and are, to produce revolution, Communism, and anarchy by means of which they hope to arrive at the hegemony of the world by establishing some sort of despotic rule'.[3] The *Morning Post* was at the time more interested in the Irish troubles, the riots in India and Egypt, and other places overseas, than in the story of events in Central and Eastern Europe, and it seemed somewhat farfetched to establish a connection between unrest in Dublin, Cairo, Delhi, and a powerful Jewish sect allegedly stirring up all this unrest. But this is precisely what the writer of the series set out to do, tracing Irish nationalism to America, and Indian and Egyptian discontent to some dark corner of Paris. Such explanations were taken perfectly

* This article was brought out by the Nazi Party as a special leaflet in 1922 or 1923: '*Aufsehenerregende Enthüllungen der* Times *über das jüdische Weltprogramm*'. There is a copy in the B.D.C.

seriously by wide sections of the population. Had not the British Foreign Office shortly before published reports very similar in character?[4] Did not Mr Winston Churchill repeatedly hint that he read the signs of the times in much the same way as the *Morning Post*? In the House of Commons he had spoken on November 5, 1919, about the 'most powerful sect of the world'. At a meeting of the Anglo-Russian Club in London in July 1919, he had called for support for Denikin against Lenin and Trotsky and the sinister gangs of Jewish anarchists around them.[5] Even later, in 1920, Churchill had contrasted (in an article for the *Sunday Herald*) the good and loyal Jews to the international terrorist Jews who were to blame for much, if not all, of the world's unrest.

The impact of the 'hidden hand' bogey on England was comparatively shortlived, but while it lasted it was powerful. The idea of a criminal mastermind undoubtedly appealed to a nation that had a traditional weakness for thrillers. The *Morning Post* provided the psychological explanation:

> The idea of a world conspiracy directed against law and order, and indeed against Christian civilization itself, would, before the war, have seemed absurd and impossible to the average Englishman. The idea that there could be an intimate connection, say, between a revolution in Portugal, a strike at home, and a murder in India would never have occurred to any ordinary man before August 1914. The war has produced a complete change of mentality, because we have had complete proof of close connection between rebellion in Ireland, disaffection in India, revolution in Russia . . .'[6]

Such theories opened up entirely new vistas for contemporary novelists and John Buchan, to mention but one, was not slow to pick up the thread. The plot of the *Three Hostages* is based on the 'Cause of World Unrest', the series of articles which popularized the *Protocols* in England. True, Sir Richard Hannay is unwilling at first to accept the theory: 'I think since the war we are all too ready to jump at grandiose explanations of simple things. I'll want a good deal of convincing before I believe in your international clearing house of crime'.* But gradually the hero is convinced of the interconnection of all contemporary anarchism. The fanatics, the young Bolshevik Jews, the moral imbeciles with their hatred of Christianity and Britain, willing to sacrifice everything, including their lives, for a mad

* John Buchan, *The Three Hostages*. Penguin edition, p. 24.

313

ideal, were but tools in the hands of a small powerful sect. 'It was a masterpiece of coldblooded, devilish ingenuity.' Now Hannay suddenly began to see the connection between the importer of Barcelona nuts with a modest office near Tower Hill, the copper company purporting to operate in Spain, the French count who was also a Highland laird and a great supporter of the White Rose League, and the gentleman in Shropshire who was a keen rider to hounds – and yet belonged to the same sinister circle. He understood that the chance of a settlement in Ireland and certain events of the first importance in Italy and America were in great danger as the result of the activities of that small all-powerful sect.*

By the middle twenties the novelty of the 'hidden hand' had worn off in England, very much in contrast to Germany, where it continued to be a most effective propaganda weapon in the hands of the rising Nazi Party. Small extremist circles continued to peddle the 'Cause of World Unrest' and similar literature, but even the less enlightened Conservatives and the more reactionary press realized that Britain's many and growing difficulties all over the globe could not be reduced to one general denominator and traced to one source.† The notion of a great world conspiracy had been attractive and easy to digest; unfortunately, it was not of much help in removing the various causes of world unrest, because it was not true. A more sober approach prevailed over the flights of fantasy.

---

* *ibid.*, pp. 23, 28, 45–7, 222. This strongly reminds one of certain passages in Winston Churchill's speech in the House of Commons on November 5, 1919: 'No sooner did Lenin arrive than he began beckoning a finger there to obscure persons in sheltered retreats in New York, in Glasgow, in Bern, and other countries, and he gathered together the leading spirits of a most formidable sect, the most formidable sect in the world.' Buchan's *The Thirty-Nine Steps* also includes hints about 'a big subterranean movement engineered by very dangerous people'. Capitalism was behind it, and the Jew ('he is the man who is ruling the world just now'). But *The Thirty-Nine Steps* was written during the war and the situation after 1918 provided infinitely greater scope for a plot on a world-wide basis.

† Among the lunatic fringe of the extreme right-wing the myth of the hidden hand lived on until well into the fifties. Colin Jordan's *Fraudulent Conversion*, (London 1955) is a fairly typical example; it repeats most of the allegations of the *Protocols*, and continues the tradition by branding as Jews all the leaders of Russian and international Communism, with the possible exception of Stalin. The *Protocols* are now more often featured in the Middle East than in Europe or the United States. President Nasser has occasionally quoted and recommended them, for instance in an interview with the editor of the pro-Communist Indian newspaper *Blitz* (*Al Ahram*, September 29, 1958). English translation in *President Nasser's Speeches and Press Interviews 1958* (Cairo, n.d.), p. 402.

BIBLIOGRAPHY

THIS GUIDE to further reading on Russian–German relations does not include all the important publications on the subject, let alone those on the many related topics that have been touched upon in this book. Preference has been given to works that contain further bibliographical references.

Unpublished sources

Of the mass of material available only a small part has so far been used in historical research. Some of the records of the German foreign ministry for the period 1867–1920 referring to Russia have been microfilmed while at Wheddon Hall by a number of institutions, including the University of California Library. For the period after 1920 a three-volume guide will eventually be available; so far only two volumes has been published – George O. Kent: *A Catalog of Files and Microfilms of German Foreign Ministry Archives 1920–1945* (1962) – but not all the files have been microfilmed; the others are now in the archives of the German Foreign Ministry in Bonn. Other important sources such as the Groener and von Seeckt papers are in the military archives (Heeresarchiv). Of great importance for German–Soviet relations during the Nazi period are the seized German records deposited at the World War II Record Division, National Archives, Washington. Of the various Guides to the records that have been microfilmed the following are the most relevant in this context: *Records of the Reich Leader of the SS and Chief of German Police* (Parts I–III), *Records of the National Socialist German Labor Party* (Parts I–III), and *Records of the Reich Ministry for the Occupied Eastern Territories*. Documents in East German and Soviet archives have so far been accessible to Western scholars only in exceptional cases.

1. General works

A. BIBLIOGRAPHIES

Bibliographie zur Zeitgeschichte in *Vierteljahrshefte fuer Zeitgeschichte*, sections 7, 10, 11 (1954–).

DAHLMANN-WAITZ, *Quellenkunde der deutschen Geschichte* (1931–2).

From Weimar to Hitler, 1918–1933 (1964) (Wiener Library, London).

GEBHARDT, BRUNO, *Handbuch der deutschen Geschichte*, Vol. III (1960), Vol. IV (1961).

MORLEY, CHARLES, *Guide to Research in Russian History* (1951).

NIKITIN, SERGE A., *Istochnikovedenie istorii SSSR*, Vol. 2 (1940).

SHAPIRO, DAVID, *Select Bibliography of Works in English on Russian History 1801–1917* (1962).

UNGAR, ERICH, *Schrifttum des National-Sozialismus* (1934).

VOLZ, H., *Daten der Geschichte der NSDAP* (1936).

B. PUBLISHED DOCUMENTS

Archivalische Forschungen zur Geschichte der deutschen Arbeiterbewegung: Die Auswirkungen der Grossen Sozialistischen Oktoberrevolution auf Deutschland (1959).

DEGRAS, JANE (ed.), *Soviet Documents on Foreign Policy* (3 vols, 1951–3).

Documents diplomatiques français (41 vols, 1929–59).

Documents on British Foreign Policy 1919–1939 (1947–in progress).

Documents on German Foreign Policy (Series C and D) (in progress).

Dokumenty vneshnei Politiki SSSR (1957–in progress).

GOOCH, G. P. and TEMPERLEY, H., *British Documents on the Origins of the World War* (11 vols, 1926).

HOETZSCH, O., *Die internationalen Beziehungen im Zeitalter des Imperialismus* (12 vols, 1931) (This is the German translation of the Russian series, ed. by Pokrovsky).

KPSS v rezoliutsiakh i resheniakh (4 vols, 1940–60).

Krasny Arkhiv (106 vols, 1922–41).

LEPSIUS, I., *et al.*, *Die grosse Politik der europäischen Kabinette 1871–1914* (40 vols, 1922–7).

Nazi-Soviet Relations 1939–1941 (1948).

Papers relating to the foreign relations of the United States.

C. GENERAL SURVEYS 1850–1919; THE FIRST WORLD WAR; GERMAN HISTORY

Most of the books in this section are well known to students of the period.

The second edition of the *Istoriya Diplomatii* is much superior to the first, published in the Stalin era. Professor Fischer's book has important sections on German war aims in Eastern Europe during the First World War. Professor E. Zechlin deals with German policy of the same period in his *Friedensbestrebungen und Revolutionierungsversuche im Ersten Weltkrieg* (a series of supplements to the weekly *Das Parlament*, 1963, *passim*). Lundin's important essay deals with the changing loyalties of the German Balts between 1905 and 1914, mainly as the result of the revolution of 1905.

ALBERTINI, L., *Le Origine della guerra del 1914* (1942).

BRANDENBURG, ERICH, *From Bismarck to the World War* (1927).

CARROLL, E. M., *Germany and the Great Powers 1861–1914* (1938).

EYCK, E., *Bismarck* (3 Vols, 1944).

—, *Das Persönliche Regiment Wilhelms II* (1948).

FAY, S. B., *The Origins of the World War* (1928).

FISCHER, F., *Griff nach der Weltmacht* (1961).

HALLGARTEN, W., *Vorkriegsimperialismus* (1935).

HARTUNG, F., *Deutsche Geschichte 1871 bis 1919* (1952).

KHVOSTOV, V. M., *Istoriya Diplomatii* (Vol. II, 1963).

LANGER, W. L., *Diplomacy of Imperialism* (2 vols, 1935).

LUNDIN, C. L., 'The Road from Tsar to Kaiser' in *Journal of Central European Affairs*, October 1950.

MANSERGH, N., *The coming of the First World War* (1949).

MOMMSEN, W., *Bismarck* (1959).

ONCKEN, HERMANN, *Das deutsche Reich und die Vorgeschichte des Weltkrieges* (1933).

Die Politischen Berichte des Fürsten Bismarck aus Petersburg und Paris (n.d.).

RENOUVIN, P., *Le XIX Siècle* (Vol. II, 1955).

SCHWEINITZ, GENERAL VON, *Denkwürdigkeiten* (1927).

TAYLOR, A. J. P., *Bismarck* (1955).

WERDER, B. VON, 'Aus Jahrzehnten deutsch-russischer Freundschaft' in *Berliner Monatshefte 17* (1939).

WILHELM II, *Briefe Wilhelms II an den Zaren 1894–1914* (1920).

YERUSALIMSKY, A., *Vneshniaia Politika i Diplomatiia Germanskovo Imperializma v Kontse XIX veka* (1948).

ZIEKURSCH, J., *Politische Geschichte des neuen deutschen Kaiserreiches* (Vols 2 and 3, 1927–30).

2. *Russia and Germany: 1830–1917*

Stammler's essay, as well as Groh's book, deal primarily with the metapolitics of Russian–German relations, and especially with the philosophy of religion and culture. The Schirren-Samarin polemic was an early manifestation of Russian–German tension though it was concerned almost exclusively with the question of the Baltic provinces and their autonomy. The debate between Haller and Hoetzsch during the First World War is of great interest, reflecting as it does the two main strands of thought about Russia among

German conservatives. Although an enormous literature on Panslavism exists, there is no systematic analysis and description of its attitude towards Germany. During the First World War both German and Russian periodicals published articles that were, not surprisingly, very outspoken in the condemnation of the other side; not all of them can be explained away as manifestations of 'hurrah' patriotism and war hysteria. Rohrbach continued to publish well after the Second World War, but his influential books on Eastern Europe appeared before and during the First.

ARNDT, E. M., *Ein kurzes Wort ueber Russland* (new ed., 1960).

BAUER, B., *Russland und das Germanenthum* (1853).

DANILEVSKY, N., *Rossiia i Evropa* (1871).

DOSTOJEVSKI, F. M., *Tagebuch eines Schriftstellers* (1921).

ECKARDT, J., *Aus der Petersburger Gesellschaft* (1873).

ERN, V., 'Ot Kanta k Kruppu', in *Russkaia Mysl* (1914, p. 116 *et seq.*).

FALLMERAYER, PH., *Gesammelte Werke* (1863).

FRANTZ, C., *Weltpolitik* (1882–3).

GERSHENZON, M., *Istoricheskie Zapiski* (1923).

GIUSTI, WOLFGANGO, *Il Panslavismo* (1941).

GROH, D., *Russland und das Selbstverstaendnis Europas* (1961).

GRUENING, J., *Die russische öffentliche Meinung und ihre Stellung zu den Grossmaechten 1878–1894* (1929).

HALLER, J., *Die russische Gefahr im deutschen Hause* (1917).

HAXTHAUSEN, A. VON, *Studien ueber die inneren Zustaende . . .* (1847).

HEHN, V., *De moribus Ruthenorum* (1892).

HESS, M., *Die europaeische Triarchie* (1941).

HOETZSCH, O., *Russische Probleme* (1917).

IVANOV-RAZUMNIK, *Istoriya Russkoi obshchestvennoi mysli* (2 vols, 1907).

KOHN, H., *Pan-Slavism* (1960).

MARX-ENGELS, *Werke* (Berlin, 1959).

MASARYK, T. G., *The Spirit of Russia* (1919).

MEYER, K., *Theodor Schiemann als politischer Publizist* (1956).

MUELLER, LORE, *Das Russlandbild der deutschen politischen Flugschriften, Reisewerke, Nachschlagwerke und Zeitungen . . . 1812–1853* (Dissertation, Mainz 1953).

NOETZEL, KARL, *Die Grundlagen des geistigen Russlands* (1917).

NOLDE, B. E., *Yuri Samarin i evo vremia* (1926).

PETROVICH, M. B., *The Emergence of Russian Pan-Slavism 1856–1870* (1956).

PUSHKIN, V. A., *Skobelev o nemtsakh* (1914).

RIASANOVSKI, NICHOLAS V., *Russia and the West in the Teaching of the Slavophiles* (1952).

RJASANOFF, N., 'Karl Marx ueber den Ursprung der Vorherrschaft Russlands in Europa', in *Neue Zeit* (Ergaenzungsheft No. 5, 1908–1909).

ROHRBACH, P., *Weltpolitisches Wanderbuch* (1915).
—, *Russland und Wir* (1915).
RUGE, A., *Russland und die Civilisation* (1834).
SCHEIBERT, P., *Von Bakunin zu Lenin* (1956).
SCHIRREN, C., *Livlaendische Antwort an Herrn Juri Samarin* (*c.* 1869).
SPENGLER, O., *Jahre der Entscheidung* (1933).
STAEHLIN, K., 'Entstehung des Panslavismus', in *Germanoslavica* (1936–7).
STAMMLER, H., 'Wandlungen des deutschen Bildes vom russischen Menschen', in *Jahrbuecher fuer Geschichte Osteuropas* (1957, pp. 271–305).
STEPUN, F., 'Nemetskii romantizm i russkoe slavianfilstvo', in *Russkaia Mysl* (March 1910, pp. 65–91).
—, 'Rossiia mezhdu Evropoi i Aziei', in *Novy Zhurnal, 69* (1962).
SUMNER, B. H., 'Russia and Panslavism in the eighteen-seventies', in *Transactions of the Royal Historical Society*, Fourth Series, XVIII (1935).
TARLE, E. V., 'K istorii russko-germanskikh otnoshenii v noveishee vremia', in *Russkaia Mysl* (December 1914, p. 173 *et seq.*).
TSCHIZEWSKIJ, D. and GROH, D., *Europa und Russland* (1959).
ZENKOVSKY, V. V., *Russkie Mysliteli i Evropa* (1926).
The collected works of Herzen, Ivan Aksakov, Kireyevsky, Konstantin Aksakov, Khomyakov, Tiutchev, and Yuri Samarin.

3. *Russia and Germany: 1917–33*

The history of Russian–German relations during the Weimar Republic has still to be written. L. Kochan's book is a useful brief outline written, however, before most of the documentary evidence from the German archives became available. Gustav Hilger was in a leading position in the German Embassy in Moscow during most of the twenties and thirties and his account is an invaluable source. There is much useful information in Professor Carr's *History*, in particular in the seventh volume covering the middle twenties. G. Freund's book covers the period 1918–25; there are a number of competent West German studies on the Rapallo policy (Helbig, Schieder, *et al.*). The East German literature on the subject published during the Stalin era is virtually useless (Klein, Norden); the more specialized investigations which have appeared more recently in East Berlin such as, for instance, Rosenfeld's work on Russia and Germany between 1917 and 1922, are of much greater interest. The same applies to the Russian literature on the subject; there were a few contemporary books of importance (such as Radek's), but nothing of interest during the late thirties, the forties, or fifties. In recent years, however, there have been some specialized studies that should be consulted by students of this period. German-Soviet economic relations have not yet found a historian. There has been much more on military co-operation between the two sides (Erickson, Speidel, Carsten, and others).

A. GENERAL

Beitraege zur Geschichte der Beziehungen zwischen dem deutschen Volk und den Voelkern der Sowjet Union (1954).

BELOFF, M., *The Foreign Policy of Soviet Russia 1929–1941* (2 vols, 1947–9).

BORKENAU, F., *The Communist International* (1938).

CARR, E. H., *A History of Soviet Russia* (1949–in progress).

—, *German-Soviet Relations between the two World Wars* (1951).

EUDIN, X. J., and FISHER, H., *Soviet Russia and the West 1920–27* (1957).

FISCHER, L., *The Soviets in World Affairs* (2 vols, 2nd ed., 1951).

FISCHER, R., *Stalin and German Communism* (1948).

HILGER, G. and MEYER, A., *The Incompatible Allies* (1953).

KLEIN, F., *Die diplomatischen Beziehungen Deutschlands zur Sowjet Union 1917–1932* (1952).

KLUKE, P., 'Deutschland und Russland zwischen den beiden Weltkriegen', in *Historische Zeitschrift* (1951).

KOCHAN, L., *Russia and the Weimar Republic* (1954).

KRETZSCHMAR, U., *Der Kampf in der deutschen publizistischen und historiographischen Literatur der Jahre 1917–1933 bei der Einschaetzung des Aufbaues des Sozialismus in der UdSSR* (Dissertation, Halle 1959).

KUCZINSKI, J. and WITTKOWSKI, G., *Die deutsch-russischen Handelsbeziehungen in den letzten 150 Jahren* (1947).

KULBAKIN, V. D., *Militarizatsiya Germanii v 1928–30gg.* (1954).

MATTHIAS, E., *Die Deutsche Sozialdemokratie und der Osten* (1954).

NORDEN, A., *Zwischen Berlin und Moskau* (1954).

RASSOW, P., *Deutsche Geschichte* (1953).

ROSENBERG, A., *Entstehung und Geschichte der Weimarer Republik* (1955).

ROZANOV, G. L., *Ocherki noveishei istorii Germanii* (1957).

SCHAPIRO, L, *The Communist Party of the Soviet Union* (1960).

SPEIDEL, HELM, 'Reichswehr und Rote Armee', in *Vierteljahrshefte fuer Zeitgeschichte* (1953).

USHAKOV, V. B., *Vneshniaia politika Germanii v period veimarskoi respubliki* (1958).

WHEELER BENNETT, J. W., *The Nemesis of Power* (1953).

ZIMMERMANN, L., *Deutsche Aussenpolitik in der Aera der Weimarer Republik* (1958).

B. 1917–23

D'ABERNON, E. D., *An ambassador of Peace* (3 vols, 1929–30).

AKHTAMZIAN, A., *Ot Bresta do Kila* (1963).

ANDERLE, A. (ed.), *Rapallo und die friedliche Koexistenz* (1963).

BLUECHER, W. VON, *Deutschlands Weg nach Rapallo* (1951).

DRABKIN, Ya. S., *Revoliutsiya 1918/19 v Germanii* (1958).

FREUND, G., *Unholy Alliance* (1957).

KOBLIAKOV, I. K., *Von Brest bis Rapallo* (1956).
RADEK, K., *Die russische und die deutsche Revolution und die Weltlage* (1919).
—, *Die auswaertige Politik Sowjetrusslands* (1921).
ROSENFELD, G., *Sowjet Russland und Deutschland 1917–22* (1960).
RUGE, WOLFGANG, *Die Stellungnahme der Sowjetunion gegen die Besetzung des Ruhrgebietes* (1962).
SALOV, V. I., *Germanskaia Istoriografiya oktyabrskoi revoliutsii* (1960).
SERAPHIM, E., *Deutsch-russische Beziehungen 1918–1925* (1925).
STERN, L., *Der Einfluss der grossen sozialistischen Oktoberrevolution in Deutschland und die deutsche Arbeiterbewegung* (1958).
TSITOVICH, I. I., *Ocherki istorii germanii 1918–1923* (1940).
WHEELER BENNETT, J. W., *The Forgotten Peace* (1956).
YERUSALIMSKY, A. S., *Germaniya, Antanta i SSSR* (1923).
ZEMAN, Z. A. B. (ed.), *Germany and the revolution in Russia 1915–18* (1958).

C. 1923–33

GASIOROWSKI, Z. J., 'The Russian Overture to Germany in December 1924', in *Journal of Modern History* (1958).
GATZKE, H. W., 'Von Rapallo nach Berlin', in *Vierteljahrshefte fuer Zeitgeschichte* (1956).
HELBIG, H., *Die Traeger der Rapallo-Politik* (1958).
MELVILLE, C. F., *The Russian Face of Germany* (1932).
RADEK, K., *Portrety i Pamflety* (2 vols, 1933–4).
SCHEFFER, PAUL, *Sieben Jahre Sowjetunion* (1930).
SCHIEDER, TH., *Die Probleme des Rapallo Vertrages* (1956).
SEECKT, H. VON, *Deutschland zwischen West und Ost* (1933).
ST N, B., *Pochemu Germaniya i SSR zakliuchili dogovor o neitralitete* (1926).
STRESEMANN, G., *Vermaechtnis* (3 vols, 1932–3).
TUROK, V. M., *Lokarno* (1949).

4 *Russia and National Socialism: 1919–33*

A. UNPUBLISHED

German records deposited at the World War II Records Division National Archives, Washington; especially records of the National Socialist German Labor Party and records of the Reich leader of the SS. Rosenberg correspondence in Centre de Documentation Juive Contemporaine, Paris. See annotated catalogue by J. Billig, *A. Rosenberg dans l'action idéologique, politique et administrative du Reich hitlérien* (1963). Documents at Berlin Centre from Hauptarchiv NSDAP., Bayrische Politische Polizei, Munich, Hauptstaatsarchiv II.

B. BOOKS:

The most relevant texts are, of course, Hitler's *Mein Kampf* and his

Second Book, Rosenberg's early writings and Goebbels' *Zweite Revolution*. Leverkuehn's *Posten auf ewiger Wache* is a biography of von Scheubner-Richter, but devoted mostly to his pre-Nazi activities during the First World War. There is no definitive history of National Socialism. Konrad Heiden's books are still of value in view of the unique opportunities the author had to watch the growth of the Nazi movement from a close angle. G. Franz-Willing's work takes a more favourable view of Hitler's party than of his opponents; the first volume of his *Hitlerbewegung* brings the story up to 1923. Nolte's book is an ambitious and provocative attempt to view Nazism in historical perspective. Professor Schueddekopf is concerned in great detail with the activities of the National Bolshevists. There is no history of the 'Black Hundred' in Russia though various collections of documents published in Moscow after 1917 include important material. Of the enormous literature published by the propagandists of the *Protocols* I have mentioned only a few characteristic books – those by Vinberg and Schwarz-Bostunich are probably the most significant. On the *Protocols*, their pre-history and political effect, Rollin's massive tome is by far the most important. Much of the relevant information for that period is contained in periodicals and newspapers rather than in books, but most of them are now very difficult to find.

C. BASIC WRITINGS BY AND ABOUT NAZI LEADERS

BAYNES, N. (ed.), *The Speeches of Adolf Hitler* (2 vols, 1942).
Der Hitler-Prozess vor dem Volksgericht in Muenchen (1924).
ECKART, DIETRICH, *Der Bolschewismus von Moses bis Lenin* (1924).
ESPE, W. *Das Buch der NSDAP* (1934).
GOEBBELS, J., *Tagebuch 1925 / 6* (n.d.).
—, *Die zweite Revolution* (1926).
HART, F. TH., *Alfred Rosenberg* (1939).
HITLER, ADOLF, *Mein Kampf*.
Hitler's Table Talk (1953).
Hitler's Secret Book (c. 1961).
JETZINGER, F., *Hitlers Jugend* (1956).
LANG, S. and SCHENK, E. VON, *Portraet eines Menschheitsverbrechers. Nach den hinterlassenen Memoiren des Reichsministers Alfred Rosenberg* (1947).
LEVERKUEHN, PAUL, *Posten auf ewiger Wache* (1938).
LUEDECKE, K., *I knew Hitler* (1938).
ROSENBERG, ALFRED, *Unmoral im Talmud* (1920).
—, *Die Spur des Juden im Wandel der Zeiten* (1920).
—, *Das Verbrechen der Freimaurerei* (1921).
—, *Der staatsfeindliche Zionismus* (1921).

BIBLIOGRAPHY

ROSENBERG, ALFRED, *Die Totengraeber Russlands* (*c.* 1921).
—, *Pest in Russland* (1922).
—, *Wesen, Grundsaetze und Ziele der NSDAP* (1923).
—, *Die Protokolle der Weisen von Zion* (1923).
—, *Politisches Tagebuch aus den Jahren 1934/5 und 1939/40.* (ed. H. G. Seraphim, 1956).
—, *Schriften und Reden* (2 vols, 1944).
SCHICKEDANZ, A., *Der Sozialparasitismus im Voelkerleben* (1927).
The Trial of the Major War Criminals before the International Military Tribunal, Proceedings, Vols 1–23, Documents in Evidence, Vols 24–42 (1947–9).

D. NATIONAL SOCIALISM

BULLOCK, ALAN, *Hitler* (1962).
DEUERLEIN, E., 'Hitlers Eintritt in die Politik und die Reichswehr', in *Vierteljahrshefte fuer Zeitgeschichte*, 1959, pp. 177–277.
—(ed.), *Der Hitlerputsch. Bayerische Dokumente* (1963).
HEIDEN, K., *National Sozialismus, Karriere einer Idee* (1932).
—, *Adolf Hitler* (2 vols, 1935–7).
HOFMANN, H. H., *Der Hitlerputsch* (1961).
NEUBAUER, H., *Muenchen und Moskau 1918–19* (1958).
NOLTE, E., *Der Faschismus in seiner Epoche* (1963).
SCHUEDDEKOPF, O. E., *Linke Leute von Rechts* (1960).
FRANZ-WILLING, G., *Die Hitlerbewegung* (Vol. 1, 1962).

E. THE BLACK HUNDRED AND THEIR SUCCESSORS

AKHMATOV, V., *Evrei i budushche mira* (1927).
BRANT, E., *Ritualnoe ubiistvo u evreyev* (1926–7).
CHEREP-SPIRIDOVICH, *The Secret World Government* (1926).
CHERNOVSKY, A., *Soiuz Russkovo Naroda* (1929).
CURTISS, J. S., *Church and State in Russia* (1940).
LEVITSKY, V., 'Pravie Partii', in *Obshchestvennoe dvizhenie v Rossii v nachale XX veka* (Vol. 3, 1914).
MARKOV, N., *Der Kampf der dunklen Maechte* (1935).
NETCHVOLODOV, A., *L'empereur Nicolas II et les Juifs* (1924).
Padenie tsarskovo rezhima (Vol. 6, 1926).
SCHWARZ-BOSTUNICH, G., *Juedischer Imperialismus* (1938).
SNESSAREV, *Kyrill Pervy, Imperator Koburga* (n.d.).
VERSHININ, E., *Mir v lapakh satana* (1933).
VINBERG, F., *Krestny Put* (1921).
ZHEVAKHOV, N. O., *Vospominaniya* (1923).
—, *Sergei Aleksandrovich Nilus* (1936).

F. THE *PROTOCOLS*

BERNSTEIN, H., *The Truth about the Protocols of Zion* (1935).
BOULACHOV, D., *Le Bolchevisme et les Juifs* (1926).

BIBLIOGRAPHY

BURTSEV, V. L., *Protokoly tsionistskikh mudretsov dokazanny podlog* (1938).
CURTISS, JOHN (ed.), *An Appraisal of the Protocols of Zion* (1942).
FRY, L., *Waters flowing Eastwards* (1931).
ROLLIN, HENRI, *L'Apocalypse de notre Temps* (1939).
SEGEL, B., *Die Protokolle der Weisen von Zion kritisch beleuchtet* (1924).
The Cause of World Unrest (1920).
The German-Bolshevik Conspiracy, War Information Series, No. 20 (October 1918).
Unpublished report of the *Protocols* trial in Berne, 1934.
VRBA, RUDOLF, *Die Revolution in Russland* (1907).
WICHTL, FR., *Weltfreimaurerei, Weltrevolution, Weltpolitik* (1936).

G. PERIODICALS, NEWSPAPERS

Alldeutsche Blaetter (Berlin).
Aufbau Korrespondenz (Munich).
Auf Gut Deutsch (Munich).
Deutsche Tageszeitung (Berlin).
Deutschlands Erneuerung (Munich).
Dvuglavy Orël (Berlin).
Der Hammer (Leipsic).
Libre Parole (Paris).
Luch Sveta (Berlin).
Mitteilungen aus dem Verein zur Abwehr des Antisemitismus (Berlin).
Monarkhicheskii Vestnik (Belgrade).
Muenchner Beobachter (Munich).
Nationalsozialistische Briefe.
Novoe Vremia (post-1918) (Belgrade).
Prizyv (Berlin).
Revue Internationale des Sociétés Secrètes (Paris).
Staatsbuergerzeitung (Berlin).
Voelkischer Beobachter (Munich).
Der Vorposten (Dresden).
Der Weltkampf (Munich).

5 Russian-German Relations 1933–60

Nazi-Soviet relations during the early years of the Third Reich have not yet been studied in detail. The essays in the symposium edited by Duroselle are the first attempts in this direction. Until material in Soviet and East German archives becomes accessible to Western scholars it is unlikely that anybody will greatly improve on Weinberg's book (covering the years 1939–41) and A. Dallin's (describing German rule in occupied Russia). The books by Fehst, Kommoss, and Greife are characteristic of both the scope and the level of Nazi *Ostforschung*. There is a surfeit of literature in Germany about military operations in Russia during the Second World War, and a fair number of books and articles on the same topic have been published in the Soviet Union. On the policy of the two countries before and during the war there is far less material. *Nazi-Soviet Relations* remains the basic collection of documents about relations between Germany and Russia during spring and summer 1939. It has been argued by Russian and by a few Western historians that the selection of documents is one-sided and tendentious; the only effective way of proving this charge would be to publish the documents held in the Soviet archives. This, however, has not been done. Several interesting books on Germany have appeared since the war, but so far there is no comprehensive account of Russian-German relations in the post-war period.

A. 1933–9

BASLER, W., *Die deutsch-sowjetischen Beziehungen in den Jahren 1933–39* (1954).

BRACHER, K. D., SAUER, W., SCHULZ, G., *Die nationalsozialistische Macht-ergreifung* (1960).

DUROSELLE, J. B., *Les relations germano-soviétiques de 1933 à 1939* (1953).

FEHST, H., *Bolschewismus und Judentum* (1934).

GREIFE, H., *Sowjetforschung* (1936).

HOFER, W., 'Die Diktatur Hitlers bis zum Beginn des zweiten Weltkrieges', in Brandt/Meyer: *Handbuch der deutschen Geschichte.*

HOFER, W., *Die Entfesselung des Zweiten Weltkrieges* (1954).

KOMMOSS, R., *Juden hinter Stalin* (1938).

KORDT, E., *Wahn und Wirklichkeit* (1948).

LEIBBRANDT, G., *Bolschewismus und Abendland* (1939).

LITVINOV, M., *Vneshniaia politika* (1937).

—, *Protiv agressii* (1938).

NADOLNY, R., *Mein Beitrag* (1955).

RIBBENTROP, J., *Zwischen London und Moskau* (1954).

ROSANOV, G. L., *Germaniya pod vlastiu Fashizma 1933–39* (1961).

SEABURY, P., *The Wilhelmstrasse* (1954).

USHAKOV, V. B., *Vneshniaia politika gitlerovskoi Germanii* (1961).

YERUSALIMSKY, E. (ed.), *Iz istorii Germanii novovo i novcishovo vremeni* (1958).

B. 1939–45

DALLIN, A., *German Rule in Russia* (1957).

DALLIN, D., *Soviet Russia's Foreign Policy 1939–42* (1942).

Der deutsche Imperialismus und der zweite Weltkrieg (2 vols, 1960–1).

Der Untermensch (published by the SS, c. 1942).

ERICKSON, J., *The Soviet General Staff* (1962).

FISCHER, G., *Soviet Opposition to Stalin* (1952).

FREUND, M., *Geschichte des zweiten Weltkrieges in Dokumenten* (3 vols, 1953–6).

GOERLITZ, W., *Der Zweite Weltkrieg* (2 vols, 1951–2).

Istoriya velikoi otechestvennoi voiny Sovetskovo Soiuza 1941–45 (6 vols, 1961–5).

IZRAELIAN, V., *Diplomaticheskaia istoriya velikoi otechestvennoi voiny 1941–45* (1959).

PHILIPPI, F., HEIM, A., *Der Feldzug gegen Sowjetrussland 1941–45* (1962).

Probleme der Geschichte des zweiten Weltkrieges (2 vols, 1958).

SCHEURIG, B., *Freies Deutschland* (1960).

SCHRAMM, P. E., STANGE, H. O. H., *Geschichte des zweiten Weltkrieges* (2 vols, 1960).

TIPPELSKIRCH, K. VON, *Geschichte des zweiten Weltkrieges* (1952).

TOYNBEE, A. (ed.), *Survey of International Affairs 1939–46*. (*The world in March 1939, The Eve of the War*, and other volumes).

WEINBERG, GERHARD L., *Germany and the Soviet Union* (1954).

C. 1945–60

ALLEMANN, F. R., *Bonn ist nicht Weimar* (1959).

Beitraege zur Geschichte der Sozialistischen Einheitspartei Deutschland (1961).

BOHN, H., *Die patriotische Karte in der sowjetischen Deutschlandpolitik* (*Ostprobleme*, 1955).

BRANT, S., *East German Rising* (1955).

DEUERLEIN, E., *Die Einheit Deutschlands* (1961).

Documents on International Affairs (Royal Institute of International Affairs, annual).

Dokumente der Sozialistischen Einheitspartei Deutschlands (Vols 1–8, 1948–62).

Dokumente zur Deutschland Politik der Sowjet Union (2 vols, 1957, 1963).

ERFURT, W., *Die sowjetrussische Deutschlandpolitik* (1956).

GROSSER, A., *Die Bonner Demokratie* (1960).

HUBATSCH, W. (ed.), *Die deutsche Frage* (1961).

MEISSNER, B., *Russland, die Westmaechte und Deutschland* (1954).

OSTEN, W., 'Die sowjetische Deutschlandpolitik in den Jahren 1952/3', in *Ost Europa* (January 1964).

REMER, C. (ed.), *Auf den Spuren der Ostforschung* (1962).

SALEKHOV, N. I., NEMCHINOV, V. I., *Adenauerovskii Reikh–Vozrozhdenie Gitlerizma* (1963).

SETHE, P., *Zwischen Bonn und Moskau* (1956).

SPEIER, H., *Divided Berlin* (1961).

STERN, C., *Portraet einer bolschewistischen Partei* (1957).

WAGNER, W., *Die Teilung Europas* (1959).

WISKEMANN, E., *Germany's Eastern Neighbours* (1956).

6 *Russia and Fascism*

Much of the relevant source material is in periodicals rather than in books. Bahne's long essay on the KPD in Matthias-Morsey, *Das Ende der Parteien*, is a most painstaking survey of the existing literature reflecting the attitudes of the German Communists and the Comintern to Nazism between 1930 and 1935. There is no similar work for either the earlier period or the years after 1935. The writings of Radek and Trotsky are still of interest, but they can hardly be considered as reflecting the official Comintern line. In Chapter 10, I have discussed the reasons for the paucity of Soviet comments on Nazism after 1933. There have been many publications in East Germany about the Nazi era, but most of them deal only with certain aspects (Communist resistance in the Third Reich, collaboration between big capital and the Nazi leaders). There is no Communist history of the Third Reich or the Nazi Party, or any attempt to explain its phenomenal growth in the early thirties and the sources of its mass support. Also included in the bibliography are some important books on Nazism and Fascism by non-Communist authors. Some of them date back to the nineteen-twenties (H. Heller), while others have appeared only recently (E. Nolte).

ALTARI, P., *Proizkhozhdenie fashizma* (1961).

ANTONOV, D., *Ocherki Fashizma v Italii* (1923).

AQUILA, G., *Fashizm v Italii* (1923 – from the Italian).

AVDEYEV, YU. I., STRUNNIKOV, V. N., *Burzhuaznoe gosudarstvo 1918–39* (1962).

BAHNE, S., *Der Trotzkismus in Deutschland 1931–33* (Dissertation, Heidelberg 1958).

—, 'Die Kommunistische Partei Deutschlands', in *Das Ende der Parteien*, E. Matthias, R. Morsey, eds. (1960).

BARTEL, W., *Deutschland in der Zeit der faschistischen Diktatur* (1956).

BECKERATH, E., *Wesen und Werden des faschistischen Staates* (1927).

BRAHM, HEINZ, 'Trockijs Aufrufe gegen Hitler', in *Jahrbuecher fuer Geschichte Osteuropas*, December 1963.

CASUCCI, C. (ed.), *Il Fascismo* (1961).

COLLOTTI, ENZO, *Die Kommunistische Partei Deutschlands 1918–33*, Bibliography (1961).

DIMITROFF, G., *Reichstagsbrandprozess* (1946).

DUTT, R. P., *Fascism and Social Revolution* (1934).

DVORKIN, I., *Ekonomicheskaia programma germanskovo natsionalsotsializma* (1933).

EDINGER, LEWIS J., *German Exile Politics* (1956).

ERBE, R., *Die Nationalsozialistische Wirtschaftspolitik im Lichte der modernen Theorie* (1958).
FAINGAR, I. M., *Ocherki razvitii germanskovo monopolisticheskovo kapitala* (1958).
GENRI (HENRI) E., *Gitler protiv SSSR* (1938).
Germanskii fashizm u vlasti (1934).
GIULIO, YU., *Fashistskaia Italia* (1929).
Grundriss zur Geschichte der deutschen Arbeiterbewegung (1963).
GUENTHER, H., *Der Herren eigener Geist* (1935).
HECKERT, F., *Was geht in Deutschland vor?* (1933).
HELLER, H., *Europa und der Faschismus* (1929).
Kommunisticheskii Internatsional v dokumentakh (1933).
KOZLOV, G., *Germanskii razboinichii imperializm* (1944).
KPSS v rezoliutsiakh i resheniakh (Vols 1–5, 1954–60).
Les Origines du Fascisme (*Recherches Internationales* 1958).
L.V., *Fashizm, evo istoriia i znachenie* (1925).
MATTHIAS, E., *Sozialdemokratie und Nation* (1952).
MILLIKAN, W., 'The Science of Soviet Politics', in *Foreign Affairs*, April 1953.
NEUMANN, F., *Behemoth* (1942).
NOLTE, E., *Der Faschismus in seiner Epoche* (1963).
O Fashistskoi diktature v Germanii (1939).
Protiv fashistskoi falsifikatsii istorii (1939).
RADEK, K., *Portrety i Pamflety* (2 vols, 1933–4).
—, *Podgotovka borby za novy peredel mira* (1934).
RAZMEROV, V. V., *Ekonomicheskaia podgotovka gitlerovskoi agressii* (1958).
ROSSI, A., *The rise of Italian Fascism* (1938).
ROZANOV, G. L., *Germaniia pod vlastiu fashizma* (1961).
SEGAL, N., *Agrarnaia politika germanskovo fashizma* (1938).
SERING, P., *Jenseits des Kapitalismus* (1946).
SIDOROV, A., *Fashizm i gorodskie srednie sloi v Germanii* (1936).
SLOBODSKAIA, S. M., *Italianskii fashizm i evo krakh* (1946).
STALIN, I. V., *Voprosy Leninizma* (1942).
THAELMANN, E., *Kampfreden und Aufsaetze* (1932).
—, *Reden und Aufsaetze zur Geschichte der deutschen Arbeiterbewegung* (Vol. II, 1956).
The Protocols of the sixth and seventh congresses of the Communist International and the reports of the tenth, eleventh, twelfth, and thirteenth plenary sessions of the Executive Committee of the Comintern.
The reports of the eighth, ninth, tenth, eleventh, and twelfth congresses of the Communist Party of Germany.
TROTSKY, L. D., *Zapad i Vostok* (1924).
—, *Die Wendung der Komintern und die Lage in Deutschland* (1931).
—, *Vor der Entscheidung* (1931).
—, *Soll der Faschismus wirklich siegen?* (1932).
—, *Was nun?* (1932).
—, *Gegen den Nationalkommunismus* (1932).

BIBLIOGRAPHY

TROTSKY, L. D.,
—, *Der einzige Weg* (1932).
—, *Ecrits* (Vol. III, 1959).
ULBRICHT, W., *Zur Geschichte der deutschen Arbeiterbewegung* (2 vols, 1954).
WEBER, H. (ed.), *Der deutsche Kommunismus* (1963).
WINZER, O., *Zwoelf Jahre Kampf gegen Faschismus und Krieg* (1955).
Zur Geschichte der deutschen antifaschistischen Widerstandsbewegung, 1933–45 (1957).
Zur Geschichte der Kommunistischen Partei Deutschlands (1955).

PERIODICALS

Beitraege zur Geschichte der deutschen Arbeiterbewegung (E. Berlin).
Bolshevik (Moscow).
Bulleten Oppozitsii (Paris).
Einheit (E. Berlin).
Die Internationale (Berlin).
Internationale Literatur (Moscow).
Internationale Presse Korrespondenz (continued as *Rundschau, Die Welt*).
Istoricheskii Vestnik (Moscow).
Izvestiia (Moscow).
Der Kampf (Vienna).
Kommunisticheskii Internatsional (Moscow).
Krasnaia Nov (Moscow).
Labour Monthly (London).
Mirovoe Khoziaistvo i mirovaia politika (Moscow).
Das Neue Tagebuch (Paris).
Novaia i noveishaia Istoriia (Paris).
Novy Mir (Moscow).
Pravda (Moscow).
Der Rote Aufbau (Berlin).
Rote Fahne (Berlin).
Rinascità (Rome).
Science and Society (New York).
Unser Wort (Paris).
Unsere Zeit (Paris, Basel, Prague).
Vierteljahrshefte zur Zeitgeschichte (Munich).
Voprosy Istorii (Moscow).
Voprosy Istorii KPSS (Moscow).
Zeitschrift fuer Geschichtswissenschaft (E. Berlin).
Zeitschrift fuer Sozialismus (Karlsbad).

NOTES

Chapter 2

1. V. T. Pashuto, 'Istoki nemetskoi fashistskoi istoriografii Rossii', in *Voprosy Istorii*, 10, 1962, p. 62.

2. *Berlin und St Petersburg*. Preussische Beiträge zur Geschichte der Russisch–Deutschen Beziehungen (Leipzig 1880), *passim*.

3. *Protokoll des internationalen Arbeiterkongresses in der Zuerlcher Tonhalle* (1893), p. 30.

4. The problem is discussed in some detail in William Maehl, 'The Role of Russia in German Socialist Policy 1914–1918', in *International Review of Social History*, 2, 1959, p. 177 *et seq.*

5. Haxthausen, *Studien ueber die inneren Zustaende . . . Russlands*, Part III (Berlin 1852), pp. 14, 19.

6. H. von Revelstein, *Die Not der Fremdvoelker unter dem russischen Joche* (Berlin 1916), p. 32.

7. C. Schirren, *Livlaendische Antwort auf Herrn Juri Samarin* (Leipzig), p. 103.

8. *ibid.*, pp. 105, 109.

9. Victor Hehn, *De moribus Ruthenorum. Zur Characteristik der russischen Volksseele*. Edited by Theodor Schiemann (Stuttgart 1892). See also Theodor Schiemann's biography, *Victor Hehn*.

10. Hehn, *op. cit.*, p. 7. This sentence has been quoted verbatim, though usually without giving the reference, countless times by latter-day adepts of the anti-Russian school, such as Rohrbach and Alfred Rosenberg; Hitler, too, repeated it on various occasions, for instance in *Secret Conversations*, p. 191.

11. Constantın Frantz, *Weltpolitik* (1882/3), Vol. II, pp. 60–1.

12. Paul de Lagarde, *Deutsche Schriften* (1905), p. 83.

13. Friedrich Lange, *Reines Deutschthum* (1904), p. 210.

14. Kurd von Strantz, 'Die Frucht des kuenftigen Krieges in Osten und Westen', in *Der neue Kurs*, November 1, 1893, p. 337.

15. *Germania Triumphans*, von einem Groesstdeutschen, pp. 10, 76.

16. Daniel Fryberg, *Wenn ich der Kaiser waer*, p. 170.

17. *Deutschland bei Beginn des 20 Jahrhunderts*, p. 212.

18. *ibid.*, p. 213.

19. *Alldeutsche Blaetter*, 1913, pp. 130–1.

20. *Vossische Zeitung*, December 25, 1914, 'Russland und Wir'. In a book published during the Second World War, Rohrbach repeated his old arguments. See Rohrbach–Schmidt, *Osteuropa, historisch-politisch gesehen* (Potsdam 1942), p. 123.

21. See *Chauvinismus und Welt-krieg*, ed. by Paul Rohrbach, Vol. II (Berlin 1919), *passim*.
22. Klaus Meyer, *Theodor Schiemann als politischer Publizist* (Frankfurt, 1956); H. Giertz, *Theodor Schiemann als Professor fuer osteuropaeische Geschichte an der Berliner Universitaet*. Unpublished Dissertation (East Berlin 1955).
23. Stuttgart 1917.
24. Revelstein, *op. cit.*, p. 8.
25. *Russische Probleme* (Berlin 1917).
26. Leo Loewenson, 'Karl Staehlin 1865–1939', in *Slavonic Review*, November 1949, p. 154.
27. F. Stepun, 'Rossiya mezhdu Yevropei i Aziei', in *Novy Zhurnal*, 69 (September 1962), p. 251 *et seq.*

Chapter 3

1. Fletcher Fullard and J. Marshall: 'The Russian Battle of Dorking', in *United Services Magazine*, 1902, p. 309.
2. F. F. Vigel (Wiegel): *La Russie envahie par les Allemands* (Leipzig 1844).
3. E. Karnovich, 'Znachenie bironovshchinoi v russkoi istorii', in *Otechestvennie Zapiski*, 10 and 11, 1873.
4. A. Lipski, 'A Re-Examination of the "Dark Era" of Anna Ioannovna', in *American Slavic and East European Review*, 1956, p. 477 *et seq.*
5. See Chapter 5, 'The Uses of History', in Hans Rogger, *National Consciousness in Eighteenth-century Russia* (Cambridge, Mass. 1960).
6. T. G. Masaryk, *Russland und Europa* (Jena 1913), Vol I, p. 135.
7. N. V. Riasanovski: *Russia and the West in the Teaching of the Slavophiles* (Cambridge 1952), *passim*.
8. Fonvizin, *Pervoe polnoe sobranie sochinenii*, quoted in Rogger, *op. cit.* p. 83.
9. von Schweinitz, *Denkwuerdigkeiten*, Vol. I (Berlin 1927), p. 395.
10. J. G. Kohl, *Russia* (London 1842), p. 297.
11. *Polnoe sobranie sochineniya* (ed. M. Gershenzon 1910), Vol. I, p. 48.
12. Bernhard von Werder, 'Immediatberichte', in *Berliner Monatshefte*, September 1939, p. 765.
13. *Preussische Jahrbuecher*, June 1914, p. 395. See also B. Huldermann, *Albert Ballin*, p. 303; and *Die grosse Politik der Europaeischen Kabinette*, Vol. 39, p. 580.
14. Report dated January 24, 1909, in *Geheimakten, Verhaeltnis Deutschland zu Russland*, No. 131, Vol. 14 (Univ. of California microfilm, reel 154).
15. 'La Svastika de l'Imperatrice', in Henri Rollin, *L'Apocalypse de notre temps*' (Paris 1940), p. 41–87.
16. Olga Novikoffa, *Skobeleff and the Slavonic cause* (London 1883), *passim*.
The authenticity of the interview was later denied, but it was widely reproduced and certainly expressed the views of many Russians.
17. *Russland 74, Acten betreffend die Presse*, Vol. 1, II (May 8, 1887).

18. See for instance: *Acten, Russland 74, Pressehetzereien gegen Deutschland*, Vols 1–4.
19. Schweinitz, *Denkwuerdigkeiten*, Vol. II, p. 328.
20. *ibid*, p. 435.
21. *Die Grosse Politik*, Vol. 34, p. 811.

22. *Geheim Akten betreffend das Verhaeltnis Deutschlands zu Russland; Deutschland, Number 131, Vol. 15*. Report dated November 1910, in University of California, microfilm 155.

Chapter 4

1. Count N. D. Zhevakhov, *Serge Aleksandrovich Nilus:* Kratkii ocherk zhizni i deatelnosti (Novy Sad 1936), pp. 67, 69.
2. *Mein Kampf* (first edition 1925, Vol. I, p. 231); E. Deuerlein, 'Hitler's Eintritt in die Politik und die Reichswehr', in *Vierteljahrshefte fuer Zeitgeschichte*, VII, 1959, pp. 177–227.
3. In the early internal circular letters (*Rundschreiben*) of the party (file 97 in the Berlin Document Centre) the Communist issue figured hardly at all.
4. *Mitteilungen* (des Verbandes fuer die Abwehr des Antisemitismus), September 18, 1919.
5. Speech in the Gasthaus 'Deutsches Reich' on February 5, 1920. Akten Wiegand, file 1315 in NSDAP Hauptarchiv (in BDC).
6. *Auf Gut Deutsch*, No. 23, August 16, 1919.
7. *Der Vorposten*, 1921, p. 196: 'Die Weisen von Zion, London und Berlin'.
8. Alexander Schilling; *Dr Walter Riehl und die Geschichte des Nationalsozialismus* (Leipzig 1933), p. 247.
9. *Muenchner Post*, February 7, 1921.
10. Compare for instance one of the few Hitler speeches preserved from summer 1922 (*Das Buch*

der NSDAP, Berlin 1934, p. 88 *et seq.*) with the writings of Rosenberg such as *Pest in Russland* (Muenchen 1922), or *Die Totengraeber Russlands* (English translation *The grave-diggers of Russia*, London, n.d.).
11. C. Leonard Lundin, 'The Road from Tsar to Kaiser: Changing loyalties of the Baltic Germans, 1905–1914'; in *Journal of Central European Affairs*, October 1950.
12. Lundin, *loc. cit.*, pp. 234–5.
13. E. F. Sommer, *Die Einigungsbestrebungen der Deutschen im Vorkriegs-Russland* (1905–1914), p. 64; 'Deutschbalten und die Vergiftung des deutschen Volkes', in *Mitteilungen* (des Verbandes für die Abwehr des Antisemitismus), November 24, 1921, p. 143.
14. Leverkuehn, p. 183.
15. 'Die Bolschewisierung Deutschlands', in *Aufbau*, September 21, 1923.
16. 'Bericht ueber die russische monarchistische Organisation in der Emigration.' This is a detailed report, dated October 18, 1935, addressed to Himmler by General Biskupsky, or a member of his entourage, quoted in the following as *Bericht*. See EAP 161-b-12/139, folder 148, correspondence with and about

General Biskupsky, National Archives, Washington.

17. *ibid.* See also Biskupsky's letter to Schickedanz, March 22, 1933, in National Archives. EAP 250-d-18-15-10/15 (NSDAP, Aussenpolitisches Amt).

18. Report of an interview with M. von Scheubner-Richter by a representative of the NSDAP, main archives, dated April 4, 1936, in BDC.

19. *Vorwaerts*, June 9, 1921.

20. See, for instance, the article against 'foreign concession hunters', *Aufbau*, August 25, 1923.

21. *Aufbau*, April 21, 1922. Exactly the same argument was used in Rosenberg's *Pest in Russland*, p. 86.

22. *Aufbau*, July 26, 1922.

23. *ibid.*, August 25, October 18, September 21, 1923.

24. *ibid.*, November 1, 1922.

25. *ibid.*, September 29, 1923.

26. *ibid.*, September 21, October 25, 1923.

27. 'Die Rote Armee', *Voelkischer Beobachter*, March 23, 1923.

28. The text of Scheubner-Richter's memorandum is in Wilhelm Hoegner (ed.), *Hitler und Kahr*, part II, May 1928, pp. 12–14.

29. *Bayerischer Kurier*, October 5, 1923. Hitler's defence of Scheubner-Richter is reprinted in Ernst Deuerlein (ed.), *Der Hitlerputsch* (1962), pp. 201–5.

30. Mathilde von Scheubner-Richter's report of April 3, 1936. Some six weeks before he had prepared a memorandum on a 'national revolution' and a coup by the nationalist forces. But it is not certain whether Hitler was decisively influenced by Scheubner-Richter's blueprint.

31. H. H. Hofmann, *Der Hitlerputsch* (Munich 1961), *passim*. See also Johann Aigner, *Als Ordinanz bei Hochverrätern. Ein Beitrag zur Geschichte der nationalen Erhebung im November 1923*, in Rehse Collection, Hauptarchiv der NSDAP. Now at the Library of Congress, Washington, Manuscript Division Acc. 11,249. Aigner was Scheubner's orderly.

32. A summary of the speeches is given in a leaflet (no title), a copy of which is in the NSDAP Hauptarchiv.

33. Poltavetz-Ostranitsa. See his *Ideologia Ukrainskovo Vilnovo Kosatstva 'Unakor'* (Munich 1936), one of the craziest documents produced by the Ukrainian, or any other group. Poltavetz-Ostranitsa remained the Baltic nazis' protégé for many years; von Kursell and Georg von Manteuffel instituted a 'world action on his behalf'; in 1932 the 'Hetman totius Ukrainae' asked Hitler for 'minimum support' of one thousand marks. See Schickedanz letters to Alfred Rosenberg dated December 21, 1931 and May 27, 1932, in Records of Reich Ministry for the Occupied Eastern territories 1941–45, National Archives, EAP 99/358, Washington.

34. Biskupsky's 'report' to Himmler, see above. Von Kursell, in a conversation with the present writer (Munich May 1962) said that Aufbau simply faded away after Scheubner-Richter's death; he regarded the link between Aufbau and the Nazi party as more or less incidental: 'It should never have been a party affair.'

35. Interview with Otto von Kursell.

36. Thilo von Trotha's introduction to A. Rosenberg, *Blut und Ehre* (Berlin 1939), p. 7.

37. See *Rote Fahne*, October 30, 1930 ('Was Rosenberg a French spy?'), based on Carbuccia's fascist paper *Je suis partout*, which claimed to have discovered incriminating material in the French foreign ministry; see also *8 Uhr Abendblatt*, October 28, 1930; *Berliner Volkszeitung*, October 30, 1930; *Vorwaerts*, November 14, 1931. Goering is said to have asked Hanfstaengl: 'Where did the scoundrel spend world war one?' (O. Strasser's *National-Sozialist*, August 10, 1930). Rosenberg won a lawsuit against the Social Democrats following a similar allegation (*Voelkischer Beobachter*, June 29, 1932). Rosenberg, of course, was not a French spy, but Chancellor Brüning was substantially right when he said about Rosenberg in the Reichstag that 'this man had not yet discovered which was his real fatherland when I was fighting in the war to the last breath'. Rosenberg's somewhat lame answer appeared the following day in the *Voelkischer Beobachter* (February 26, 1932).

38. *Memoirs of Alfred Rosenberg*, ed. Serge Lang and Ernst von Schenck (New York 1949), p. 20.

39. *ibid.*, p. 24.

40. 'Nirwana und Persoenlichkeit', in *Schriften und Reden*, Vol. 1; *Schriften aus den Jahren 1917–1921* (Munich 1943), pp. 12, 16, 20.

41. *Schriften und Reden*, Vol. 1, p. 71. His impressions of the March revolution were written in Russian.

42. *ibid.*, p. 77.

43. 'Das Verbrechen der Freimaurerei', in *Schriften und Reden*, Vol. 1, p. 585.

44. *Mythus des zwanzigsten Jahrhunderts* (edition of 1930), p. 601.

45. *Dietrich Eckart: Ein Vermaechtnis* (Munich 1935), p. 45.

46. *Memoirs of Alfred Rosenberg*, pp. 48, 62.

47. *ibid.*, pp. 70–1.

48. *Schriften und Reden*, Vol. 1, p. 79 (written in June 1918).

49. *Voelkischer Beobachter*, July 17, 24, August 4, 21, November 26, 1921.

50. 'Schicksalswende in London', *Voelkischer Beobachter*, March 6, 1921; 'Genua', *ibid.*, April 19, 1922.

51. 'Vernichtung und Verhoehnung deutscher Arbeiter', *ibid.*, March 29, 1922.

52. 'Von Brest Litowsk nach Versailles', *ibid.*, May 8, 1921.

53. *Voelkischer Beobachter*, April 7, 1923, October 5, 1921, quoting *Russkaia Tribuna* (Zürich), *Ukrainski Kazak* (Lvov), and *Novoe Vremya* (Belgrade), respectively.

54. 'Erkenntniskritik und Marxismus', *Voelkischer Beobachter*, July 12, 1922.

55. These were *Unmoral im Talmud* and *Die Spur des Juden im Wandel der Zeiten* (1920); *Das Verbrechen der Freimaurerei* (1921); *Pest in Russland* and *Der staatsfeindliche Zionismus* (1922); *Wesen, Grundsaetze, und Ziele der NSDAP* and *Die Protokolle der Weisen von Zion* (1923). Rosenberg translated Gougenot des Mousseaux, *Le Juif*.

56. August Rohling, *Der Talmudjude* (1871); Johann Andreas Eisenmenger, *Entdecktes Judentum* (1711).

Chapter 5

1. Alfred Levin, *The Second Duma* (1940), p. 23. I am also indebted to Hans Rogger's unpublished essay 'Was there a Russian Fascism – The Union of Russian People' (1963).
2. N. Markov, *Der Kampf der dunklen Maechte* (Erfurt 1935), p. 4. See also chapters one and two of H. Rollin, *op. cit.*
3. *Soyuz Russkovo Naroda* (ed. A. Chernovskii) (Moscow, 1929), p. 411. This is an important collection of documents on the activities of the Union including the transcript of the interrogation of the Union's leading members in summer 1917. For the testimony of Markov II in July 1917, see *Padenie Tsarskovo Rezhima*, Vol. VI (Moscow 1926), pp. 175–265.

   On the anti-Jewish propaganda see *Yevreiskaya Entsiklopediya*, Vol. II, pp. 745–52.

   On the foundation of the Union, 'Dnevnik Borisa Nikolskovo', in *Krasny Arkhiv*, Vol. II (36), 1934, p. 87.

   It is probably of some political interest that apart from one collection of documents, and a few more dispersed documents elsewhere, there has been no historical study in the Soviet Union of the Union of Russian People, the Black Hundred, or indeed of the extreme right in general, despite the many references to these groups in Lenin's writings and elsewhere.
4. S. Lyubosh, *Russki Fashist* (Leningrad 1925). This short biography of Purishkevich showed no doubts about how to classify Purishkevich politically; it has a swastika on its cover at a time when the swastika outside Germany was not yet well known. At the same time it is quite fair to 'a Fascist who set the style ten years before Fascism as a political movement arose in Europe' (p. 29), and says that he was both intellectually and morally head and shoulders above the other extreme right-wingers.
5. Purishkevich's description of the plot was published first in Kiev, and subsequently in many foreign editions, the last in Paris in 1953. More interesting, from a political point of view, is his *Diary* (*Dnevnik*) published in Riga in 1924, of which the description of the anti-Rasputin plot is a part, and the 'Pavel Dupenski' (Vladimir Purishkevich) *Dnevnik* published in Petersburg in 1913.
6. On the attitude of the Black Hundred to the revolutionary movement see A. A. Maikov, *Revoliutsionery i Chernosotentsy* (St Petersburg 1907); on their attitude towards the intelligentsia and government officials, see B. Nazarevsky, *Biurokratiya i Intelligentsiya* (Moscow 1907); on the national question in Russia, see A. Budilovich, *Po Voprosu ob okrainakh Rossii* (St Petersburg 1906); there was an enormous literature against Jews and freemasons, especially Butmi's books, or such pamphlets as A. Lavrov-Kaluzhsky, *Druzheskii Sovet Yevream* (St Petersburg 1906), D.G.I.'s *Ob Ozhidovlenie byvshei gosudarstvennei Dumy* (1907), or Baron M. F. Taube's tract against spiritualism which ap-

peared in the same publishing house.

7. *Russkoe Znamya* (the Union newspaper edited by A. Dubronin), January 11, January 25, February 8, 1912. See also the Union magazine *Zemshchina*, January 18, 1912. It was not strictly speaking a new invention; it is found in anti-Semitic literature in both Russia and Germany (Stöcker) in one form or another since the eighteen-eighties.

8. In a speech in the Duma on April 18, quoted in Alexander B. Tager, *The Decay of Czarism* (Philadelphia 1935), p. 44. On occasion, one finds racial motives coupled with religious in the anti-Semitic ideology. The programme of the *Russkaya Narodnaya Partiya* (Russian Popular Party), a group close to the Union, maintained that the 'Jewish nationality is anti-human in its religion, parasitic according to its racial characteristics'.

9. On the social composition of the Union see V. Levitsky, 'Pravie partii', in L. Martov and others (ed.) *Obshchestvennoe dvizhenie v Rossii v nachale 20-ovo veka*, Vol. III, Book 5 (St Petersburg 1914).

10. Reinhart Maurach, *Russische Judenpolitik* (Berlin 1939), p. 382.

11. J. S. Curtiss, *Church and State in Russia* (New York 1940), p. 210. Professor Curtiss analyses in detail the complex relationship between the Orthodox Church and the right-wing radical organizations on the basis of rare sources of material. See specifically pp. 209–35.

12. *Vera i Razum*, December 1907, p. 859; Curtiss, p. 269.

13. Levitsky, p. 381.

14. Maurach, *op. cit.*

15. G. Butmi's evidence in *Soyuz russkovo Naroda*. Butmi, whose real name was apparently de Katzman, hailed from Bessarabia, as did many other prominent members of the Union. His book, appropriately enough, was published by the local society for the deaf and dumb. For a list of the Black Hundred newspapers and periodicals, see Nikolskii, *op. cit.*, p. 380.

16. 'Programma Soyuza Russkovo Naroda', in *Krasny Arkhiv*, 1 1927. It is interesting that in this confidential document, which was not designed for outside consumption, there was no anti-Jewish propaganda.

17. 'Zagovor monarkhicheskoi organizatsii V. M. Purishkevicha', in *Krasny Arkhiv*, 1 (26), 1928, p. 169. According to Vinberg (*Put Kresta*) the plotters were in contact with Buchanan, the British ambassador, who wanted the younger Duke of Leuchtenberg to marry his daughter. Vinberg is a notoriously unreliable source. Buchanan, at any rate, did not help the plotters.

18. V. Denikin, *Ocherki russkoi smuty*, Vol. V, p. 161. *V Moskvu* was edited by Izmailov, a lawyer who was editor, with Ivan A. Rodionov, of the Novocherkassk edition of the *Protocols*. Rodionov, a Cossack officer with literary ambitions, had attained some notoriety with his novel *Nashe prestupleniya* (Moscow 1909). In another novel, *Zhertvoe Vecherniya* (Berlin 1922), he describes the situation (as he saw it) in Rostov and Novocherkassk during the civil war.

19. Denikin, V, 160.

20. Denikin, V, 159. *V Moskvu* had the subtitle 'Take a stick and chase the Jew to Palestine' (Beri khvorostinu i goni zhida v Palestinu).

21. . . . après la revolution de 1917, on se prit à envisager les Protocols de façon différente. Ce qui avait fait rire avec mépris comme 'une invention absurde des quelques deplorables chernosotents' se réalisait alors aux yeux de tous avec l'exactitude foudroyante d'une prédiction prophétique qui s'accomplit (A. Netchvolodov, *L'Empereur Nicolas II et les juifs* (Paris 1924), p. 251). See also *The Cause of World Unrest*, p. 175, for an almost identical explanation.

22. See the leaflets quoted and reproduced in N. B. Shekhtman, *Pogromy dobrovolcheskoi armii na Ukraine* (Berlin 1932), pp. 21, 263–4. One of the earliest of these, dated November 24, 1918, had been issued by a monarchist unit created by the Duke of Leuchtenberg in German-occupied Ukraine. Members of this group later reappeared in Munich, and belonged to the circle of Russian emigrants which supported the young Hitler movement.

23. *ibid.* 'Golos k russkomu narodu Yuzhnoi Armii.'

24. *Donskie Vedomosti*, reprinted in Shekhtman, p. 265.

25. *Pest in Russland*, p. 31. The 'Jewish capitalism' of Trotsky and Zinoviev was to prepare (according to this source) the sell-out of Russia to Jewish finance capital. See also *idem, The grave-diggers of Russia*, p. 8.

26. 'Kuhn, Loeb and Co. calls Coughlin Charge False', in *New York Herald Tribune*, November 29, 1938. One Nazi work said: 'Trotsky was commissioned by Jacob Schiff and Max Warburg to bring about the revolution' (Rudolf Kommos, *Juden hinter Stalin*, 3rd ed. (Berlin 1942), p. 25).

27. See, for instance, G. L. Rozanov: *Germaniya pod vlastiu fashizma*, (Moscow 1961), pp. 24–6. The story has been disproved many times; in greatest detail in Hermann Lutz, 'Faelschungen zur Auslandsfinanzierung Hitlers', in *Vierteljahrshefte fuer Zeitgeschichte*, October 1954, p. 386 *et seq.*

28. *The German–Bolshevic conspiracy*. Issued by the Committee of Public Information (October 1918), p. 27.

29. See Chapter 22, 'The Sisson papers', in George Kennan, *Russia Leaves the War* (London 1956).

30. Zhevakhov, *op. cit.*, p. 35.

31. *Mitteilungen*, February 1, 1905.

32. Wilhelm Müller, *Politische Geschichte der Gegenwart* (1881); Harold Frederic, *The New Exodus* (London 1892) thinks that 'anti-Semitic agitation in Russia . . . had begun months before the outbreak in Germany', but the German riots did 'point the means to a practical demonstration of anti-Semitism in Russia', p. 115.

33. S. M. Dubnow, *History of the Jews in Russia and Poland*, Vol. I, pp. 57, 95; elsewhere he says that 'the bacillus of German anti-Semitism had penetrated even into the circles of the Russian radical intelligentsia', Vol. III, p. 278, and he mentions German anti-Semitism as one of the formative influences on Ivan Aksakov.

34. *Der gefaehrdete Wiederaufbau* (Berlin 1925). For another contemporary witness of the impact of German anti-Semitism on Russia, see Anatole Leroy Beaulieu, *L'empire des Tsars et les Russes, passim.*
35. *Manifest an die Regierungen und Voelker der durch das Judentum gefaehrdeten christlichen Staaten laut Beschluss des Internationalen Kongresses zu Dresden,* 1882–3 (Chemnitz 1883), p. 4.
36. *Manifest*, p. 10.
37. *Flugblatt 23.* Deutsch-Soziale Partei. n.d.
38. *Flugblatt 47, Die geheimen Ziele des Judentums,* n.d. It was also included in Fritsch's *Antisemiten Katechismus,* pp. 385–92.
39. *Antisemitische Korrespondenz,* February 1901.
40. *Deutsch-Soziale Blaetter,* quoted in *Mitteilungen,* 1906, p. 310.
41. *Enthuellungen,* p. 223.
42. 'Judenheit und Politik', in *Auf Gut Deutsch,* 17/18, June 13, 1919. Rosenberg advanced fast in his reading; a year later he had discovered the existence of Zionism and from then on hardly ever mentioned the AIU.
43. The number of books and booklets published on this subject in the twenties and thirties is truly staggering. The most substantial investigations, Rollin's book apart, are: Benjamin Segel, *Die Protokolle der Weisen von Zion kritisch beleuchtet* (Berlin 1924); Herman Bernstein, *The Truth about the Protocols of Zion* (New York 1935); V. L. Burtsev, *Protokoly Tsionistkikh mudretsov dokazanni podlog* (Paris 1938) and the evidence given in the Bern trial about the authenticity

of the *Protocols* in 1935. As late as 1942 a committee of leading American historians published a report on this subject: John S. Curtiss (ed.) *An Appraisal of the Protocols of Zion* (Columbia, N.Y. 1942).
44. Quoted in Curtiss, p. 92.
45. *Luch Sveta,* Vol. III, May 1920, p. 240. The first Moscow subways were built in the 1930s.
46. Among them J. Brafman, *Kniga Kagala* (St Petersburg 1882), (German edition, 2 vols., 1928).
47. Zhevakhov, *op. cit.* Du Chayla's evidence in *Poslednie Novosti,* Paris, May 1, 1921, *La Tribune Juive,* May 14, 1921, and as a witness at the Bern trial, 1935.
48. Schwartz-Bostunich, *Juedischer Imperialismus,* p. 359. See also A. P. Rogovich's introduction to the Russian edition of the *Protocols* (Berlin 1921), pp. 6–7.
49. *Die Geheimnisse der Weisen von Zion.* First German edition. Verlag 'Auf Vorposten' (Charlottenburg 1919). Some details about the history of this edition are given in *Der Vorposten* 4/5, 1921, p. 100. With the ninth edition in 1929, this book passed to the Nazi Party publishing house in Munich (Franz Eher).
50. *Die zionistischen Protokolle.* Fifth edition (Leipzig 1924).
51. Such as *Die Protokolle der Weisen von Zion und die juedische Weltpolitik,* first published in Munich in July 1923, of which some fifty thousand copies were sold; Alfred Rosenberg: *Der Verschwoererkongress in Basel; um die Echtheit der zionistischen Protokolle* (Munich 1927); Alfred Rosenberg: 'Echt oder gefaelscht', *Der Weltkampf,* 4, 1925, pp. 145–63.

52. *The International Jew. The World's foremost Problem* (a reprint of a series of articles appearing in the *Dearborn Independent*, May 22 to October 2, 1920 (Dearborn, Michigan 1920). See also Chapter 19 in H. Rollin, *op. cit.*
53. Gwyer, *op. cit.*, p. 127.
54. C. A. Loosli in the Bern trial

(1935); see Alexander Stein, *Adolf Hitler – Schueler der Weisen von Zion* (Karlsbad 1936); Ruben Blank, *Adolf Hitler – ses aspirations, sa politique, sa propaganda, et les Protocoles de Sion* (Paris 1938); 'La similitude de l'idéologie politique de M. Hitler avec celle des Protocoles des Sages de Sion est indéniable', p. 201.

Chapter 6

1. Biskupsky, 'Bericht', *loc. cit.; Der Kampf*, Munich, June 10, 1921.
2. *Vorwaerts*, June 9, 1921; *Rote Fahne*, June 9, 1921. *Neue Zuercher Zeitung*, June 12, 1921.
3. *Rul*, June 8, 11, 1921; *Golos Rossii*, June 5, 1921. The *Protocols* of the conference were not published but the contents of some of the main speeches are given in four numbers of *Dvuglavy Orel* (Berlin), published between May 15, 1921 and July 1, 1921; these include A. M. Maslennikov's report 'Ideologia rossiiski imperatorskoi vlasti' (May 15) as well as the speech of Markov (June 15), the text of the resolutions (June 1), N. Talberg's article ('Paris i Reichengall') (June 1), and 'Vpetchatleniya na sezde' (July 1). The German press was not admitted to the conference, with the exception of a Balt, Baron Engelhardt, writing for a Munich newspaper.
4. *Der Kampf* (Munich), June 7, 1921; *Schlesische Zeitung* July 2, 1921; *Koenigsberger Allgemeine Zeitung*, June 30, 1921.
5. *Frankfurter Zeitung*, June 7, 1921.
6. *Muenchener Neueste Nachrichten*, June 6, 1921.

7. *Reichswart*, May 28, 1921.
8. Biskupsky, 'Bericht' to Himmler.
9. Reports of a conversation with Biskupsky, dated September 8, 1939, in *Records of the National Socialist German Labour Party*, T-81, roll 11, National Archives, Washington. On the same occasion, Biskupsky claimed that he had been an early member of the Union of the Russian people and had collaborated with Dr Dubrovin.
10. Biskupsky 'Bericht' to Himmler (1935); a great many people claimed to have had a hand in the formulation of Kyrill's manifesto, including Scheubner-Richter and Snessarev. The programme has been discussed in detail in: 'K': *Mit oder ohne Moskau* (Dresden 1927).
11. Snessarev, *op. cit.*, p. 90.
12. On the switch from a pro-German to a pro-French orientation on the part of the *emigré* right-wing, see A. Bulatsel (a former Black Hundred leader): *Na Rodinu iz stana Belikh* (Moscow 1924), p. 58 *et. seq.* Markov, Shirinsky-Shikhmatov the elder, Metropolit Antoni and others had already moved from Germany to Paris in 1922.
13. Biskupsky, 'Bericht' to Himmler.

14. *ibid.* It has been impossible, unfortunately, to trace the text of this letter or of Hitler's reply.
15. Biskupsky to Rosenberg, October 22, 1931; Rosenberg to Biskupsky, December 30, 1931, National Archives, Washington, see note 17, Chapter 5.
16. Biskupsky to Rosenberg (with a request to submit this to Hitler – but to no military or political institution), March and April, 1933, National Archives, Washington, see note 17, Chapter 5. On other occasions Biskupsky claimed to have American contacts as well.
17. E. Kuskowa-Prokopowitsch made some pertinent observations on this dilemma in her *Die Elemente des russischen Faschismus* in C. Landauer and H. Honegger (eds.), '*Internationaler Faschismus*' (Karlsruhe 1928).
18. *Lagebesprechungen im Fuehrerhauptquartier*, ed. Helmut Heiber (Munich 1963), pp. 114–15.
19. F. Vinberg: *Krestny Put*, Part I (Munich 1921), p. 94.
20. See his evidence during interrogation in *Krasny Arkhiv*, 1 (26), 1928. See also H. Rollin, *op. cit.* pp. 154–8.
21. *Luch Sveta*, March 1919, *passim.*
22. *Krestny Put*, p. 284.
23. 'Velikii Zagovor' in *Luch Sveta*, 4; *Krestny Put*, Chapter 2; also pp. 240–5, 250–65, 346. Similar views are expressed in a book published in Graz in 1922: V. N. Gladky, *Zhidy.*
24. *Krestny Put*, pp. 240–65 and epilogue. There is a shortened German version: Th. von Winberg, *Der Kreuzweg* (Munich 1922). The second part of the book was announced but never published.
25. For further biographical details see N. D. Zhevakhov, *Svetloi pamyati shtallmaistera vysochaishevo dvora Th.V. Vinberg* (Paris 1928), and the privately published memorial booklet by Olga Loginova (Paris 1927). I have not been able to locate a copy of Vinberg's *Captive of the Monkeys* (Kiev 1919), dealing mainly with masonic conspiracies and his own experiences in 1917–18.
26. *Der Mythus des Zwanzigsten Jahrhunderts* (Munich 1930), p. 202.
27. *Voiny temnykh sil*, 2 vols (Paris 1928); *Der Kampf der dunklen Maechte* (Erfurt 1935).
28. *Prizyv*, February 3, 1920.
29. *Prizyv*, September 21, 1919.
30. See his *The Secret World Government or The Hidden Hand: 100 Historical Mysteries Explained* (New York 1926), also *Pamyati Grafa Cherep-Spiridovich*, ed. N. D. Zhevakhov (New York 1926).
31. Evgenii Brant, *Ritualnoe Ubiistvo u Yevreev* (Belgrade 1926–7). Under the Nazis he called himself Erwin Brant.
32. V. Akhmatov, *Yevrei i budushche mira* (Belgrade 1927), p. 124.
33. *Vospominania*, Vol. I (Munich 1923); Vol. II (Novy Sad 1928) p. 435.
34. He died in December 1920: see N. D. Zhevakhov, *Knyaz Aleksei Aleksandrovich Shirinsky-Shikhmatov* (Novy Sad 1934).
35. See Geoffrey Bailey, *The Conspirators* (New York 1960), *passim*, also the articles by Voitsekhovsky and Vraga in *Vozrozhdenie* (Paris) 7, 8, 9, 11; 1950.

36. See xxx: 'Legenda i Deistvitelnost' (Trest) in *Vozrozhdenie*, May–June 1951, pp. 114–29. The younger Shirinsky-Shikhmatov moved to France, was arrested by the Germans during the occupation of that country, and perished – apparently in a German camp.

37. Evgenii Vershinin, *Mir v lapakh Satany* (Berlin–Shanghai 1933), pp. 146, 157.

38. Most of the biographical data are from his *Juedischer Imperialismus*, third edition (Leipzig c. 1938), and the extensive correspondence between him and Himmler in *Records of the Reich Leader SS and Chief of the German Police*, National Archives, Washington, EAP 161–b–12/66 folder 269. Bostunich's autobiography was to have been published in the *Illustrierter Beobachter* in 1942, the main Nazi illustrated magazine, but the SS central office apparently refused to clear it for publication. See also Albert Norden, *Faelscher* (East Berlin 1961), pp. 249–50, for some documents now in East German archives.

39. *Masonstvo i Russkaya revoliutsya* (Novy Sad 1922).

40. *Juedischer Imperialismus*, p. 7.

41. *Jude und Weib. Theorie und Praxis des juedischen Vampyrismus* (Berlin 1939).

42. *Juedischer Imperialismus*, p. 7.

43. Bostunich–Himmler correspondence in the National Archives, Washington.

44. Letter dated November 8, 1935, Bostunich–Himmler correspondence.

45. In his *Juedischer Imperialismus:* in this book another highly revealing personal statement occurs: All great impostors in Russian history were called Grigori . . .

Chapter 7

1. Among the literature on the subject published since the Second World War: Gerald Freund, *Unholy Alliance* (London 1957); Lionel Kochan, *Russia and the Weimar Republic* (Cambridge 1954); Herbert Helbig, *Die Traeger der Rapallo-Politik* (Goettingen 1958); Gustav Hilger and A. G. Meyer, *The Incompatible Allies* (New York 1953), ought to be mentioned; all include bibliographies. The most detailed East German work on the early period is Guenther Rosenfeld, *Sowjetrussland und Deutschland 1917–1922* (Berlin 1960); Alfred Anderle, *Die Deutsche Rapallo-Politik* (Berlin 1962), gives the fullest account of relations in the mid-twenties from the Communist viewpoint.

2. John Erickson, *The Soviet General Staff* (London 1962), *passim*; G. Castellan: 'Reichswehr et Armée Rouge 1920–1939', in J. B. Duroselle (ed.), *Les relations germano-soviétiques de 1933 à 1939* (Paris 1954).

3. Gustav Hilger and Alfred G. Mayer, *The Incompatible Allies*, p. 118.

4. E. E. Dwinger, *Wir rufen Deutschland*, pp. 438, 514.

5. von Seeckt, *Deutschland zwischen West und Ost* (1933), pp. 38, 45.

6. *Zeitschrift fuer Geopolitik*, 6, 1929, p. 578.

7. *Wehrgeographische Betrachtungen der Sowjet Union*, Schriften

342

zur Geopolitik, 4, 1933, p. 11.
8. Many of these attacks are listed in the bibliographical essay by Gerd Voigt: 'Zur Rolle der faschistischen Ostforschung vor dem zweiten Weltkrieg' in *Der*

deutsche Imperialismus und der zweite Weltkrieg (East Berlin 1961), pp. 237–64.
9. Hermann Greife, *Sowjetforschung*, 1936, p. 62.
10. *ibid.*, p. 58.

Chapter 8

1. *Hitler's Secret Book*, p. 137.
2. *ibid.*, p. 1936.
3. *Mein Kampf*, p. 755.
4. *ibid.*, p. 750; *Hitler's Secret Book*, p. 138.
5. *Mein Kampf*, p. 742.
6. *ibid.*, p. 743.
7. *Hitler's Secret Book*, pp. 135, 139.
8. *ibid.*, p. 133.
9. *ibid.*, pp. 133–5; *Mein Kampf*, p. 748.
10. *cf. Mein Kampf*, p. 750.
11. *Hitler's Secret Book*, p. 139.
12. *St Petersburg 1910* reprinted in *Weltpolitisches Wanderbuch*, 1915, pp. 72–3. Certain early racialist writers had argued this all along: 'The Russians are today what they have always been, a confused mob, without movement and consequently without history, polished on the surface but sunk in darkness. They are a certain danger for our civilization.' Friedrich Lange, *Reines Deutschthum* (1904), p. 210.
13. *Burg Grobin*, 1915, *Spala*, 1915, reprinted, *ibid.*, pp. 284–5.
14. O. E. Schueddekopf, *Linke Leute von Rechts*, p. 194.
15. *Das Russische Problem* in *Die Zweite Revolution*. p. 47.
16. *ibid.*, p. 41, also published in *Nationalsozialistische Briefe*, October 1925, and *Voelkischer Beobachter*, November 14, 1925.
17. *Die Zweite Revolution*, p. 54.

18. *ibid.*, p. 53.
19. *ibid.*, pp. 53, 42.
20. *Voelkischer Beobachter*, October 22, 1925.
21. Goebbels in *Nationalsozialistische Briefe*, January 15, 1926.
22. Gregor Strasser, *ibid.* Another participant in the *Voelkischer Beobachter* controversy was G. Nemirovich-Danchenko, who belonged to the Rosenberg circle in Munich. On Nemirovich-Danchenko's rôle in the Russian Civil War, see his *V Krimu pri Vrangele* (Berlin 1922).
23. J. Goebbels, *Der Bolschewismus in Theorie und Praxis* (Munich 1936), p. 7.
24. *Der Weltkampf*, 1926, p. 263; Schwarz Bostunich in *Weltkampf*, 1929, p. 49.
25. *Weltkampf*, 1924, p. 26.
26. *Nationalsozialistische Briefe*, October 15, November 15, December 15, 1927.
27. *Weltkampf*, February 1929, p. 49; April 1930, pp. 150–1.
28. These include *Die internationale Hochfinanz als Herrin der Arbeiterbewegung aller Laender* (Munich 1925), the postscript to Katharina Haug-Haough, *Hinter den Kulissen des Bolschewismus* (Leipzig 1926), *Das Wesen des Bolschewismus* (1924) and various essays.
29. *Die sibirische Tragoedie* in *Weltkampf*, May 1925, p. 433 *et seq.*
30. *Der Weltkampf*, July 1928, p. 293; see also *Voelkischer*

Beobachter, September 22, 1926, October 10, 1928.
31. *ibid.*, p. 311.
32. von Manteuffel and von Kursell, two of the Nazi Balts, launched a campaign for the Ukrainians in 1931. See Schickedanz letter to Rosenberg, dated December 21, 1931, in their file of correspondence EAP 99/358, National Archives, Washington.
33. In a letter to Rosenberg dated May 27, 1932, the Hetman asked Hitler for 'minimum support of 1,000 mark', *ibid.*
34. *Weltkampf*, December 1927, p. 529.
35. *ibid.*, January 1930, p. 23.

36. *Nationalsozialistische Monatshefte*, June 1931, p. 247.
37. *Weltkampf*, January 1931, pp. 13–15.
38. *Nationalsozialistische Monatshefte*, October 1932, p. 484.
39. *ibid.*, January 1932.
40. *Das Wesen des Bolschewismus*, *op. cit.* p. 2.
41. *Weltkampf*, December 1927, p. 533.
42. Speech in Duesseldorf, January 27, 1932, quoted in Gordon Prange (ed.), *Hitler's Words*.
43. *Voelkischer Beobachter*, April 19, 1932.
44. L. Luedecke, *I Knew Hitler*, p. 422 (New York 1938).

Chapter 9

1. *Documents on German Foreign Policy*, series C, Vol. I, p. 851.
2. von Twardowski on a conversation with Radek; January 1, 1934. *Documents*, Series C, Vol. II, pp. 297–8.
3. German Foreign Ministry (reel 1806 H); 429734 (Enukidze) 429645 (Krestinski).
4. German Foreign Ministry, 1908 H; 429484.
5. *ibid.*, 429508.
6. *ibid.*, 429585.
7. *Documents*, Series C, Vol. I, p. 21.
8. German Foreign Ministry, 1908 H; 429585.
9. Radek in *Pravda*, May 10, 1933; *Documents*, Series C, Vol. I, p. 388.
10. German Foreign Ministry, 1883 H; 425248–57, and 425298–300.
11. Dirksen report, May 16, 1933 in *Documents*, Series C, Vol. I, p. 449.

12. *Voelkischer Beobachter*, November 7, 1933.
13. *Reichswart*, January 14, 1934.
14. *Documents*, Series C, Vol I, p. 744.
15. Report dated October 30, 1933. German Foreign Ministry, 9339/ E 661809–22.
16. *Documents*, Series C, Vol. I, p. 901.
17. *Documents*, Series C, Vol. II (Litvinov to Twardowski; October 16, 1933), p. 19.
18. *Documents*, Series C, Vol. I, p. 421.
19. *Documents*, Series C, Vol. II, November 1, 1933, p. 81.
20. *Documents*, Series C, Vol I. Report by German military attaché in Moscow dated June 28, 1933, p. 609. Since many files pertaining to 1933 have been lost, important details are not known. On September 15 another dispatch announced that 'the stations have been discontinued'

(*ibid., loc. cit.* p. 820). The first message indicating that the Russians might discontinue the military co-operation was in a Dirksen report dated June 5, 1933 (1806 H; 429639). But a month later Milch, subsequently State Secretary for Aviation, in a letter to Dirksen expressed the conviction that it should be possible to have good relations with the Russians *at least* in the military field (1806 H; 429675).

21. *Documents*, Series C, Vol. II, p. 322 *et seq.*
22. *Documents*, Series C, Vol. II, p. 860. This memorandum, on the lines of Nadolny's policy recommendations was drafted by Meyer and Gaus, German Foreign Ministry officials.
23. *Documents*, Series C, Vol. II, p. 863.
24. *Documents*, Series C, Vol. III, p. 521.
25. *ibid.*, p. 532.
26. *Documents*, Series C, Vol. II, p. 333. On the same occasion Radek also predicted that technology would make enormous advances during the next ten years; that it would be possible then to fly to New York in the stratosphere in seven hours, that present war materials and defences would be ridiculous and that the frontier lines drawn in little Europe would then really have become senseless.
27. *Documents*, Series C. Vol. IV, p. 19. On the extent of German re-armament and its implications; Tukhachevsky in *Pravda*, March

31, 1935, and *Krasnaia Zvezda*, April 1, 1935; he thought that in case of war Germany could already muster 108 divisions – which was a very much exaggerated figure at that date.

28. German Foreign Ministry, 1906 H; 429057.
29. *ibid.*, 1906 H; 429076.
30. *Documents*, Series C, Vol. II, p. 333.
31. Schacht, of course, informed the government departments concerned.
32. *Documents*, Series C, Vol. IV, p. 933.
33. *ibid.*, p. 899.
34. *ibid.*, p. 818.
35. *ibid.*, p. 779.
36. *Weltkampf*, September 1934, p. 7.
37. *Weltkampf*, November 1934, p. 330.
38. *Voelkischer Beobachter*, May 22, 1935.
39. *Hitler's Speeches* (Baynes), Vol. I, p. 668; interview with Baillie of the United Press.
40. *Hitler's Speeches* (Baynes), *loc. cit.*, p. 675.
41. 'Der Bolschewismus als Aktion einer fremden Rasse', reprinted in *Nationalsozialistische Monatshefte*, October 1935, p. 866 *et seq.*
42. J. Goebbels: *Der Bolschewismus in Theorie und Praxis* (Muenchen 1936), p. 3, p. 5.
43. *Voelkischer Beobachter*, February 21, 1938.
44. *Deutscher Volkswirt*, August 17, 1934.

Chapter 10

1. The following abbreviations are used with regard to hitherto unpublished sources about the Anti-Komintern: 'Amt Osten': these are the files of the Eastern department of the Foreign Political Office (APA) of the Nazi Party headed by Rosenberg, 1933–41; they now constitute a section of the German documents held in the National Archives, Washington, D.C. Their serial numbers are

EAP 250–d–18–05, 1–12
EAP 250–d–18–10, 1–13
EAP 250–d–18–15, 1–16

Other Anti-Komintern material and correspondence is now in the Hoover Library, Stanford. They have been microfilmed as T 81/Series 11, 14, 16, etc.

Taubert: this refers to a final report, written in January 1945 by the father of the Anti-Komintern, a high official in Dr Goebbels' Ministry of Propaganda. The full title is 'Querschnitt durch die Taetigkeit des Arbeitsgebiet Dr Taubert (Anti-bolschewismus) des RMVP bis zum 31 December, 1944', and the original is kept in the YIVO Archives, New York.

2. The only exceptions are a few pamphlets such as Karl Bartz, *Bolschewismus ueber uns* (Berlin,

1932), or Heinz Franke, *Der Schwindel des Bolschewismus* (Munich 1931), or Hardefuss, *Was hat uns der Bolschewismus gekostet* (Munich 1932), which dealt chiefly with German Communism. See also list in Erich Unger, *Das Schrifttum des Nationalsozialismus, 1919–34* (Berlin 1934).

3. *Hier spricht Sowjet Russland* (Gaupropagandaleitung Essen 1932).

4. See Goebbels' announcement of January 10, 1936, designated a state secret, that for the purpose of covering up ('*zum Zwecke der Tarnung*') the Anti-Komintern was to appear in public as an independent organization. Amt Osten: T 81, roll 14.

5. *cf.* Taubert, p. 9.

6. The order was revoked in January 1936. Amt Osten, Leibbrandt to Rosenberg 27/1/1937.

7. *Osteuropa und Deutscher Osten,* 1934.

8. Letter dated October 1, 1935 in Amt Osten.

9. *loc. cit.* letter dated June 14, 1935: this refers apparently to an article by Mehnert in the *Muenchner Neueste Nachrichten*, No. 173, 1935, and an article in *Bolshevik*, March 15, 1935.

10. Dr Hermann Greife, *Sowjetforschung* (Berlin 1936). *cf.* also his and Ehrt's articles in *Das Volk*, April 1936, March 1937, *passim*. This politico-literary monthly, which was not of a specialized character, found very few people interested in its message; its circulation was about three thousand, most of which were given away. Yet it could speak with

346

authority because of its influential backers.

11. Greife, *op. cit.* pp. 37–8, 42, 54–7.

12. W. von Kielpinski, 'Deutsche Wissenschaft und Sowjet Union', in *Volk im Werden*, February 1937, p. 77 ff.

13. Bolko von Richthofen: 'Bolschewistische Wissenschaft und Judentum' in B. von Richthofen (ed.), *Bolschewistische Wissenschaft und Kulturpolitik* (Koenigsberg 1938).

14. Undated, unsigned memo, in Amt Osten file.

15. Taubert, p. 8. On Niedermayer's activities in the twenties, see F. Carsten, 'The Reichswehr and the Red Army', *Survey*, October 1962.

16. Taubert, p. 8.

17. Leibbrandt to Rosenberg, October 2, 1934, October 10, 1934. Amt Osten roll 14 (which means that Dr Goebbels fooled even his colleagues).

18. *Das Volk*, September 1936, p. 258.

19. See, for instance, the protocol ('strictly confidential') of the 'Erste Vertrauliche Internationale Antikommunistische Konferenz in Feldafing bei Muenchen, November 4–10, 1936.'

20. On lack of means, see Leibbrandt to Rosenberg, September 28, 1935. Amt Osten.

21. German Foreign Ministry, 1949 H; von Neurath circular dated April 17, 1937.

23. '*Es hat immer zu den unvergesslichen Anekdoten der Anti Komintern gehoert, dass die Saarbrueckener Pfaefflein nie geahnt haben wessen Geschaefte sie besorgt haben.*' Taubert, p. 16.

24. *Abrechnung mit Moskau* (Berlin 1938). Mrs Reese also collaborated with Ernst Torgler, who had been a leading German communist and one of the main defendants in the Reichstag fire trial, in yet another book on German communism and the Comintern. Hitler decided against immediate publication 'until the old wounds are healed' (Taubert, p. 20). Only two copies of the manuscript existed and they may have been destroyed in 1945.

25. *Die groesste Sklaverei der Weltgeschichte, Wettlauf mit der GPU, Fuenf Jahre Sowjet Flieger, Bauern unter Hammer und Sichel, Russische Passion.*

26. Leibbrandt to Rosenberg, No. 1, 1939 – Amt Osten.

27. *Warum Krieg mit Stalin? Das Rothuch der Anti-Komintern* (Berlin 1941).

28. *Zeitschriftendienst*, May 30, June 24, 1939.

29. *ibid.*, August 26, 1939.

30. Duerksen to Rosenberg, September 2, 1939. Amt Osten.

31. December 31, 1938. Leibbrandt to Rosenberg, Amt Osten. If Dr Taubert's announcement was true, it throws fresh light on Hitler's foreign policy, for in this case Hitler must have envisaged a reconciliation with Stalin as early as December 1938, not only in April or May 1939 as most historians are inclined to believe. Yet it is by no means certain that Hitler really had given such an order; the propaganda ministry was probably just waiting for a pretext to sabotage the activities of Rosenberg's office.

32. Amt Osten, July 1, 1940.

33. Gottlieb Leibbrandt: *Bolschewismus und Abendland* (Berlin 1939), pp. 40, 93. See also the

same writer's 'Die rassisch-voelkische Bedingtheit der bolschewistischen Revolution' in *Nationalsozialistische Monatshefte*, November 1937, p. 1021.
34. 'Die Protokolle der Poale Zion' in *Nationalsozialistische Monatshefte*, November 1938, p. 1006.
35. *Wille zum Reich*, February 1935; *Fridericus*, February 1934.
36. Hermann Greife, *Ist die Entwicklung der Sowjet Union zum nationalen Staat moeglich?* (Berlin 1939).
37. *ibid.*, pp. 25, 32, 36–8.
38. Hermann Fehst, *Bolschewismus und Judentum* (Berlin 1934), and Rudolf Kommoss, *Juden hinter Stalin* (1938), became the two standard works.

39. Fehst, *op. cit.* p. 90.
40. Kommoss, *op. cit.* p. 33.
41. 'Anti-Kommunistischer Propaganda Feldzug im Inneren' (Confidential). Two such sets of instructions have been found, one dated October 1935, the other March 31, 1937 (Amt Osten). They probably emanated from the propaganda ministry, either from Taubert, or from Goebbels himself.
42. See for instance 'Mitteilungen zur Lage in der Sowjet Union. Reichsführer SS Chef des Sicherheitshauptamtes', 1939. These monthly bulletins of about 60–80 pages each were apparently prepared by the Wannsee Institut headed by Akhmeteli.

Chapter 11

1. K. Radek: *Portrety i Pamflety* (Moscow 1933), Vol. 2, pp. 353, 365.
2. *Inprecorr*, December 21, 1922, p. 1820.
3. 'L.V.': *Fashizm, evo istoriya i znachenie* (Moscow 1925), p. 26; a wholly negative appraisal was given by Guilo Aquila: *Der Faschismus in Italien* (Hamburg 1923), also published by *Krasnaya Nov* in Moscow in 1923.
4. *Jahrbuch fuer Politik, Wirtschaft, Arbeiterbewegung, 1923/4* (Hamburg, n.d.), p. 579.
5. Theses on tactics adopted by the fourth Comintern Congress, quoted in J. Degras (ed.), *The Communist International 1919–43, Documents*, Vol. I, pp. 421–2.
6. In an article first published in *Lo Stato Operaio*, June 1928, reprinted in Paolo Alatri (ed.)

L'antifascismo italiano (Rome 1961), Vol. II, p. 84.
7. *Inprecorr*, September 16, 1924.
8. See, for instance, the resolutions of the Lyons Congress of the Italian Communist party in 'Trenta anni di vita e lotte del P.C.I.', *Quaderni di Rinascita*, (2) Rome (n.d.).
9. 'A proposito del fascismo', republished in *Società* (December 1952) p. 591, reprinted in *Il Fascismo*, ed. C. Casucci (Bologna 1961), p. 281.
10. *Kommunisticheski Internatsional v dokumentakh*, ed. Bela Kun (Moscow 1933), pp. 448–9; Stalin *Sochineniya* (Moscow 1947), Vol. 6, p. 282.
11. Arthur Rosenberg was, I believe, one of the first to make this distinction: 'Historicus': *Der Faschismus als Massenbewegung* (Karlsbad 1934), p. 8.

12. Title of an article on Venezuela in *Novy Mir*, 6, 1929, p. 184.
13. Palme Dutt in *Labour Monthly*, July 1925, quoted in R. P. Dutt, *Fascism and Social Revolution* (London 1935), p. 89.
14. *Inprecorr*, July 5, 1923, p. 989.
15. *Inprecorr*, June 20, 1923, p. 859. This episode is discussed in detail in Joseph Rothschild: *The Communist Party of Bulgaria* (New York 1959) pp. 117–132.
16. Most of the literature on the 'May Error' is mentioned in M. K. Dziewanowski: *The Communist Party of Poland* (Cambridge 1959), pp. 116–35.
17. *Jahrbuch fuer Politik, Wirtschaft, Arbeiterbewegung* 1923–4, p. 26.
18. *ibid.*, p. 579.
19. Manifesto of the CC of the German Communist Party, dated April 2, 1924, quoted in H. Weber (ed), *Der deutsche Kommunismus* (Koeln 1963), p. 92.
20. *Rote Fahne*, June 21, 1923, January 24, 1923.
21. *Izvestia*, November 13, November 17, 1923.
22. *Rote Fahne*, May 6, 1924.
23. P. Froelich in *Bolshevik*, 5/6, 1924, p. 104 *et seq.*
24. Entry on Gitler, Adolf, *Bolshaya Sovetskaya Entsiklopedia*, first edition, Vol. 17, p. 124.
25. *Protokoll des 6. Weltkongresses der Kommunistischen Internationale* (Hamburg 1928), Vol. 1, p. 598. (Schneller).
26. *ibid.*, p. 449.
27. *Die Internationale*, XIV, p. 491. For more detailed bibliographical references about Communist policies toward the Social Democrats, the reader should refer to S. Bahne '*Die Kommunistische Partei Deutschlands*' in *Das Ende der Parteien* (Erich Matthias and Rudolf Morsey, eds. Duesseldorf 1960), pp. 655–739.
28. *Der Rote Aufbau*, November 15, 1932, p. 1020.
29. *ibid.*, January 1931, p. 18.
30. *ibid.*, December 15, 1931, p. 859.
31. 'Fascism, the danger of war and the tasks of the Communist parties' (speech at the 13th plenum of the ECCI) (London n.d.), p. 62.
32. D. Manuilski: *The Communist parties and the crisis of capitalism* (London n.d.), p. 112.
33. V. Knorin: *Fascism, Social Democracy and the Communists* (London n.d.) 1933–4 , p. 28.
34. *Protokoll des 6. Weltkongresses* etc., Vol. I, p. 590.
35. *Der Rote Aufbau*, February 15, 1933, p. 211.
36. See, for instance, the editorial 'Krizis Kapitalizma i fashizatsia mezhdunarodnoi Sotsial-Demokratii', *Bolshevik*, August 15–16, 1933.
37. *Rundschau*, Basel, April 26, 1934, p. 1006.
38. Hans Guenther: *Der Herren eigener Geist. Die Ideologie des National Sozialismus.* (Moscow-Leningrad 1935), p. 32.
39. Palme Dutt: *Fascism and Social Revolution* (London 1935), p. 155.
40. O, Piatnitsky in *Bolshevik*, October 15, 1932.
41. *German Foreign Ministry Files*, Germany–Soviet Union, Vol. 5 (Sept. 1931–Dec. 1933) roll 1882 H, frame 424964 (Litvinov); also 424898 (complaint by the Tass representative about the *Nationalsozialistische Monatshefte*, July 1932).

42. *German Foreign Ministry Files, ibid.* frame 424792. Report on a talk by Lunacharsky after his visit to Western Europe.

43. *Protokoll des 12. Parteitages der KPD*, pp. 213–4.

44. *Rote Fahne*, June 15, 1930. Resolution of the Politburo of the KPD.

45. *Der Rote Aufbau*, August 1930, p. 410.

46. According to current East German historiography, the German Communist leaders became aware of the Fascist danger in October 1929 and decided to modify their policy accordingly. See Klaus Mammach, 'Ueber die Wende der KPD zum Kampf gegen den Faschismus' in *Beitraege zur Geschichte der deutschen Arbeiterbewegung*, 4, 1963, p. 672. If Dr Mammach's account were correct, Thaelmann's policy after October 1929 would appear altogether incomprehensible, unless one assumes the existence of an overwhelming death wish among the party leadership, which there is no good reason to do. The true explanation is far easier; the Communist leaders did *not* realize the full magnitude of the Nazi danger until well after Hitler's seizure of power.

47. *Der Rote Aufbau*, August 1930, p. 410; November 15, 1931, p. 786.

48. *ibid.*, January 1931, p. 18.

49. Karl Radek: *Portrety i Pamflety*, Vol. II, p. 353 *et seq.*

50. *ibid.*, p. 347.

54. Thaelmann speech in Berlin, February 19, 1932, in *Der revolutionaere Ausweg und die KPD* (Berlin 1932), p. 23.

52. For a detailed discussion of Communist tactics in 1932 see Bahne, *loc. cit.*, also the circular letters and the 'Referenten Material' sent out by the Central Committee of the German Communist Party in EAP, 175-b-16-05/240 and 242.

53. See *Thesen and Resolutionen, XII Plenum EKKI* (Moscow, 1932).

54. *Inprekorr*, XII, p. 2197 *et seq.*

55. *Bolshevik*, 21, 1932, p. 21; Kuusinen's article in *Bolshevik*, 23/4, 1932; Radek in *Izvestia*, quoted in *German Foreign Ministry Documents*, press report from German Embassy, Moscow (frame 415028).

56. *Communist International*, December 1, 1932, p. 698.

57. Piatnitsky in *Bolshevik*, 19, 1932; *Communist International*, December 1, 1932, p. 700.

58. *Zapad i Vostok* (Moscow 1924) p. 128; see also I. Vardin's critique of Trotsky's early theories on Fascism in *Krasnaya Nov* (1), 1925, p. 201, *et seq.*

59. *Die Wendung der Komintern und die Lage in Deutschland* (Berlin 1930), p. 9.

60. *ibid.* Many of Trotsky's writings on Germany have been republished in the third volume of the French edition of his works, *Ecrits*.

61. *What Next*, p. 38.

62. '*Was Nun*', p. 50.

63. *Pravda*, November 16, 1932; *Kommunisticheskii Internatsional*, 4–5, 1933, p. 7.

64. Bela Kun in *Der Rote Aufbau*, November 15, 1932, p. 1020.

65. East German historians have put great emphasis on these activities in January and February 1933, and on one or two isolated appeals for common action. This is to prove that the Communists

were for a united anti-Fascist front all along and that it was only due to Social-Democratic cowardice and shortsightedness that such action was not taken. Some documents that have recently come to light (such as a circular letter by the KPD Central Committee dated March 25, 1933) suggest that the Communists seriously contemplated some form of co-operation with the socialists – but this was already after Hitler had taken over. (Copy of the circular letter in *Records of the Reich Leader SS-EAP* 173-b-16-05/176, frame 2801330). See also the Central Committee circular published in May ('On the causes of the temporary victory of Fascism in Germany'), EAP 173-b-16-05/240, frame 2811253 *et seq.*).

66. Ex Insider, 'Moscow–Berlin 1933', in *Survey*, October 1962, p. 163.

67. Letter dated January 30, 1942, in Berlin Document Centre.

68. *Records of the Reich Leader SS*, roll 357, frames 2867093/6.

69. *Pravda*, January 31, 1933; *Unsere Zeit*, February 15, 1933.

70. *Bolshevik*, 3, 1933, pp. 39–57.

71. F. Heckert in *Unsere Zeit*, February 15, 1933, p. 211.

72. Knorin in *Kommunistische Internationale*, XV, p. 197; declaration by the Central Committee of the party; in *Rundschau*, II, p. 543 (dated June 21, 1933).

73. F. Heckert, *Was geht in Deutschland vor?* (Moscow 1933) pp. 3, 9, 11, 14, 36; *Pravda*, March 4, 1933.

74. *O fashistskoi diktature v Germanii* (Moscow 1934), p.129.

75. Only a short time previously *Pravda* (September 2, 1932), had called the KPD the 'best section of the Third International'.

76. J. Stalin, *Problems of Leninism*, (Moscow 1947), p. 467.

77. Louis Fischer: 'Moskau und die Weltrevolution', in *Neue Weltbuehne*, October 19, 1933, p. 1311.

78. Louis Fischer, *loc. cit.*

79. 'Krushenie Dollara i Votsarenie Gitlera', *Izvestia*, May 1, 1933.

80. 'Yaponski i mezhdunarodnyi Fashizm', *Bolshevik*, 21, 1933; *Izvestia*, January 1, 1934.

81. 'Antisovetskaya Politika germanskovo fashizma i mezhdunarodny proletariat' in *Bolshevik*, 11, 1933; *Podgotovka borby za novy peredel mira* (Moscow 1934) p. 167.

82. Ernst Henri, *Hitler over Russia*, (London 1936), p. VIII.

83. Ernst Henri, *Hitler over Europe* (London 1934), p. 223.

84. *ibid.*, pp. 4, 107, 110, 175.

85. *ibid.*, pp. 60, 184.

86. Dust cover of *Hitler over Russia*.

87. *Hitler Over Russia*, pp. 38–53; p. 82 *et seq. Hitler Over Europe*, p. 184.

88. *13th Plenum of ECCI* (London n.d.), pp. 6–8. (Theses and Decisions).

89. D. Manuilski, *Revolutionary Crisis, Fascism and War* (London n.d. probably 1934), p. 8.

90. Wilhelm Pieck, *We are Fighting for a Soviet Germany* (London n.d.) p. 77.

91. *ibid.*, p. 84.

92. See Bahne, *loc. cit.*, pp. 706–20, for details about German Communist publications during 1934.

93. *Pravda*, January 4, 1934.

94. *Rundschau*, July 1934, *passim*.

95. *Deutsche Volkszeitung*, October 18, 1936.

96. *VII Congress of the Communist International*. Abridged stenographic report of proceedings (Moscow 1939), pp. 21, 34, 36, 75, 136, etc.

97. *ibid.*, pp. 133, 179.

98. *ibid.*, p. 242 (Florin).

99. Stalin, *Problems of Leninism* (Moscow 1947), p. 603.

100. Stalin, *War Speeches* (London n.d.) p. 9.

101. *ibid.*, p. 20.

102. *ibid.*, pp. 29–30.

103. Yu.I. Avdeev and V. N. Strunnikov, *Burzhuaznoe Gosudarstvo v period 1918–1939 gg.* (Moscow 1962.)

104. V. D. Kulbakin, *Ocherki noveishei istorii Germanii* (Moscow 1962), p. 357.

105. G. L. Rozanov, *Germaniya pod vlastu fashizma 1933–1939* (Moscow 1961), pp. 182–93.

106. Rozanov, p. 25, based on I. G. Schoup *De Geldbronnen van het National Socialisme. Drie Gespreken mit Hitler door Sidney Warburg*, published in 1933. It was investigated in detail by Hermann Lutz: 'Faelschungen zur Auslandsfinanzierung Hitlers', *Vierteljahrshefte fuer Zeitgeschichte*, October 1954, p. 386 *et seq.*

107. Avdeev and Strunnikov, *op. cit.* pp. 29–30.

108. The records of the Nazi Party treasurer, Xaver Schwartz, unfortunately no longer exist, but there is sufficient documentation from other sources. See Fritz Thyssen, *I Paid Hitler* (New York 1942); George F. W. Hallgarten, *Hitler, Reichswehr und Industrie* (Frankfurt 1955); Daniel Guerin, *Fascism and Big Business* (New York 1939); in addition there have been many East German contributions on the subject; for instance, Fritz Klein, Die Vorbereitung der faschistischen Diktatur durch die deutsche Grossbourgeoisie, 1929 –1932 in *Zeitschrift fuer Geschichtswissenschaft*, 1953, p. 872 *et seq.*; much evidence emerged from the Nuremberg trials, particularly in the trial of Friedrich Flick.

109. For instance, L. Lochner, *Tycoons and Tyrant. German Industry from Hitler to Adenauer* (Chicago 1954) or Deutsches Industrieinstitut, *Die Legende von Hitler und der Industrie* (no place, no date, *c*. 1963).

110. Joseph Goebbels, *Vom Kaiserhof zur Reichskanzlei* (Berlin 1933) *passim*.

111. Thyssen exaggerates when he says that until the Nazi takeover Krupp was Hitler's 'most bitter enemy', and that he warned Hindenburg as late as January 29, 1933, against appointing Hitler (*loc. cit.* pp. 103–4). But Krupp certainly did not support Hitler at that time.

112. R. Michels, *Sozialismus und Faschismus* (Muenchen 1926).

113. See Nuremberg Trials IMG, Vol. 33, p. 531, also Hallgarten, *op. cit.* p. 114 *et seq.*; Albert Schreiner, 'Die Eingabe deutscher Finanzmagnaten, Monopolisten und Junker an Hindenburg fuer die Berufung Hitlers zum Reichskanzler' in *Zeitschrift fuer Geschichtswissenschaft*, 1956, p. 366 *et seq.*; Deutscher Gewerkschaftsbund, *Hitler und die Industrie* (Duesseldorf 1963), p. 6.

114. See for instance Gerhard Volkland on the 'Gelsenkirchen affair'

(the support given to one group of steel producers during a crisis) in the East German *Zeitschrift fuer Geschichtswissenschaft* 2, 1963, p. 289 *et seq.*

115. See Klaus Brobisch: 'Der Freundeskreis Himmler' in *Zeitschrift fuer Geschichtswissenschaft* 2, 1960, p. 316. The subtitle of the article is 'An example of the subordination of the Nazi Party and the fascist state apparatus to the oligarchy of finance'. Yet the facts contained in the article prove the opposite, namely, that the 'financial oligarchy' prostrated itself before the Nazi leaders.

116. Konrad Heiden: *Adolf Hitler. Das Zeitalter der Verantwortungslosigkeit* (Zurich 1936), p. 311.

117. *Rapallo und die friedliche Koexistenz* (East Berlin 1963), p. 123.

118. Hallgarten, *loc. cit.*, p. 117.

119. See Iring Fetscher: 'Faschismus und Nationalsozialismus', in *Politische Vierteljahresschrift*, 1962, 1, p. 52.

120. R. Hilferding; 'Das historische Problem' in *Zeitschrift fuer Politik*, December 1954, p. 293 *et*

seq. Hilferding did not live to finish his study. See also his remarks about state capitalism and the totalitarian state economy in the *Modern Review*, June 1947, pp. 266–71.

121. *Die deutsche Tragoedie* (Prague 1933), p. 342.

122. *Behemoth* (Left Book Club edition, London 1942), p. 267.

123. Otto Bauer, *Zwischen zwei Weltkriegen* (Bratislava 1936) pp. 113–41. Paul Sering: series of articles in *Zeitschrift fuer Sozialismus*, September–December 1935, March 1936. Historikus (Arthur Rosenberg), *Der Faschismus als Massenbewegung* (Karlsbad 1934) *passim.*

124. Curt Geyer: *Die Partei der Freiheit* (Paris 1939), p. 13.

125. Such as Leo Lania (in *Tagebuch*) and Willi Schlamm (in *Die Neue Weltbühne*).

126. The most ambitious, and, I think, most successful attempt at an explanation has been made by Dr Nolte in his *Der Faschismus in seiner Epoche* (Munich 1963). If the communists overrate economic factors, Dr Nolte somewhat neglects them in his brilliant work.

Chapter 12

1. *Istoriya velikoi otechestvennoi voiny Sovetskovo Soyuza 1941–1945*, Vol. 1 (Moscow 1961), p. 176.

2. See, for instance, Kurt Krupinski, *Die Komintern seit Kriegsausbruch* (Berlin 1941); the most complete collection of such material.

3. *Voelkischer Beobachter*, October 4, 1941.

4. See for instance *Deutsche Soldaten sehen die Sowjet Union* (ed. Wolfgang Diewerge) (Berlin 1941) and the countless personal reports published both before and after 1945.

5. Melvin Croan, 'Reality and Illusion in Soviet–German Relations', in *Survey*, October 1962, p. 14 *et seq.*

Appendix

1. *Daily News*, September 15, 1917.
2. Robert Wilton, *The Last Days of the Romanovs* (London 1920), p. 148.
3. *The Cause of World Unrest* (New York–London 1920) p. viii; this is a book edition of the articles originally published in the *Morning Post* between July 12 and July 30, 1920.
4. The reports by Lord Kilmarnock and the Rev. B. D. Lombard to Earl Curzon in *Russia 1919*, p. 32, p. 56.

5. General S. A. Lukomsky, *Vospominania*, p. 251. Churchill seems to have been influenced at that time by the writing of Mrs Nesta Webster, an expert on the conspiracy theory of history who specialized in tracing back the 'hidden hand' to the French revolution and beyond. He mentioned Mrs Webster's writings in his article.
6. *The Cause of World Unrest*, p. 175.

INDEX

Some inconsistencies in spelling have been unavoidable—especially with regard to the transliteration of Russian names into English, and whenever a Russian author has also published in English, French and German.